1777

1777

Tipping Point at Saratoga

DEAN SNOW

OXFORD
UNIVERSITY PRESS

OXFORD
UNIVERSITY PRESS

Oxford University Press is a department of the University of Oxford. It furthers
the University's objective of excellence in research, scholarship, and education
by publishing worldwide. Oxford is a registered trade mark of Oxford University
Press in the UK and certain other countries.

Published in the United States of America by Oxford University Press
198 Madison Avenue, New York, NY 10016, United States of America.

Library of Congress Cataloging-in-Publication Data
Names: Snow, Dean R., 1940– author.
Title: 1777 : tipping point at Saratoga / Dean Snow.
Description: New York, NY : Oxford University Press, 2016. |
Includes bibliographical references and index.
Identifiers: LCCN 2016005200 (print) | LCCN 2016006469 (ebook) |
ISBN 9780190618759 | ISBN 9780190618766 | ISBN 9780190618773
Subjects: LCSH: Saratoga Campaign, N.Y., 1777.
Classification: LCC E241.S2 .S69 2016 (print) | LCC E241.S2 (ebook) |
DDC 974.7/4803—dc23
LC record available at http://lccn.loc.gov/2016005200

1 3 5 7 9 8 6 4 2

Printed by Sheridan Books, Inc., United States of America

Contents

To Samuel Snow and Nathaniel Barnett,
Soldiers of the Revolution

Preface

I have thought about writing this book ever since I received a polite telephone call from John Cotter at the Philadelphia office of the National Park Service in the spring of 1971. He asked me to consider taking on the first of a series of archaeological projects at the Saratoga National Historical Park. The start of the nation's bicentennial celebrations was only five years away and the park needed help in preparing for the events that would culminate there in 1977. I was a young assistant professor at the University at Albany, having taken up the position there in the fall of 1969.

The current park contains 3394 acres of land. The armies of 1777 occupied the battlefield for only a month, and I wondered then how an archaeologist might design a research project to investigate such a short occupation of such a large site. Because it seemed like such a difficult problem, Cotter's invitation was irresistible. In 1972 and subsequent years, crews made up of faculty, students, and staff from the university carried out archaeological projects on the battlefield that cleared up some lingering questions that documentary history could not satisfactorily answer, and further illuminated features and events already reasonably well known.

I started reading journals, letters, and other first-hand narratives of the battles as I conducted archaeological projects on the landscape they described. There is a compelling immediacy about these accounts that I thought deserved retelling, not just the usual scholarly mining of sources for facts. The artifacts and archaeological features we had uncovered related directly to the actions of real individuals, some of whom we could name and come to know better through their writings. I was struck by the profound humanity of the words of men and women who had experienced the tragic reality of war on both sides here in 1777.

I have made inferences regarding the motives, strengths, weaknesses, proclivities, and ambitions of the main historical characters that appear here. Few of these are new because the personalities of the principals have long been understood by historians. My purpose here is to lead the reader to a deeper understanding of the people involved in the brief but momentous culmination of the Saratoga Campaign. If some individuals appear to receive more coverage or greater sympathy it is because there are more sources for them, or they were more explicit about their thinking. It is also the case that I regard them to have been mostly good people caught up in the tragedy of war.

There is a tendency to view history in terms of the momentous decisions taken by leaders of various kinds. At the same time, historians explore the details as thoroughly as they can, but in the end they necessarily have to generalize, and their generalizations are usually stated in terms of the same momentous decisions taken by the same leading figures. But in the real world, conflicts are not simply games played by a few chess masters. There are thousands of participants, many layers of authority, and many people capable of taking action on their own. In a single battle soldiers in one sector might perceive a weakness in the enemy's position and charge spontaneously to a reckless but isolated victory, while soldiers in another sector might break and flee in the face of what they genuinely perceive in the moment to be overwhelming odds and certain death. The random and chaotic dynamics of battle often sort otherwise similar people into heros and cowards, victors and vanquished, living and dead. Capable officers understand these dynamics and the limits they impose on their planning and execution of battlefield operations.

The need for the historian to clarify the big picture thus often means that the details that make up the lives of individuals get left behind in the archives. The Saratoga campaign offers an opportunity to explore those details because it was a crucial turning point for the American Revolution that was played out over a relatively brief span of time in a relatively small space by a reasonably small number of people. I have used direct quotes extensively, I have reported known conversations from eyewitness accounts, and I have re-created some conversations from letters and journals. But I have not invented either fictional characters or fictional dialog. All the words in quotes are words that were spoken by real people at the time. I have attributed to those people only the thoughts and emotions they explicitly expressed, or that historians have agreed they must have had. The result is a microhistory of thirty-three days that straddled what was arguably America's most important historical tipping point. The time span covered is brief and the number of players few by modern standards. This is how most of us remember our personal histories, it is how we prefer to tell stories, and it is how our primary sources tended to write about Saratoga. I hope that this approach conveys meaning to readers that they might not find in more traditional historiography.

My approach is perhaps predictable because I am a professional archaeologist, a science that depends heavily on inference. For example, in our 1972 test excavations we found a skeleton that had been buried face down in the Balcarres Redoubt foot trench. We inferred that it was a foot trench because we had looked at British construction techniques at several points nearby and so understood the materials and techniques the soldiers there had used in constructing the fortification. Study of the skeleton later led us to infer that the skeleton had belonged to an elderly woman. We found that the facial bones had been driven into the interior of the cranium by a charge of buckshot. We knew from historical records that the Americans had loaded their muskets with both ball and buckshot on October 7, 1777, so we inferred that she had been shot by an American during the unsuccessful assault on the redoubt that afternoon. We knew that the Balcarres Redoubt was defended mainly by the British Light Infantry Battalion, and we knew that some British noncommissioned officers had their wives with them, so we inferred that the woman was most likely one of those dedicated wives. That is the basis for the account I have written of some of the events that took place in the redoubt around four o'clock that afternoon.

I have laid out the story line day by day, sometimes hour by hour. Into this narrative I have inserted occasional maps and organizational charts. In the case of written correspondence that I have included, either all or in part, the contents are presented indented and in italics. In these cases, I have only rarely altered spelling, punctuation, and capitalization so that the reader can get the flavor of the written correspondence of the time.

I have been mindful that while most of the English language of 1777 is remarkably clear to modern readers, there are occasionally obsolete or special terms that can be confusing. Terms that are not clarified in context are typically defined in the chapter notes. A few controversial issues are also explained briefly in the notes, which are otherwise used mainly to lead readers to documentary sources.

Few of the participants wrote long thoughtful memoirs after the campaign, and those who did had agendas that require them to be read critically. Burgoyne was focused on escaping blame for his army's loss, the first such capitulation in British history. When he wrote his memoirs late in life James Wilkinson was similarly focused on salvaging his reputation at the end of a long and checkered career. Thomas Anburey apparently copied from many sources without attribution and has been damned as a plagiarist in more recent years. Some, such as Arnold, Gates, and Fraser, left little beyond their letters and the testimony of others. Fortunately, each man's character becomes clear through those works, and I have used them as much as I could. I have also been able to draw upon several orderly books from both the American and British records.

In 1777, people set their watches by the sun, adjusting to twelve o'clock noon when the sun was at its highest point in the sky. Thus the sun rose at 5:47 a.m. local time on September 15, 1777, as it still does on that date. Modern computer programs that calculate the times of past sunrises tell us that the sun came up over the Saratoga battlefield at 5:34 a.m. EST (6:34 EDT) that day. But there was no standard time in 1777, let alone a daylight-savings version of it. Standard national time zones were not instituted until 1883. Because of this I have adjusted all times that specific events occurred in 1777 to local time. Our standard time thus runs thirteen minutes behind local solar time. Our modern daylight time runs forty-seven minutes ahead of local time. These corrections help us better understand the timing of specific events with the rising and setting of both the sun and the moon.

All of the people involved in the battles used watches set to local time. On the other hand, their memories and accuracies varied considerably, and there are many contradictions. I have found over five dozen specific time references for September 19, 1777, and about half that many for October 7, 1777. Many of the precise times I have provided are merely plausible estimates based on the preponderance of evidence. I judge that the most important thing is to get the unfolding of events in the correct sequence, a difficult task in the fog of any battle, when events on different parts of the battlefield often unfolded independently and were reported by people aware mainly of the action in just their immediate surroundings.

Among many park professionals I am especially indebted to five, beginning with John Cotter, mentioned earlier. Michael Phillips, park historian in the 1970s, provided knowledge of the documentary history and military archaeology that I initially lacked. Eric Schnitzer, who constructed and still maintains an invaluable online resource on Saratoga, on several occasions provided help in more recent years from his own vast knowledge. Christopher Martin, like Eric a Park Service professional, provided me with electronic resources and pleasant expert company on various battlefield excursions in recent years. Christine Valosin, Saratoga Park Historian, has helped me repeatedly with archival and collections resources at the park. William Griswold's eye for maps and figures was especially important in the late stages. Donald Linebaugh's unsurpassed editorial skills caught dozens of gremlins that others had missed.

I am grateful for the support I received over the years since 1972 from colleagues at the University at Albany, fifty-six undergraduate and graduate students who made up the crews that carried out archaeological and documentary research at the Saratoga Battlefield, rangers and administrators at the Saratoga National Historical Park and elsewhere in the National Park Service, and several other authors and researchers whose advice and support might not be apparent among the references I have cited. They are too numerous to list here, but some deserve special mention. Richard Wilkinson has been a constant friend and colleague from the beginning, and his contributions can be found in several places in this book. William Starna's advice and support began at Saratoga and have endured ever since. Charles Gehring, who knows well both the Dutch-American and German components of the Saratoga story, provided me with critically important advice. While I was overall director of operations from 1972 to 1974, Dwight Wallace and John Palter supervised field operations in two of those years, and Stuart Reeve authored much of the report in 1974. David Starbuck, Susan Bender, and Karen Hartgen generously shared the results of their later archaeological projects on and near the battlefield. After I moved from the University at Albany to The Pennsylvania State University I had the advice and assistance of George Chaplin, Nina Jablonski, and George Milner in my continuing efforts to improve our understanding of 1777 Saratoga and bring this book to a successful conclusion.

Park personnel, from a succession of superintendents to part-time seasonal employees have been unfailingly supportive. No American taxpayer should underestimate the contributions of these dedicated people, which often extend well beyond their official duties. They are truly remarkable government employees. Hugh Gurney, Glen Gray, and Joe Finan were park superintendents at times when I was active on the battlefield, a position that Amy Bracewell holds now. They and several others have been unfailingly supportive.

I am especially grateful to several relatives and friends who labored through earlier versions of this book and provided me with excellent advice on ways to improve it. My wife, Janet Snow, who has always been my most dependable critic and is the most reliable of copyeditors, has read drafts of this book, in some instances multiple times. Little would be possible without her. My daughter Barbara Snow helped me stay grounded and focused on the book's primary audience. My son Joshua Snow and my daughter Kate Snow brought skills from their own professions that enabled them to give me advice I could not have acquired any other way.

Roy Hammerstedt, Dan Douthitt, James Hurteau, Douglas Gonzalez, Bob Bailey, and Dieter Aumann all read earlier drafts of the book and provided valuable suggestions for improvement from the points of view of people who did not previously know much about Saratoga in 1777. I am grateful to Frank Harvey for pointing me toward sources on the building and firing of rifles in the late eighteenth century.

The repositories that hold and protect the unpublished manuscripts and artwork that document history are staffed by helpful, dedicated, but typically anonymous people. Among those who made this book possible are Edward O'Reilly at the New-York Historical Society, Andrea Ashby at Independence Hall, Megan Welchel at the Frick Collection, Heidi Hill and Ronna Dixson at the Schuyler Mansion in Albany, and Tim Weidner at the Chapman Historical Museum in Glens Falls.

Finally, I am very grateful to Oxford University Press, to two anonymous reviewers, and to my editor, Stefan Vranka, for supporting, facilitating, and improving my approach to the subject. Sarah Svendsen and John Veranes shepherded the manuscript and artwork with gentle skill. Jeremy Toynbee and Ginny Faber provided copyediting that accommodated differences between American and British styles, both past and present, and many special usages. Angela Messina, Sarah Russo, and Lauren Hill provided promotion and publicity.

Oxford University Press has created a website to accompany *1777: Tipping Point at Saratoga*. Material that could not be made available in the book is provided here, namely color images, detailed electronic maps, lengthy supporting documentation, chapter timelines, and tabular data. The reader is encouraged to consult this resource in conjunction with chapter subheadings and the index. Doing so will facilitate following character, military unit, or topical threads through the crucial thirty-three days of American history at Saratoga.

1777

Introduction

At its core, any authentic account of the American War of Independence has to be about human endurance. For the rebellious Americans it was about self-government and freedom from political, economic, or religious exploitation, but they discovered that they would have to endure a long war to secure that freedom. At the onset of the conflict they lacked a standing army, the trained men and equipment to create one, the money to pay for the effort, or a bureaucracy to manage it, and they had little more than the self-appointed Continental Congress to provide leadership. What sense of unity the citizens of the separate thirteen colonies of Great Britain in North America possessed ironically derived more from sharing a common enemy than from sharing common goals. The fractious Americans had to find ways to come together to maintain a rebellion that would endure long enough for them to form a new kind of government through protracted debate and compromise. It would take a dozen years for the basic structure of a new federal government to emerge, and even then it was uncertain whether the new democratic system could endure for the long term. In the meantime, the colonies moved forward with an improvised national government, an improvised navy, an improvised army, and an improvised economy, all while holding off the finest armed forces of the day.

England's army and navy were as formidable as any on earth in 1776, but they were deployed far from home at the ends of stretched and vulnerable supply lines. The British Army in America was large and well-trained and supplemented by German regulars but required to deploy across a largely forested landscape that was vaster than most of them had previously imagined possible and inhabited by hostile rebels, sullen undecideds, and fewer Loyalist supporters than they had hoped for. Consequently, the British had to endure a long campaign to suppress a popular rebellion that enjoyed local support, adequate supplies of food, a huge theater of operation, and the tactical advantage of being able to escape repeatedly to fight another day.

The war that broke out in the spring of 1775 in Massachusetts would test the endurance of nations, of institutions of many kinds, and of the individual men and women who found themselves caught up in it all. Most of the histories of the war take a broad view, which is characteristic of traditional historical writing. There are notable exceptions, such as Scheer and Rankin's *Rebels and Redcoats*, which uses letters, diaries, journals, and other first-hand reports to tell the story at a more personal level.[1] However, even their book can only sample the history of the war from Lexington to Yorktown, seven years of conflict. More coherent personal accounts have been published, but most of them are too idiosyncratic and too limited in scope to be of more than biographical interest. To bridge the chasm between the endurance of conflict told at large scale and the endurance of the individual human beings who lived and died over the course of it, this book tells the story of a pivotal thirty-three days in the autumn of 1777 from the personal points of view of a few dozen people. Taken together, their narratives make up the threads of these critical thirty-three days in American history during which, on a little patch of ground in upstate New York, the future of a new nation tipped from uncertain to inevitable.

BACKGROUND

The political agenda of the American Revolution was driven by ideas derived mainly from the political and scientific advances of the Age of Enlightenment. Thomas Paine's *Common Sense*, which articulated many of these ideas, had a big impact when it was published in 1776. However, because the ideas expressed by Paine and others were debatable, they did not constitute parts of a single coherent political ideology. Instead, they were the elements of what would be an emergent political process. The Articles of Confederation had been drafted by November 1777, but it would take more than three years for this stopgap document to be ratified. The founders would require much more debate before formalizing a better Constitution of the United States in 1788. Even then, it would remain subject to amendment and thus forever tentative, unlike the rigid and static religious ideologies that already existed or some similarly rigid political ideologies that would remain or become popular in later centuries.

The founders tended to be Deists, or at least sympathetic to Deism, people who were skeptical of religious ideology, skeptical of institutionalized religion in general and of Christian doctrines in particular. This predisposed them to favor flexible democratic processes over rigid absolutes. The Constitution eventually accomplished the intended objective, emerging as an amendable document subject to improvement. However, it would prove to be tragically crippled from the outset by the institution of slavery.

For the time being, the Continental Congress acted collectively on nearly all matters and in the near absence of anything like the later American executive and judicial branches of government above the state level. John Hancock was elected president of the Continental Congress on May 24, 1775, and remained in that position until October 31, 1777. This meant that he served as president from almost the opening shots of the war through the creation of the Continental Army, the appointment of George Washington as commander in chief, the Declaration of Independence, the siege of Boston, the British occupation of New York City, and the Saratoga Campaign. It was a tumultuous year and a half, during which a fractious set of former colonies sought to invent a new kind of government, even while at the same time fighting desperately for survival.

The War Begins

It was 1777. People joked that it was the year of the hangman because the three sevens looked like a row of gallows. But gallows humor always has a serious side. A year earlier Benjamin Franklin had quipped, "We must hang together, gentlemen ... else, we shall most assuredly hang separately." The occasion had been the signing of the American Declaration of Independence in July. The signers had come to depend on Franklin for humor and wisdom. They had truly needed both at the time, and the more irony in it, the better.

Franklin was also fond of saying that there had never been a good war or a bad peace. But the Americans were in the middle of a war now and there was little to do but see it through to the finish. They had been fighting since 1775, and George Washington had long since taken up the role of commander in chief. Yet for over a year it had remained just a rebellion.

Initially, complete political independence was not even necessarily the goal for many people. In this fractious set of colonies opinion often ran against the idea of independence. Washington's troops fought under a flag bearing thirteen red and white stripes, but which still had the union flag of Great Britain in its upper canton, where the national flag now displays stars. Many of the Americans and the British believed that reconciliation was still possible. Washington and his improvised army were still retreating more often than advancing, hoping that the British war machine would exhaust itself trying to quell an insurrection in the vast and rugged countryside of eastern North America. An outright American victory was not something that very many people expected.

By the summer of 1776, Congress had declared independence. The rebellious Americans were now all in and hoping for a tipping point, the point at which American independence from Great Britain would shift from uncertain to something more likely. George Washington was still in overall command, but he, other officers, and thousands of volunteers were trying to win against the best army in the world with a makeshift army of amateurs. It is a familiar story today, but in the late eighteenth century it was a quixotic novelty.

THE SARATOGA CAMPAIGN

Fighting began in 1775 near Boston with the famous "shot heard 'round the world." American militia units converged on Boston and besieged the British garrison there. The fighting around Bunker Hill is the most widely known episode of that siege. By June the Continental Congress had concluded that militias would be an insufficient fighting force. They accordingly created a regular force, named it the Continental Army, and appointed General George Washington as commander in chief. The British evacuated Boston and moved on to Long Island and New York City, where they would enjoy more freedom of movement and more Loyalist support. They defeated Washington's forces in southern New York and forced the Americans to retreat into New Jersey.

One of the senior British officers in Boston had been John Burgoyne (Figure 0.1), who began thinking about a plan to sever the particularly rebellious New England colonies from the other less rebellious colonies. Burgoyne was fifty-five years old and supposedly the son of a British Army captain of the same name. But it was rumored that he was actually

Figure 0.1 John Burgoyne (1722–1792). Painted by Joshua Reynolds in May 1766. Burgoyne's uniform is that of the 16th Light Dragoons as it was worn until that month. Copyright: The Frick Collection.

the illegitimate son of his godfather, Lord Bingley. Bingley had died when Burgoyne was nine years old, leaving a will that specified that the boy would inherit his estate should Bingley's daughters fail to produce male heirs. A year later Burgoyne entered the Westminster School, which put him on a track to become an army officer. His inheritance would allow him to follow the practice of the day, which was to buy an expensive army commission. It was a system that ensured that British officers would be gentlemen from privileged families. By 1737 he was able to purchase a commission in the Horse Guards and had acquired a reputation as "Gentleman Johnny" on the London social scene. He later had to sell his commission to cover his debts. He was subsequently able to acquire a new lieutenant's commission in the 1st Royal Dragoons, a commission that he did not have to purchase. Still later he was able to find enough money to purchase a captaincy. The conclusion of the War of the Austrian Succession, however, paused his military career in 1748.

In 1751 Burgoyne eloped with Lady Charlotte Stanley, the daughter of Lord Derby, a well-known politician who had opposed the marriage. Burgoyne again had to sell his commission to pay his living expenses. The couple reconciled with Derby after the birth of a daughter. With the support of his father-in-law Burgoyne had renewed prospects. He joined the 11th Dragoons and eventually saw action in the Seven Years' War, distinguishing himself in the Portugal campaign. The war was fought in several theaters; in America it would be known as the French and Indian War.

Burgoyne was a major-general by 1775, when he was sent to help quell the American rebellion around Boston.[2] In 1776 he helped drive the Americans under Benedict Arnold out of Quebec. It was while he was there that he worked out the details of a plan to sever New England from the rest of the rebelling colonies. His idea was to lead a main force south from Montreal, Canada, by way of the natural corridor provided by Lake Champlain and the Hudson River and to seize Albany (Figure 0.2). A second, smaller British force led by Barry St. Leger was to be sent as

Figure 0.2 Burgoyne's strategy for the 1777 campaign. Three British expeditions were supposed to converge on Albany by way of forts (♦) and settlements (•).

a diversion by way of Lake Ontario to Fort Stanwix and the headwaters of the Mohawk River in central New York, with the idea that if they were lucky they could push down the Mohawk and attack Albany from the west. A third British force was expected to come northward up the Hudson River from New York City, which after the fighting of 1776 was now in British hands. The three-pronged attack was expected to capture Albany and create a line of garrisons from New York City to Montreal that would split the colonies and facilitate the suppression of the American rebellion.

The British repeatedly forced Washington to retreat southward from New York through New Jersey and Pennsylvania. From his new headquarters in New York City the British commander, Sir William Howe, seemed poised to defeat Washington through any of six different military initiatives he had at hand. For a while Howe even imagined that he could carry out all six at the same time.[3] One of his ideas was to send forces to converge on Albany and sever New England from the rest of the colonies. Thus the plan that Burgoyne took back to London in the fall of 1776 was an endorsement and elaboration of an option already promoted by Howe.

Burgoyne wanted the command of the expedition from Montreal for himself. He had discussed the idea with his friend, Major-General William Phillips of the Royal Artillery, and Phillips was eager to join him in the effort. Burgoyne had also discussed the proposal with another good friend, Lieutenant-General Sir Henry Clinton (not to be confused with the American Major General George Clinton). Sir Henry might have gained command of the expedition himself, but he deferred to his old friend Burgoyne and remained under Howe's command in New York. They both hoped that Clinton would be assigned the task of attacking northward up the Hudson River and meeting Burgoyne at Albany.

Overall it seemed like a good strategic plan, but it had some serious tactical flaws. The farther south Burgoyne's army moved from Montreal, the weaker it would inevitably become. Troops would have to be left behind along the way to garrison strong points and protect an ever-lengthening supply line. Thousands of people, horses, and oxen would have to be fed from supplies the army either carried or could acquire along the way. Burgoyne hoped, unrealistically as it turned out, for food, horses, and volunteers from Loyalist communities in northern New York. It would be relatively easy going while the supplies could still be floated southward down the lengths of Lake Champlain and Lake George. But it would become difficult once the expedition had to shift to land transportation when they were still seventy miles short of Albany. Consequently, the plan contained the seeds of its own eventual failure.

Burgoyne left Montreal in June 1777 with a force of 9500 officers and men; 138 pieces of artillery; and thousands of horses, carts, tents, and all the rest of what any army needed to operate in the field. The entourage also included civilian employees, hundreds of women, and even some children. As he moved south Burgoyne dropped off boats, cannons, and infantry units to garrison strong points along the route so that his supply line would be protected. Of the strong points, Fort Ticonderoga was the most significant.

Fort Ticonderoga had been built as Fort Carillon by the French twenty years earlier to defend Canada against British attacks from New York. The British won that war and renamed the fort, which still stands where Lake George spills into Lake Champlain. In 1777 the fort was defended by the American Northern Army under the command of Philip Schuyler (Figure 0.3). It had been over a century since the English had conquered

Figure 0.3 Philip Schuyler by J. H. Lazarus. Courtesy of the Schuyler Mansion State Historic Site, Albany, NY, New York State Office of Parks, Recreation, and Historic Preservation.

New Netherland and changed its name to New York, but the Schuylers and other old Dutch families still dominated there. They grew up speaking both Dutch and English, husbanded their inherited wealth, and encouraged their children to marry into only the best of the Dutch and English families. Many of them supported the rebellion. Philip Schuyler had thus been a natural choice to command the Northern Army in New York at the time. He was wealthy and very well connected. His primary residence was in Albany, and his country mansion was in Saratoga, now called Schuylerville, well up the Hudson toward the American military outposts.

Schuyler decided that Fort Ticonderoga could be defended without artillery from atop nearby Sugar Loaf Hill. It was a fatal mistake that allowed Burgoyne's army to quickly force the abandonment of the fort by its American garrison. Burgoyne's army took Ticonderoga by dragging guns up the undefended hill to exploit the American tactical error, and that was that. Congress was shocked by the loss of Ticonderoga and removed Schuyler from his command of the Northern Army.

After the fall of Fort Ticonderoga, the Americans fell back slowly in the face of the British advance. They stood and fought from time to time, and did what they could to roads and bridges in order to slow the British advance. Burgoyne's army took steady losses as a result. In July, Burgoyne lost 229 killed and wounded at Hubbardton and skirmishing around the southern end of Lake Champlain.[4]

Horatio Gates Assumes Command

Congress then appointed Major General Horatio Gates (Figure 0.4) as the new American commander of the Northern Army. When the Continental Army was created in 1775 Congress had appointed Gates to serve as adjutant general under George Washington. It was a position that required Gates's management skills, and he had impressed the New Englanders during the long American siege of Boston. The aristocratic Schuyler was not much admired by the many New Englanders in the Northern Army, so the replacement of Schuyler by Gates was a popular decision.

Gates had once been a young officer in the British Army, but he did not come from a wealthy family. Fortunately for him, Gates's father had earned the patronage of the Duke of Bolton. His patron found a place for the young Horatio Gates as an ensign in the 20th Regiment of Foot; this was one of several favors that prompted rumors that Bolden was actually

Figure 0.4 General Horatio Gates, 1777. Painted with permission from Independence National Historical Park, Philadelphia, PA, after Charles W. Peale. Courtesy of the artist, Ruth Major.

Gates's biological father. In due course Gates was made a lieutenant in Bolden's regiment. Gates and Burgoyne were old acquaintances from these early days of service together in the British Army.[5]

Gates was younger than Burgoyne but looked and acted like his senior. Gates was forty-nine years old, but even at a distance he looked older. He had thinning gray hair, wore his spectacles perched low on his nose, and stooped when he walked. Even Gates himself appeared to think of Gates as an old man, and he behaved accordingly.[6]

Gates was a veteran of the unfortunate British expedition against the French at Fort Duquesne in 1755. He had been wounded there, but like the young George Washington, who had been there too, Gates had escaped. Washington, unlike Gates, came from aristocratic stock, which contributed to his long-term success. Gates eventually realized that he had scant future in the British military. He simply could not afford it. At the same time, his association with Americans in the colonies had instilled republican and democratic notions in him. So Gates left the British Army and settled in Virginia.

Gates had adopted the country as his own, and he volunteered to serve it when the fighting broke out around Boston. Now Gates found himself commander of a new kind of army. There was nothing like it in Europe. The men were all volunteers, mostly amateurs. Not one of them had signed up in order to buy his way out of jail. Few of them expected to be paid, or if they did, they expected it to be scrip rather than hard coin. They were driven by a combination of idealistic sentiment and pragmatic obligation. Some expected to elect their officers and to go home when their terms of service were up, no matter what the military circumstances might be at the time. Militia volunteers in particular often committed to only very short enlistments. It was an army of rabble in the eyes of the British, but Gates was ready to make the most of it.

As Washington's adjutant general Gates had taken on the tasks of procuring and distributing supplies, organizing the medical department, and ensuring proper sanitation. He wrote a manual for military routine and instructed recruiters on whom to recruit and whom to reject. Immigrants were welcome if they were settled and with families, but "vagabonds, British deserters, and negroes" were specifically barred from service.[7] Those around him thought Gates was a good administrator. Whether he could command an army in the field remained to be seen.

Burgoyne Presses On

In August Burgoyne sent a detachment toward Bennington, Vermont, in the belief that it would be able to secure much-needed horses, supplies, and Loyalist supporters there. It was a risky move and Burgoyne knew it. The prospect of acquiring more horses to mount the German dragoons and help with the transport of provisions was a strong attraction. Better yet, Burgoyne had intelligence reports that the residents in and around Bennington favored the British cause at a ratio of five to one. He thought his army needed only to show itself for more Loyalists to come to his aid, despite the British tendency to treat Loyalists as inferiors when they showed up as volunteers.[8] However, by this time, he was in the chaos of what the French Canadians called *la petite guerre*. Every day the rebels poked and prodded at his forces, a prisoner taken here, a camp picket killed there.[9] The numbers were negligible so far, but the effect of the attrition on morale was not. He had warned his men about this in his general orders way back in June, but that was of little consolation in the middle of September.[10]

The Americans destroyed bridges and felled trees across forest roads, slowing the British advance to a crawl south of Skenesborough. Burgoyne refused to fall back to Ticonderoga from Skenesborough so that his army could take an easier water route down Lake George to Fort George and thence across a relatively short portage to the Hudson. It would have seemed too much like a retreat. Instead, he had struggled overland from Skenesborough through Fort Ann to Fort Edward (Figure 0.5).[11]

Burgoyne depended on Brigadier-General Simon Fraser, commander of the Advanced Corps, and a couple other senior officers for daily advice. Fraser was a Scot, the youngest son of Hugh Fraser of Balnain and one of many in the large military Fraser family. Fraser had served with the Fraser Highlanders and had been with Major-General James Wolfe at Quebec in the French and Indian War. He had been promoted to lieutenant-colonel of the British 24th Regiment of Foot and sent back to Canada again in

Figure 0.5 Routes used by Burgoyne's army. The British garrisoned the forts (♦) but not the settlements (•) they took. The attack on Bennington failed.

1776. Now temporarily promoted to brigadier-general under Burgoyne, he left the 24th in the command of a major and took command of an entire brigade.[12]

Fraser had not objected to the Bennington excursion in August, but he had disliked the idea of sending the Germans.[13] Fraser had wanted the assignment for his own corps, but significant portions of it were by then already on the west side of the Hudson, and it would have been difficult to get them back to the east side.[14] In Burgoyne's view it was the German dragoons who needed the horses, and it was those troops who needed more seasoning in the kind of warfare fought here in America. So it happened that Lieutenant Colonel Friedrich Baum had been sent up Batten Kill with just over two hundred unmounted dragoons, some British marksmen, some Canadian volunteers, two light cannons, a hundred Indians, and some Loyalists who said they knew the ground.[15] This polyglot detachment was commanded by a German who spoke hardly a word of either English or French.[16]

Baum's force of just over five hundred should have been adequate to overcome the four hundred green American militiamen said by British intelligence to be defending Bennington. American militias were largely made up of untrained men aged sixteen to sixty, and career military men tended to not regard them as a serious threat. The problem was that no one on the British side knew that militia Brigadier General John Stark would arrive with a thousand additional men just as Baum was about to attack.[17] Worse for Baum, Seth Warner's regiment was not far behind Stark with hundreds more militiamen as well as their Stockbridge Indian allies. Trained or not, there were simply too many Americans facing Baum for his detachment to have any chance of achieving its objective in Bennington.

Baum had recruited some Loyalists around Bennington, but he had not anticipated that dozens of rebels would easily dupe the expedition by pretending to be Loyalists and infiltrating the British camp.[18] No one had anticipated that Stark could muster so many farmers and shopkeepers and overwhelm Baum's dragoons. At the end of the day perhaps 80 dragoons were left, but 127, including Baum, were still missing and presumed dead or captured. Worse, a relief force Burgoyne had sent under Heinrich von Breymann's command arrived too late after an exhausting march. Von Breymann was lucky to be wounded only once in the left leg; his coat had five holes in it.[19] Four cannons were left behind as the Germans retreated, the horses needed to pull them all dead. A half-dozen officers were dead for sure, and nearly as many had been captured.[20] Far from acquiring more horses to mount the dragoons, the expedition fell back with net losses of both and none of the supplies they had hoped to capture.

Von Breymann came back wounded, having lost 220 of his 664 men, killed, wounded, captured, or missing.[21] The Bennington expedition had cost Burgoyne twenty-six officers and nearly a thousand men, most of them taken prisoner, and had gained him nothing. His only consolation was that prisoners and deserters were telling him that the Americans had suffered many more killed and wounded. Even if true (it was not), it was cold comfort. Burgoyne had lost 15 percent of his command. Whereas the Americans could replace their losses in men and supplies, Burgoyne could not. That was the reality Burgoyne faced as he sat down to write a private letter to Lord Germain in London.[22]

George Germain, 1st Viscount Sackville, was the secretary of state for America during the war. Germain was in charge of the effort to put down the American rebellion, the dispenser of resources, and the approver of plans. Burgoyne's formal report to Germain had been written in a different tone, for Burgoyne knew that it would be promptly published in the *London Gazette*.[23] His private letter contained a more honest assessment. The side expedition to Bennington had ended in disaster only four days before he wrote this letter, and the western prong of his coordinated attack on Albany was still stalled at Fort Stanwix. Of the expected southern prong coming up the Hudson from New York City there had been no news at all. Burgoyne was beginning to have doubts. "The consequences of this affair, my Lord, have little effect upon the strength of spirits of the army. But the prospect of the campaign in other respects is far less prosperous than when I wrote last," Burgoyne wrote.

The commissary could no longer bring supplies forward fast enough to keep up with their consumption, let alone add to the thirty-one days' worth of supplies currently in hand. It was time to either cut loose from the supply line and advance on Albany or fall back toward Fort Ticonderoga. The second option was simply unacceptable.[24] Burgoyne made the decision on his own. Perhaps he should have called a council of his generals, but he judged that there was simply no choice. He reasoned that "the preemptory tenor of my orders and the season of the year admit no alternative."[25]

It had taken two days to get the army across the Hudson on a temporary bridge of boats, but just minutes for the bridge to be carried away by a surge of high water, leaving him with nothing to show for the Bennington diversion, little hope for resupply from the north, little room for retreat, few means of communication, and little choice but to press on to Albany before New York's cold autumn froze his army in place.[26] Instead of Loyalists, he seemed surrounded by rebels. Burgoyne observed that a dozen years earlier, at the end of the French and Indian War, most of the land off to the east was vacant wilderness. Now it was full of rebels proud enough to declare themselves citizens of a new state they called "Vermont." Burgoyne characterized them for Germain: "The Hampshire Grants [Vermont] in particular, a country unpeopled and almost unknown the last war, now abounds in the most active and most rebellious race of the continent, and hangs like a gathering storm upon my left."

It was worse than that. The Loyalists whom Burgoyne had expected to flock to his banner had not materialized. Burgoyne had already lost close to a thousand men killed, wounded, captured, or missing. The Americans had destroyed or carried off the grain, cattle, horses, and forage Burgoyne had expected to find for his army. Dispatches intended for General Howe in New York City were regularly intercepted and Burgoyne's messengers hanged as spies. The few Loyalists who came into the camp expected to be fed from the dwindling provisions, more burden than help. Now he was facing American General Horatio Gates, who had at least two brigades, perhaps four thousand men, between Burgoyne and Albany, with more apparently on the way.

Had I a latitude in my orders, I should think it my duty to wait in this position, or perhaps as far back as Fort Edward, where my communication with Lake George would be perfectly secure, till some event happened to assist my movement forward. But my orders being positive to "force a junction with Sir William Howe," I apprehend I am not at liberty to remain inactive longer than shall be necessary to collect twenty-five days [of] provision, and to receive the reinforcement of the additional companies, the German drafts and recruits, now (and unfortunately only now) on Lake Champlain. The waiting the arrival of this reinforcement is of indispensible necessity, because from the hour I pass the Hudson River and proceed towards Albany, all safety of communication ceases. I must expect a large body of the enemy from my left will take post behind me. I have put out of the question the waiting longer.

Burgoyne thought it was still the only course. He had his orders. They could only be countermanded from above, and despite his invitation to Germain and his pleading with General Guy Carleton in Montreal, they had not been. No one could blame him later for persisting against these odds as winter approached. He thought he had no choice in the matter but to push on.

> By moving soon, though I should meet with insurmountable diffi-culties to my progress, I shall at least have the chance of fighting my way back to Ticonderoga.
>
> I yet do not despond. Should I succeed in forcing my way to Albany, and find that country in a state to subsist my army, I shall think no more of a retreat, but at the worst fortify there and await Sir W. Howe's operations.
>
> Whatever may be my fate, my Lord, I submit my actions to the breast of the King, and to the candid judgment of my profession, when all the motives become public, and I rest in the confidence that whatever decision may be passed upon my conduct my good intent will not be questioned.
>
> I cannot close so serious a letter without expressing my fullest satisfaction in the behavior and countenance of the troops, and my complete confidence that in all trials they will do whatever can be expected from men devoted to their King and country.

It was a noble finish to the letter. Circumstances all but guaranteed failure, but he would make the best of it. He was, after all, still in command of the finest of armies. The letter absolved Burgoyne in advance without blam-ing either his subordinates or his superiors in case the expedition failed.[27] At this point Burgoyne had 4646 rank and file left, including three hun-dred replacements who had finally arrived.[28] It was still enough to match Gates's untrained army.

Between the Fort Stanwix and Bennington fiascos August had cer-tainly not been Burgoyne's month. To make matters worse, General Howe had decided to take the bulk of his forces toward Philadelphia, leaving Burgoyne's friend Lieutenant-General Henry Clinton with a portion of the British Army in New York to launch the planned attack northward along the Hudson toward Albany. A British force of four thousand was north of New York City, but that was too small a force, and they were not moving in any case. In Burgoyne's view the feckless Howe had merely promised to pursue Washington northward if the American commander in chief decided to move up the Hudson in support of the Northern Army facing Burgoyne. If Howe thought this promise would console Burgoyne, he was deluded. But Burgoyne could only plead with Howe, who was his superior; he could not order his assistance. The situation again demonstrated that the British command structure was badly fragmented, lacking a single commander in chief in the colonies. This would prove to be disastrous in the long run. Burgoyne and Barry St. Leger both had orders to join with Howe and place themselves under his command. St. Leger had been turned back, and Burgoyne would apparently have to chase the man down to make that happen.[29]

The Army from Canada

Burgoyne's army had three major divisions (Figure 0.6). Typically, each division comprised three or more brigades, but in this case each division was made up of units assigned according to that division's special tasks.[30]

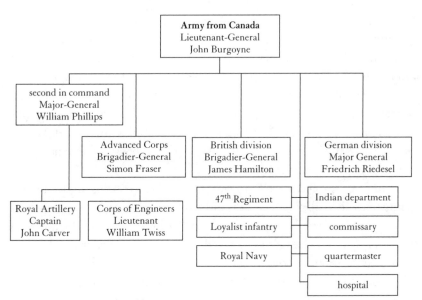

Figure 0.6 Basic organization of the Army from Canada. Chart by the author based on Schnitzer (2016).

Burgoyne's second in command was his old friend Major-General William Phillips of the Royal Artillery. It was Phillips who had managed to put guns on Sugar Loaf Hill above Fort Ticonderoga, which had prompted the Americans to swiftly abandon the fort. Phillips was also a Member of Parliament and a distinguished veteran of battles on the European continent. On one occasion during the Seven Years' War he had brought ponderous artillery into action so swiftly and decisively that the other officers could scarcely believe what they were seeing. His reputation as an artilleryman was legendary. Burgoyne had good reason to value his company.

It was appropriate that Burgoyne's second in command was a senior artillery officer. The expedition had begun with 126 pieces of artillery, a huge number by any standard, some of them monstrous 24-pounders, big guns that could throw five-and-a-half-inch solid cast-iron balls of that weight. They were designed for laying siege to solidly built fortifications. The smaller cannons could also be used in the field to fire canister at infantry units, cans of smaller shot that spread out when fired and could account for many casualties.

Some of the biggest cannons and the heavy 12-pounders, twenty-six big guns in all, had been dropped off or sent back before the overland trek from Lake Champlain had begun. Despite losing some cannons at Bennington and leaving others behind with garrisons, Burgoyne still had thirty-nine pieces of artillery, including two 24-pounders. Two of the 3-pounders and most of the 6-pounders were assigned to support infantry regiments. The rest were held back in the artillery park. It was still a huge amount of firepower, especially when the protracted toil of dragging it all along rough forest trails and across bogs and rivers was considered. Some officers and men still grumbled that the expedition had more cannons and more weight than would be needed to lay siege to the unfortified Albany or in any action along the way. But Burgoyne was convinced that he would need the big guns sooner or later.

A practical problem for Burgoyne and Phillips was that under British regulations an artillery officer was forbidden to command infantry or cavalry regiments. Another commander had been admonished by the king for ignoring that rule, so it had to be taken seriously. Burgoyne decided to deal with the problem by taking command himself in the field and having Phillips always at his side so that orders to all units would always come directly from Burgoyne, even if they originated with Phillips.

Burgoyne also liked to use Phillips as a sounding board, testing new ideas or repeating already expressed opinions and waiting for Phillips to assure him that they were still valid. He agreed that the Americans had ample supplies behind them and that they could afford to fight a defensive campaign. Burgoyne had no choice but to take the battle to them and to dislodge them with cannons and light infantry if necessary. But Phillips also knew as well as Burgoyne that now, in the middle of September, time was not on their side.[31]

The regiment was a fundamental administrative unit in the British Army as it was in the American Continental Army. Each British regiment had an authorized strength of 647 men and 560 muskets, although few regiments were at full strength. All British infantrymen wore brick-red coats, the lapels folded back to reveal long facings of yellow, light green, orange, buff, white, red, or blue, depending upon the regimental colors. Artillery units sported blue coats. Most of the German infantrymen wore lighter blue coats, trimmed with regimental colors, similar to the British uniforms. The variations in colors, hat styles, and other details allowed anyone familiar with them to identify military units at a distance. Even an American officer could, with the help of a spyglass, identify the units he was facing across a battlefield, even though regiments at Saratoga did not risk the capture of their colors by carrying flags into battle.

A standard regiment comprised ten companies, eight of them called line or battalion companies, the remaining two being specialized "flank" companies, one of light infantry and one of grenadiers. The men of the battalion companies usually wore brimmed tricorn hats, unlike the special bearskin or felt headgear worn by the grenadiers or the small caps worn by the light infantry.[32]

In action the regiment was often identical with the operational unit known as the battalion, and everyone from Burgoyne down the chain of command seemed to use the terms *battalion* and *regiment* interchangeably. But there was an important difference. The flank companies could be detached from their regiments and formed into specialized battalions. It was common for flank companies of all the available infantry regiments to be detached and consolidated as battalions of all grenadier or all light infantry companies, and that's how they were organized here under Burgoyne. The grenadier companies formed one special battalion, and light infantry companies formed another. In this army the two special battalions were both assigned to the Advanced Corps. Their home regiments, including the four in Hamilton's brigade-sized British division, would each necessarily fight as battalions of eight infantry companies when the time came.

THE ADVANCED CORPS

Brigadier-General Simon Fraser had command of the "Advanced Corps" (Figure 0.7), an agile brigade that was the tip of the British spear pushing toward Albany. He had both Acland's grenadier battalion and Lindsay's light infantry under him. For weight he had his own 24th Foot and some artillery. Most of the time he also had Burgoyne's Indian allies, along with some Canadian and Loyalist volunteers. Finally, there were Fraser's Rangers, not originally from the 24th Foot, but selected marksmen from the 34th Regiment of Foot that had been organized by his nephew, Captain Alexander Fraser. The company of marksmen had been all but destroyed in the August foray to Bennington, Vermont, but Alexander Fraser had rebuilt it within weeks with sixteen new men and one noncommissioned officer detached from each of the British infantry regiments under Burgoyne's overall command. As a result, the Advanced Corps was now well designed to be the vanguard of the army and to cover its right flank.

THE GERMAN DIVISION

Another of Burgoyne's key subordinates was Major General Friedrich Riedesel (Figure 0.8), who commanded the German troops from Brunswick and Hessen-Hanau.[33] Riedesel led the Brunswick division of four infantry regiments, including his own, along with an infantry regiment and two artillery units from Hessen-Hanau (Figure 0.9). His

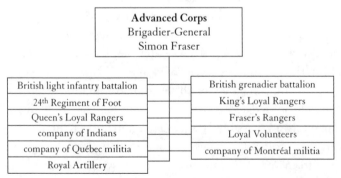

Figure 0.7 Fraser's brigade, the Advanced Corps. Chart by the author based on Schnitzer (2016).

FRIEDRICH ADOLPH VON RIEDESEL.

Figure 0.8 Painting of Friedrich Riedesel, n.d., unknown artist. Courtesy of New York Public Library.

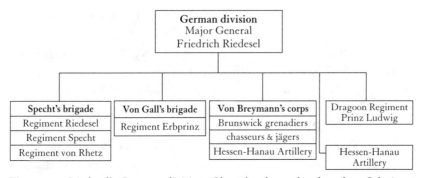

Figure 0.9 Riedesel's German division. Chart by the author based on Schnitzer (2016).

Brunswickers made up about a fifth of the twenty thousand German troops serving Great Britain in America in 1777.[34]

Riedesel's command had no brigadier generals, so he had arranged for Wilhelm von Gall, a colonel, and Johann Specht, a lieutenant colonel, to be temporarily promoted to that rank so that he could create two infantry brigades. It was a small matter, perhaps, but it was important to Riedesel that he have a proper division, one with no fewer than two infantry brigades along with artillery and some special units. Von Gall had only the Regiment Erbprinz, the lone Hessian infantry regiment among the Brunswickers. Most of the Regiment Prinz Friedrich, which would otherwise have also been assigned to von Gall, had been left behind to garrison Fort Ticonderoga. On paper at least, this arrangement brought Riedesel into a position of equality with Major-General Phillips. That the formality seemed necessary at all revealed the undercurrent of potential friction between the British and German halves of Burgoyne's army.

The German grenadier companies were detached from their five regiments and combined to form a Brunswick grenadier battalion under the command of Colonel von Breymann. Like their British counterparts, the German grenadiers were big men. They wore tall, polished miter caps of brass or tin over hair that on good days was tightly curled and powdered white. Most had long, stiff mustaches, waxed black and twisted into sharp points. This was intended to emphasize their size and ferocity. The men had long practiced keeping their faces expressionless, their eyes wide. It was designed to make them look fierce, and it worked. The German soldiers moved methodically and deliberately, deadly serious in their precise discipline.[35] Many had not come back from Bennington, but those who did were recovering quickly. They would be ready for action again in a few days.

The light infantry companies of the five German infantry regiments were similarly detached and formed into a dark-uniformed chasseur battalion under Major von Bärner. The green-uniformed Brunswick company of Hessen-Hanau jägers (hunters) was also part of this battalion. But the battalion had been badly cut up at Bennington. Von Bärner himself had been severely wounded, and the chasseurs lost 129 of their 317 men.[36]

The German jägers wore coats of woodsman's green and carried short-barreled rifles that approached but did not equal the American rifles in accuracy. Like the German grenadiers, they had a reputation for ferocity, but that was a blade that cut both ways. English officers told the German troops that the Americans were brutal savages who had adopted the cunning and unspeakable practices of American Indians. Americans in shaggy dress, particularly Morgan's riflemen, were given to cannibalism, they said, brutes that had to be exterminated quickly. The wide-eyed

German troops gave little thought to desertion in the early days of the campaign. Worse, the demonizing of the enemy prompted them to act brutally on occasion themselves, killing surrendering Americans on the spot rather than risk taking such monsters prisoner.[37]

Riedesel looked older than his thirty-nine years. He was a portly and homely man, though his adoring wife Frederika ("Fritschen" within the intimate circle of their family) would have bristled at the description. He and Frederika had married in 1762, when Friedrich was a lieutenant colonel in the Black Hussars. Riedesel was nothing like the dashing figure cut by Burgoyne, but Frederika was devoted to him just the same. She was here with the army, as were their three very young daughters and some servants.

Both Frederika and Friedrich ignored the fun the common soldiers made of their officers, such as when they would emphasize the last two syllables of Riedesel's name. *Esel* meant "ass" in German; it was just the kind of joke one should learn to overlook in the lower classes. British soldiers called him "Red Hazel," with more simple English humor than malice. Riedesel deserved and got better from his aide-de-camp and others who were in daily contact with him.[38] After all, the man usually declined to use either his title (he was a baron) or the "von" that preceded the surnames of senior German officers from the nobility.

Weeks earlier Simon Fraser had rushed into action without waiting for Riedesel's support at Hubbardton, and then complained that Riedesel had been slow to assist him. As far as Riedesel was concerned, the German troops had arrived in the nick of time and saved Fraser from possible disaster. Later on Fraser complained again, this time that Riedesel had moved too quickly. But the two generals had been comrades in the Seven Years' War, and by September 15 they had put these disagreements behind them. Now, having crossed to Saratoga on the west side of the Hudson and moving ever closer to Albany, Burgoyne's generals appeared united.[39]

THE BRITISH DIVISION

Brigadier-General James Hamilton commanded the British Division (Figure 0.10), which comprised just four British infantry regiments and some artillery. They were, however, the best infantry regiments in the army from Canada. It was also the brigade that would take the brunt of the coming battle and with which both Burgoyne and Phillips would ride when it was joined.

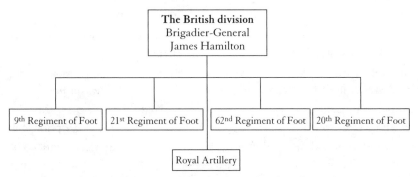

Figure 0.10 The British division. Chart by the author based on Schnitzer (2016).

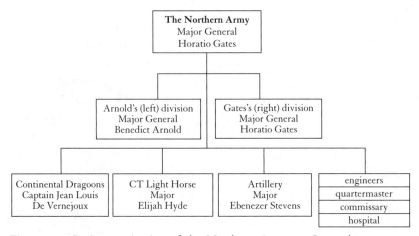

Figure 0.11 Basic organization of the Northern Army on September 15, 1777. Chart by the author based on Schnitzer (2016).

The American Northern Army

If Burgoyne was growing weaker as his army advanced southward, Gates was experiencing the reverse. The Northern Army (Figure 0.11) was slowly retreating south before the British advance and was gaining strength. Thanks to Schuyler and others there were good supply lines northward from Albany, the Hudson Valley, and the Mohawk Valley. Militia regiments from New York and the New England states were rallying and joining the Northern Army. As the Americans fell back they were joined by more units, both short-term militia regiments and long-term Continental regulars. The Continental Army was only months old, and the men in it were not well trained, but with the Continental regiments the United States finally had a regular army made up of men who had made long-term commitments to serve. Philip Schuyler had, of course, not liked being replaced by Gates as commander of the Northern Army. He had gone into seclusion for two days in August. But if any pique remained he was no longer showing it. As autumn approached, Schuyler threw himself into the task of supplying the Northern Army, using his influence and committing his private resources without any expectation of repayment. Gates had the core of a real army, which he divided into two main divisions, keeping one of the divisions and some smaller units under his direct command.

By August Gates also had the skills of Polish military engineer Colonel Thaddeus Kościuszko (Figure 0.12) to help him find and prepare a place to stop the advance of Burgoyne's army.[40] They found the right ground at Bemis Heights, a few miles north of the little town of Stillwater.

Jotham Bemis was a family man, farmer, and cattle trader in addition to running the only tavern on this stretch of road between Stillwater and Saratoga. The bluffs above his establishment were an excellent place to position cannons to command the road along the river. The floodplain of the Hudson, narrow and constrained for its entire length, was especially pinched here. The width of the plain on the west side of the river was no more than 450 feet at Bemis Tavern, and much of that width was impassable swampy ground. It was a constriction that the Americans could use to stop Burgoyne's advance along the river road.[41] Any army attempting to push south past Bemis tavern was compelled to stick to the narrow road and come under steady fire from guns posted on the heights above. Because of the terrain, the British failure at Bennington, and the threat of New England militias to the east, it was almost a certainty that Burgoyne would have to stay on the west side of the Hudson from now on. Thus the choke point below Bemis Heights was unavoidable (see Figure 0.13).

Lumber had been floated down from Philip Schuyler's mill in Saratoga before Burgoyne occupied the village there, and Gates's engineers used it to build an American bridge of boats across the Hudson not far south of Bemis Tavern. The bridge was cleverly designed to swing with the flow of the river if detached from one end. If Burgoyne were successful in pushing this far along either bank the Americans could easily fall back across the bridge to the opposite side of the river and deny the crossing to the

Figure 0.12 Painting of Thaddeus Kościuszko by Julian Rys, after an unidentified source, 1897. Courtesy of Independence National Historical Park.

pursuing British by simply detaching it at the western end and letting it swing with the current.[42]

Gates still fully expected that Burgoyne would try to force his way along the main river road, so he posted the division of the army that was under his direct command there. This right wing of the army was made up of brigades under Generals Glover, Paterson, and Nixon (Figure 0.14). They were posted west to east in that order between Neilson's farm

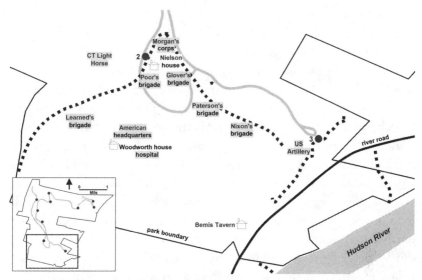

Figure 0.13 American positions on September 15, 1777. Defensive lines are shown as dotted lines. The current National Park property (shaded) and its tour road provide context.

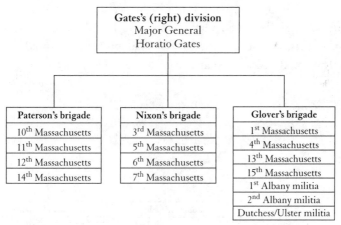

Figure 0.14 Organization of Gates's (right) division on September 17, 1777. Chart by the author based on Schnitzer (2016).

three-quarters of a mile northwest of Bemis Tavern and the bluffs overlooking the Hudson River, with Nixon's brigade dug in on the bluffs. Gates still thought it would be best to stay within Kościuszko's defensive positions and let Burgoyne bring the battle to him.

ARNOLD'S DIVISION

Gates had put the left wing of the Northern Army under the command of Major General Benedict Arnold (Figure 0.15). Of that division, Morgan's corps, Poor's brigade, and some of the militia were posted around Neilson's farm. There the American line turned and angled southwest, running three-quarters of a mile to a ravine protecting the left flank. Learned's brigade, which was also part of Arnold's division, was posted there.

Benedict Arnold was thirty-six years old, a modest five feet nine inches tall, and possessed of a nervous energy that worried his friends and unsettled his enemies. Black hair, icy gray eyes, and a swarthy complexion added to his charisma, which would prove to have its dark side. He still limped from the gunshot wound to his left leg he had received during the disastrous winter assault on Quebec City nearly two years earlier, but this only added to his reputation. He had stamina and fearlessness other men admired, but with those traits came a narcissistic self-confidence that could alienate his peers and lead the mercurial and impulsive Arnold to seize the initiative when more cautious minds around him hesitated. Most of all, it made him doubt, even dismiss, any authority but his own, and for this he had already risked disgrace more than once.[43]

Arnold admired the urbane Philip Schuyler for his wealth and social standing, but he also liked Gates. After all, he and Gates had similar modest origins, and it was Gates who had protected Arnold from accusations of malfeasance a year earlier at Fort Ticonderoga.[44] Gates had

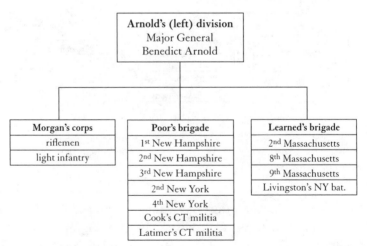

Figure 0.15 Organization of Arnold's (left) division on September 17, 1777. Chart by the author based on Schnitzer (2016).

written to Hancock at the time, saying that "the warmth of General Arnold's temper might possibly lead him a little farther than is marked by the precise line of decorum." But he went on to add that "the United States must not be deprived of that excellent officer's services."[45] It was an assessment that Gates had believed in August but would revise in September.

Colonel Daniel Morgan (Figure 0.16) arrived in Albany with his corps of riflemen the same day as Arnold. The large and flamboyant Daniel Morgan had been born in New Jersey in 1736, the son of Welsh parents. At seventeen he had run away from home and become a farm laborer in Virginia. He had later been a wagoner on the Braddock campaign against the French and came to be known for his strength and courage. While in this service he struck an officer who had slapped him with his sword, the kind of response the officer might have expected from a headstrong American. But in the British Army offenses of this kind were not excused for their predictability. The penalty was a severe whipping, the number of lashes later being the subject of much debate. It was four

Figure 0.16 Daniel Morgan, painted by Charles Willson Peale, from life, ca. 1794. Courtesy of Independence National Historical Park.

hundred.[46] Morgan stayed conscious through the ordeal, counting off the lashes with the drummer, even noting when the drummer miscounted, quitting after only 399. He loved to recount the story, claiming that he was still owed a lash by the British Army. Now he carried both scars and a lasting contempt for privileged British officers who could not even keep count properly.

Morgan had married and become a Virginia farmer, but when war broke out in 1775 he formed a company of Virginia riflemen, crack shots who used rifles made mostly by Pennsylvania Dutch craftsmen around Lancaster.[47] Morgan marched them six hundred miles to Cambridge, Massachusetts, in twenty-one days. After that he was with Arnold on the awful trek through northern Maine in the winter 1776 attack on Quebec. The British had taken Morgan prisoner, but he was later exchanged and rejoined his unit, the last lash still uncollected.

Later that year George Washington proposed to John Hancock that Morgan be given a rifle regiment as soon as his exchange was finalized. Morgan was made a colonel in command of the 11th Virginia. But the unit proved to be too small to be effective, so Washington gave Morgan a new command of a specially created new and larger corps of riflemen. These men were drawn largely from the western counties of Pennsylvania, Maryland, and Virginia, those from Virginia coming mostly from the 11th regiment.[48]

Morgan's riflemen were rough mountain men who dressed in hunting shirts and leggings. Few soldiers in the new American Army had proper uniforms, but the riflemen looked particularly unmilitary. Despite this, or more likely because of it, Morgan insisted on neatness and cleanliness. The purpose was to provide a counter to the impressive irregular force of Indian allies the British Army enjoyed.

Washington had persuaded Congress to assign Benedict Arnold to the Northern Army. Around the same time New Yorkers began requesting that Morgan's corps be sent north as well to help stop Burgoyne. Washington reluctantly sent Morgan to join the Northern Army, with the stipulation that the riflemen were subject to immediate recall to the main army should Washington need them. Now Morgan and Arnold found themselves together under Gates's command.

The American men were poorly shod and poorly clothed, most without any semblance of uniform. Many did not even have blankets. Supplies were starting to come in for the Continental Army troops: shoes, uniform coats, shirts, and other badly needed articles. But the new coats were made of a variety of cloths and colors, hardly uniform in any sense of the word. The new coats came in red, blue, green, and brown, with facings white, green, blue, and so forth. Few were standard blue. To signal their rank most of the senior American officers wore color-coded sashes: purple for major generals like Gates, pink for brigadier generals. Aides-de-camp wore green sashes, while lower-ranking commissioned officers wore color-coded cockades on their hats. Noncommissioned officers, sergeants and corporals, got by with strips of red or green cloth on their right shoulders. Those were the Continental regulars. The militiamen were even worse off; most of them wore civilian clothes with no insignia of rank at all.

By September 15 the erosion of British strength and the growth of American strength had brought the two armies to near parity in numbers. Both Gates and Burgoyne believed they could prevail, and the scene was set for a major battle. But their tactical preferences were quite different, partly from necessity and partly because of their personalities. Burgoyne, with his crack troops, was inclined to take the offensive; those were his orders and the approach of winter left him with no options other than to attack or to accept at least a partial retreat. Gates was inclined to fight defensively, waiting for the enemy to attack him and letting his green troops fight from behind strong defensive lines. This would have been his preference even if circumstances had not dictated it. But circumstances did dictate it; nothing else made military sense to him. The heights above Bemis Tavern provided the ground where he could make such a stand. Gates believed that Thaddeus Kościuszko had designed defenses that would hold, and the confident young Polish engineer had said that this was the place to dig in. Gates knew that Burgoyne had to reach Albany by winter, and that the Northern Army had the resources to block the way. As autumn began turning the New York countryside scarlet, the scene was set for a confrontation that would decide the future of the new United States of America.

The Opening

MONDAY, SEPTEMBER 15, 1777

6:05 AM, an American Scout, South of Saratoga

Alexander Bryan was a popular innkeeper who kept his business two miles north of Waterford, where the Mohawk River emptied into the Hudson.[1] Today he was scouting the British advance along the same road, which Burgoyne hoped to follow all the way to Albany. He was forty-four years old and thus not a young man, but his age granted him an amiable steadiness that his patrons admired. His hospitality was enjoyed by Whigs and Loyalists alike, and in his place of business he made sure that his affable smile and stock of spirits gave free rein to the flow of opinions and information of all kinds. Simple patience had rewarded him with a wealth of useful information.

The rebellion had hit what seemed like bottom only a few months before. Washington had begun the field season with only a couple thousand men. Now Washington's army in New Jersey comprised over thirty thousand men, and the Northern Army in New York also seemed to be growing steadily under Horatio Gates. There was a chance that the Northern Army could actually stop the British invasion from Canada, perhaps even force it to fall back to Fort Ticonderoga.

The local Committee of Safety knew full well that Bryan was not one of the third of Americans who found it best to stay neutral in this war. His inn was a constant source of information for the committee, facts and rumors that they sifted for fresh intelligence. Bryan was committed to independence, and right now he was doing his duty as he saw it.

Bryan had spent days and nights in the woods on the west side of the Hudson, watching Burgoyne's army make its way slowly toward Batten Kill on the east side. He knew the northern Hudson Valley well. Yesterday he had watched the rest of Burgoyne's army shuffle down what passed for a road and across a temporary bridge of boats into the village of Saratoga. When the last of them had crossed, he had circled around to take a new hidden post along the road leading south from the village. There he had waited for signs that the British Army was about to move again.

The advance British scouts were nearly on Bryan by the time he realized that this was the movement he had been waiting for. He escaped with only minutes to spare, trotting through the woods to put distance between himself and the advancing scouts. He had to reach American headquarters, eight miles to the south on Bemis Heights, and report in. The British Army was marching and a battle could not be far off. General Gates needed to know, and the sooner the better.[2]

8:00 AM, John Burgoyne, the British Camp at Saratoga

Lieutenant-General Burgoyne wrote out his orders for the day.[3] That done, he emerged from his tent in a uniform as red as madder or Mexican cochineal dye could make it, the color of brick rather than the color of blood. Burgoyne's staff were dressed in less ornate versions of the British red uniform. Major Robert Kingston, was his adjutant-general. His aide-de-camp and private secretary was Sir Francis Clerke. Burgoyne regarded Clerke as a promising young officer and was convinced that he would one day make a fine general, probably before reaching the age of thirty. He certainly had the breeding, having succeeded to a baronetcy at the age of twenty-one. Clerke had done well in the army since 1770. He had been promoted to lieutenant in the 3rd Foot Guards two years earlier, which, because of the peculiar benefits enjoyed by that unit, made him a captain in the larger army. Captain Charles Stanhope and another aide-de-camp attended Burgoyne as well. Stanhope was the eldest son of the Earl of Harrington, Viscount Petersham, Baron Harrington, and as such heir to that fine collection of titles. He was also, more or less in his own right, a Member of Parliament for Westminster in Middlesex. It was the custom for the son in this circumstance to use one of his father's secondary titles while waiting to inherit the lot. Stanhope was consequently addressed as Viscount Petersham of the 29th Regiment of Foot. It was a happy corps of officers, one in which Burgoyne encouraged intelligent conversation and socialization.[4]

The officer of the day absorbed the specifics of Burgoyne's latest orders and added them to the standing orders that had been in effect since summer. Each brigade would provide a picket made up of a captain, one subaltern, one sergeant, one corporal, and twenty-five soldiers from each regiment. The captain in each case brought along a drummer from his own regiment. The picket assembled before the morning gun and practiced marching and charging with bayonets under the watchful eye of the brigadier of the day. They had been doing this for weeks, but Burgoyne remained concerned that the British and German troops might revert to bad habits and lose coordination. When night fell they would post half the picket well in advance of the camp so that the alarm would be triggered if the Americans attempted a night attack. It should be enough to keep skulking rebels at a safe distance.[5]

Burgoyne handed his general orders to Kingston, who left to dictate them to the general officers of the day and to the brigade-majors, all of whom were waiting, ready to write them down on paper or on wax writing tablets. Each brigade-major would then leave for his brigade headquarters, where he would dictate the orders to the various majors or adjutants of the regiments. These men, in turn, would read them to their colonels and lieutenant-colonels. Sergeant-majors then dictated the orders to company sergeants, and the distribution of orders was complete. At every step in this process, orders were often written down more or less as dictated, but with more than occasional copy errors and paraphrasing.[6]

More than nine hundred men had been left behind to garrison Fort Ticonderoga: 462 British and 448 Germans. Now, after the losses at Bennington and elsewhere, Burgoyne had an army of just under three thousand British and about seventeen hundred German rank and file. If Guy Carleton, military governor of Canada, would send forward men from Montreal to garrison Ticonderoga, Burgoyne would have nine hundred more men to use at Saratoga, but it seemed to Burgoyne that in his jealousy, the scoundrel would rather let the expedition wither under Burgoyne's command than send him the men he needed. To make matters worse, Burgoyne had in fact assumed way back in July that Carleton would be sending a garrison force forward and had even said so in his report to London. An excerpt from that report had been published in the

London Gazette, and now he had to live with the embarrassment of having spoken too soon. His consolation was that Carleton should be even more embarrassed.[7]

Carleton had wanted command of this expedition for himself, but he was stuck in command of the garrison in Montreal instead while Burgoyne seemingly marched off to glory. Each man blamed and resented the other for his current circumstances. Both of them now held the military rank of lieutenant-general, but Sir Guy Carleton was also a knight of the realm, something Burgoyne could only hope for, and that, in turn, depended upon the outcome of the current expedition. Meanwhile, Carleton's title gave him a subtle edge over Burgoyne. It was yet another indication of the flaws in the British command structure.

Various attached units filled out Burgoyne's command. He even had a few sailors with him to manage the bateaux[8] and engineers to rebuild bridges and design fortifications. The engineers had managed the construction of the bridge of boats that got the army across the Hudson, and Burgoyne knew he might have need of those talents again.

The men of the various British regiments now moved about, engaged in the routine business of camp life. When the army was not moving, the troops paraded every day from ten to noon, sometimes longer. After that, the generals dined in the early afternoon and the troops paraded again from five until the evening gun.[9] It was an elaborate marching routine that was designed to instill discipline through force of habit.

Burgoyne's officers were gentlemen, many of them of the first order. The common soldiers often came from the lower ranks of British society, of course, some of them criminals who had opted for the army over jail or illiterates looking for a way out of poverty. Little wonder that the army was held in such little esteem at home. Still, this army had acquired a degree of discipline that Burgoyne thought enviable. The number and severity of punishments had been low enough to show that infractions were not epidemic but high enough to keep the lower classes mindful of their station and their obligations. Witnessing a man receive a punishment of a few hundred lashes of "the cat"[10] was a powerful deterrent.[11]

The Brunswickers were another matter. Two-thirds of the Germans King George had acquired from his friends and relatives in the petty German principalities were Hessians who had been supplied by the Landgrave of Hesse-Cassel. But most of the German troops under Burgoyne's command came from the Duke of Braunschweig. It was a name that most English gentlemen could not pronounce, so the anglicized "Brunswick" was usually substituted in their conversations.

Burgoyne often conversed with Riedesel in French. Both men spoke the language well, whereas Burgoyne knew little German and Riedesel's English was accented in a way that seemed to put him at a disadvantage. It was an inequality that disappeared when the two spoke in French, at least from Burgoyne's point of view.[12] Other officers followed suit if they could. Broken French was often the only common language spoken by the German and English officers. For the common soldiers the language barrier was almost absolute, and there was little fraternizing across it.

9:00 AM, Horatio Gates, American Headquarters

Horatio Gates wrote a brief letter to John Hancock, president of the Continental Congress. The advice of Schuyler's officers had been unanimous in August, when Gates's predecessor had moved the army to Stillwater, but unanimity did not necessarily mean that it had been the right thing to do. The British juggernaut had in quick succession taken Fort Ticonderoga and embarrassed the Northern Army at Hubbardton (Figure 0.5). All the American armed vessels and bateaux had been lost. At least 128 pieces of cannon were lost, and who knew how much ammunition, stores, and baggage as well. Now Burgoyne had crossed to the west side of the Hudson and was driving south from Saratoga, less than ten miles away. As a precaution, Gates had ordered all soldiers to sleep in their clothes and with their weapons.[13]

Gates had plenty to worry about. Administration was his personal strength, but he needed all he could muster. Today there was confusion over the daily password and countersign for the sentries on picket duty. Some units thought they were "Gordon" and "Roxbury," while others thought they were "Morris" and "Clymor." Gates would be lucky if the Americans did not end the day firing on each other when they heard passwords they did not recognize.

Gates was making progress in supplying the Northern Army. Wagonloads of supplies were arriving, and he now had enough staff to manage their distribution. This was largely because of the efforts in Albany of Schuyler, the general Gates had replaced and a rival he preferred to distrust. Today he appointed issuing commissary officers for each of the five brigades and Morgan's corps. That would take some of the pressure off headquarters.

Gates reasoned that if he were defeated he could probably fall back and prevent the construction of a new British bridge of boats across the Mohawk River, the main tributary of the Hudson that flowed in from the west just fourteen miles to the south of Bemis Heights. This would force Burgoyne to detour miles westward in order to use the fords closer to Schenectady. The idea suited Gates's inclination to fight a defensive campaign that depended more on delaying the enemy than defeating him. But the reality was that he could first risk defending the heights here north of Stillwater. Gates could wait here for Burgoyne to attack. If forced to retreat, he still had the fallback position south of the Mohawk.

Thaddeus Kościuszko had the engineers throw up breastworks for nearly a half mile along the brow of the bluff, placing strong batteries at the ends and a third one near the middle. He placed another line of breastworks across the river flats from Bemis Tavern to the bank of the Hudson. Today the men were finishing a second line across the flats a half mile northward below the northern battery and along the south bank of Mill Creek. There American forces could at least delay the enemy for a time and allow the guns on the bluffs behind and above them to pour devastating fire over their heads and into the enemy column. Burgoyne's way forward would lead him into a bottleneck with multiple corks. But what if Burgoyne detected the trap and tried a flanking movement around the American left flank, to the west and away from the river? Kościuszko's work was clearly not yet done. The fresh units arriving daily would have to be put to work fortifying the interior western flank of the American Army.

Gates had moved his headquarters from Stillwater to Bemis Tavern once the decision was taken to make a stand here. Once Kościuszko had completed the river bluff emplacements on Friday the twelfth, the American units had moved up from the river flats and on to Bemis Heights. Gates then moved his headquarters again, this time from Bemis Tavern to the Woodworth farm. By this time, he commanded at least nine thousand men, and more were on the way.[14]

Woodworth lived in a farmhouse (Figure 1.1) northwest of Bemis tavern, and it was to this house that Gates shifted his headquarters. A barn east of Gates's new headquarters would serve as a hospital if the need arose, and Gates was grimly certain it would. The Woodworth house sat a

Figure 1.1 The Woodworth house, the American headquarters on Bemis Heights. Source: Lossing (1851: 46).

third of a mile south of the Neilson farmstead, which was the apex of the American line.[15] It was an easy seven-minute hike between the two farmhouses. North of the Neilson house Morgan's riflemen were busy turning the Neilson barn into a fort; this was the point everyone expected would receive an attack if Burgoyne was smart enough to avoid the river road and try a flanking movement though the woods and scattered farm clearings west of the river.

The Neilson house (Figure 1.2) was small, but it sat on high ground that overlooked the surrounding countryside. Just north of it was Neilson's log barn, becoming fortified by American troops on all but the south side with a double tier of logs. Trenches and breastworks were built so that they curved from the barn around the house and back to the barn again, enclosing about half an acre. This the men decided to call Fort Neilson. It was the strongest point on the western portion of the American line. Other emplacements were dug and built on open ground and along a ravine lying between the fort and the river bluff emplacements three-quarters of

Figure 1.2 The Neilson house on Bemis Heights. Photo by the author.

a mile to the southeast. All along this line and the second long line stretching southwest from the fort, men were still felling large trees outward to form an abatis.[16] The felled trees presented an impenetrable tangle to any attacking force. Soldiers turned engineers made the tangle even more formidable by sharpening the ends of the branches so that the American line bristled like a giant porcupine. Ironically, even if he could bring them into action, Burgoyne's big guns would have a much harder time with the American abatis than they would with the brittle stone walls of a proper fort.

Kościuszko built an ammunition magazine between Fort Neilson and Gates's headquarters in the Woodworth house. This he made bombproof under a cribwork of timbers and earth. The temporary nature of the fortification bothered the Americans not at all. One way or another, their need for it would be gone before winter. Morgan's 451 riflemen were camped immediately north of the fort, but many spent their days and nights getting to know the woods and fields northward and serving as pickets to detect the first movements of the British there.[17]

Gates's service in Massachusetts had made him a good many friends among the Yankees who made up a major portion of his army. The New

Englanders also trusted John Stark and his Vermont militiamen. They had won big, defeating the Baum detachment at Bennington. But now Stark was refusing to bring his brigade across the Hudson to join the Northern Army. Gates begged him to "not tarnish the glory you have gained," but Stark seemed obstinate.[18] Gates knew that Stark had been passed over for a promotion by Congress, and he also knew that had to be part of the problem. What Gates did not know was that the terms of service for most of Stark's militiamen were about to expire. Few of them showed much inclination to abandon the harvest back home and spend a cold autumn in tents with the Northern Army.

The officers and troops under Gates's command were generally pragmatic men, full of republican and democratic ideals that Gates admired. Many were Deists, if they thought much about religion at all, and not a few of the officers were Masons. Gates did not have much time or patience for religion himself, but he thought that army chaplains helped morale. Nevertheless, it was a secular army, and the few chaplains who were allowed to attend it treaded lightly.

From the point of view of an ex-British officer like Gates the militiamen were even less disciplined than the Continentals. Like most other American generals, he worried that the militia regiments would break under pressure when they faced a bayonet charge from Burgoyne's disciplined professionals. On the other hand, his were citizen soldiers who were motivated by revolutionary zeal, not paroled convicts whose main motivation was to avoid the lash. This was something the idealist Gates seemed to understand even better than the aristocratic George Washington did.

The scouts reporting back to Gates were suitably impressed by the size of the British artillery park they saw at Saratoga and the large number of tents set up by Burgoyne's army. There had to be a thousand of them, they said.[19] The scouts were going to try to get closer and send back more detailed information. It was enough to prompt Gates to write a letter to Major General Benjamin Lincoln, who was still ranging with his militia somewhere off to the south and east, between Gates's position and Albany. It occurred to Gates that Lincoln might have a chance to gall the portion of Burgoyne's army that was still on the east side of the river, where British artillery and reinforcements would be unable to assist them. Gates looked at his draft letter, and then changed "gall" to "defeat." He was feeling more confident in the future outcome every day. Yet the letter was more a piece of advice to Lincoln than an order; Gates was still not sure of his authority over Lincoln, and he would remain uncertain about it until Lincoln came into camp and placed himself under Gates's direct command. Just as important, he knew the steady and self-effacing Lincoln well, and he was sure that a polite suggestion would serve at least as well as an order in this case.[20]

Lincoln might or might not be able to keep the cranky, independent John Stark engaged with him on the east side of the river, but neither Lincoln nor Gates would succeed at giving the man orders. These were touchy Americans, after all. Gates was also sure that Stark was still disgusted that Congress had promoted Lincoln over him. Gates handed the draft letter off to his adjutant, James Wilkinson, and told him to append the written report from the scout detailing what they knew about Burgoyne's position. After that, Gates drafted a letter to John Hancock, bringing him up to date and acquainting him with the ever-improving prospects of the Northern Army.[21]

9:30 AM, James Wilkinson, American Headquarters

Lieutenant Colonel James Wilkinson (Figure 1.3) was only twenty years old. He had been born in Maryland and educated for a career in medicine. But war changes plans and ambitions, and so Wilkinson rode to Cambridge in 1775 to volunteer his services. The young man was a charming and ingratiating member of a family that had once been well off. He had risen quickly, becoming a company captain in time to be sent to Canada as part of the reinforcements intended to aid Benedict Arnold's ill-fated attempt to take Quebec. The retreat from Canada brought him into contact with Gates, on whom he made a good impression. When Gates was appointed to command the Northern Army, Wilkinson left his previous regiment and joined Gates's staff as adjutant general, with the rank of lieutenant colonel.[22]

The ambitious young Wilkinson had grabbed three of Burgoyne's soldiers on a Saturday while the men were too busy raiding a garden just south of Saratoga to notice the American patrol approaching. The information gathered from these prisoners made it clear that Burgoyne was once again on the move. Now the British were moving to Dovegat, just six miles north of the American entrenchments.[23]

This morning it was again Wilkinson's duty as adjutant general to read out Gates's orders for the day. The confusion over passwords continued.

Figure 1.3 James Wilkinson by Charles Willson Peale, from life, 1796–1797. Courtesy of Independence National Historical Park.

That would have to change. Wilkinson drew himself up before Arnold, the brigadier generals of the five brigades, Colonel Morgan, and their respective staff officers. The brigade commanders were mostly in their forties, one was fifty-three, and another only thirty-three. They might have smiled at such a young adjutant general, but this was a young man's war and they all focused on writing down what he was saying word for word, or close to it. Guards and soldiers assigned to fatigue duty would be deployed as usual. One of the doctors had lost a case of surgical instruments, and a reward was offered for its safe return. Burgoyne's army was now estimated to number eight thousand. Finally, Wilkinson listed the number of soldiers each of the infantry brigades was expected to provide to parade with the artillery in the evening. Wilkinson finished, and the officers dispersed to repeat the orders to the units they commanded.[24]

Henry Brockholst Livingston was in the crowd of officers that were gathered to hear the orders. He was an old friend of Philip Schuyler, one of the New York Livingstons, and alert to any slip Gates might make.

He struggled to control his amusement when he heard Gates estimate Burgoyne's strength at eight thousand. Only days earlier, Gates had guessed that Burgoyne had only five thousand men, but now that growing American strength was passing that number it was in Gates's interest to exaggerate enemy strength. Arnold had taken Livingston and some other friends of Schuyler on as aides, and the arrangement was not pleasing to Gates.[25]

10:00 AM, Oliver Boardman, the American Camp on Bemis Heights

Oliver Boardman had left Middletown, Connecticut, on the second of September, marching with Colonel Thaddeus Cook's Connecticut Militia along rough roads, and not reaching Stillwater until the twelfth. It had taken most of eleven days, 150 more or less, at twelve or fifteen miles a day. Now Boardman and the rest of the Connecticut militia were camped with Arnold's division on Bemis Heights. He was glad to be led by a New Englander, particularly one from Connecticut. Arnold seemed like a natural leader: quick, sharp-eyed, direct, and apparently fearless.

Boardman saw some excitement around the northern defenses of the camp, where men were still working hard to build defensive walls and trenches behind the abatis. Word came back that Burgoyne's Indians had driven American scouts back. Now Morgan was sending out a hundred of his riflemen to return the favor. Things were heating up.[26]

11:00 AM, Benedict Arnold, the American Camp on Bemis Heights

Benedict Arnold was pleased that he had done well in the Mohawk Valley, turning back the attempted British attack on Albany from the west. He and Morgan had rejoined the Northern Army in Albany on August 31, and Gates seemed pleased to have both of them. Gates and Arnold had got along well enough at Ticonderoga in 1776, and Gates had even deflected charges brought against Arnold by another officer at that time. But it remained that Arnold and Gates were opposites in temperament. For the time being, Gates chose to use Arnold's impulsive aggressiveness as a balance to his own reserved inclination to play a defensive game. He had given Arnold command of the left wing of the army. It was a division made up largely of New Englanders, happy to serve under the charismatic Arnold.

Yet despite the outward appearance of collegiality, the seeds of dispute were already germinating in the mix. Arnold was still fuming because

Congress had passed him over, as it had John Stark, when it had promoted five more-junior brigadier generals to the rank of major general back in February. Meanwhile, the list of promotions included Benjamin Lincoln and Arthur St. Clair, men whom both Arnold and Stark regarded as their juniors. The problem was that Congress had just adopted a set of state quotas to deal with political complaints of favoritism. According to the new formula, Connecticut already had more than its share of major generals. Knowing this did nothing to mollify Arnold.

Arnold had written to a sympathetic George Washington in March, saying that he presumed that Congress was hoping he would resign. The commander in chief had tried to mollify him, but the truth was that while Washington's own sense of commitment to the American cause was deep and enduring, Arnold's was shallow and dependent on personal gratification.[27] Arnold had finally been promoted to major general in May, but the delay had made him junior to Benjamin Lincoln, who, having been promoted earlier, had held the rank longer. Now Lincoln was ranging somewhere south and east of here with his troops. If and when Lincoln joined the main body of the Northern Army commanded by Gates, he would be senior to Arnold, and he would displace him in the command hierarchy. It was a thought that Arnold neither liked nor could forget.

Congress made more than a few such mistakes as American government struggled to invent itself. The proper balance between the national whole and the constituent states was unclear from the beginning. Washington had been named commander in chief in 1775, a popular decision that ensured that New England and the southern states would cooperate in fielding a national army. But when Congress selected Gates to command the Northern Army it did not explicitly place him under Washington's command. For his part Washington had declined to ratify a foregone conclusion by also appointing Gates himself.[28] Gates had served well as Washington's adjutant general during the siege of Boston, but now Gates was technically independent from his old friend. As a result of the action of Congress, Gates now increasingly saw Washington as a rival rather than as his superior.

Meanwhile, Arnold created his own potential discord by taking on Richard Varick and other close associates of Philip Schuyler in Albany. Varick had been born in New Jersey to a middle-class family of Dutch origins. He grew up speaking both Dutch and English, and eventually practiced law in New York. By 1777 he was a twenty-four-year-old aide, first to Philip Schuyler, now to the mercurial Arnold.[29]

Arnold also took on Henry Brockholst Livingston and Matthew Clarkson as aides. Like Varick they were both scions of the New York aristocracy and friends of Schuyler. Schuyler had the resources to maintain express riders to carry letters between his Albany mansion and friends serving in the Northern Army. Varick was especially diligent in writing Schuyler and using the express service, his letters reflecting the self-assuredness and strong opinions common in young men. Gates for his part regarded each of Schuyler's young friends with deep annoyance, and they returned it in kind. To their more astute fellow officers it seemed now to be only a matter of time before Gates and Arnold would clash.

When Henry Brockholst Livingston had first showed up in camp and dined with Arnold, Gates had made a point of issuing general orders countermanding Arnold's assignments of two newly arrived militia units. Since he had initially directed Arnold to take care of the assignments himself, it was a public way of taking the man down a notch. No one, least of all Arnold, could mistake Gates's intention. Arnold took umbrage and complained. Gates relented and promised to rectify the error, though he never would.

Arnold shared with Enoch Poor and Daniel Morgan the tiny Neilson farmhouse and its outbuildings at the apex of the left wing. Matthew Clarkson had sat next to him a few days earlier as Arnold wrote out a new version of his will. Clarkson joked wryly, "I should do the same, but God knows I have nothing to leave."[30] There were many like him in both armies. For his part, Benedict Arnold's youthful problems as a headstrong soldier, the recent death of his wife, the refusal of Betsy Deblois to replace her, his experiences early on in the war, and the peculiarities of his personality had brought him to a morbid enthusiasm for battle, and a resignation that went beyond mere fatalism. No one doubted his bravery, self-confidence, and ambition—or his intolerance of being thwarted. But no one knew him well enough to perceive the death wish that could smolder behind his cold gray eyes when he was frustrated.

For the time being, all was well with Arnold. Today he went out with a large detachment, probing for the British Army, trying to discern their intentions, following up on observations made on Sunday. Richard Varick had been out the previous day, scouting with Arnold, some other officers and three troopers from Major Elijah Hyde's Connecticut Light Horse. They had fallen in with Morgan and a party of two hundred of his riflemen around Sword's house. From there some of the mounted men went still farther north, looking for Burgoyne's advanced pickets. They went as far as Dovegat, where they saw Burgoyne's forces at a distance, apparently parading without drums. They doubled back, found Arnold, and decided to return with their information rather than risk an engagement only two miles from the British Advanced Corps.[31]

12:00 Noon, John Burgoyne, the Road South from Saratoga

The whole army marched at noon. Prior to this day the brigades and their regiments had marched in train, each often camping on the ground vacated in the morning by the regiment just ahead of them in the long line of troops that had previously stretched mostly along the east bank of the Hudson. They had assembled the night before on the west bank, in and around the small village of Saratoga, the entire army at last now on the west side of the river. Today the march would take them only a few miles, but they moved more as an army now. Fraser's Advanced Corps began to move along roads a mile or more west of the main body, away from the river. Hamilton's British brigade was moving south along roads and trails closer to the river, while Riedesel's German brigade and the bulk of the artillery kept to the river road and the meadows between the road and the river (Figure 1.4).

The artillery took the river road for good reason. The big guns needed firm footing and good bridges. (See Figure 1.5.) Neither of these was often encountered even on the road, but movement off the road was much worse. The gruff but admired Major Griffith Williams had direct command of the guns not assigned to any particular column, nearly twenty British artillery officers, and over 250 artillerymen. Yesterday General Phillips had reminded them that there would be no fresh supplies of shot or powder. Success would probably not be determined by a single action, and they had to husband their ammunition. There could be no wasted firing at a retreating enemy, and gunners were cautioned to use their own judgment and cease firing even when commanded to fire by field officers if the situation seemed to require it. The exceptions were direct orders from Phillips himself or from Burgoyne.[32]

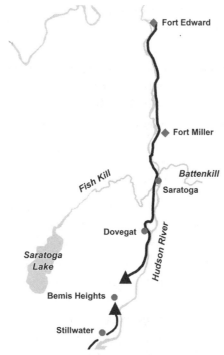

Fort Edward

Fort Miller

Fish Kill

Battenkill
Saratoga

Dovegat

Hudson River

Saratoga
Lake

Bemis Heights

Stillwater

Figure 1.4 The final approach of the army from Canada.

Figure 1.5 American field artillery (*left*) and a British howitzer (*right*). Photos by the author.

The four companies of artillery were each supposed to have a captain, a captain-lieutenant, a first lieutenant, three second lieutenants, and a hundred enlisted men. Some companies were already below those numbers. Second Lieutenant James Hadden marched as part of Captain Thomas

Jones's artillery brigade, assigned to Hamilton's brigade in the event of engagement. Hadden was the son of a Royal Marine, and the product of the Royal Military Academy at Woolwich. Like many other officers in Burgoyne's army, he had never known any other life. Now he had to function in the field, where gunners were encouraged to refuse orders from field officers. It was yet another of the disconnects and logical inconsistencies in the command structure of the British Army, problems that would eventually put the whole expedition at risk.[33]

The British Army had started out with about four hundred horses just to haul the artillery train. Nearly a hundred of these were needed to pull just the eighteen light 6-pounders, the six light 3-pounders, and the two 8-inch howitzers[34] that were normally attached to the infantry battalions (see Figure 1.5). The artillery park required the rest. Yet four hundred horses for the artillery were just the beginning. The total number of horses required by the army was astonishing. Burgoyne had six mounts of his own available, as did each of his two major generals. Four brigadiers had four each, and so forth. Even the surgeons needed thirty horses. Each battalion needed fifty-four horses for its field officers and their staffs. Because of their greater numbers, the German battalions needed seventy each. The total just for officers came to 1268 mounts. Artillery and baggage horses brought the total to around two thousand, all of them hungry. The supply of oats was nearly gone and forage was scarce. Each horse ideally needed about twenty pounds of forage a day, but few of them got anything close to that. Burgoyne knew that he would have over two hundred horses available for other tasks if the guns in the artillery park did not burden his army, but he simply could not imagine leaving any more guns behind.[35]

Neither was Burgoyne inclined to leave behind his personal baggage, which included prodigious amounts of wine and champagne. Phillips had discovered to his astonishment way back in August that Burgoyne's personal baggage alone filled about thirty carts. Phillips could only guess at how many additional carts were needed to supply the rest of the many officers on the expedition, not to mention a horde of wives, servants, and even children who accompanied the army. A spreadsheet kept by Burgoyne's commissary general, estimated that a force of five thousand men would need 1688 two-horse carts to stay in the field for three months. The expedition had already been in the field much longer than that, and even with its huge herd it had nothing like that number of horses and carts available.

As short of horses and as short on supplies as the army was, it was still an enormous undertaking.[36]

Four companies of the 47th Regiment brought along the provisions and the hospital in the rear. The sailors floated the bateaux down the river and broke up the damaged bridge of boats the army had used to cross the Hudson. The rear guard was commanded by the stern but still limping Lieutenant Colonel von Breymann. His wound at Bennington had not yet fully healed. The rear guard included the Brunswick chasseurs and grenadiers as well as the jägers, and Hessen-Hanau artillery. Captain Georg Päusch commanded the German artillery, which included two light 6-pounders, two light 3-pounders, and enough men to serve them.

1:00 PM, Simon Fraser, on the Bluffs above the Hudson

Brigadier General Simon Fraser moved out with his Advanced Corps, pushing ahead tentatively on the high ground to the west and away from the Hudson. He had been promoted to his current rank under Burgoyne for this campaign. Fraser appreciated his promotion, but it came with an onerous condition, as did the promotions of four other brigadiers under Burgoyne's command. The condition was that once Burgoyne's expeditionary force linked up with Howe's army in New York, the entire force would come under Howe's command and the brigadiers would revert to their lower permanent ranks. The problem was that there were lieutenant colonels in Howe's army, who according to the dates of their commissions were senior to Fraser and the other officers serving under Burgoyne. It would not do for the four newly minted brigadiers to jump past them. This conundrum, which had been created back in London by Lord George Germain, upset Burgoyne as much as it did his brigadiers, and he said so. "Were this to be put in execution, I should find myself at the head of an army without a single intermediate British officer between the Lieutenant General and a Lieutenant Colonel." No one under his command disagreed with Burgoyne's assessment of the unhappy situation. He had restated it in a letter to the adjutant general back in June, but there was no solution forthcoming from London. Burgoyne could not have really expected that there would be. The British Army was rife with a confusing mix of local ranks, regimental ranks, and army ranks. Individual officers often had two, even three, separate ranks depending on what units they were in and where they were stationed. If Phillips could be major general in

Burgoyne's army while at the same time being a colonel in the army and a mere major in the Royal Artillery (and he was), almost any crazy combination of ranks seemed possible. Simon Fraser could not have been much comforted by the knowledge that his current situation was far from unique. Like the others, he soldiered on.[37]

2:00 PM, Friedrich and Frederika Riedesel, the British Camp at Saratoga

Major General Friedrich Riedesel was concerned as he waited for his turn to move out of Saratoga and down the river road toward the Americans. Not far away, the Baroness Frederika Riedesel was also worried. Burgoyne had told her only a few days earlier that "the English never lose ground," and her spirits were elevated accordingly. But it bothered her that the other officers' wives seemed to have advance knowledge of the army's movements while she did not. There were many women with the army, but only a few ladies. Perhaps only these few had intimate knowledge of what was planned, but it was disturbing to be left out nonetheless. She was painfully aware that the wives of other senior officers seemed to know more than even her husband did, despite his rank. When she had followed Friedrich in the Seven Years' War everything had been kept quite secret, even from the wives. But here everything seemed generally known within Burgoyne's inner circle, and Frederika worried that if the British wives knew what was going to happen next, the Americans probably did too. She did not think it was an accident that the Americans seemed to be waiting for them at every turn.[38]

Frederika fussed over her three daughters with the help of two maids and their faithful man servant. It took her mind off the weightier matters of the men's world around her, and her exclusion from the inner circle. The oldest, Gustava, was only six years old. Frederika, the middle child sharing her mother's name, was three, and little Caroline was only one, yet here they all were in the middle of a war in the vast forests of America.[39]

Today Frederika's husband, Friedrich, was as annoyed as he usually was with things as they stood in the expedition. From the beginning Burgoyne had not felt it necessary to share the overall plan with him as he did with his British generals. Riedesel was routinely left outside their councils, less often invited to dine, and condescended to when he was. But unhappy duty was duty all the same, and Riedesel would carry it out to the best of his ability.

The German and British soldiers did not speak the same language, leading to inevitable misunderstandings and flashes of conflict. Most of the women following the army were British and would have nothing to do with the Germans; the men could not even pay them to wash their clothes. The women simply refused to offer the same services to the Germans as they did to the British soldiers. Worse, it was a new kind of warfare for troops accustomed to formal set-piece engagements on the broad open fields of Europe. Little wonder that Riedesel's command of military step-children from Brunswick was already starting to be eroded by desertions.[40]

Years ago Fraser and Riedesel had been comrades in the European fighting. General Phillips had been with the Riedesels in the Seven Years War as well. He had remained a good friend to them ever since. Phillips, at least, was one senior officer whom Riedesel felt he could count on. Riedesel was grateful that circumstances kept Phillips close to Burgoyne's side. Riedesel could not ignore the fact that his German troops had taken the brunt of the disaster at Bennington. Men and cannons had been squandered and Riedesel's dragoons, what were left of them, were still un-mounted. Now the entire army had crossed the Hudson and thereby cut its supply line back to Fort Edward and Fort George. Perhaps Burgoyne was right. If they garrisoned enough posts along the way to keep the supply line open, they would not have enough men left to take Albany. Riedesel was not happy to be part of an isolated command, one that had only enough provisions for a month and no future but to do or die on the road to Albany.[41]

2:00 PM, *Horatio Gates, the American Headquarters on Bemis Heights*

Gates invited his senior officers to dine with him in the early afternoon. He had just finished drafting a brief statement for release to the press.[42]

Gates had been handed a propaganda coup when some of Burgoyne's Indian allies killed and scalped the beautiful, blond Jane McCrae. It had mattered not at all to Gates that young Jane was a Loyalist and betrothed to a British officer, and it seemed not to matter to the outraged public either. Gates had made good use of the Jane McCrae affair, and the American newspapers were happy to help out. When Burgoyne wrote a letter com-plaining to Gates about the conduct of American forces at Bennington, Gates had responded quickly and in public.[43]

Jane McCrea's fiancé had recently joined the corps of provincials attached to Burgoyne's army. He had engaged some Indians to find her, separate her from the Americans, and deliver her safely to him. The two Indians who had been bringing Jane to him had a falling out over who would get the expected payment. One of them then impulsively killed Jane with his tomahawk in order to prevent the other man from getting the reward. Burgoyne ordered the killer to be turned over to him, and the man was delivered up. Burgoyne spared the man's life after the Indians agreed to some new rules of engagement, thinking that if he executed the man the rest of the Indians would promptly desert him.

Burgoyne had in fact been ready to execute the killer regardless of the consequences, but he was dissuaded by the French Canadian who was in charge of the Indian contingent. Burgoyne's initial reaction was, "I would rather lose every Indian in my army than connive at their enormities." After he cooled, Burgoyne said, "I have ever esteemed the Indian alliances, at best a necessary evil, their services to be overvalued; sometimes insignificant, often barbarous, always capricious, and that the employment of them was only justifiable, when by being united to a regular army, they could be kept under control."[44]

No one thought it odd that the two commanders would write each other letters in the midst of a campaign. They were gentlemen, after all, and they had known each other back in 1745. Burgoyne's answer to Gates was just as florid as Gates's letter but much longer. When the American press acquired copies of the exchange Gates's public relations victory was complete. Officers in both armies knew that politics were part of warfare in this modern age. The gradual departure of Indians from the British Army began in the wake of the death of Jane McCrae.[45]

6:20 PM, *John Burgoyne, the British Camp at Dovegat*

The British Army made camp at Dovegat as night fell. It was a spot where a rare, old oxbow in the Hudson had created a looping backwater on the west side of the river. The bateaux could be drawn up along the bank of the backwater, giving them more protection than they enjoyed through most nights. The river road bent westward here to get around the backwater, and for the first time in many days the main channel of the Hudson was a mile away from where they camped.

The entire army had lumbered forward barely three miles. Burgoyne thought he could sense the Americans hanging in the shadows to the west away from the river and in the forest in front of him. American scouts peered at them from across the river. Every small bridge they came to along the west bank of the Hudson was destroyed, every big tree felled across the road. It was clear that the Advanced Corps would soon feel the pressure of active resistance. The Americans were dug in somewhere ahead, and Burgoyne sensed that their lines could not be far away. They might even attack. The engineers had repaired a major bridge for the morning advance, and it was no time to be taking chances. Burgoyne scrawled his last order of the day; the men would sleep dressed and with their weapons tonight.

That night Simon Fraser's Advanced Corps would camp atop the bluffs west of the Hudson. The rest of the army camped below on the river plain. The English regiments camped just south of the Dovegat house. Some of the German regiments camped facing a small stream on the right, while others camped on the left, facing the Hudson and overlooking the supply bateaux lined up there. The troops were delighted to find broad fields of wheat and rye for feeding the horses and for straw bedding for their tents. There were fresh vegetables; the men had not enjoyed such comfort since the expedition had begun. The Germans in particular were impressed with the abundance and quality of maize, the American crop they called "Turkish wheat," despite it being neither of those things.[46]

8:30 PM, *John and Harriet Acland, the British Camp at Dovegat*

John Acland was from Somersetshire. His wife, Lady Harriet, was the sister of the Earl of Ilchester. She was twenty-seven years old, pretty, poised, and completely devoted to her husband. John had persuaded her to remain behind in Canada during the campaign, but she had come south to join him. John was now the envy of most of the men in Burgoyne's army. John and Harriet retired to the tent they shared, the canvas glowing dimly from the candle they liked to burn as a night light and to drive off the damp.

There was not a British soldier who did not admire the polite and amiable Lady Harriet. Officers were solicitous and common soldiers gawked and grinned in her presence. She was invariably considerate. They all remembered that as the army was setting off from Montreal, Harriet had sent each of thirty officers a half of a large wheel of Cheshire cheese. It was no trifling gift; English cheese was selling at a dollar a pound at the time.[47]

John Acland was thirty years old, having purchased the rank of major in the 20th Foot less than two years earlier. In Montreal General Carleton had appointed Acland to command the battalion of grenadiers in the Burgoyne campaign. It was made up of ten grenadier companies that were detached from their respective regiments to form the battalion.

Each of the same ten regiments had also given up their light infantry companies to form a separate light infantry battalion, in this case one commanded by Alexander Lindsay, the Earl of Balcarres, a major in the 53rd Foot. Both battalions thus had companies drawn from regiments having slightly different uniform styles and facing colors, and the distinctive headgear of both kinds of flank companies, which led them to be known as "hatmen."[48]

The standard infantry line companies of three regiments had been left behind to carry out garrison duty in Canada. All but one of the rest of them were now with Burgoyne at Saratoga. The 53rd Foot, the "Brickdusts," was the exception. Its line companies had been sent back to garrison Fort Ticonderoga after the action at Hubbardton. The flank companies of the 53rd now commanded by Acland and Lindsay were the only men of that regiment still with the main force. Lindsay and his men from the 53rd enjoyed their nickname, "Brickdusts," because they wore the only red uniforms in Burgoyne's army that also had red facings.

Acland's grenadiers were the best-looking and tallest men in their respective regiments, made taller by the wool felt caps and fancy uniforms they wore. Grenadiers no longer carried grenades, but in addition to bayonets their belts still held short swords. The grenadiers were skilled with both flintlocks and blades, and they were used as a shock force whenever special coolness under fire and selfless bravery were called for.

Unlike Acland's grenadiers, the Earl of Balcarres's light infantry soldiers were the smallest, fastest, and most agile men that could be found in the regiments. They wore short jackets and small hats to keep themselves as unencumbered as possible. Flank company men of both the grenadier and light infantry battalions were expected to be able to travel easily at four miles an hour and to cover twenty-four miles a day without complaint. Flank company officers, whether grenadier or light, were the youngest, toughest, and most ambitious gentlemen available. Battalion commanders like Acland and Lindsay were thus cut from the same cloth. They and their battalions were assigned to

Fraser's Advanced Corps, the column expected to see action first, and the two flank battalions were at its front.[49]

The circumstances that had led Harriet Acland to join her husband arose when John was wounded at Hubbardton. Harriet had found out about it and begged to be allowed to join and tend to him. She was brought south across Lake Champlain on a supply boat, and once she found him she refused to leave her husband during and even after his recovery.[50]

John recovered quickly and Harriet decided that she was not going back to Canada. After all, General Riedesel had his wife with him, and children and servants as well. Acland had resumed his command of the grenadiers on August 5, and Harriet made it clear that she expected to stay with him for the remainder of the campaign. At Fort Edward, or soon thereafter, accommodating artillerymen had contrived to supply Harriet and her two maids with a two-wheeled tumbrel to carry her along as the army slogged toward Albany. This she sometimes rode in dressed in the finest fabrics and wearing small gold slippers. None of this detracted from her angelic reputation.[51]

The sun had set at Dovegat by twenty past six and a nearly full moon had risen in the east. Their night candle flickered, and John's big Newfoundland dog, Jack Ketch, was curled up at their feet in the tent. The candle somehow got tipped over and the tent caught fire. The fire spread rapidly, and the commotion roused the whole camp. With the fire spreading up the canvas wall John's orderly sergeant dove through the front of the tent and grabbed the first person he found, dragging John out of the flaming tent. Harriet saved herself by crawling under the back wall of the tent to safety. Out front the rescued John looked around and did not see her. John then lunged back into the tent thinking she was still inside. Seeing Harriet outside, the sergeant went back in to rescue his major a second time.

John suffered burns on his face and arms, giving Harriet a new set of wounds to nurse. Jack Ketch took the blame for knocking over the candle. The incident did nothing to reduce Harriet Acland's cheerful resolution to remain with her husband for the duration. Nor did it reduce the long roster of her admirers.[52]

John Acland's reputation was another matter. The men admired and followed him cheerfully, but the Baroness Frederika Riedesel thought that though he was a fine officer, he was a plain and rough fellow who drank too much and clearly did not deserve such a fine young wife.

Being certain of this only increased Frederika's admiration of the devoted Harriet.[53]

9:00 PM, *An American Scout, the American Camp on Bemis Heights*

A full moon was above the hills to the east when Alexander Bryan, the innkeeper and part-time scout, finally reached Gates's headquarters. It had taken him all day to elude the British scouts and make his way through the woods back to Bemis Heights. Major Henry Dearborn had also been out with his American light infantry, scouting quickly through the woods as far west as Saratoga Lake. Like Bryan, he returned in the evening bringing further intelligence that Burgoyne might attack tomorrow. A fuller report from Lt. Colonel Colburn from Scammell's 3rd New Hampshire had also come in. Andrew Colburn and his men had been prowling the east bank of the Hudson since Sunday morning. Colburn said the enemy had struck most of their tents in Saratoga at noon and that the whole British Army was moving this way. Captured British grenadiers confirmed all of this. Gates had already ordered the entire army to stay fully clothed, lie upon arms, and be up at four o'clock. In the morning Bryan would head south, back to the listening post at his inn. His contribution in the field was at an end for the time being.[54]

TUESDAY, SEPTEMBER 16, 1777

8:00 AM, *John Burgoyne, the British Camp at Dovegat*

It was good news that the 47th Foot had come in this morning with provisions. The advance of his army was certain to come up against some resistance any day now. The Americans had to be close, but Burgoyne's scouts were not coming back with much information. The forest cover was so thick and chance encounters with American advanced pickets so frequent that they had not been able to move far enough out to observe what fortifications the rebels and thrown up or where. Burgoyne's men were being picked off, especially when they decided to venture too far from camp in search of food for themselves or forage for the hungry horses. Burgoyne needed to tighten discipline, to issue a few orders that would convey his sense of urgency and signal the impending battle. He assigned the field officer of the day. The password and countersign were in place. He wrote out his orders for the day and handed them off to his staff for the daily briefing.[55]

9:00 AM, Horatio Gates, American Headquarters on Bemis Heights

Gates was still nervous, and cautious to a fault. He did not fully trust the information he was receiving and worried incessantly about what he could not know. Today he'd had the army turn out again at four in the morning just in case Burgoyne attacked at dawn, despite the absence of any evidence that he was close enough to do so. The regiments of Glover's brigade were put to work throwing up breastworks and felling trees to make additional abatis defenses ahead of their lines.[56]

Additional militia regiments were appearing in the American camp. To Gates's great relief, General John Stark finally arrived with his brigade of Vermont militia. The rumored British attack failed to materialize, but everyone could sense that Burgoyne was not far away and still creeping toward the American lines.[57]

Gates was also still feeling his way forward as the commander of the army in the Northern Department. There were problems every day that were outside his experience, and two of them stood before him now. Burgoyne had sent two American prisoners through the lines under a flag of truce, both of them captains, both sick and distressed. Burgoyne had provided them with horses, and they were escorted through the lines by one of the British General Fraser's servants. They carried a letter of explanation from Burgoyne.

> Captains Lane & Watkins having earnestly solicited permission to return to their respective houses upon account of their ill state of health & exigencies of their private affairs. I have consented to their request for a limited time, upon their parole, & under certain conditions which they will communicate to you. Should any hindrance be meant by your Commander in chief or yourself to the punctual fulfilling of these conditions on the part of the prisoners you will please, Sir, to inform me that I may be prepared how to act upon other occasions. This is a matter of good faith to which I do not conceive you can have any objection.[58]

What in the world was Burgoyne trying to accomplish? What sort of game was this? There was no existing cartel for the exchange of prisoners. Gates held prisoners, too, but he had no interest in giving any of them up, and there was no protocol for doing so even if he were inclined to it. Yet Burgoyne had sent over two sick officers, apparently as a gesture, under vague unwritten conditions that he simply could not be foolish enough to imagine would be met. Maybe Burgoyne was simply tired of feeding his prisoners. Gates simply congratulated the two men on their good fortune, and sent them home.

The second part of Burgoyne's letter inquired about Dr. Wood, his senior physician, who had come over to check on wounded British and German officers being held prisoner by the Americans. Wood had stayed longer than anticipated and Burgoyne was clearly worried that he might not be coming back. So that seemed to explain it. Burgoyne had sent over two prisoners as an incentive for Gates to send Dr. Wood back.[59]

Gates wrote back to Burgoyne. He would agree to receive the two released American prisoners under the unwritten conditions Burgoyne had intimated to them. Why not? They would both be soon forgotten in the wake of the battle that was coming soon. But he then made it clear that there could be no more bargains of this kind, at least not until General Washington negotiated a general cartel. As for Wood, the doctor had behaved suspiciously, with the result that he had been detained in Albany. Nevertheless, Gates would send him back on Thursday, September 18. There, it was done. Burgoyne would get his physician back in exchange for two sick Americans.[60]

That done, Gates handed his orders of the day to Wilkinson for the morning briefing. This Wilkinson carried out with his customary pleasure.

The General is pleased with the gallant appearance of the troops this morning. The General is satisfied they mean to beat the enemy. By the best intelligence from General Burgoyne's Army it is clear they were yesterday marching this way. When the General is assured they continue their march this way he will order the tents to be struck and the baggage to be loaded. But the army may rely upon it that he will not abandon this camp until they submit to be defeated by an enemy in every respect their inferiors. This order to be read to the army. Every man on the ground is to have two days provisions by evening.

The officers scribbled, compared notes, and made corrections before breaking up to pass the orders along down the chain of command.[61]

1:00 PM, James Hadden, the British Camp at Dovegat

Second Lieutenant James Hadden watched as Burgoyne left camp with Generals Riedesel and von Gall at one o'clock. They took with them two thousand men from the English grenadier and light infantry battalions, as well as some from the 9th and 62nd regiments and the German Specht and Hessen-Hanau regiments. None of the men took packs or tents. The purpose of the excursion was to reconnoiter the routes Burgoyne expected his columns to take on Wednesday. Bridges had to be repaired and roads cleared. They made a circuit of the terrain west and south of Dovegat, dropping off teams of men to prepare the way, placing sentries to detect American scouts and provide cover if the men had to get back to camp in a hurry.[62]

Hadden moved out at about the same time the generals departed. He was with Captain Jones's artillery brigade and an infantry detachment of nearly two thousand men. They had four 6-pounders, two each to cover the interior road Burgoyne was exploring and the main road closer to the river. Some of the infantry were put to work repairing bridges that the Americans had pulled apart. The supply bateaux were drawn up along the shore of the backwater at Dovegat, and four companies of the 47th Regiment came up to protect them. Men peered southward along the river road, wondering if the Americans would come at them from that direction. Some artillery pieces were moved to the front on that road, just in case.[63]

2:00 PM, Oliver Boardman, the American Camp on Bemis Heights

Oliver Boardman had been up since three in the morning. Cook's Connecticut militia had been rousted and paraded early, just in case an attack came at dawn. Of course it had not, and the men lapsed into a state of sleepy boredom by afternoon. Most countered this by helping to strengthen the American defenses.

A soldier came back into camp having spent a little time sick in the new American hospital in Woodworth's barn. The man seemed fine now, and he sat down to share a hearty dinner of pot pie. Boardman thought that the pie was a bit undercooked, but the usual low quality of camp food did not fully explain what happened next. The man just released from the hospital collapsed in agony, and within a half hour he lay dead on the ground. Help was summoned from the hospital and a pair of French doctors arrived to examine the corpse. An autopsy was performed on the spot, and the Connecticut militiamen gathered around to view the process. The pot pie lay like a clod in the dead man's stomach.

To the surprise of no one, the doctors could not offer much more in the way of an explanation. The soldier's body was carried back to an improvised burial ground near the hospital. Everyone suspected that the poor man was just the first of many who would be buried there in the days to come. Colonel Thaddeus Cook was not looking forward to writing to the man's family; he knew that it probably would not be the last such letter he would write, assuming that General Poor would not instead be writing the same sort of letter to Thaddeus Cook's family.[64]

3:00 PM, *Philip Van Cortlandt, the American Camp at Bemis Heights*

Philip Van Cortlandt was still a young man, not yet thirty, but he was also the scion of one of New York's eminent Dutch families.[65] Well-born young men like Van Cortlandt enjoyed privilege unencumbered by the need for experience. New York had ceased to be New Netherland over a century ago, but like the Schuylers and other leading Dutch families, the Van Cortlandts still maintained political, social, and economic positions of importance. Van Cortlandt had been appointed colonel of the 2nd New York less than a year ago. Now he was serving alongside his mercurial cousin Henry Beekman "Harry" Livingston, colonel of the 4th New York, in Enoch Poor's brigade.[66] It was a proper assignment in the Northern Army. Van Cortlandt had been comfortable under the command of Philip Schuyler before the general had lost his job to Horatio Gates. Schuyler's mother had been a Van Cortlandt, so the connection was close. And he thought that Congress's dismissal of Schuyler after the fall of Fort Ticonderoga had been unfortunate and undeserved. But Van Cortlandt was also mindful that, however unjustly, the real politics of the matter ran against Dutch New Yorkers. New England regiments, particularly the militia regiments, were unlikely to serve gladly under Schuyler. Gates was more acceptable to them, and that was that.

Today Van Cortlandt found himself at dinner with Benedict Arnold and some of the other commanding officers in General Arnold's division. Van Cortlandt was pleased to be sharing the table with Richard Varick and Henry Brockholst Livingston. These last appointments by Arnold had annoyed Gates as much as they pleased Van Cortlandt, although there were things about Arnold that Van Cortlandt did not admire. The appointments signaled to everyone Arnold's persisting connection to Schuyler. Van Cortlandt knew that it was a reminder that Gates did not like at all.

Arnold had a dark side, and Van Cortlandt knew that well, too. A year earlier Van Cortlandt had been posted to Fort Ticonderoga, which was then commanded by General Gates. Arnold reached Ticonderoga from the opposite direction, having retreated from his failed attempt to seize Quebec after the horrific overland expedition through Maine that had lasted into the early winter. Arnold's left leg was wounded in the failed attack, but he had soldiered on. He had then retreated to Montreal and served as military governor there through the spring of 1776. It was there that he apparently swindled the local merchants out of food and other supplies, some suspected partly for his own personal gain. Later the arrival of fresh British regiments forced Arnold and his men to retreat to Ticonderoga. Van Cortlandt found out about Arnold's swindling from the men who had retreated south with him. In Van Cortlandt's mind the offenses warranted a court-martial trial of Arnold.

As it happened, a court-martial was instead called to try another officer, a colonel who had been charged with disobeying orders issued by General Arnold. Gates assigned Van Cortlandt to sit on the panel of officers that would decide the case. The accused colonel was certain to reveal Arnold's alleged crimes as part of his defense, so Arnold persuaded Gates to transfer Van Cortlandt to Skenesborough, a move that effectively dissolved the court-martial proceeding. The colonel got off without a trial, but so did Arnold. Van Cortlandt had been a convenient pawn in that game. Now Van Cortlandt was a guest at Arnold's table, and like every good officer, he was polite and genial, as such social circumstances required. Van Cortlandt was now serving under Arnold, a man he distrusted and disliked, but his Albany friends were also there and he would make the best of it. Conversations over dinner and otherwise were both frequent and animated.

Today Arnold's dinner guests also included Colonel Daniel Morgan and Major Henry Dearborn. Both were assigned to Arnold's division, and Arnold was convinced that when action came their units would be critical to American success. Henry Dearborn was another survivor of Arnold's quixotic attack on Quebec. Like Morgan he had been captured and later exchanged. Following the exchange, he had been able to rejoin the army and was appointed to Colonel Alexander Scammell's 3rd New Hampshire with the rank of major. Scammell was thirty-three years old, a Harvard graduate, and a dedicated army officer. When he was not fretting over the wretched conditions suffered by the men under his command, he was writing long love letters to Abigail Bishop back in Mystic, Connecticut.

His desire to marry "Nabby" was surpassed only by his duty to country, which he begged her to understand in every letter.[67]

When the army had retreated from Ticonderoga, Dearborn had been with part of the picket ordered to act as rear guard. At Hubbardton, Colonels Cilley and Scammell, along with Dearborn, had tried twice to persuade General Poor to convince General Arthur St. Clair to leave more units at Hubbardton. But Poor refused to take the proposal to St. Clair. Dearborn was still bitter about it, and occasionally said so in private conversations. "If the measure had been adopted as we proposed, there can be little doubt but the party of the enemy which arrived at Hubbardton a little after daybreak and defeated our troops with a very severe loss on our part, would have been completely destroyed." It was a good thing that Poor was dining with Gates and not present at Arnold's table to hear Dearborn's grumpy assessment. Such were the recriminations that flavored the discussions of the old comrades over dinner.[68]

In the three days Scammell had camped at Stillwater, Gates had detached three hundred handpicked men from their regiments to form five companies of a special light infantry battalion. To Henry Dearborn's joyful surprise, Gates ordered him to command the new unit. Dearborn would miss the 3rd New Hampshire, and Scammell was sorry to see him go, but both of them knew it was an exciting promotion. Gates attached Dearborn's new light infantry battalion to Morgan's corps of riflemen, and Dearborn now found himself leading part of this elite unit of the American Northern Army. Between the light infantry and the riflemen, the corps numbered nearly seven hundred.[69]

The purpose of the light infantry was to support the riflemen in close action. Rifles were slow to load, and they had been designed to be hunting weapons that lacked bayonets. The riflemen would need agile light infantrymen to provide covering volleys of musket fire and bayonets if the British regulars got too close. Dearborn was pleased with his new command and for the pleasant company of officers who were both old friends and trusted colleagues.

The dinner conversation moved on. Arnold informed his officers that Burgoyne had a reconnoitering boat on the Hudson. The boat came down the river every night until its sailors caught sight of the American pickets. At that point it was rowed back up against the current to wherever Burgoyne was camped for the night. Van Cortlandt snapped up Arnold's bait. "If I were permitted to take a command of my men

I could capture them tonight, if a few bateaux with muffled oars could be fitted for me."

The discussion become more animated as the men worked through how the trap could be set and sprung. Everyone realized that the moon would be full tonight, providing enough light for such an adventure, but not enough to make it too risky. At length Arnold summed it up. "Proceed up the river in bateaux within two miles of the enemy. Then draw your boats to the shore and conceal them as much as possible until those of the enemy have passed. If you succeed this far you will come on their rear with your boats and attack them from the shore with small arms. Prepare your men. Four boats are at your service." Van Cortlandt excitedly excused himself and got up to leave; Matthew Clarkson followed him. After they left the table, talk shifted to other subjects.[70]

5:00 PM, William Digby, the British Camp at Dovegat

Lieutenant William Digby was a grenadier, a member of one of the companies detached from their regiments and combined into a grenadier battalion under the command of John Acland. Digby's regiment was the 53rd Foot, the "Brickdusts." Digby was not so sure that the British expedition would succeed, and he said so to his closest friends. "They never will allow us to go into winter quarters till we have gained some great advantage over them. Should that be the case many of the country people will join us, but not till then. They choose to be on the stronger side." Digby could see the fundamental problem facing Burgoyne. The Americans had a huge supply of armed men available. Most of them were not well trained, but their militias could be called out almost on a moment's notice and supplied without great difficulty. Improvised or not, such an army could absorb huge losses and still persevere. It was not a happy thought for Digby.[71]

The river road detachment that had left earlier pushed out about two miles, then pulled back to Dovegat by five o'clock. Burgoyne and the rest of his reconnaissance detachment returned at six, having also ranged as far as two miles out but seeing no trace of the enemy. Before pulling back they had fired the evening gun at sundown as far south as they could, hoping that the Americans would think they were making camp there. Digby watched as they all returned to camp. Burgoyne and his generals decided with some satisfaction that the Americans had probably withdrawn to

Stillwater, pulling back their advanced troops accordingly. Burgoyne then gave orders for the army to be ready to march in the morning.[72]

The men of the combined British and German expeditionary force were still happy for the most part. Luxuries such as wine, rum, and coffee were increasingly expensive, but fresh vegetables and meat on the hoof could be purchased locally for reasonable sums. The army was well supplied for at least the coming four weeks and at the current rate they would reach Albany with time to spare.[73]

6:00 PM, American Soldiers, the American Camp on Bemis Heights

In the American camp the ragged discipline of this improvised army led sometimes to raucous enthusiasm, at other times to angry confrontations. This evening Major Chester, a supernumerary aide to Arnold, and yet another officer named Livingston fell into a dispute that quickly escalated into a duel. They managed to stage the confrontation in a way that injured neither party and both men went away with umbrage satisfied. By the time senior officers found out about it the storm had passed, but dueling was still a bad option.[74]

Elsewhere in the sprawling camp, men found ways to entertain themselves at the expense of the British enemy rather than make enemies of each other. Burgoyne had issued a manifesto before attacking Fort Ticonderoga, and distributed it as best he could through the scattered settlements of New York and the New Hampshire grants that were now called Vermont. It was filled with the most foreboding predictions of death and destruction that awaited all who dared to resist the British Army.

A few of the men carried worn copies of the August 21 issue of the *Pennsylvania Evening Post*, which contained Burgoyne's condescending pronouncement to the rebellious Americans. The article's byline alone ran on and on, finally ending in an insinuating series of et ceteras. Burgoyne had signed it as "Lieutenant-General of his Majesty's Armies in America, Colonel of the Queen's Regiment of Light Dragoons, Governor of Fort William, Member of the House of Commons, Commander of the Expedition from Canada." It was all too glorious for words, and the Americans literate enough to appreciate its ironies could not stop quoting from it, to the applause and peals of raucous laughter from those who could not read it for themselves.

The tone of Burgoyne's manifesto was grave and ponderous, which made the readings in mock seriousness all the funnier. Its effects on the Americans were completely contrary to Burgoyne's hope and intent. The men he expected to be cowed, shamed, and frightened by his message heard only self-parody and unintended irony. They roared with delight after the recitation of each labored paragraph, the noise increasing in the evenings, when rum lubricated what was already a convivial atmosphere. The mocking words never failed to elicit peals of laughter and shouts of disgust from the American rank and file. There was also no shortage of more formal American replies mocking Burgoyne's words. Not least of them was Washington's own response, which would also come to be widely published.[75]

8:00 PM, Van Cortlandt, on the Hudson River near the American Lines

The sun had set about a quarter past six. A half hour later it was nearly dark, but a rising full moon gave the men enough light to maneuver. The four bateaux crossed the river and crept up the Hudson's east bank, away from both the strong current in the middle and the British scouts they assumed were prowling the west bank north of the American positions. It was a long pull, ten miles from Bemis Tavern to the mouth of Fish Kill on the south edge of the nearly deserted village of Saratoga. It took them half the night, and the British boat they hoped to snare never appeared. What Van Cortlandt did not know was that the British Army was camped on the back channel away from the main river, around the oxbow at Dovegat. Van Cortlandt's little detachment pulled silently past the British boat and the entire British camp, all of which was hidden by trees off to the west of the main channel. It was going to be a long night for Van Cortlandt and his men.[76]

WEDNESDAY, SEPTEMBER 17, 1777

5:00 AM, Philip Van Cortlandt, the Village at Saratoga

Saratoga was empty. The British gunboat was gone. So too were all the supply bateaux that were part of Burgoyne's expedition. Van Cortlandt was dumbfounded for a moment, then he realized what must have happened. Burgoyne had moved his entire army forward three miles to Dovegat. It was the only backwater on the entire length of the river and Burgoyne had taken advantage of it. The back channel curved away for over a half mile from the main river. It was here that Burgoyne must have beached his boats. The army was camped west of the oxbow, even farther from the main river. Van Cortlandt's bateaux had paddled past the side-channel cul-de-sac during the night, gliding quietly past the entire British Army in the dark.

It was still dark out, and the morning fog was rising. There was a full moon low in the west, and the first hints of gray to the east, but it was hard to see anything because of the fog. The men looked for occupied houses and began waking people up. The locals assured Van Cortlandt that Burgoyne was now camped southwest of Saratoga, beyond the house of someone known as "blind Moore," they said. Their pickets were only a half mile away on this road, someone said, the northeastern approach to the British camp. Van Cortlandt figured that the bulk of the British Army was a good three miles away and saw an opportunity to snatch the rear guards covering the northeastern perimeter. Burgoyne would never expect such an action from this direction behind his lines. It seemed like a good idea.

Van Cortlandt led his men southwestward past blind Moore's house and stopped at a fence line. It was starting to lighten. The full moon was behind the hills to the west and opposite it the sun was about to rise. Despite the glow in the sky, no one could see more than a few yards because of the fog. No one realized that they had moved past the British sentries until they were challenged. "Who goes there?" The men froze, seeing nothing in the fog, not knowing where they were or where fire might come from at any second. The British password was "Saint Honora," but no one in Van Cortlandt's detachment had any reason to know that. The countersign was "England," but there was no way for them to know that either. No one moved. Each man struggled to maintain a slow, noiseless breathing. A cough now would be fatal. They remained frozen there. The sentry who had challenged them apparently concluded that he had been mistaken, and he did not repeat the challenge. Still nobody moved.

The sky gradually turned lighter. The fog thinned just a little. Now Van Cortlandt could see tents and men moving around, adding fuel to fires, getting ready for the day. He had led his men into the northern part of the main British camp. They slowly turned and crept back the way they had come.

It seemed a miracle that they were able to get back to the river without being fired on, apparently undetected. Van Cortlandt gathered his men at an abandoned house and sent a noncommissioned officer hurrying back with one bateau to the American lines with a message for Arnold, Poor, and Morgan. The British were on the move and it was urgent that units be deployed to check their advance. If he continued to the southwest Burgoyne might get around the left flank of the American lines and have a clear path to Albany. It was crucial that British progress through the woods be impeded so that Burgoyne would have to continue advancing mainly along the river road. That was what Van Cortlandt thought and that was what the messenger was urged to convey to Arnold.

The rest of his detachment piled into the remaining bateaux and pushed off to paddle southward past the British Army again. Their luck held, and they reached their starting point at Bemis Tavern by eleven, feeling more relief than success. Nevertheless, having paddled past the British Army during the night, blundering into the camp at dawn, and then paddling past the British Army again, Van Cortlandt now convinced himself that if his messenger had reached Arnold in time, he, Philip Van Cortlandt, would eventually be credited with having saved Albany.[77]

8:00 AM, Benedict Arnold, the American Camp on Bemis Heights

A colonel had been sent out with a detachment to scout around Saratoga Lake five miles west of the American camp. Now he was back with a report that a breastwork had been thrown up around Walsine's house and that perhaps three hundred of the enemy were stationed there. The colonel guessed that these were new levies, along with a few Indians. Arnold found the report hard to believe and wanted to know more, so he sent a captain off with another scout west to Saratoga Lake to have a second look.

8:30 AM, John Burgoyne, the British Camp at Dovegat

The drummers rattled "The General" at eight-thirty in the morning. By ten the fog would be lifting and the army would be moving again. Everyone had received and followed Burgoyne's terse order issued yesterday: "The whole army to lie accoutered and be under arms an hour before daybreak and continue so until it clears up."

Fraser had sent down more detailed orders for the advance the previous evening. Now as the fog lifted from the hills it was turning into a fine autumn day. It would take longer for the fog to dissipate below in the valley. Consequently, Fraser's Advanced Corps started out as usual, taking the interior road explored Tuesday, followed by Hamilton's division of

English infantry. Brigadier General James Hamilton still had the four strongest British regiments of foot, plus four pieces of British artillery under the command of Captain Thomas Jones.[78]

Riedesel's German division advanced southward along the river flats in fog that persisted along the river, some of them having the advantage of marching along the main road, others having to trudge through fields alongside. The bloodied, dispirited, and still largely unmounted Brunswick dragoons were now down to about forty men. Those who were mounted had only scrawny horses that would soon be meat for the infantry. They had become a reluctant headquarters guard, a bitter fate for men who had once been dashing cavalrymen. Twelve more cannons were part of the artillery park that traveled with the Germans, brigaded into three batteries, but not yet detached for service.[79]

2:00 PM, Horatio Gates, the American Camp on Bemis Heights

Gates dealt with the petty annoyances first, leaving many of them for his staff to resolve. Two soldiers had quarreled in the morning and one ended up slashing the other's jugular vein. Having disposed of the annoyances, he wrote an order extending the practice of the last two days; the men would lie with their arms and be up at four in the morning to load tents and baggage. The army might be makeshift, but as long as he had his command it would also be mobile. The men had to be ready to advance or retreat quickly, come what may. If he kept them busy enough perhaps they would be less likely to stick knives in each other.[80]

Gates thought he could see what was coming. He needed as much help as he could muster, and he needed it soon. He summed up his thoughts for his brigadier generals. "General Burgoyne has caused Skenesborough, Fort Ann, Fort George, Fort Edward, and the posts he lately occupied to the southward of Lake George and Skenesborough, to be all evacuated. The artillery, stores, and provisions are to be brought to his army at Van Vechten's mills, seven miles north of this camp. Except some heavy cannon which are carried to the island in Lake George. From this it is evident the General's design is to risk all upon one rash stroke." He had just written a letter to Governor Clinton, which contained this information and Gates's interpretation of it. The letter went on to urge the governor to send militia from every possible source with all possible expedition. "It is the indispensible duty of all concerned to exert themselves in reinforcing the army."[81]

Gates wrote another letter saying much the same thing to the Committee of Safety in Bennington, asking that the message be forwarded to other committees farther east. He asked them to send all available militia. The decisive battle was at hand and Gates needed all the support he could get from New England. Morgan and Arnold were in camp and other units were arriving daily. This was good news as far as it went, but Gates wanted more. He now had over seven thousand men under his command, the majority of them Continental Army regulars, such as they were. Gates felt a growing confidence, but the Northern Army still needed more militia support. Later in the day, Gates's appeal reached Albany, where seventeen regiments of militia were organized on paper but not yet mobilized. Supplies were coming in daily from that direction, many of them drawn from the farms farther south along the Hudson or from the Mohawk and Schoharie valleys to the west. But Gates needed militiamen too, the more the better.[82]

Gates then wrote to General Lincoln, who was still operating independently even though he was technically under Gates's command. Gates was more than careful with his wording. Wilkinson could be forgiven if he wondered who was subordinate to whom in this exchange as he copied over the final version. But Gates was still not sure that he could treat Lincoln as a subordinate. The result was that his message sounded deferential.

> I entirely approve of all your plans to Distress the Enemy ... Would it not be right you take some Station near or upon the North River ... Your posting Your Army somewhere in the Vicinity of mine must be infinitely Advantageous to Both.[83]

Gates dined with Dr. Potts, Colonel Baldwin, and other officers in the afternoon. With Potts present the table talk inevitably drifted toward medicine and the accomplishments of the hospital, which was now set up on Woodworth's barn. After the dinner broke up, Gates's guests returned to their respective quarters to prepare yet again for the expected fighting.[84]

5:00 PM, Benedict Arnold, the American Camp on Bemis Heights

The scouts who had been sent to Saratoga Lake were back in only seven hours. With them were an ensign and four other captured Loyalists whom they had surprised and taken in Walsine's house. Where the other 295 of the enemy that had been previously reported to be around the house were was anybody's guess. They found no breastworks and no Indians, and there was nothing else of consequence to be reported. Henry Livingston wondered what they could believe of any scouting report when two of them could contradict each other as completely as these two did. Livingston shrugged. "They seldom bring any intelligence that can be depended on."

The ensign and two of the others were deserters from the Northern Army. Livingston thought all three deserved to be hanged, and said so. But they all knew that the fates of the men would depend upon a court-martial, and it might be months before one was organized. The glum prisoners were sent off to captivity and an uncertain future in Albany.[85]

8:30 PM, John Burgoyne, the British Camp at Sword's House

The ponderous British war machine had again traveled only three and a half miles. Burgoyne had his new headquarters set up at Sword's house, and waited while the slow train of something now approaching six thousand officers, men, women, and other civilians snaked into camp. The five hundred Indians who had been part of the army on Lake Champlain were now down to only fifty. The rest had left in the wake of the death of the unfortunate Jane McCrea and Burgoyne's prohibition of looting and other acts of warfare unbecoming of gentlemen.[86]

It would be one in the morning before von Breymann's last regiments passed through the camp and joined Fraser's Advanced Corps on the bluffs. The regiments lined up in order of battle, *en potence*, angled back to protect the flank. The Americans were close and unpredictable. No tents were pitched. No soldier got out of uniform. It was going to be a long night.

Sword's house was a mess. Thomas Sword was a Loyalist. He had been imprisoned by the rebels months ago. His wife, Mary, had been unable to stay in the house during the weeks before Burgoyne took it over as his temporary headquarters, and Indians and local patriots had vandalized the place. But it was a house with a roof and Burgoyne's servants quickly made a decent headquarters of it.[87]

The Americans were not far ahead, probably just three miles. But the inability of Burgoyne's scouts to range very far without being picked off and made captives kept him blind to the details. Maybe Thursday would bring more news and greater clarity. Like his men, Burgoyne stayed in uniform, and sleep would be a long time coming. He decided to invite Major Lindsay to remain with him and play cards.[88]

THURSDAY, SEPTEMBER 18, 1777

6:00 AM, Benedict Arnold, near the British Camp

It was going to be a fine day, but this morning it was foggy again.[89] Scouts now reported that the British Army was camped around Sword's house, south of Dovegat and just three or four miles from the American lines. Gates decided to have Arnold send out large detachments to scout and harass Burgoyne's forces. Arnold set out early with 1500 men from his division. The men had been ordered to strike their tents at three in the morning and to leave them with their packs so that they could get started before sunrise. Oliver Boardman and other men from Cook's Connecticut militia were among those who went with Arnold. Dearborn and his light infantry were also along. If the excursion turned into something bigger, their equipment and baggage would be cared for by others. Meanwhile, speed and agility were what Arnold needed.[90]

Arnold detached a lieutenant colonel and a second body of men from Scammell's 3rd New Hampshire and sent them across the bridge of boats near the Bemis Tavern to the far side of the Hudson. Their orders were to scout northward along the east side of the river and climb trees or do whatever else would help them to observe the movements of Burgoyne's forces.[91]

From Morgan's riflemen Arnold sent Lieutenant John Hardin with a detachment from Van Swearingen's company to probe the woods around to the west and north behind the British, and try to take a prisoner and gather intelligence in that sector. Morgan's men knew the upland territory well. They had been getting to know it ever since their arrival, but it was still a dangerous mission.[92]

All three detachments groped forward through the dense fog rising from the Hudson River and low wet patches on the uplands, expecting to encounter large British units at any moment. Instead, what the men of Arnold's main party saw when the fog suddenly lifted were a few dozen men digging potatoes a quarter mile into no man's land. Arnold's detachment immediately began firing on the men. They all tried to flee back to their camp but three of them were caught, one of them wounded.[93]

With prisoners and potatoes in hand the Americans fell back to a hilltop and waited to see if more would come their way. Arnold drew his small force into a line; they stood there, daring the British to come out and attack them. There they would remain for most of the day, taunting the British and German troops who were just out of musket range.[94]

7:00 AM, *Horatio Gates, the American Camp on Bemis Heights*

Gates had been up early reviewing the daily orders that he had written out last night. Wilkinson could polish them a bit and read them to the brigadiers and other officers at the daily briefing. Gates liked his rum and believed that the men would benefit from it too as the mornings got colder. He raised the allocation from a quarter gill to a half gill for each man. This meant the commissary had to be ready to deliver a gallon of rum for every sixty-four men, but that did not appear to be a difficult task. Supplies were coming in even faster than the new militia units. A single keg was enough to easily supply a half gill to each of the men in two regiments, and Gates was pleased to see that kegs were arriving by the wagonload. As further inspiration for the men, he selected "Bennington" to be the password for the day. Although many of the men were now referring to the fort on the upper Mohawk that Arnold had rescued in August as Fort Schuyler, Gates pointedly made that day's countersign "Fort Stanwix," the older British name for the place. Let the friends of Schuyler clustered around Benedict Arnold send *that* news back to Albany by the next express rider. Gates's last order was to the commissaries, who were instructed to give each soldier his half gill of rum in the morning.

Gates still expected an attack at any moment. He had let most of the men sleep until half past three in the morning, still ridiculously early. The sun would not rise until around six, and no sane person expected Burgoyne to attack in the dark. The men struck their tents and loaded their baggage in order to be ready to either flee or pursue, nobody knew which. Once that was done they drew bread and their half gill of rum for breakfast. The combination drove off the chill and elevated their enthusiasm.[95]

Arnold was somewhere to the north harassing Burgoyne's men but, Gates hoped, not doing much more than that. Lieutenant Colonel Andrew Colburn from Scammell's 3rd New Hampshire was across the river, there more to observe than anything else. Meanwhile, Colonel John Brown was probably in the vicinity of Ticonderoga by now with his men from the battalion of middle Berkshire County militia, but no one knew what would become of that detachment.

Most men spent the day with their arms grounded, working to strengthen their breastworks. They braced for attack. They marched. They heard gunfire in the distance. And they lapsed into the boredom that afflicts most armies most of the time. Later, American scouts brought in the two prisoners taken by Arnold, both British regulars. The third was brought in a bit later. This was the wounded man, who had not been able to move as quickly.[96]

11:00 AM, John Burgoyne, the British Camp at Sword's House

The British and German soldiers got little sleep overnight. Everyone had stood to arms ready to march an hour before dawn. The men of Fraser's Advanced Corps farther up on the bluffs above the camp had been up early, too. Foragers, both men and women, had gone out with armed detachments to protect them. They had found more than they expected, standing crops yet to be harvested and gardens full of unpicked produce. The attractions had been too great. The men moved out too far, separating into happy groups that were too small and too scattered to be safe in the morning fog. Some were five hundred yards out gathering potatoes from a field.

The American scouts had been waiting, of course. In a matter of a few minutes some of the isolated British foragers had been picked off. Back in the British camp, Lieutenant William Digby of the grenadier battalion heard the small arms fire in the distance. The Americans pulled back after armed British soldiers were sent out to rescue the foraging party. But men had been killed, wounded, and captured. Reports were that the Americans had seized about twenty prisoners. The rest had fled back into camp. Those who escaped described what had happened to their appalled officers. The Americans had fired on unarmed men. What next? Fourteen men had been wounded or captured came a revised report. The Americans had no sense of fair play, thought the British officers. Something had to be done about it.[97]

The incident caused a new rumor to spread rapidly through the entire army. The Americans were moving against Fraser's Advanced Corps on the bluff. Drums rolled throughout the sprawling British and German camps; the men of every regiment stood to arms and made ready to move to support Fraser. Fraser himself soon reported to Burgoyne with chagrin that it was all an overreaction to the reports of his careless foragers.[98]

Burgoyne was furious. He had been up all night with Major Lindsay, drinking and playing cards. He would have been grumpy in the best of circumstances, but this was too much. There would be action soon, and it was apparent to him that there was a laxity that had to stop. He was hungover and on edge. If his subordinates were not also on edge they would be as soon as his new orders were read out to them. He sat down at his desk and wrote out supplementary orders for the day.[99]

To the great reproach of discipline, and of the common sense of Soldiers who have been made Prisoners, the Service has sustained a loss within Ten days that might in action have cost the lives of some hundreds of the Enemy to have brought upon it in Action. The Lieutenant General will no longer bear to lose Men for the pitiful consideration of Potatoes or Forage. The life of the Soldier is the property of the King, and since neither friendly admonition, repeated injunctions, nor corporal punishments have effect, after what has happen'd, the army is now to be informed (and it is not doubted the commanding officers will do it solemnly) that the first Soldier caught beyond the advance Sentries of the Army will be instantly hanged.[100]

Burgoyne's mood improved when an American deserter was brought to him. The Americans were moving toward him, the deserter said. This confirmed what the British command already sensed. Every time they sent engineers out to rebuild a destroyed bridge they needed a larger detachment of infantry to protect them. At some place and at some time soon Gates would attempt to stop them entirely.[101]

Burgoyne's message to his troops on June 30 at Crown Point on Lake Champlain now seemed ironic. It had taken him nearly three months to get his army from there to this spot, and they were still a long way from Albany. There had been a victory at Ticonderoga, a near defeat (but still a victory) at Hubbardton, and then the disaster at Bennington. The army was intact and willing to fight, but it had suffered terribly as it inched along with its heavy train of artillery and baggage, slowed constantly by bridges that had been destroyed and trees felled across roads everywhere by the obstinate American rebels.

> The Army embarks tomorrow to approach the Enemy. We are to contend for the King and the Constitution of Great Britain, to vindicate the Law and to relieve the Oppressed. A cause in which His Majesty's Troops and those of the Princes His Allies, will feel equal Excitement.
>
> The Services required of this particular Expedition are critical and conspicuous. During our progress occasions may occur, in which nor difficulty nor labour nor life are to be regarded. THIS ARMY MUST NOT RETREAT.[102]

It had been a gamble to cross the Hudson to the Saratoga side a few days ago. The bridge of boats was gone now, leaving the entire army at the end of a slender, perhaps already broken supply line stretching all the way back to Montreal. It was getting colder. Albany was still many miles away, and the needed help from Howe and Clinton at the mouth of the Hudson was still just a vague promise.

12:00 Noon, Friedrich Riedesel, the River Road South of Sword's House

A single gun fired on each side of no man's land. Ideally, each army would hear the noon gun of the other army a few seconds after its own, the delay caused by the time it took the sound to travel the two miles between Gates's and Burgoyne's respective headquarters. But such precision was rarely realized. Artillery officers had to depend upon imprecise reckonings of solar noon, which was especially difficult in cloudy weather. Officers who had watches checked to be sure that the hands both pointed straight up at twelve. In the event of action, they had to be synchronized, and this was the one time of day they could be reasonably sure of the correct time.

General Riedesel stared glumly southward along the river road. The Americans had burned every bridge across every creek and kill crossed by this road. There was no reason to think that any were left standing between where he stood and Stillwater. It had fallen to his brigade's men and engineers to repair each ruined bridge they encountered on the march.

Riedesel had sent a hundred men forward to rebuild a bridge, and another hundred to protect them while they worked. The German troops were getting good at this task, and it did not take long for the detachment to finish their work on the first bridge and move on to help another detachment with the next one. This time Riedesel's men found Americans waiting to harass them with musket and rifle fire. As many as four hundred of them seemed to be concealed in the woods around the second ruined bridge.

The detachment major reported back that more American regiments were coming into view as rebel reinforcements moved north on the river road. The major thought that this might be the beginning of the fight they all knew was coming, but Riedesel was not convinced. The Americans were dug in somewhere up ahead and Gates would most likely fight a defensive battle from behind whatever fortifications he had been able to construct. Just the same, Riedesel decided that at six o'clock he would order up two 6-pounders to cover the repaired bridge through the night. It would be another long one. Once again the men would be ordered to remain in uniform and fully armed through the night. They would all be up and ready again an hour before dawn.[103]

Burgoyne ordered Colonel von Breymann's German grenadiers and chasseurs to move up from their rear guard position to the rear of Riedesel and join Fraser's Advanced Corps on the high ground away from the river. Two guns of the Hessen-Hanau artillery under the command of Captain Georg Päusch, both 6-pounders, were detached and assigned to von Breymann's battalions. Von Breymann's unit, which had embarrassed itself by being late to the party at Bennington, had been assigned to rear guard duty ever since. Now von Breymann's unit was moved up to Fraser's division, out of Burgoyne's doghouse and in position to redeem itself if the occasion arose. The trek up was steep enough to impress the Brunswickers from the flatlands of northern Germany, some of whom called it a "high mountain." They would spend the night there without tents.[104]

Almost four miles due east across the Hudson a party of men led by the American named Willard strained their eyes toward Burgoyne's camp. They were atop a peak, what would from now on be called Willard's Mountain, and they had a glass. But the truth was they would see little at this distance until night fell. Then the scatter of campfires would clearly show the concentration of Burgoyne's forces. Gathering more specific intelligence for Gates would take an effort more dangerous than this.[105]

3:00 PM, Abraham Ten Broeck, the American Camp on Bemis Heights

Men of additional Albany County militia regiments were starting to straggle in. Their commander, Brigadier General Abraham Ten Broeck, was among the first to arrive. He was forty-three years old and in the prime of a privileged life. Together, the Albany militia regiments had been known as Schuyler's brigade. The name would not do now that Gates was in charge and fighting was at hand. Now it was called Ten Broeck's brigade, and Gates was happy to have it.

Ten Broeck was already a wealthy and suitably portly patrician in the 1760s when he married Elizabeth Van Rensselaer, the sister of Stephen Van Rensselaer II, the ninth patroon of a vast estate on the east side of the Hudson known as the Manor of Rensselaerswyck. When his brother-in-law died young, leaving the entire estate to his young son Stephen III, Ten Broeck had been made co-administrator of the estate until the boy came of age. Now Ten Broeck was also a member of the New York Provincial Congress, chairman of its Committee of Safety in 1777. Who better to lead the Albany County militia than the forty-three-year-old Ten Broeck?

The 1st and 2nd Albany County militia regiments were already in camp and attached to Glover's brigade. Governor Clinton had ordered Ten Broeck to form his own brigade from draftees drawn from all but one of the rest of the Albany militia regiments, fourteen regiments in all. The men of the 15th Albany regiment were still needed to protect settlers in the Schoharie Valley, but all the other regiments were made available for the expected battle against Burgoyne. It had been a slow process, but Clinton had thought if Gates could slow the progress of Burgoyne's army there would perhaps be time for Ten Broeck's brigade to help turn the tide. Burgoyne's slow progress had allowed the strategy to work. A mix of Dutch and English names made up the list of colonels and other officers Ten Broeck had available to assemble the militia units. They had started as quickly as they could and now were seeing results.

If anything, it was easier now to find supplies for Gates's Northern Army. Ten Broeck had enlisted his sister and their compliant young nephew to persuade the many tenant farmers living on Rensselaerswyck Manor to contribute as much livestock, grain, and other farm products as they could. Caravans of wagons had dutifully wound northward, leaving the tenants with just enough to get their families through the coming winter. Granaries and barns were all but emptied. After the contributions had been made, the young patroon, still only twelve years old, had invited all his tenants to Albany for a celebration. To their surprise and delight he had presented them all with permanent titles to their farms while Ten Broeck stood smiling in the background.[106] There was clearly much more to this revolution than political independence from Great Britain. At least in New York there was a social revolution playing out as well, as the title transfers proved. Now Ten Broeck stood before Gates, reporting for duty. Behind him thousands of volunteer Albany militiamen were following him north to Bemis Heights, though few would be with him soon enough to assist in the coming battle.

6:00 PM, Oliver Boardman, the American Camp on Bemis Heights

Morgan's riflemen seemed to spend every night abroad in the forest, getting to know the lay of the land and picking up unwary British prisoners. This time they were back in camp before dark. Arnold also returned at nightfall with the news that they had taken thirty-six prisoners and killed four. With all the detours, advances, feints, and retreats, Oliver Boardman figured he had marched nine miles that day, quite enough. Tonight they would sleep on their arms again, but without much apprehension. Andrew Colburn remained on the east side of the river, his men in trees with glasses, counting the fires in the British camp. Everything pointed to action tomorrow.[107]

11:30 PM, John Stark, the American Camp on Bemis Heights

Against his better judgment, Brigadier General John Stark had brought his regiment of Vermont militia from Bennington to Gates's army on Bemis Heights. The prickly Vermonter was still angry with Congress, but Stark's commitment to the cause of independence had brought him here anyway. Now here he was, uncomfortable in the company of Ten Broeck, like Stark a militia brigadier. Stark did not like New Yorkers, especially the Dutchmen. Had Schuyler still been commanding the Northern Army he would never have come at all. But Gates was another matter. He and his men liked the new commander.

However, now Stark had a still bigger problem. The terms of service of the militiamen in his regiment would expire at midnight. He had thought that by marching them here he would inspire at least some of them to remain and fight Burgoyne's main force, but it now appeared to be no use. It appeared that they would vote differently with their feet.

Gates needed Stark, that much was clear. And the men had fought wonderfully at Bennington; these were no backsliders. Stark knew how to get the most out of untrained militiamen. His speech to them before the battle at Bennington was retold uncounted times. "There are your enemies, the Red Coats and the Tories. They are ours, or this night Molly Stark sleeps a widow!" There was no way he could repeat, let alone top, those words now, no way to keep men who had done their duty to stay and do it again when their commitments had expired and there was a harvest to be taken in back home. More than that, when Stark had agreed to take command of his militia brigade with the rank of brigadier general it had been with the condition that he would never be subject to the command of the Continental Army. He had violated his own principled stand just by showing up here, and the thought of it did not sit well with him. His men knew Stark, and they shared his views.

So that was that. Stark had brought them here thinking his men might be persuaded to fight again, but they were having none of it. They were packed and ready. In fact, they had never unpacked. Stark's aide-de-camp went to Gates's aide-de-camp, young James Wilkinson, and asked for the password needed to pass through the sentry line. Wilkinson gave it to him. In a wonderful irony the password of the day was still "Bennington." At five minutes past midnight, under the light of a waning full moon, John Stark and his militiamen left camp, crossed the Hudson on the American bridge of boats, and headed east for home.[108]

Gates knew what Stark was about, and he did not question the man's commitment to American independence or the man's bravery under fire. Stark truly thought that there were worse things than death, and occasionally he said so. Maybe Stark and his militia would come back again, maybe not.

2

The Battle of Freeman's Farm

FRIDAY, SEPTEMBER 19, 1777

6:00 AM, Friedrich Riedesel, the River Road South of Sword's House

Word had reached the British camp at dawn that some of Colonel Morgan's American riflemen had been observed to be in advance of the American lines, settled in on what appeared to be a strong position. It was time to confront the enemy.[1] Today was the day. It was clear to Burgoyne that his army could not force its way much farther down the river road. The Americans were on the heights, just three miles south. Swampy ground near the river caused the road to angle westward across the flats, right at the American artillery on the bluffs. American guns on the high ground would tear Burgoyne's forces to pieces if he tried to push through that way.[2]

Burgoyne had already divided his army into three columns (Figure 2.1). Two of them, Fraser's Advanced Corps and Hamilton's division, were already camped on the heights above Sword's house. Burgoyne would send the Advanced Corps west to cover the right flank. Then he would ride with Hamilton's center column of British regiments, marching first south along an upland road, then up a great ravine to the flat farmland above the valley, and then turning south again to attack the Americans. He did not like having to direct the action this way but he had no choice. The woods were infested with Americans and he found out afresh every day that his scouts could not venture far without risking death or capture. With his intelligence about the terrain ahead of him so limited Burgoyne simply had to be close to the expected fighting to direct it properly. Besides, it was

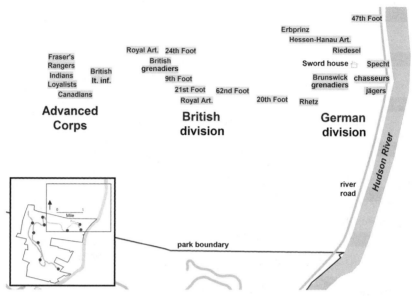

Figure 2.1 Prelude to the Battle of Freeman's Farm, 6:00 a.m., September 19, 1777.

the only way he could make use of General Phillips in the coming fight. Phillips could issue advice and commands only through Burgoyne.

Riedesel would keep most of the Germans and some British units on the river road to repair bridges, protect the stores, and provide a feint that might convince the Americans that Burgoyne was going to walk into their trap. Riedesel had three thousand men there, a tactical anchor for Burgoyne's army on the left wing. Despite Riedesel's obvious personal doubts about Burgoyne's regard for him, the German general was a skilled leader. Burgoyne knew he could depend on the man.[3]

Riedesel busied himself and his men with minor redeployments. At eight o'clock Riedesel ordered the Regiment Specht and the Hessen-Hanau artillery company commanded by Captain Päusch to join the rest of the column on the river road (Figure 2.2). Päusch had four light 6-pounders and eighty-two artillerymen, all of them highly trained. Päusch had also brought along a servant and two horses of his own, as was fitting for his rank and social station.[4]

Most of Riedesel's German regiments and Päusch's artillery moved south along the river road, the cannons and their crews behind the infantry. He had six companies of the British 47th Regiment of Foot behind

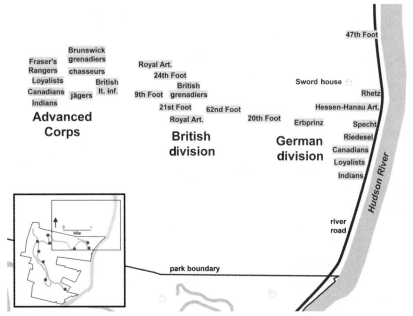

Figure 2.2 The Battle of Freeman's Farm, 8:00 a.m., September 19, 1777.

him to guard the bateaux that were in turn brought along at the same pace. He also had all the unassigned artillery, all the army's baggage, and the hospital following in the rear of his column. It was slow going because of the destroyed bridges that still needed repair and the trees the Americans had felled across the road. Reconstructing and clearing took time.

As Riedesel's units advanced slowly southward a detachment of Indians, Canadians, and Loyalists from Fraser's corps jogged past them along the edge of the woods at the bottom of the bluffs overlooking the Hudson. These irregulars would test the American positions just down the road. The main road ran along the flats near the river, but there was also a path along the base of the bluffs, which the local people used when the water was high and the river flats were flooded. The task of the detachment was to probe the American right flank and create a diversion. The American scouts were not far ahead. It would not be long before they would detect the approach of Burgoyne's irregulars and send word back to Gates at his headquarters. Perhaps Gates could be lured into committing troops to resist this feint along the river road, reducing the resistance he might put in the way of Fraser's and Hamilton's columns off somewhere to the west.

8:30 AM, Horatio Gates, American Headquarters at Bemis Heights

The morning was bright and clear above the American headquarters on Woodworth's farm. Everything not covered up was white with a coating of hoarfrost.[5] To the north away from camp, small American detachments moved furtively through the woods in front of the British Army like packs of wolves. They were the eyes and ears of the American general staff.

The army had been turned out and put on parade by five-thirty, and they had stayed on parade until after the sun rose.[6] Gates's improvised Northern Army was as ready as it could be made to be. His orders for the day were fussy and probably unnecessary. Gates was making nervous work, like an expectant father, and many of his subordinates were doing the same.

Yet even a general known for his organization and attention to detail could forget things. In the midst of issuing dozens of different commands Gates neglected to set the daily password and countersign. Perhaps it was not so much a lapse as a measure of his certainty that there would be action today. Passwords and countersigns would count for little once the fighting started.

Gates was in a dark mood. Stark and his men had refused to join the Northern Army just as the likelihood of battle was increasing. Gates grumbled to Wilkinson, who was of a more charitable frame of mind regarding Stark and his New Hampshire militiamen. "These citizens have fought once," Wilkinson said. "They are desirous to tell the tale of feats performed and look into their private affairs, after which they will be ready again to take arms."[7] Stark was gone, and that had to be the end of it. Gates had to do what he could with what he had to prepare for what was coming. Among other things, he appointed two special adjutants to assist him.[8]

A messenger came in from scouts on the far side of the Hudson and opposite Burgoyne's camp. They reported that tents were being struck and columns of the British Army were streaming westward up the roads leading into the countryside north of the American lines.[9] Gates sent the messenger back and found another to alert Morgan, some of whose men were serving as pickets a mile to the north: "Should you find the enemy approaching, hang on their front and flanks to retard their march, and cripple them as much as possible." Then another message came from pickets forward of the American lines on the river flats below Bemis Heights. Indians and other irregulars were approaching there.

Gates was ready to believe that the main attack would develop near the river, so he did not hesitate to order the detachment of about three hundred men from the portion of Nixon's brigade that was posted around Bemis Tavern. The detachment moved north and encountered the British irregulars on flat ground near Mill Creek, just northeast of the most advanced American line across the flats. The skirmish was smart; the firing was heard by everyone on both sides. The number of Americans was more than equal to the party of British irregulars, and the rebels' preferred style of fighting matched that of the attackers. The Americans had the advantage because they already knew the ground. Before long, the British detachment had lost thirteen dead and thirty-five taken prisoners. It was the first engagement of the day.[10]

The remnants of Burgoyne's probe of the American right fled back toward the lines being set up by Riedesel's men. There they picked up reinforcements and decided to try again. This time they drove the Americans back into their line on the south bank of Mill Creek. About a hundred of them saw a chance to dislodge the Americans and attacked. At the same moment more American troops from Nixon's brigade came up as well. There was another round of sharp fighting that lasted for about fifteen minutes; then the Americans surrounded the outnumbered attackers, taking all of them prisoner.[11] It was an auspicious beginning for the Americans, but just as Burgoyne had hoped, it had drawn American attention in the wrong direction.

Gates did not stir from his position just north of his headquarters. There was no need to. Not only was it his personal preference to command from the rear, but unlike Burgoyne, Gates had good intelligence regarding the terrain of no man's land. So long as there was any uncertainty about how the action would unfold, Gates thought he would be more effective where he was, directing his subordinates using mounted messengers, playing the game like a remote chess master.[12]

9:00 AM, Simon Fraser, at the Head of the Advanced Corps

Simon Fraser's Advanced Corps was ready to move on the heights above Sword's house, having taken to the roads on the high ground after leaving Dovegat yesterday. To Fraser, Burgoyne had given the task of covering the army's right flank, telling him to "make a circuit in order to pass the ravine commodiously without quitting the heights. Afterward cover the march of the line to the right. Have the Indians, Canadians, and Provincials upon your front and flank."[13] Fraser had most of these irregulars with him, all but the detachment that had been sent south ahead of Riedesel's division down by the river (Figure 2.3).

Fraser's Advanced Corps was composed primarily of Acland's grenadier battalion, the light infantry battalion commanded by Alexander Lindsay, Fraser's own 24th Regiment of Foot, and a brigade of Royal Artillery. He also had a unit of rangers. To this Burgoyne had added von Breymann's German grenadiers, as well as von Bärner's chasseur and jäger battalion. Fraser had a total of nearly three thousand men to protect the right flank of Burgoyne's army, not as many men as Riedesel had down by the river, but enough.[14]

The entire Advanced Corps had been designed from the beginning for speed and agility. Captain Alexander Fraser commanded the single company of British rangers, rifle sharpshooters handpicked from various British regiments. Alexander was Simon Fraser's nephew, an officer Burgoyne described to his generals as "one of the most distinguished officers in his line of service that ever I met with."[15] Now Captain Fraser was in the middle of what looked like a remarkably disorderly advance. His rangers scampered through open woods alongside Indians, chasseurs, and

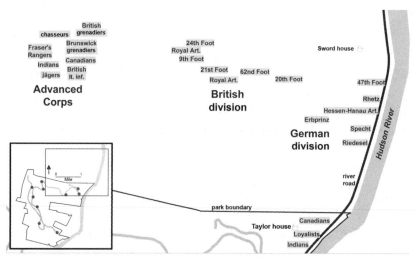

Figure 2.3 The Battle of Freeman's Farm, 9:00 a.m., September 19, 1777.

German jägers, while the regular troops slogged westward along a cart path that was the nearest thing to a road they could find.

Each British soldier had a leather cartridge box with thirty-six rounds of ammunition hung from a broad white belt that crossed the chest. He carried another twenty-four rounds in his knapsack. Another forty rounds were kept in the regimental baggage so that there were ideally a hundred rounds available for each infantryman.[16] A narrower belt around the waist held a scabbard and bayonet, and of course each man carried a 10-pound Brown Bess musket. In addition, every man had a knapsack, canteen, hatchet, haversack containing four days' provisions, blanket, and a fifth of the tent and equipment he shared with four mess mates. It was a load of about sixty pounds for *each* man. German grenadiers were even more heavily encumbered than their British equivalents, with additional armor, heavy clothing, and gallon canteens. Most of their baggage would be dropped behind the lines once it was clear they were going into action.[17]

Burgoyne had ordered that at eleven o'clock guns would fire to signal that it was time for all three columns to advance to the staging points the scouts had found over the previous two days. Simon Fraser, with the farthest to go, had estimated that it could take him two hours to reach his initial goal. The generals had agreed that Fraser would fire his 6-pounders as a second signal when he was in place. At that signal the columns would advance toward the Americans. It was important that all three columns be aligned at that stage and able to move forward in concert despite the expanses of forest and fields that would keep them out of sight of each other.[18]

9:30 AM, *John Burgoyne, British Headquarters at Sword's House*

The main British column, the smallest of the three, was made up of nearly seventeen hundred men: the 9th, 20th, 21st, and 62nd Regiments of Foot under the command of Brigadier-General James Hamilton. Burgoyne accompanied Hamilton, as did Major-General Phillips. Their entourage of aides, servants, and spare horses also rode with the column. So did two brigades of artillery, each made up of two 6-pounders.[19]

The center column moved off first from its overnight position to the west above Sword's house. Then it turned south along a narrow road through the forest and fields away from the Hudson. It was actually a column of two double files, barely able to march along the narrow roads.

In Europe they would have advanced over open ground in broad platoon ranks, but the American wilderness prohibited military elegance. The 9th regiment marched in two files on the right of the road, followed by the 21st, also marching in two files. On the left side of the road were two files of the 62nd, followed by two of the 20th.[20] The regiments tended to get strung out along the road as individual soldiers stumbled or when their equipment got caught up in the brush or branches that hemmed them in, and it was difficult to keep order.

Each regiment advanced as best it could in company order. Their two long files would be turned into ranks if and when they deployed for battle. Had they marched in three files and fought in three ranks as they usually did in Europe, the regiments would have had less tendency to get strung out, but that was impracticable here.[21]

The officers had anticipated that the long files of the 62nd and the 20th Regiments would march off to the left when they encountered the Americans, so the tall men of the first rank marched near the center of the road. Anticipating eventual deployment to the right, the tall front ranks of the 9th and the 21st also marched nearest the center line of the road, with the shorter men to the right. The spacing of the men was as precise as the road would allow, their cadence timed with the regular drumbeat. Each man focused on the precision of his movements and pushed any thought of what might lie ahead out of his mind. Strict discipline in the smallest of things had its purpose. The men were too busy attending to details to allow their minds to wander into fear.[22]

Colonels rode at the heads of their regiments, accompanied by other officers, everyone in his proper place according to rank and seniority. Sergeants marched alongside the rank and file, carrying halberds and making sure that the lines remained properly dressed. They had left their colors behind in camp; the officers wisely left their more elaborate uniform decorations behind as well. Flags and fancy uniforms were the Americans' favorite targets. There was no need to accommodate them.

About a mile from the camp above Sword's house the British column came to a deep ravine. At the bottom was a stream flowing eastward toward the Hudson. To their delight, the scouts found a bridge across the stream that the Americans had neglected to destroy. The column descended into the ravine, crossed the bridge, and ascended the southern side of the ravine on a small road, still without incident (Figure 2.4).

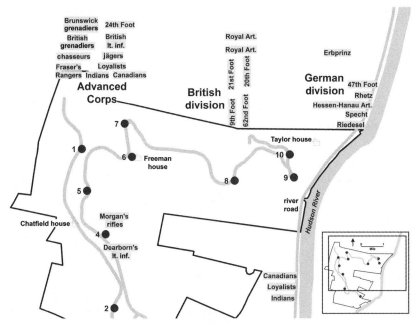

Figure 2.4 The Battle of Freeman's Farm, 10:00 a.m., September 19, 1777.

10:00 AM, Daniel Morgan, No Man's Land

Daniel Morgan's four hundred riflemen were mostly quick and rangy Appalachian mountain men who were well adapted to hunting, living, and fighting on the western frontier of the colonies. Each man carried a custom-made long rifle, most of them made by Pennsylvania Dutch craftsmen. Each man had demonstrated his marksmanship by consistently hitting a target the size of a pie plate at two hundred yards.

The long rifle was the descendant of German hunting rifles, but with improvements made by American gunsmiths. Every man in Morgan's corps could hit a squirrel at thirty yards and a man at three hundred yards.[23] The secret was the rifling of the long, narrow bore of the weapon. Gunsmiths took particular care to forge a four-foot-long, dead-straight bore, usually filing the outside of the barrel to give it an octagonal cross-section. A special wooden rack was used to pull a cutter through the barrel as many times as was needed to cut the parallel twisting grooves into the interior that would impart spin to the often smaller rifle ball. Although the windage of smooth-bored muskets made them inaccurate beyond fifty to seventy yards, the rifleman remained deadly accurate at four times that distance. This was the great advantage of the rifle. But there were also some disadvantages. The octagonal barrel was not designed to take a bayonet; the rifle was designed for hunting, not military operations.

But that was just one of the rifle's disadvantages. There were more, and most regimental officers did not care at all for the rifle as a weapon of choice. Each rifle was expensive to make and maintain. Worse, it could take a rifleman up to a full minute or more to load and fire. After measuring powder into the barrel, the rifleman had to retrieve a cloth patch from the brass box in his fancy stock, and then force the patch and the small ball into the tight-fitting bore. Some men carried a short ramrod and a small hammer to get it started. Then the patch and ball had to be pushed or tapped home using the main ramrod. Only then did the rifleman put powder into the frizzen pan of the flintlock firing mechanism and make ready to fire.

By comparison, the standard infantry soldier could load the loose-fitting cartridge holding powder and a ball into his musket and fire in fifteen seconds. Even better, the round barrel of the standard musket was designed to receive a bayonet. Regiments that carried muskets made up for their inaccuracy by simultaneously firing massive volleys of lead, often following up with bayonet charges. Both the American Continentals and the British soldiers were trained to fight this way. No amateur army, least of all one mainly equipped with rifles, could stand up to an assault by an army of seasoned regulars equipped with muskets and bayonets.

But Daniel Morgan had no intention of fighting that way. His corps was valuable to American commanders for its other skills. He had explored the woods and farm clearings north and west of the American line and knew them well. Some of his men were already out ahead of his main body, having spent several nights serving as pickets and scouts. Some were in Chatfield's house, just a half mile north of the American lines. A few were farther north in Freeman's house. The order from Gates was enough to get the rest of Morgan's corps out and moving quickly.

Morgan's riflemen who were not already deployed forward trotted along the narrow road through the woods like the individual athletes they were, irregular in every way but the one that counted. Fifteen minutes northwest of Fort Neilson they came to a fork in the road. They took the road to the right that angled off to the north, knowing that it led directly to Freeman's farm. It took them only a little more than another fifteen minutes to reach the southern edge of the deserted farm clearing. The field widened north of them. Here at the south end, the farm clearing was only a hundred yards wide. The riflemen stopped and waited. Some moved cautiously out through the stubble and stumps of the abandoned field. Freeman, a Loyalist, was busy helping out Burgoyne somewhere to the north. The farm was deserted. Some of the men climbed trees.

One of them, Timothy Murphy, had a double-barreled weapon. It was a little heavier than most rifles, but no heavier than a Brown Bess musket. Its twin barrels were designed to rotate so that each engaged with the flint-lock firing mechanism in turn. Murphy could scale a tree and fire twice before having to reload. Some men could reload a rifle on a perch, but even when it was possible this, too, took time. So as snipers went, Murphy was twice as effective as most. Murphy was twenty-six years old, stocky, strong, and short limbed. He was what people would call Black Irish, with black hair, black eyes, and a swarthy complexion. His upbringing in the wilds of central Pennsylvania had equipped him with ample measures of strength, endurance, stealth, passion, and profanity.[24] Yet, apart from his custom rifle, in this corps he was typical, not exceptional.

A few men moved out to the Freeman farmhouse and the fences nearby, getting there in less than ten minutes. The house was on a ridge that ran northeast–southwest. From the house the advance men could see that Freeman's farm clearing was much broader here than it was on the southern end, a good quarter-mile wide. Most of the riflemen waited at the edge of the woods, in or behind the trees. Somewhere behind them were Dearborn and his light infantry, presumably coming up to provide support in case the riflemen fell in with British regulars. It was still quiet.

Morgan's roster listed seven companies of varying sizes, ranging from twenty-six to eighty-seven officers and men, but they were already a bit scattered. He told his riflemen to concentrate on the British and German officers when the time came. "Boys, shoot at those who wear epaulettes rather than the poor fellows who fight for sixpence a day."[25] This republican attitude appalled the British gentleman officers, who were still not accustomed to the notion that their uniforms might attract anything but respect, and every American rifleman knew it.

10:15 AM, Henry Dearborn, No Man's Land

Major Dearborn looked over the five companies of his brand-new light infantry battalion. Young, strong, disciplined, and quick, they were the best of the best. They had followed Morgan northward from Fort

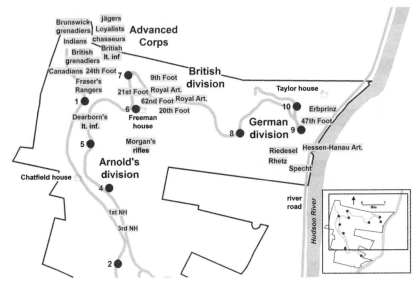

Figure 2.5 The Battle of Freeman's Farm, 11:00 a.m., September 19, 1777.

Neilson. Scouts came back to tell Dearborn that there were British units to the northwest, close enough to threaten Morgan's left flank. Dearborn decided that his best course was to angle toward that threat and prevent the possible flanking move rather than come up immediately behind Morgan. When they reached the fork in the road they took the left road that led off toward the threat to the northwest, not the northward route Morgan's men had followed. It was a decision that would bring Morgan to the edge of disaster (Figure 2.5).

10:30 AM, Benedict Arnold, American Headquarters at Bemis Heights

It had been an hour since scouts had confirmed that nearly the entire British Army was on the move and headed for the American lines in three heavy columns. Yet Gates still waited. The contrast between Gates and Arnold was coming into sharp focus. Gates still wanted to fight a defensive battle from behind the abatis, trenches, and breastworks that protected much but still not all of the American position. More to the point, it was not yet clear which of the three British columns would attack in earnest and which would act as diversions. Gates had fresh intelligence from the skirmish down on the river flats around Mill Creek. Over a hundred of Burgoyne's men had been captured there and some of them had plenty to say about Burgoyne's plans for the day. Gates still thought that the main attack was coming down the river road, and that the other two columns were designed to lure the American forces westward and away from the river.[26]

Arnold argued that waiting was too dangerous. They had to engage the British in the fields and woods a mile to the north of Neilson's farm, lest Fraser's Advanced Corps flank the American left. Burgoyne had to know better than to try to force his way down the river road. No, Burgoyne would surely come at them from the northwest. Arnold's view was that to delay sending units out to meet him any longer risked catastrophe.[27]

Gates finally relented. He had to admit there was still no evidence of a concerted attack along the river road. He had already ordered Arnold to send Morgan and Dearborn forward, and now he ordered him to reinforce them as necessary from Enoch Poor's brigade. Arnold seized the chance to get the rest of his division into action. Arnold rode over to Brigadier General Poor and ordered him to begin sending forward some of the regiments of his brigade. Poor turned to Colonel Joseph Cilley of the 1st New Hampshire, then to Colonel Alexander Scammell of the 3rd New Hampshire. The Continentals in the two regiments got themselves ready to march.

Gates still refused to commit more units from the right wing under his direct command. And he refused to let Arnold commit any part of Brigadier General Ebenezer Learned's brigade, which was defending the left flank of the American line, even though Learned was part of Arnold's division. Burgoyne might do something unexpected. Gates stayed back, convinced that caution was the better part of valor.[28]

At around eleven Arnold rode forward and found that Morgan's men had taken cover in the trees, around the Freeman house, and behind the farm's fences. They could see the first of the advanced British pickets emerging from the woods. Several of them looked like Indians. Arnold rode up even with Morgan, who was watching from the edge of the woods on the south side of the farm clearing. Arnold pointed. "Colonel Morgan, you and I have seen too many redskins to be deceived by that garb of paint and feathers. They are asses in lions' skins, Canadians and Tories. Let your riflemen cure them of their borrowed plumes."[29] With that he turned and rode back toward headquarters, where he could start lobbying Gates anew.

12:00 Noon, John Burgoyne, the British Column at Freeman's Farm

The center British column was ironically the smallest of the three. Hamilton had fewer than seventeen hundred men under his command; yet this was where Burgoyne and Phillips had decided to be, and this was the column most likely to see hard action. They had marched westward along a road through the woods until they came parallel with a farm clearing just to the south. This had to be the farm of John Freeman, a Loyalist who had abandoned his home to join Burgoyne. Freeman himself was somewhere to the west with Fraser's Advanced Corps, presumably providing accurate guidance. The British column stopped and rested, its four infantry regiments strung out along the woods path on the north side of the farm. It was noon. The day was pleasant and the sky not threatening. Could it be that the Americans had fallen back yet again? Pickets were deployed to investigate the buildings and fields of the small farm. Time dragged. The men in the long files in the woods relaxed.

At Fraser's order the second set of signal guns set all three columns advancing southward.[30] There was a shot ahead of the British column. Then more shots. The pickets were engaging, but it was not yet a firefight. Some of the shots were clearly coming from the American side, and some of the soldiers thought they could distinguish the distinctive snap of rifles. Hamilton sent forward a hundred skirmishers under Major Gordon Forbes. Yesterday Forbes had been merely in charge of the pickets around Sword's house; today he appeared to be at the point of the attack. When they reached the clearing around Freeman's farm, Forbes led his men forward and fell in with Americans posted in and around the farmhouse. The two advance parties began skirmishing.

The Americans were riflemen, lead elements of Morgan's corps. They fired at Forbes's men in a ragged, seemingly harmless spatter of fire. But one or another of Forbes's men seemed to fall with each shot. Forbes noticed that there were fewer of the riflemen than he had expected. It might take them each a minute to reload their rifles. Meanwhile Forbes pushed his skirmishers forward to seize the advantage. But they were too scattered to be effective and Morgan's men were too far away and moving too fast to be brought down by muskets. Still, Forbes thought that he had the Americans badly outnumbered.

12:00 Noon, Daniel Morgan, Freeman's Farm

It was noon before Morgan's men saw the red coats of Forbes's skirmishers coming into the Freeman clearing from the north. They could see motion off to the northwest as well, but their immediate attention focused on the hundred or so redcoats advancing slowly to investigate the farmhouse. Some of his pickets who had been in and around the house had already fired and were falling back. Morgan could see a few British skirmishers lying on the ground, but many more were advancing across Freeman's farm. Morgan knew that his men in cover on the south side of the farm clearing would wait until there were as many targets as possible around the farmhouse before firing. They held their fire, each man marking a red uniform coat in the middle distance. To Morgan's riflemen, Forbes's detachment was like a herd of deer walking unknowingly toward them across a frozen winter deer yard. When it finally came, the firing was ragged but lethal. Most of the British skirmishers fell. Forbes himself was wounded. All but one of his fellow officers also fell, either dead or wounded. The British detachment was clearly in desperate trouble.[31]

It would take the riflemen at least a minute to reload, but seeing the British skirmishers falling prompted more of Morgan's men to move out on to the field. Major Morris rode out on horseback and Captain Van Swearingen moved out as well. Meanwhile British regulars started to emerge from the woods, too many for the riflemen, who were now mostly in the open with empty rifles. Where was Dearborn? Morgan needed light infantry support and he needed it quickly. Some of the riflemen got off one more shot, then all of them began their dash back to the cover of the woods on the sides of the farm clearing.

Across the field more and more British regulars were lining up and turning to face the Americans. Survivors of the detachment of British skirmishers were struggling to their feet and falling back even as Morgan's men were doing the same. A British infantry company somewhere along the line fired a volley before receiving any orders, and more of Forbes's pickets fell, this time to friendly fire.[32] But the American riflemen now realized that there was a large force of regulars behind the British pickets, and lacking close support from Dearborn they were scattering like quail (Figure 2.6).

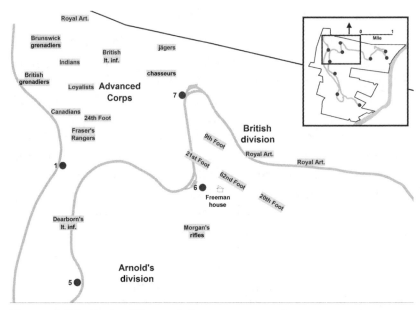

Figure 2.6 The Battle of Freeman's Farm, 12:00 noon, September 19, 1777

12:00 Noon, Henry Dearborn, Coulter's Farm

Dearborn's light infantry came into the southwest side of the Coulter farm clearing at about noon. The clearing was about the same size as the Freeman farm clearing. Dearborn could see that Morgan's men were already skirmishing almost half a mile off to his right. He might have gone directly toward the sound of rifle fire to support Morgan, but he could also see movement ahead of him and even some off to the left. British troops were on the high ground in that direction and they looked ready to fall on Morgan's position in a flanking attack. Dearborn saw it as his task to prevent that from happening, even though it would take him even farther away from Morgan.

Dearborn's men filed off to the left along the tree line, then made a right turn to create a skirmish line. Facing them to the north across the farm clearing were what appeared to be about two companies of British light infantry and some militiamen. These were Captain Alexander Fraser and his rangers, along with a mix of Loyalist irregulars. Here was an isolated detachment from Fraser's Advanced Corps ripe for picking. Dearborn's men moved forward at a trot in a line long enough to envelop the British detachment. They closed the two-hundred-yard gap between them quickly, stopped at fifty yards and loosed a volley, then set off faster with bayonets. Some of Dearborn's men fell, but a larger number of the smaller British and Loyalist detachment fell, retreated, or dropped their arms in surrender.

Dearborn's men took twenty-three prisoners, but there was no time to relish the accomplishment. In a matter of a few minutes, many more British troops appeared out of the woods just to the north of them. There were many more regulars and irregulars facing them now and Dearborn could see that while he had enjoyed an advantage just minutes before, he was now seriously outnumbered. He had run into the front line of Fraser's Advanced Corps. Having nearly enveloped the little detachment of British rangers, Dearborn was now acutely aware that he was about to be enveloped himself by a much larger main force. British troops were passing his light infantry on the right. Any farther and they would completely cut him off from contact with Morgan. He could see Fraser's rangers doing the same thing off to his left. Both flanks of his light infantry were about to be turned.

Now, almost a half mile to Dearborn's right, Morgan's men were scattering as the main British column deployed against them. The two components of Morgan's corps had both separately run into two of Burgoyne's main columns. There was nothing for it but to fall back. Dearborn's only rational option was to retreat 275 yards to safer high ground southwest of the farm clearing, and he took it. Within minutes the light infantry was back where it had started less than an hour earlier, bloodied but intact, and in possession of a couple dozen prisoners. He could only hope that Gates would send more forces forward soon, or both he and Morgan would have to fall all the way back to the American lines.[33]

1:00 PM, *Friedrich Riedesel, on the river road*

Down near the Hudson, three German regiments had crossed the bridge they had repaired on Thursday. The repair detachment had joined the column and they marched together to the second bridge, only a few hundred yards farther on. Harassing American scouts had prevented the completion of repairs the day before, but Riedesel had been sure that today his force was large enough to get the job done. This bridge crossed a bigger stream that flowed down what everyone would soon start calling the Great Ravine.

Riedesel had next ordered his own regiment up the river bluff to his right. From there they could see any American advance coming from down the valley and provide protecting fire for the units below them on the flat. Another German regiment moved up the narrow road that led west toward the Great Ravine, along the north side of the stream that issued from it, leaving their left wing in contact with the bridge. Still another deployed just west of them along the same road. Both regiments contributed men to rebuild the ruined bridge with as much speed as they could muster.[34]

Riedesel ordered two companies of another regiment to the top of a prominent hill they could see to the southwest, on the south side of the Great Ravine. A major battle was probably unfolding out of their sight and they needed eyes on the high ground. The two companies moved quickly up the narrow road into the Great Ravine, passing troops already deployed along it. Eight hundred yards along this road they found the bridge across the stream that the Americans had neglected to destroy. It was the same bridge that Hamilton's column had used a few hours earlier. But unlike the British column, once the Germans were across the bridge, they veered off to the left to climb the hill overlooking the river.[35]

It was now one o'clock. They had heard the spatter of musketry from Hamilton's center column first, but soon the signal guns were heard from Fraser's more distant right column, then a confusion of more and more firing of all kinds. Riedesel needed to support Burgoyne's center column as best he could. But he also had to protect the immense baggage train, the hospital, the artillery park, and the bateaux just behind him on the river road.[36]

Riedesel sent one of his adjutants up the hill with orders for his own Regiment von Riedesel to advance toward the fighting. He then sent Captain Georg Päusch off up the Great Ravine with a detachment of men, two cannons, ammunition, and an equipment cart from Päusch's Hessen-Hanau artillery brigade. For this the undestroyed bridge was not just convenient, but crucial. Päusch would otherwise not have been able to get his artillery in position without a long delay.[37]

When reconstruction of the bridge on the river road was done, the Germans fired guns to let the companies on the hill known that they had succeeded. It was another of a series of coded signals the generals had agreed to at the start of the day. Two regiments crossed over the repaired bridge on the river road but they had only gone a short distance when they found yet another that had been destroyed and needed reconstruction. The regiments stopped again, and again they changed from soldiering to construction. By this time the Regiment von Riedesel was on the bluff above them, and it became that regiment's duty to cover the right flank of the two regiments below. A party of forty men was detached from the Regiment von Riedesel to move to an observation post on a barren hilltop even closer to the Americans. The new bridge repair took more than an hour.[38]

Another four hundred yards farther on, the Germans encountered yet another destroyed bridge. Two companies were already at work on it, protected only by their own muskets and the advanced detachment on the bluff above. It was then that they realized just how close to the American lines they were. The last bridge was repaired, but not crossed. Scouts came in saying that the Americans appeared to be getting ready to strike north along the river road. It was time for the German troops to dig in.[39]

1:00 PM, Simon Fraser, the Advanced Corps

Fraser could see much of what was going on from his vantage point on high ground on the west. To the east of his position he could see Hamilton's main British column filing out of the woods and deploying across the northern side of Freeman's farm. Americans continued to fire from the woods and behind fences around the farm clearing. The British pickets under Forbes's command who had not been killed or wounded were falling back.

Fraser ordered two British light infantry companies from Lindsay's battalion to move left in support of Hamilton's column, along with a single piece of artillery. It was not much more than a hundred men, but it was enough to give relief to the dwindling British skirmishers. The light infantrymen trotted forward in pairs. It was a loose, shallow formation, the men taking turns firing so that one was always able to cover the other with a loaded musket.[40] The single cannon fired canister as the two companies of light infantry moved forward in skirmish lines on either side of it. At this the remaining Americans, all of them riflemen, scattered into the woods.[41]

Captain Van Swearingen of Morgan's corps was captured by some of the Indian irregulars under Fraser's command. They were about to strip him of his clothing when one of Fraser's batmen[42] came up and rescued the American. The batman recovered Van Swearingen's pocketbook, which contained all of his papers, including his commission. The American was so grateful that he offered the batman all his paper dollars.

Van Swearingen apologized for not having any hard cash to offer as a reward. This the batman politely declined.[43]

The American captain was taken to General Fraser, who had come up to the two detached companies. Fraser peppered him with questions, but Van Swearingen said only that the American Army was commanded by two major generals, Gates and Arnold. Fraser flushed with anger. "If you do not immediately inform me as to the exact situation of your army, I will hang you up directly." Van Swearingen tensed himself and said, "You may if you please." They both knew it was an empty threat, but Van Swearingen could not be as certain of it as Fraser was. Fraser wheeled his horse and rode off, leaving the prisoner in the charge of an artillery officer. They were joined by another British officer and the three men sat down to share a canteen of water. They tried a gentler approach to interrogation, but with little more luck than Fraser had. After a series of evasive answers one of them got to the point. "Captain, do you think we shall have any more work upon our hands today?" Van Swearingen nodded pleasantly. "Yes, yes, you'll have business enough for there are many hundreds all round you now."

As if Van Swearingen's words had been a signal, heavy fire suddenly began to spray the farm clearing. The artillery officer jumped up and ran toward the four 6-pounders that made up the brigade's artillery, calling over his shoulder to the other officer, "You must take charge of the captain." He in turn gave Van Swearingen over to a sergeant and told him to take the captive to the house where other prisoners were being kept, cautioning him that General Fraser had ordered that they not be ill-treated. Van Swearingen would not be hanged this day. The artillery suppressed the firing from the Americans, but there were casualties. The fighting was growing hotter.

The British grenadier battalion came up and filed east to form an east–west line. To their left and behind them were more scattered companies of the British light infantry battalion. Still farther to their left the 24th Foot had moved even farther off to the east in support of the main British column. The 24th was now close enough to the center column to support it if needed. Fraser deployed von Breymann and his four companies of German grenadiers to protect the right flank of the Advanced Corps. Von Breymann formed up his troops facing west so that he made a right angle with the line of the British grenadiers.

With Dearborn pulled back and Morgan's men scattered, it was quiet now. Fraser could see Americans along the woods edge at the south side of the Freeman farm clearing as silence passed over the battlefield. The initial fighting had lasted only a half hour or so. Fraser's men waited. Somewhere in the distance a turkey was squawking.

Down on the river road the men of both armies noticed the lull. Breathing became shallow as everyone at a distance strained to hear any clue to what might be happening. Around Freeman's farm the two armies squinted through the dissipating gunsmoke, each trying their best to understand their circumstances. It was quiet enough for both sides to hear the faint cries and groans of the wounded on the field. Nothing could be done for them for the time being.[44]

1:30 PM, John Burgoyne, the British Column

The leading regiments of Hamilton's center column had deployed in a brick-red line along the north side of Freeman's farm. The line drew out to the west as the 9th filed off, followed by the 21st. The 20th deployed east in the opposite direction, stretching out and followed by the 62nd. When the head of each regiment advanced as far as it could, the companies began to separate. When this was accomplished a simple left face would turn the 9th and the 21st into firing lines two ranks deep. A right face accomplished the same change for the 20th and the 62nd. Their appearance on the north side of Freeman's farm had quieted the skirmishing. Now they waited.

An immediate problem was that the farm clearing was only about a quarter-mile wide, 440 yards, not enough to accommodate all four regiments deployed in two ranks.[45] The 20th and the 21st each had 450 men and needed at least two hundred yards apiece, more to provide small gaps between companies, space for artillery, and the open spacing between men that the British Army in America preferred.[46] The 62nd with three hundred men needed at least another 150 yards. Hamilton and Burgoyne conferred about this and decided to pull the 9th back to a reserve position behind the 62nd, which would then be centered between the 20th on the left and the 21st on the right. This made sense, as the 9th was down to only about 250 men after a tough fight at Fort Ann back in July, and many of those left had been part of Forbes's battered party of skirmishers. Two companies of the 9th were sent off to occupy two little structures in the gap between the British column and Fraser's Advanced Corps. The rest were ordered to wait in reserve in the woods (Figure 2.7).

In minutes, the remaining three regiments of Hamilton's column were in double ranks and ready to advance.[47] The line ran at an angle to the east–west axis of the farm, facing southwest toward the woods where the scattered American riflemen were concealed.[48] The 62nd was on the north end of a ridge in the middle of the long red line, where Freeman's house and farm buildings were located. Morgan's riflemen were beginning to shoot at the main line from the woods.

Major Kingston, Burgoyne's adjutant, suggested that a gun be fired to get the attention of the infantry so that officers could make the command to cease fire heard before more of the pickets were lost to friendly fire. Burgoyne agreed. Lieutenant James Hadden's guns were the closest, and so it was that he later claimed the honor of firing the first cannon shot of the day, not at the enemy, but merely to restore order. It had the desired effect, and order settled once again on the British line while the surviving bloodied skirmishers got back to safety.[49]

Hamilton's brigade was supported by four light 6-pounders, and these were to be set in pairs between the three regiments. Captain Jones of the

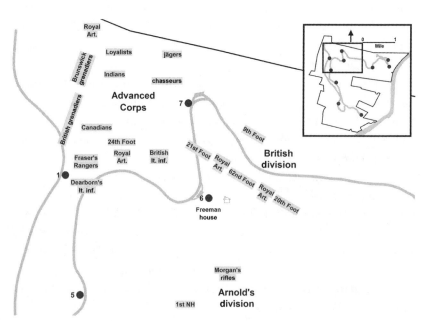

Figure 2.7 The Battle of Freeman's Farm, 1:30 p.m., September 19, 1777.

British artillery commanded both pairs of 6-pounders in action. Once the field was cleared of British pickets, Jones was ordered to put a ball through Freeman's farmhouse. He passed the order on to Hadden, who did his best but missed. Jones then stepped forward and laid a gun himself. This time the ball holed the farmhouse, but the expected swarm of Americans did not explode out the door and windows. This house was where the shot that had wounded Forbes had come from, but it was empty now.

By a quarter to two, Hadden's two 6-pounders had been drawn up behind the left end of the 62nd Regiment. The two easternmost infantry companies pulled back to form a protective angle, into which Hadden set his guns. It seemed clear that the 20th Regiment to their left was going to see less action than the other regiments; the Americans were appearing ahead and to the right on the other side of the fields. Jones took a lieutenant and the other two guns to a position between the 62nd and the 21st Regiments 150 yards off to Hadden's right.

Each 6-pounder cannon was four and a half feet long, mounted on a two-wheeled carriage and drawn by a two-wheeled limber. No matter what combination of elevation and powder they used, each gun had an effective range exceeding a thousand yards. Shot, powder, ropes, and an array of rammers, ladles, sponges, wad hooks, hand spikes, levers, and other specialized tools brought the total weight of each gun and associated equipment to over a ton and a half. Each of the four guns was served by a crew of a dozen men, all in blue artillery coats with red facings. Each gun was drawn by two horses harnessed in tandem, managed by a civilian driver who was not part of the gun crew. The gun crews were well trained.[50] When the crews arrived at their positions in the line, they unlimbered the guns, turned them around, pulled them into position, and stood ready to load and fire in only a minute and forty-five seconds. Today the target would probably be American infantry at close range, almost point blank, and the guns would fire mostly deadly canister with almost no elevation.

Loading and firing required the precise coordination of the dozen men. There were a hundred ways for the team effort to go wrong. If the man serving the vent dropped his woolen thumb stall, the heat of the metal would prevent him from stopping the vent, putting the sponger at risk of losing his arms. If the men behind the gun did not get clear quickly enough, the recoil could crush them under the wheels. If the man bringing the cartridge from the cartouche failed to keep it on his left side and under his coat while taking it to the loader, a spark could kill him, along with half the crew. The crews had practiced the precise sequences of steps required to prevent fatal mistakes hundreds of times.[51] They had trained for long hours under varying conditions, playing out various scenarios. Jones's crews would not kill themselves because of inadequate training. Just as important, their attention to habitual detail would keep them working smoothly for as long as the gun was in action. What the Americans might do to them was another matter.

2:00 PM, James Wilkinson, Freeman's Farm

At noon Wilkinson had been able to hear the rifle fire from the direction of Morgan's assignment. At one o'clock they had all heard the British field piece that signaled the advance of Fraser's and Hamilton's columns. The minutes had dragged. At last Wilkinson asked Gates for permission to ride forward to see what was happening. Gates refused his young adjutant. "It is your duty, sir, to wait my orders." The scattered small arms fire had ceased for a minute or two, then there was much more of it. Wilkinson had made an excuse about having to check the picket on the left for intelligence. A preoccupied Gates was examining a battery on the American left and seemed not to notice. Wilkinson had mounted and ridden his horse toward the picket, but as soon as he was safely out of sight he had spurred the horse toward the more distant gunfire.[52]

Five hundred yards into the woods Wilkinson had come up behind Major Dearborn and the light infantry regiment. The firing had ceased again. Wilkinson had ridden on and had run into Morgan's Major Joseph Morris riding alone. Morris had explained that the corps had been advancing across Freeman's farm when they unexpectedly fell in with the British line west of Freeman's farmhouse. Several men and officers had been taken prisoner. Morris himself had escaped only by riding hard through the ranks of the British and doubling back through the woods.[53]

Now Morris showed Wilkinson Freeman's farmhouse. Once Morgan's men had fallen back, the British pickets had taken it over, then the main British line had come up as well. Now there were dead and wounded all around the farmhouse, but the British main line appeared to be waiting. Wilkinson's curiosity pushed aside caution. He spurred his horse to leap the fence and started across the weedy fields. Lieutenant Colonel Richard Butler, second in command of the rifles and behind cover with three men, shouted and stopped him. "Enemy sharpshooters are on the opposite side of the ravine. Being on horseback you should be shot." Wilkinson thought about it and decided to leave investigation of the farmhouse until later. "What are Morgan's orders?" asked Butler. "I have seen a heavy column moving toward our left."

Wilkinson had no idea what Morgan's orders might be. He decided that he had gathered enough information and should return to report to Gates. As he rode off he heard the squawk of a turkey from the woods, the last thing he would expect to hear in this growing noisy confusion. He rode toward it and ran into Morgan with two of his men. Morgan was using his turkey call, a contraption made of three turkey wing bones, to rally and assemble his riflemen, who were now scattered through the woods south of the farm clearing. Morgan was distraught. His horse had been shot out from under him and his men were scattered. "I am ruined by God! Major Morris ran on so rapidly with the front that they were beaten before I could get up with the rear and my men are scattered God knows where."[54]

Morgan always brought up the rear, more herder than leader; it was the only way to be sure that his irregulars actually got where they all were supposed to be going. "It is to see that every man does his duty, and that cowards do not lag behind while brave men are fighting," he had often said. This time, his leading men had been eager to a fault and had been scattered like turkeys by the British regulars. They were now starting to gather around Morgan, who was calling them to the woods south of the weed-choked fields of Freeman's abandoned farm. Wilkinson glanced at the turkey call again and smiled a bit at the irony. "You have a long day before you to retrieve an inauspicious beginning. I have seen your field officers." Wilkinson rode off toward headquarters. There were already three men from one company missing and presumed dead. It would be a long day for sure.[55]

The lull in the fighting lasted over an hour. During this time Morgan reassembled most of his riflemen, gathering his wits at the same time. Morgan had already lost several—a handful killed so far, another handful wounded, some missing and presumed captured. Dearborn's light infantry already had losses of twice that many, but Morgan was not sure what Dearborn and his men were doing way off to his left. The fact was that Dearborn's men were ready to fight on from their position southwest of Freeman's farm clearing, but they were still in no position to support Morgan in any direct way.[56]

2:30 PM, Benedict Arnold and Horatio Gates, American Headquarters

Wilkinson got back to the American lines and reported what he had observed to Gates. If the general was annoyed that his adjutant had been insubordinate, he did not say so. The news that Morgan's men had been scattered and there was a large force in front of him and another somewhere off to his left was troubling. Gates still preferred to wait behind his defenses and let Burgoyne attack him, but the truth was that the defenses on the American left and in the center had barely begun. The American camp was largely unprotected even by abatis.[57] There were log ramparts in front of Glover's and Paterson's brigade camps, but Morgan's, Poor's, and Learned's camps were mostly not defensible. It would be days more before they had continuous fortifications to protect them. Meanwhile Cilley finished his advance with the 1st New Hampshire, having marched through the woods for about a mile. Scammell was behind him with the 3rd New Hampshire. They had followed the road taken earlier by Morgan's men, then came up on the southwestern side of the Freeman farm clearing. As they approached they came up on Morgan's men from the rear around three o'clock. At about the same time Arnold back in the American camp ordered Cook's battalion of Connecticut militia forward as well.

3:00 PM, Joseph Cilley, Freeman's Farm

Colonel Joseph Cilley was forty-three years old, and like Scammell a dedicated republican. He was old enough to have served with Rogers' Rangers almost two decades ago. He had married Sarah Longfellow around that time; over the course of two decades they had nine children, and Sarah now carried a tenth, due in December. Joseph thought that if the child were a boy they should name him Horatio Gates Cilley. By the outbreak of the revolution he had been ready to move up to a more senior appointment. Now he was here in command of the 1st New Hampshire Continentals.

The New Hampshire regiments were coming up on Morgan's left just as he was restoring some order to his reassembling riflemen. Morgan was relieved to now have the New Hampshire muskets and bayonets at the edge of the clearing. The 1st New Hampshire files turned right to deploy along the southern side of Freeman's fields, following the main body of Morgan's riflemen as they shifted east. Morgan's riflemen found perches in the trees and provided covering sniper fire for the advancing

Continentals. Scammell's 3rd New Hampshire regiment was following but it was not yet up.

Cilley could see that he had the three British regiments of foot in front of them. He could see three sets of regimental uniforms, but there were no regimental flags to identify them.[58] Artillery sat in the two gaps between the three regiments. The regiment farthest to the west appeared to have uniforms with blue facings. At this distance it was hard to see them even with a glass. The entire British regiment on the west was wearing bearskin hats, and at first they appeared to be grenadiers. But their uniform facings were all the same royal blue, so this was no battalion of grenadier companies drawn from different regiments. The regiment in the middle had buff uniform facings. The men all wore cocked hats. The third regiment also had cocked hats, but their uniform facings were a light yellow. The American officers scanned the line with their glasses. Three regiments of foot it was, probably the 21st, 62nd, and 20th. If Burgoyne pushed all of them forward against the two New Hampshire regiments, the Americans would be badly outnumbered, but there was nothing for Cilley to do but try it.

There were 250 yards between the American and British lines. The 1st New Hampshire was lined up in two ranks. Cilley watched as the center British regiment stepped off toward him. The British artillery on both sides of it began firing at him as well, and he knew they would keep it up as long as there was no danger they might fire into the backs of their own infantry. Scammell and the 3rd New Hampshire were still not up. Cilley ordered his regiment forward. In a few minutes the two regiments would be within fifty yards of each other, the killing zone between them, close enough for both regiments to fire their first and best volleys.

The gap narrowed, a hundred yards, now seventy, now fifty. The British cannon fire had taken some of Cilley's men down, but the rest were steady. Both regiments were ordered to halt and present. Bayonets glittered at the ends of muskets on both sides. The Americans knew what would happen next. The British would start by firing volleys by company, the roar measured and steady. Then they would advance and keep firing. Then, when all muskets were loaded and primed they would fire one more battalion volley, a simultaneous explosion of balls in the direction of the 1st New Hampshire from every musket the British regiment had. Then they would lower and level their empty muskets to their waists and come on at quick step, then a trot, then at a dead run, yelling in an all-out bayonet charge. It was their favorite shock tactic.

3:00 PM, John Burgoyne, the British Column at Freeman's Farm

Burgoyne rode behind the center of the line with General Phillips, Major Kingson, and Captain Stanhope. Burgoyne's three aides-de-camp were there as well, as was Phillips's aide-de-camp, Captain Green.

Hamilton commanded both his own regiment, the 21st, and the column as a whole. The men of the 21st were fusiliers.[59] Their regiment was the oldest in the expeditionary force, and they had stubbornly retained an old-fashioned hat style that made them look almost like grenadiers, even after they were supposed to have cut down both their coats and their hats to styles more like those of light infantry.

Lieutenant Colonel John Lind commanded the 20th to Hamilton's left; Lieutenant Colonel John Anstruther, the 62nd in front of him.[60] Burgoyne watched the action with the studied detachment expected of a British general. He delivered his orders with cool precision. If any man looked at him, there had to be no expression other than intrepidity, even serenity. It was his duty.

The dispersal of the American riflemen had been reasonably easy, but now there were many more of them in the woods 250 yards in front of them, too far away for the British muskets but close enough for the American riflemen. Officers of all kinds were falling as the American rifles found their marks. Hamilton's eyes ran up and down the long line of the 20th, 62nd, and 21st, facing whatever the Americans had on the other side of Freeman's fields. It was time.

Sergeants stood at the flanks of their platoons, halberds erect, checking from time to time to ensure that the ranks were dressed straight. Colonels and their subordinate officers took their places in front, all carefully positioned by rank and seniority. They could not remain there when the firing began, of course, and as that moment approached they retired to the flanks and rear.

Each soldier stood straight with his Brown Bess on his left shoulder, the butt in his left hand, his right hand hanging, palm toward the right thigh. His left hand was slightly rotated so that the trigger guard pressed against his chest. His left elbow was rotated slightly outward. His feet were a step apart, heels in line with the others of his rank, his toes rotated slightly outward as required.

Some of the men were grizzled veterans, some young and inexperienced. The veterans tried to calm the nerves of the green youngsters. "There is no danger if you hear the sound of the bullet which is fired against you. You are safe, and after the first charge all your fears will be done away."[61]

The order came, calmly: "Fix your bayonet." The command initiated what was really a series of five well-practiced steps, each requiring two to five specific motions that the men accomplished with rigid precision. At the end their arms were back where they began, but now with bayonets glittering at the ends of their muskets.[62]

The generals conferred and ordered the 62nd forward. The British regiment marched forward in two long ranks, the tallest men in front, as planned. The second rank followed exactly one step behind, offset slightly to the right. They were moving southwestward along a low ridge, across the fields and toward the woods from which the Americans had now emerged.

A little later the 20th was mistakenly ordered forward as well.[63] But the action was not in front of them, so they stopped and held their ground. The Americans were advancing, too. Now the armies were only fifty yards apart.

Anstruther gave the order to halt. The order repeated down the command chain, ending a few seconds later with bellows from the sergeants. The lines halted. Here and there an American rifle ball found its mark and a man fell out of the front rank. Other rifle balls fired from high in the trees snapped overhead, seeking British officers and Loyalists.

"Make ready." The simple command unleashed a long series of coordinated movements: right hands to firelocks, firelocks poised, left hands to firelocks, firelocks cocked. Each man of the front rank dropped to his right knee, putting the butt of his musket on the ground but keeping his thumb on the cock and his index finger at the trigger. Each man in the second rank stepped forward at the same time with musket recovered and put his left foot just to the left of the right foot of the kneeling man in front of him. The second rank thus staggered to the right; all the men in the second rank could now easily aim past those kneeling in front of them.

"Present." In a single motion all the muskets went from vertical to horizontal, all the 42-inch barrels parallel, all the butts brought up to shoulders. Right hands gripped polished walnut stocks, their index fingers poised over triggers, not quite touching them yet. Bodies leaned slightly forward to take the recoil, right knee stiff in the second rank, left knee slightly bent. It was more important to keep muzzles level than it was to take careful aim, so faces were not pressed against stocks, and unlike hunters, the soldiers were not squinting along the tops of their musket barrels. Sixty-nine-caliber balls rested loosely at the bottoms of their 75-caliber bores, allowing enough windage to make individual aiming a waste of time and effort. The object was to throw a cloud of lead in the direction of the enemy, not to fire well-aimed shots at individual soldiers.

"Fire." The companies fired in a complex sequence so that volleys came from different parts of the line every two or three seconds. By the time the last company fired, the first had reloaded and was ready to fire again. The volleys flew out in staggered roars and the army disappeared in a cloud of gunsmoke. The smoke covered the long complicated series of steps necessary for each company to reload and get ready to fire another volley.

After firing, the front rank of each company stood up and the men behind stepped back to their previous positions. It had required twenty-one steps, a total of sixty-three discrete motions that each man had practiced hundreds or even thousands of times. Each of them focused on the precision of those motions; each blocked out all the other sights, sounds, and thoughts that competed for his attention. That was the nature of military discipline, and it was why Burgoyne was sure he led the best army in the world. But even in this highly disciplined army the elaborate sequential firing began to break down after the first volley.

Some of the muskets had failed to fire, but the men holding them went through all the same motions, not opening a new cartridge, but otherwise repeating all the steps required to reload. A few younger and less experienced men whose muskets misfired mistakenly put another charge and ball on top of the one still in the barrel. Every man primed, closed the pan, poured powder and ball into the muzzle, crumpled the cartridge paper and inserted it as a wad, pulled out the steel ramrod, rammed the charge home, replaced the ramrod, recocked, and made ready to present again. Hands and arms moved in concert for the time being. The groans of the wounded were ignored. It had taken less than twenty seconds.[64]

3:15 PM, Joseph Cilley, the 1st New Hampshire at Freeman's Farm

The two opposing regiments volleyed almost simultaneously, but with different effect. The British infantry companies were trained to fire as one, and the main object was to keep musket barrels level and parallel. Most of the balls passed harmlessly over the heads of the New Hampshire men. The British, on slightly higher ground, had overshot them.

The New Hampshire men were less thoroughly trained. They tended to pick targets and aim individually, even when told not to. Their initial volley had more effect as a result. The British line advanced a few yards, fired another volley, then another. The Americans were returning fire, almost volley for volley. They were a little more ragged and not quite as fast, but they were effective.

The big guns on the flanks of the 62nd had been firing as fast as their crews could load, three shots per minute. A half-dozen men pulled each gun forward to keep up with the infantry and reset the gun after the recoil. At this range they could use canisters, each filled with eighty-five small balls that spread out and shrieked as they flew toward the enemy.[65] The artillerymen would not fire into the backs of their own infantrymen. They stopped firing as the infantry advanced.

There was no sign of an American retreat. Burgoyne suggested that it was time to force the issue, and Hamilton agreed. The command for the bayonet charge rippled down through the chain of command before the men could even prime their pans, unheard by many men who by this time were temporarily half deaf from the noise. The British started forward at a walk, the drummers rattling along behind them, the line ragged at first as the more deafened soldiers caught visual cues from the men beside them. Then by quick step, then by the double quick, leaving the artillery far behind. Few armies could stand up to a well-coordinated bayonet charge by this finest of all armies, and no one was surprised to see the Americans falling back toward the woods on the south side of the farm. For the British line it was a dash of perhaps a hundred yards, about as much as could be expected from heavily armed men who were gasping and shouting encouragement as they went. From the trees to the left came rifle balls that Morgan's men could now fire from the flank as the British line passed by, a lethal infilading fire.

There was a chance they could hold if reinforcements came up, but it was time for the Americans to fall back into the woods. When they reached the trees they turned, took cover, and made ready to fire again.

The British bayonet charge slowed. The panting British soldiers had still not reloaded, and they could not sustain a charge into the woods. The New Hampshire men were loading, aiming, and firing as rapidly as they could from cover. The American infantrymen could hear Morgan's rifles behind them and off to the right, harassing the redcoats from perches in the trees.

Rifle balls from the woods plucked at British officers waving their swords to encourage their men. Then the return fire increased, not volleys of it, but the kind of erratic, ragged firing that the American frontiersmen preferred. The British muskets were empty and their bayonets were ready, but all most of them could see in front was smoke, a worm fence, and trees. The most eager of them began to notice that there was no longer movement in their peripheral vision. The charge stalled. Muzzle flashes from the woods increased. The men of the British 62nd stopped and began to fall back.[66]

Cilley's men moved back out on to the field and began to re-form their lines. The tension of the moment and the dullness of their hearing made it difficult for the noncommissioned officers to form them up, but in a few minutes they would be ready again.

3:30 PM, Alexander Scammell, the 3rd New Hampshire at Freeman's Farm

Scammell's 3rd New Hampshire was now finally deployed on Cilley's left. Now there were two regiments and both could advance together. It took the Americans a few more minutes to form up on the edge of the field. The British were falling back but it was difficult for the Americans to get organized quickly enough to follow up their advantage. Most of them managed to fire when the first volley was ordered. They reloaded, moved forward twenty yards, and fired again. This time it was the Americans' turn to attempt a charge. The British line was in disarray and the British cannons were either already exposed or soon would be. While it lacked the precision and martial beauty of the British charge, the American one was just as effective. Men leapt over fallen British and American soldiers.[67] The 62nd fell back toward the woods on the north side of Freeman's farm (Figure 2.8).

The 62nd turned and re-formed. This time the British command also sent the 21st Regiment forward. It was a repeat of the previous assault,

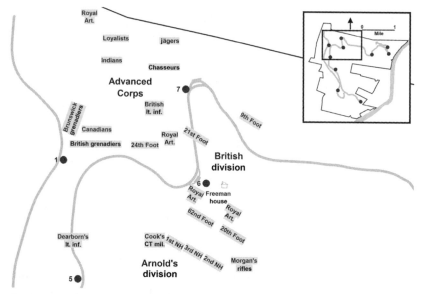

Figure 2.8 The Battle of Freeman's Farm, 3:30 p.m., September 19, 1777.

but with nearly twice the number of men involved. The Americans had advanced, now they were falling back.[68] The New Hampshire men of the two American regiments dropped back into the trees again.

The fighting had taken twenty minutes. At least three dozen men in the 1st New Hampshire were wounded and another dozen were missing. Wounded and missing in the 3rd New Hampshire were less than half that, but Scammell already had a half dozen killed or mortally wounded, including his lieutenant-colonel and a lieutenant.

It had been a hot fight, and both commanders were proud of their men. The ground was already littered with fallen soldiers but Scammell was pleased to see that no one in his regiment thought of plunder. An American soldier would occasionally run short of ammunition, stoop down, and take cartridges from one of the fallen, but that was all.[69]

Scammell, always at the front of his regiment, took a ball through the breech of his fusil and another through his coat. The first made a loud impact, and he doubled over as his damaged weapon punched him in the stomach. His reaction caused some of the men to think he had been wounded, and word spread quickly that he had been hit, badly wounded, and carried from the field.[70] The New Hampshire regiments turned once again and pushed the British 62nd and 21st back past their artillery support. Around the cannons the Americans saw only dead horses and dead artillerymen. A few of the Americans tried to turn the guns and pull them off, but the ground was too rough. They needed horses to capture the big guns, but none were to be had. Meanwhile the British were re-forming again in the cover of their own woods. They would be coming at them again. It was no use. The captured guns had to be abandoned again.[71] The two New Hampshire regiments backed across to the south side of Freeman's farm once again as the British made another push.

The New Hampshire Continentals had done what they could, but the fighting seemed stalemated. Cilley decided that he could not continue without more reinforcements. He ordered his regiment to retire back toward the American lines.[72] The fatigued 1st New Hampshire started back. Almost immediately they met more fresh troops coming up through the woods south of Freeman's fields. The sight of reinforcements renewed the spirits of Cilley's men, and they were willing to turn and fight again.

Thaddeus Cook and his battalion of Connecticut militia were the relieving force. They came up and deployed off to the left, allowing Cilley to redeploy his regiment, this time also off to the left of Scammell's 3rd New Hampshire, where he could see Cook's regiment and Dearborn's light infantry still farther off.[73] After what seemed like a very long time Winborn Adams brought the 2nd New Hampshire up to take its place on the field as well, replacing Cilley's 1st on Scammell's right. More than half of Poor's brigade was now in action. Four American regiments were now deployed in a ragged line across the southwestern side of Freeman's farm. Back behind the American lines, and off to the east on the river bluffs, soldiers on both sides listened to the rolling thunder of battle and wondered what it meant.

4:00 PM, Benedict Arnold, American Headquarters at Bemis Heights

Reports came back that Cilley and Scammell were having a hard time of it. There were at least three British regiments in front of them and artillery and some grenadiers on their left flank. Arnold had already sent four regiments forward, but they needed more assistance.

Gates mulled over this news. Morgan's corps and four of Poor's seven infantry regiments already in action and Arnold wanted to send more.

This was not what he had intended should happen. Force Burgoyne to attack the American lines; don't meet him in the open field. That had been his battle plan. He did not like what was unfolding now in the least.

Messengers rode back and forth between headquarters and the forward units fighting around Freeman's farm. They were fast, but it still took a half hour for each to ride out and return with news. Meanwhile, it was taking a half hour for each regiment ordered out to get into position to attack. The long lags in both the execution of orders and the receipt of intelligence about their consequences was maddening to everyone back at headquarters.

Arnold was mounted on a gray horse that churned under him. Gates was mounted but still, listening to the dull roar of gunfire to the north. Arnold shouted, "General, the British are reinforced. We must have more men." Gates hesitated. Here they were, the British still far from the American fortifications, and Arnold wanted more regiments to march out to meet them. How did this take advantage of the defensive strategy? How many more regiments would Arnold demand? It seemed the worst of all options: to expend men and ammunition in open field combat and to weaken the defensive line that was their best chance for success in the longer term. Gates also had another reason to hesitate. The American Army was short of shot and powder. Only he and his immediate staff knew it. They could use up most or all of their ammunition today, and if they did, what might happen tomorrow?

But Gates could see that it was not just Arnold who was agitated and ready to commit more units. He could also see for himself that the American lines were not yet strong enough to be effectively defended. The other officers around him were staring at him, and the message was clear. At last he gave in. "You shall have them, sir." Gates ordered Arnold to let General Poor send the rest of his brigade forward. Van Cortlandt's 2nd and Harry Livingston's 4th New York Regiments marched off. So too did Latimer's Connecticut militia regiment. The last units of Poor's Brigade marched out.

4:15 PM, John Brooks and William Hull, the American Lines at Bemis Heights

William Hull was the regimental major in Jackson's 8th Massachusetts Continentals. Colonel Jackson was sick, and Lieutenant Colonel John Brooks now led the regiment. Hull was in command of a picket stationed north of the main line of Learned's brigade on the left wing of the American Army. They had heard the initial action between Morgan's men and Burgoyne's pickets, including the three cheers shouted by the Americans when they all but annihilated the British skirmishers around Freeman's farmhouse. But they could also hear the more intense firing that erupted when Burgoyne's main force moved out on to the field and forced Morgan's men to scatter. For the time being they could only listen and wonder what was going on. They were responsible for protecting the left flank of the American line, and Gates had forbidden Arnold to deploy any of the four regiments in Learned's brigade.

Arnold rode up on his gray horse. He gathered the officers he could find, which included two colonels, John Bailey and John Brooks. How many men did Hull have? Arnold wanted to know. From which regiment? How many regiments were close at hand? He needed three hundred volunteers to move forward to support the units already engaged. Hull hesitated. He had command of the guard detachment of only 250 men and was under orders of Lieutenant Colonel James Wilkinson, the adjutant general. Hull explained this to Arnold, and said, "If I can be excused from that duty, I will be happy to command the detachment." As usual, none of the impediments of custom and order deterred Arnold. With neither authority nor hesitation he said to Hull, "I will excuse you." He then turned to the two colonels and asked them for three hundred volunteers, along with a suitable number of captains and subalterns to command them.

Gates had been clear about forbidding deployment of regiments from Learned's brigade, but he had not precluded the use of volunteers, or so Arnold rationalized. It took only a few minutes for four companies to form up. Arnold gave Hull command of the detachment and told him to move forward and put himself under the command of General Poor.[74] With that Hull found himself suddenly detached from Learned's brigade, reattached to Poor's brigade, and no longer under Wilkinson's orders. Hull wondered what Wilkinson would have to say about it at the end of the day, but he put it out of his mind and marched forward with his new detachment.

Arnold tore off toward the fighting as Brooks and Hull assembled their men and set off in double quick time. Gates saw Brooks leaving with his men and asked where they were going. Someone explained Arnold's action to him. "No more troops will go. I will not suffer the camp to be exposed." But it was too late. There was no stopping them.[75]

4:30 PM, *Joseph Cilley, Freeman's Farm*

Cilley's men made another push, this time with the fresh troops beside them. The British artillery opened up again with canister. They again took turns with the British troops, driving forward then retreating. Long minutes dragged by. It seemed like several hours since Cilley had first engaged. The New Hampshire Continentals were nearing exhaustion. Cilley was again preparing his dazed men to march back to camp. At that critical moment the rest of Poor's brigade started to appear behind them.

Van Cortlandt's 2nd New York fell in just to the right of Dearborn's light infantry, which had been doing their best to hold the left flank since noon. Van Cortlandt thought that Harry Livingston should reinforce him with the 4th New York, and told him so. After all, Poor had instructed Livingston to provide support for Van Cortlandt. But the two cousins were of equal rank, and the prickly Livingston decided on his own to move his 4th New York to the right of the 2nd and closer to Cook's Connecticut militia, leaving Van Cortlandt's regiment to contend with the German riflemen on the left along with Dearborn's light infantry[76]

Latimer's Connecticut militia regiment came up and fell in between the 2nd and 4th New York Regiments. The three fresh regiments had orders to extend the front to the left and to support those points in the action where the need seemed to be greatest. The right flank seemed not to be threatened because it was protected by thickets and ravines.[77] It was enough to again persuade Cilley's weary New Hampshire men to stay in the action.

The American line was now continuously manned from Morgan's rifles in the trees on the southeast side of Freeman's farm all the way to Dearborn's position on Coulter's farm on the far left flank, nine regiments in all. Each was acting on its own, its officers responding to the perceived needs of nearby units and the opportunities that the British opposite them provided (Figure 2.9).

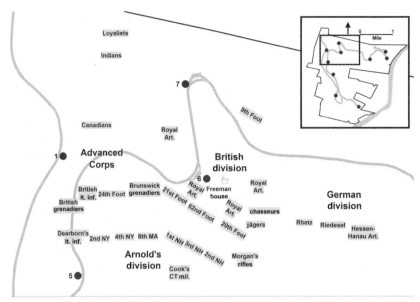

Figure 2.9 The Battle of Freeman's Farm, 5:00 p.m., September 19, 1777.

4:45 PM, John Brooks and William Hull, Freeman's Farm

The Massachusetts detachment of impromptu volunteers moved forward through the woods in columns of eight platoons, following the last of Poor's regiments forward. When Poor heard that Brooks's detachment from Learned's brigade was coming he sent his brigade major back to tell Brooks how to deploy. The 1st and 3rd New Hampshire Regiments were already fully engaged. The center and the left were doing well, but Cook's regiment of Connecticut militia was hard pressed and needed support. The whole of Poor's brigade was now in line or soon would be.

When Hull's platoon columns got to Freeman's farm fields they met Cook's retiring militiamen. They had seen enough action and were falling back. Now the British were threatening to move into the new gap in the line and turn the left flank of the New Hampshire regiments still fighting on Freeman's farm.[78] Brooks's detachment came up and filled the gap in support. Arnold urged Brooks to try to flank the British forces of Hamilton's division that were facing Cilley and Scammell. They could see Freeman's farmhouse a little more than a quarter mile to the northeast. But they could also see Fraser's Advanced Corps waiting off to the northwest. They could help the New Hampshire Continentals by flanking the central

British column, but if they did so they risked being attacked from their left by Fraser's men. Brooks saw that because of this, Fraser might attempt a flanking movement of his own. Some of Brooks's men deployed to face this threat while Hull's portion turned toward Hamilton's British column.

Brooks ordered Hull to take two hundred men and do his best to clear the Freeman farmstead. Hull was as enthusiastic as Brooks and set about the task quickly. Hull scanned the open fields in front of him. There were a few large dead trees, the girdled remnants of the forest Freeman had cleared in recent years. An unharvested crop of wheat had stood among the skeletal trees. Now it was badly trampled by the contending armies. Hull moved his detachment out on to the killing ground. At first he did not see the battery of two pieces of field artillery positioned near Freeman's farmhouse on the north side of the fields. Flanking the battery were two double ranks of Burgoyne's best infantry, perhaps 165 yards away.[79]

Hull was on slightly higher ground than the British unit opposing him. He gave orders to his men to hold their fire until he gave the signal, and then to fire at the knees of the enemy soldiers. If they simply fired a volley as usual from the higher ground, they would shoot over the heads of the enemies unless they took particular care not to.

The British artillery began firing at Hull's detachment, but it had little effect. The British regiment opposite them began to advance. There seemed to be about three hundred of them. Hull could see that they were led by an officer in a uniform with buff facings. Hull was beginning to have doubts. He was facing a crack British regiment with eight green American platoons that might never have fought together before. A hundred yards, then eighty. The artillery continued to fire and a few of Hull's men fell. The British regiment reached the middle of the field. Fifty yards. Hull gave the order to fire. Dozens of British fell in the smoke. Their lines stumbled into disorder, still they came on. Then they halted, the front rank kneeled, and the return volley came. Hull's double lines held. His men had reloaded. Now was the moment when the British would probably bring a bayonet charge. But their muskets were empty and Hull seized the moment, ordering a bayonet charge of his own. The Americans lunged forward with their muskets leveled, inexperienced men catching the insanity of battle. The exposed British regiment, scrambling to reload, fell back in disarray. Hull's men pursued, jumping over fallen redcoats, pursuing them all the way across the field until the retreating British disappeared into the woods on the north side.

Hull was shouting, pointing at the artillery battery, urging the platoons on the left to seize the guns. Gunfire came from Freeman's farmhouse, taking down a few of his men. Some of the Americans on the left diverted to the farmhouse, forced the door, and brought out a sergeant-major and nineteen privates before they were able to reload. All the British horses were dead or had been led off behind the British line; Hull could not draw off the cannon without them. Neither would he be able to hold the salient for long, once Burgoyne discovered the threat. Hull had succeeded, but it was temporary, and accomplished at a high cost. Hull knew what would happen next, so he shouted orders for his men to retire to their original positions, taking their prisoners with them.[80]

Hull collected his wounded and some of the dead as he moved back across the field. He had lost nearly a third of his detachment. The walking wounded and his twenty prisoners were sent back to the American lines. A captain was dead; so was a lieutenant, and who knew how many rank and file. The men were tired and Hull was not sure that they could repeat the action. Now another British regiment moved forward on the right, clearly intending to try to turn the American flank, and Hull's battered detachment was their target. Hull turned his line so that his units faced northeast toward the new threat. This time there was no charging, but instead a grinding struggle of mutual attrition. The British gave ground, then Hull's Americans did, back and forth, with no clear advantage for either side.[81]

4:45 PM, Simon Fraser, the Advanced Corps at Freeman's Farm

For the most part Fraser had stayed where he was, on elevated ground where he was positioned to fall upon the Americans if they made a concerted attempt to flank Hamilton's British column.[82] Hamilton's 21st Regiment had been in trouble for a while. Fraser could see that the American forces were moving around the right flank of the 21st, which endangered the entire center column. Fraser had ordered five companies of his own 24th Regiment forward into the woods to stop the American flanking move. Within minutes they had been beaten back. The American attack had been ferocious and Hamilton's flank was still exposed. Fraser tried again, sending the entire 24th Foot. This time they had gained the position in the woods and held it, but at the cost of fifty men lost.[83]

Fraser could see that still more Americans were advancing in a new attempt to flank Hamilton's line. The entire 24th Regiment was fully engaged but might not be able to hold the critical patch of woods they had just taken. Fraser ordered von Breymann forward with his German grenadiers and light infantry. They had been covering Fraser's own right flank off to the west, but there was no indication that the Americans had the ability or inclination to attack from that direction now. Lieutenant Colonel von Breymann's leg wound still bothered him, but he was ready. The grenadiers moved quickly toward the Americans attempting to break through. At last there was enough force between Fraser and Hamilton to stave off the American effort there.[84]

Fraser and the American Colonel John Brooks had observed each other and had come to similar conclusions. Just as Brooks had seen both opportunity and threat in their relative positions, so too did it occur to Fraser that his units might find themselves rotating counterclockwise with the newly arrived American units. This could allow him to flank them but at the risk of letting them sever his connection to Burgoyne's center column. The last thing either side wanted was a whirlpool action with men chasing each other in a large circle. The action was fierce and bloody, but at last von Breymann's units poured such a galling fire into the American units that Brooks and his Massachusetts men were forced to fall back in line with the New Hampshire regiments.[85]

4:45 PM, Horatio Gates, American Headquarters at Bemis Heights

Arnold was still badgering Gates for more units and Gates was exasperated. Gates had allowed the remaining three regiments of Poor's brigade to be sent forward into the battle. He had seen Brooks detach from Learned's brigade with several companies of volunteers. Nearly half his army was committed to fight a mile north of where he would have preferred them to be, and it was all Arnold's doing.[86]

Arnold and Gates sat on their horses listening to the din of musketry through the forest. Arnold was agitated, unhappy to be at such a distance from the action. Colonel Lewis rode up with a new report from the action, which was disappointing. The fighting was indecisive, he said. Gates was torn. He could still pull back into his lines and wait to fight a defensive battle, but what if the British forces still waiting on the high ground to the left were strong enough to threaten his flank? What if the German forces still at the river started to move down the river road after all? What if all of the American shot and powder were used up? He had already committed more forces than he had wanted to on this day and now still more were being requested. He had not wanted to fight at all today, but now the future of his defense of Albany was hanging in the balance.

Arnold was ready to explode. The battle was not the only thing that seemed indecisive to him at this moment. "By God I will soon put an end to it." He dug his spurs and his gray was at a full gallop toward the fighting in three lunges. Lewis and Gates twisted to face each other as their horses pranced in anticipation of following Arnold. "You had better order him back. The action is going well. He may by some rash act do mischief," advised Lewis. Gates sent Wilkinson after Arnold with orders for Arnold to return to camp. Then, with customary uncertainty, Gates ordered Marshall's 10th Massachusetts Regiment to move forward from Paterson's brigade.[87]

4:45 PM, Friedrich Riedesel, the German Column on the River Road

Riedesel could hear the fighting, but he still had heard nothing from Burgoyne, so he sent a captain to Burgoyne for orders. Riedesel was nervous. He could tell from the noise of it that the fighting was ferocious beyond his sight to the west, but he knew nothing about exactly what was happening there. He had positioned his troops to move quickly since they might be needed, but he had too little intelligence to act. He had already sent out a sergeant and four men with orders to make contact with the units that were in action and let them know that the Germans were available on their left if they were needed. A half hour later he had sent out another patrol with the same orders, and a half hour after that a third. None had returned. He hoped the captain would bring him news.[88]

Over a mile to the west the captain found Burgoyne. It took the commander only seconds to shout new orders for Riedesel, "Please tell General Riedesel to take the best measures to cover the artillery, baggage, and bateaux, and then with as many troops as he can spare, come to my assistance and endeavor to attack the enemy on the right flank."[89] The captain turned to go back and find Riedesel.

The firing seemed to be getting closer. No one among the German officers found it possible to draw an optimistic conclusion from that fact. None of the patrols had returned. The strain of inaction was almost unbearable. Riedesel looked around at his staff and found a major. There was still no word from the patrols, but they had been sent off on foot. The captain he had sent off had not returned either. The major was mounted, a distinct advantage, and Riedesel told him to ride as quickly as he could to make contact with Burgoyne. "Tell him that I stand here in readiness with my own regiment, two companies of the Regiment von Rhetz, two six pounders, and I am waiting for orders to reinforce him."[90]

As the major rode off, the first of the missing patrols at last returned. The captain too finally came back and found Riedesel at five o'clock. The second patrol came in also and reported that the ground between the German units and the 20th Regiment in action was open. Another messenger also arrived from Burgoyne requesting two more cannons.

That was more than enough for Riedesel. He sent orders down to the river flat for Major Williams to set off with two more Royal Artillery 6-pounders to help Burgoyne, hauling the guns up the Great Ravine road as fast as they could be drawn. Riedesel handed off command of the left wing of his column and galloped off to the top of the hill where the Regiment von Riedesel and the two companies of the Regiment von Rhetz were waiting.[91] The German advance westward through the woods and toward the action finally began. Captain Georg Päusch put his two cannons on the only road leading through the woods. Fences on their left had already been knocked down in order to deny the Americans cover should they advance from that direction, so only the woods slowed their advance.[92]

Riedesel ordered that the march into battle be a noisy one. The men marched to the beating of drums and the men cheered with the cadence. Halfway there they were met by the major returning on horseback, who repeated Burgoyne's orders to do what they were in fact already doing. "Attack the enemy on their right and if possible follow them up," he had said unnecessarily. Riedesel urged his men on.[93]

4:45 PM, John Burgoyne, the British Column at Freeman's Farm

Back behind the center of the British line Hamilton and Phillips conferred with Burgoyne, ignoring the occasional rifle balls still stripping leaves off the branches above them from time to time. Their field uniforms were relatively plain, a concession to the American sharpshooters' seeming preference for senior officers. Their staffs stayed close, all of them mounted, all of them looking not too much unlike the senior officers. The exception was Captain Charles Green, Phillips's aide-de-camp. Green's horse sported a fancy white-fringed saddle cloth that made both him and his mount stand out in the crowd.

To the south, in the trees beyond the American infantry, an American rifleman saw the fancy saddle cloth and thought it could only belong to

Burgoyne himself. The man was 250 yards distant, maybe more, but it was a shot he knew he could make. The rifleman held his breath, squinted along the top of his rifle barrel, and squeezed. The officer fell from his horse, his left shoulder shattered. The rifleman scrambled down the tree to reload, elated that he had shot the British commander. He shouted the news to the rifleman closest to him. A rumor that Burgoyne had been killed or badly wounded quickly spread through the American ranks.[94]

5:00 PM, James Hadden, the Royal Artillery at Freeman's Farm

With his right flank now secured by von Breymann, Hamilton ordered the 62nd and the 21st to have it out with the stream of fresh American regiments rotating into the field. Thunderous fire erupted ahead of the center column. A grenadier officer of the 21st who had not been detached to Acland's battalion took a fatal ball through the heart on the first American volley. When he was hit he sprang almost to his own height and was dead before he hit the ground.[95]

Now the Americans were trying the other flank of his line, falling repeatedly on the left of the 62nd in the gap left when that regiment advanced farther than the 20th. Jones's two artillery positions, once securely sandwiched between the three infantry regiments, now found themselves at opposite ends of the 62nd with no cover for the left battery. Hadden's men had advanced their two guns at the left end of this shortened line in support of the 62nd, but they could not pull back fast enough when the Americans counterattacked and the surge flowed against them. Each time the Americans counterattacked they captured the cannons. Each time the British line rallied and took them back again.

The charging and countercharging went on for hours as the sun moved through the late afternoon. Hadden had lost and regained his guns over and over. The same thing was happening to the other battery off to the west, but less frequently. The fighting dragged on. His friends fell beside him one by one, but somehow the lethal balls never seemed to find Hadden. How many times had the fighting surged back and forth? Three, four? Hadden could not be sure. His guns were no longer firing. He looked around and realized that he had lost all but three of his twenty-two men, either killed or wounded. The Americans could not carry off his guns but neither could Hadden fire them with only three men. He trotted back through the noise and smoke and found

Brigadier-General Hamilton. He begged the commander for a few infantrymen to help him get his guns back into action. As they spoke, an American rifle ball tore through Hadden's hat, tugging at his hair. A ball had found him at last, but still no real harm done. Hamilton could not help him. Hamilton told him to speak to Major-General Phillips about his problem.

Hadden dashed off and found Phillips with Burgoyne near a couple of Freeman's log huts. Hadden repeated his request, his voice strained almost to impoliteness as he made his case to the two serenely detached senior officers. Phillips thought about it, then he sent orders for Captain Jones to let Hadden have all the men from one of the guns on the right of the line. Jones was ordered to go back with Hadden to make sure that the order was carried out and to help Hadden secure his position.

By the time Hadden and Jones returned with at least a partial crew, they found that the guns had been taken by the Americans again, and that the 62nd had lost twenty-five men prisoners in the attempt to retake them. The infantrymen had succeeded, but the fighting had gone on so long and the 62nd had taken so many losses that the regiment was beginning to disintegrate in confusion. Jones and Hadden got the guns back into action with the men they had brought from the other end of the line. What was left of the men of the 62nd milled about them and seemed unable to pull themselves together for another assault. The 9th Regiment remained where it was, still behind them in reserve in the woods.

Hadden still eluded the shots that now started taking down the men he and Jones had brought along. Soon nearly all of those men had also been wounded or killed by the galling fire still coming from the American riflemen in the trees across the field and the American infantry forces arrayed against them. Jones himself then fell, severely wounded, and Hadden was once again without enough men to continue firing the cannons.

5:00 PM, an American Rifleman, Freeman's Farm

The rifleman climbed down from his perch to reload. It took precision and concentration; just the right amount of powder, the patch set properly under the ball before they were rammed home. He used the tree as cover, ignoring the occasional buzz of a ball through the leaves, ignoring the busy confusion of the officers and men scattered around him.

Benedict Arnold had ridden straight for the loudest firing. He rode to where Morgan's men were still firing selectively over the heads of the American infantry, still trying to pick off British officers. Arnold spotted the rifleman through a gap in the smoke and urged his horse up behind him, jumping to the ground and limping up alongside the man. Arnold grabbed the rifle away from the startled man, who could do nothing but gape at the general. Arnold stepped forward, steadied his left arm and the gun, and fired at a distant redcoat. Arnold turned, nodded at the dumbfounded rifleman, and handed his empty rifle back to him. Arnold's stunt allowed Wilkinson to catch up with him and give him Gates's order to return to camp. The rifleman turned to reload his rifle as they rode off.[96]

5:00 PM, Stephen Harvey, the British Column at Freeman's Farm

Lieutenant Stephen Harvey of the 62nd Regiment was not far away from Hadden's guns. He was young for his rank, but well connected through his uncle, an adjutant general with the same name. The younger Harvey was wounded early in the afternoon, but this was his first real action and he was not about to let a scratch force him from the field. Then he was wounded again, and later still again. The American riflemen in the trees on the far side of the field seemed to be taking a special interest in him. He was hit several times as the battle reached its peak, and nearly each time he was struck he was ordered by Lieutenant Colonel Anstruther to go to the rear. He ignored each order until a ball smashed one of his legs. It was a crippling wound; this time it was clear that he had to be moved to the rear. As he was being helped from the field yet another ball struck him in the midsection, tearing through his gut. Such wounds were invariably fatal. Anstruther watched the young lieutenant be carried away, but the colonel stayed in the field and was soon wounded himself.[97] So were Major Henry Harnage and Ensign Henry Young. They were four of the eleven officers from the 62nd killed or wounded in the course of the afternoon.[98]

The 62nd was no longer an effective regiment. By now over 160 officers and men, more than half the regiment, were dead, wounded, or captured.[99] What was left of the 62nd fell back, leaving Hadden's guns once again in American hands. The Americans seemed to be bringing up new regiments at will. Time and again the British line had charged. Time and again it had fallen back again before yet another countercharge by fresh American troops.

5:15 PM, British and German Reinforcements, Freeman's Farm

General Phillips was relieved when he saw Major Griffith Williams approaching behind the 20th with the two additional 6-pounders from the artillery park and fresh artillerymen to man them. The guns, Williams's "thunderers," were brought forward, propelled by Williams's constant loud groans and curses. The British center column was hard pressed by superior American numbers and its men were close to breaking. Phillips broke away from Burgoyne and rode through heavy fire to help bring the additional pieces of artillery up to support the 20th Regiment. The British line stabilized for the moment.

Off to the left Phillips could see Riedesel's men finally emerging from the woods and engaging the right flank of the Americans. Williams swung his guns into position and began pounding at the American front. At last it was enough to hold back the American tide.

When Riedesel emerged into the Freeman's farm fields he saw both armies fully engaged. The German troops were close to the right flank of the Americans, and the English left flank in front of it was on the point of retreating. The two companies from the Regiment von Rhetz arrived first and began firing on the American flank. The Regiment von Riedesel came up behind them and began firing by platoon. The soldiers of the 20th saw this and took heart. The attack rallied the beleaguered 20th one more time. Hadden's guns were retaken one last time.

When Captain Georg Päusch emerged from the woods with his Hessen-Hanau artillery brigade he saw that Riedesel had stopped the American advance. Päusch wheeled his two 6-pounders into the line and began sending murderous quantities of canister into the American flank as rapidly as his crews could fire. It was too much even for fresh American troops. The Americans fell back.[100]

Now Päusch was informed that Burgoyne needed his cannons on the right flank of the 21st Regiment, at the far western side of the British division. They had lost Jones and one entire gun crew when he had moved it to support Hadden's position on the left. Päusch had to move his artillery unit across Freeman's farm, to the rear of all the current fighting, and he needed to do it quickly. Päusch's wagonmaster was mounted on his own horse, so Päusch sent him ahead to scout around the woods and cornfields to find ditches and swampy ground that might slow or stop their progress. Firm ground was found, but Päusch's detachment was raked by American fire as it rushed across the rear of the British line. Päusch reached the hill Burgoyne had sent him to support just as the 21st and 9th Regiments were about to abandon it. General Phillips was riding back and forth, trying to get the exhausted infantry to turn and fight yet again for ground they had by now contested for hours. The two British guns were silent here on the right wing, their ammunition gone and their remaining crews all dead or wounded.

The appearance of Päusch's guns made the difference. The British infantry and Brunswick chasseurs who had come to their assistance grabbed ropes and helped the wheezing horses drag the guns up the hill and into position to fire on the surging line of Americans on the fields south of them. Along the line the British troops were cheering. They turned and readied for one more bayonet charge. What had minutes before been a hopeless prelude to defeat had been reversed. The rebels were within pistol shot as Päusch's men loaded and fired a dozen or more rounds of canister and forced the Americans to stop firing and fall back. Far off to the left Riedesel's infantry companies still fired by platoon, driving hard against the vanishing American right flank (Figure 2.10).

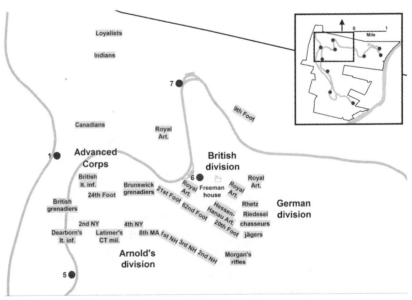

Figure 2.10 The Battle of Freeman's Farm, 5:30 p.m., September 19, 1777.

5:30 PM, Frederika Riedesel, the British Camp near the Hudson

The Baroness Riedesel, her servants, and her children had been put up in a reasonably nice house. The house had a large main room. Both the doors and the wainscoting were made of solid cedar. Cedar was plentiful here and they burned it in the fireplace too, for the odor kept insects away. While this was a benefit, Frederika knew that cedar smoke could also be bad for one's nerves, and was likely to cause premature births in pregnant women. It was just another of the many hazards in the American wilderness.

Frederika had also acquired a one-horse calash, which was large enough to accommodate her, all three of her children, and her female servants. They had entertained the marching troops along the way by singing songs and shouting encouragement. Frederika had imagined entering Albany this way, with Friedrich riding alongside.[101]

John Acland had made Harriet promise to follow the artillery and baggage, which were far to the rear and unlikely to be in danger. On this day Harriet was in the house near the artillery park with Frederika and the wives of Major Harnage of the 62nd and Lieutenant Reynals of the 24th. The distant firing of small arms and cannon rumbled on for hours, and each woman was terrified for the life of her husband. There was a rumor that the rebel riflemen took a particular interest in officers. Luckily, the children were all too young to understand the danger signaled by the incessant rumble.

Late in the day Major Harnage, who had already been injured in previous fighting, was brought back to the hospital, badly wounded. His wife did what she could to care for him. A little while later the news came that Lieutenant Reynals had been shot dead. Both wives were distraught. At least Harnage's wife had a wounded husband on whom to focus her attention. Reynals's wife found herself suddenly widowed and desolate in the American wilderness. Harriet and Frederika tried to comfort both women while they waited and wondered who would be next.[102]

They brought in Ensign Henry Young of the 62nd Foot, whose family had been kind to the baroness in England. Young had been shot in the leg, and though the surgeons wanted to amputate he would have none of it. Frederika decided to look after him personally. Lieutenant Harvey was brought in as well, another brave officer of the battered 62nd, full of wounds and certain to die. Frederika was shocked to see how young he was. The surgeon advised him to take a powerful dose of laudanum to ease his passage and the young lieutenant agreed. They took Harvey to a tent and laid him next to Major Harnage. The older officer asked him if he had any affairs to settle, to which Harvey said, "Being a minor everything is already adjusted." Then he added, "Tell my uncle I died like a soldier." Harnage said he would. Then the laudanum carried the young officer away. He was sixteen years old.[103]

6:00 PM, Henry Dearborn, Coulter's Farm

Most of Morgan's riflemen had moved to the extreme right, beyond Scammell's regiment, in the middle of the day. There they had climbed trees and taken shots at selected targets. Thaddeus Cook had come up with his Connecticut militia and joined in the fight. Cook had lost eleven killed, thirty-six wounded, and three missing. The chaos and noise had rolled on for hours. Dearborn's light infantry had held the left flank through all of it, getting support from two New York regiments and Latimer's Connecticut militia near the end of the day.[104]

Latimer's militia had fought for less than an hour, but Ephraim Squier could see that they had lost eight or nine killed. The men around him were repeating the names of the dead they had seen on the field the last time they had pulled back to their starting position. Another thirty had been wounded, some so severely that they would surely die. Others could walk and were making their way to the rear. The sun was already slipping down behind the hills to the west. It would be dark soon.[105]

The entire American line was back at the southern side of farm clearings. On the western end of the line they had fallen back for the fourth time since the fighting began.[106] The field was strewn with the dead and the writhing wounded of both armies. The sun was out of sight behind the hills and trees. A red glow silhouetted trees on the ridge to the west. In a half hour it would be completely dark, and the waning moon would not rise until eight o'clock. It was no time to be this far forward of the American lines. Perhaps an hour from now it would be too dark to see. There was no choice for the Americans but to withdraw.

Wilkinson looked out over the dusky carnage. It had been a fortuitous battle, one that had not been intended by either side, yet it had happened. Had it not been for scouting reports in the morning they would all probably be secure back in their fortified lines. The men lying dead in the field before him would still be alive. As it was, the armies ended the day more or less where they had begun it.[107]

Hull's men were nearly out of ammunition; some of them were completely out. Hull sent a messenger to Poor. Would General Poor or any other officer superior to Hull be good enough to send him orders? His troops and their cartridge boxes were all exhausted. Colonel Cilley of the 1st New Hampshire got back to him. Cilley was taking his regiment back to camp; he ordered Hull and his detachment to join him. Hull had never received a more welcome order. He had lost half his men killed or wounded. Most of those still fit for duty had only their bayonets with which to face the enemy. Hull got back to camp to be told that Lieutenant Colonel Brooks and the rest of the detachment from the 8th Massachusetts were still in the field, unwilling to quit the fight.[108]

The American regiments were made up of companies comprising neighbors and friends. The dead and wounded still on the field were as often as not the friends, cousins, even the brothers of men still standing. The small sizes of the communities from which many companies were drawn guaranteed that even men not related by blood were still linked in many ways. They carried off as many as they could find, and it was hard to leave the rest behind.[109]

Back behind the American lines, General John Glover strained to make sense of the distant sounds. Men were straggling back with fragmentary reports. As far as he could determine, Gates had committed about three thousand men. Exhausted soldiers from Poor's brigade were telling Gates that Burgoyne had at least seven thousand in action. They also reported that Burgoyne himself had been wounded in the shoulder. Glover's brigade had waited in reserve the entire day. It was too late to go forward now. Dusk was beginning to settle.[110]

6:00 PM, James Hadden, the British Column at Freeman's Farm

It was going to be dark soon. Hadden had supported the wounded Jones in his arms for a long time. The Americans had been getting closer; they were only a hundred yards away as the position of the 62nd collapsed. For a time, it had looked like the 20th would not hold either. Hadden had watched as the 20th moved forward, stalled, then fell back again. The 20th had rallied from the edge of the woods when the Germans arrived, which had saved what was left of the 62nd from being flanked and destroyed. But the Americans had been much too close. Hadden had come close to being captured. Now he had to get Jones off the field. He ordered the handful of men still standing to do their best to tend to the wounded all around them. Hadden picked up his captain and began carrying him toward one of farmer Freeman's huts, hoping that this shelter would be far enough to the rear to be safe from the fighting. Behind him the German troops who had arrived in such a timely way under Riedesel's command were securing the east end of the battlefield. The little hut was already full of wounded men. It took him a long time to find a place to lay Jones down. As he did he could see that Jones was finished.[111]

6:30 PM, Thomas Marshall and Philip Van Cortlandt, Coulter's Farm

Some of the American officers wondered at how the British troops could do it. Some of Burgoyne's men had been fighting all afternoon, without respite for at least two hours, probably more. The British appeared to have comparatively few reserve units, so it was the same regiments over and over. Yet there seemed to always be one more bayonet charge in them, even as they faced fresh American regiments.[112]

It was dusk when the men of Marshall's 10th Massachusetts finally saw action, sent forward by Gates at the end of the day. They came up on some British grenadiers and infantry on a rise west of Freeman's farm. The British officer in command was killed and his men retreated. The fighting continued here as the sky darkened. Van Cortlandt was now facing some Germans on his left and companies of Major Lindsay's British light infantry in front of him. He pulled his men down to a footpath at the bottom of the low hill they had been fighting on. The depression provided them with about three feet of cover. There was time for him to tell his officers to have their men wait until the enemy soldiers fired, then fire themselves at spots in the dark just below the muzzle flashes. It worked. The enemy soldiers were only about twenty-five yards away when they fired, but all of their shot went over the heads of the Americans. The return fire was devastating. It was the worst result of the day for Lindsay and his light infantry. It was now too dark to pursue, so both sides pulled their men back and retired. Some British units mistook the dark uniforms of the Germans for American ones as the sky darkened and nearly fired on them. The British could hear the moans of the wounded that night but they could not go out to help them, not knowing where the Americans might be. The night was going to be very cold.[113]

7:00 PM, John Burgoyne, the British Camp at Freeman's Farm

The battlefield was silent except for an occasional random shot. Six times the Americans had surged across Freeman's fields. Six times the British regiments had volleyed and charged. Only on this last bayonet charge had they finally succeeded, and then only because darkness kept the Americans from pushing them back one more time. The armies had advanced and fallen back perhaps a hundred yards at a time. The temperature began its descent toward freezing, and the wolves began to slink down from the hills to the west. Burgoyne, who was unharmed, watched as the British and German units found places to camp and a few careful fires were lit.[114]

Georg Päusch camped between the 21st and 9th Regiments. As he was moving to his camp he passed by General Phillips. "What artillery brigade is that?" asked Phillips. Päusch replied, "It is my own detachment," his German accent matching his uniform. Phillips gave Päusch his compliments for the day's successes.[115] So it went down the exhausted British line. They had not been defeated. The Americans appeared to have used almost all of their forces. The British and Germans had been vastly outnumbered yet had held their ground. They were proud of their accomplishment.[116] It felt like a draw, but in fact it was a technical victory for the British because they still held the ground on which they had fought.

Some officers and men even speculated that had night not fallen they might have carried the American lines that lay somewhere through the woods. Others grumped that most of the Americans had been drunk when they reached the battlefield, the only way their generals could have got them to fight.[117] Päusch had lost neither men nor horses. That was a good thing, for the surgeon had been nowhere near the action all afternoon. Later Päusch would at last find the man drunk with a group of English drummers.[118] It appeared to him that both sides probably had more rum than was absolutely necessary.

Burgoyne had seen for himself that the Americans could fight. They had superior numbers, no shortage of courage, and lethal marksmanship. It had been a long and revealing day. Despite the technical victory Burgoyne knew that his options were once again diminished. While some of his subordinates would huff that only nightfall had denied them a more complete victory, Burgoyne knew that he was in trouble.

Riedesel was one of those who were sure that had night not fallen they could have routed the Americans. As darkness grew Riedesel returned to the bulk of his command on the river flat. Frederika was relieved when she saw him. Fortifications were being built on the heights north of the Great Ravine overlooking the flat. Construction of a new bridge of boats across the river was started, and a *tête de pont* was set up on the other side to protect it.[119] But these were half-hearted efforts. As the moon rose, the army sank into exhaustion.

8:00 PM, *John Brooks, Freeman's Farm*

Brooks and his Massachusetts Continentals had been engaged with von Breymann's grenadiers since he had arrived on the field. The sun had set shortly after six o'clock, and gunfire had tapered off quickly as the two armies withdrew to opposite sides of the darkening farm clearings. Twilight had lasted a half hour longer, but Brooks had lingered. In the gloom they had received fire from rifles and thought briefly that Morgan's men might still be in the field and mistaking them for the enemy. But the dull glint of brass match cases on their chests had revealed them to be German jägers. The attackers had broken off and disappeared. The moon, only a day or two past full, came up brightly by a quarter after eight, and still Brooks stayed, not wanting to give Burgoyne the technical victory that American withdrawal back to camp would afford him. He also wanted to wait until the moon rose so that his men could slip onto the field and take off as many of the wounded as they could find. A few of the men were caught looting the dead, and there would be hell to pay for them, but most tended gently to the wounded and the dying. At last Brooks relented, and the 8th Massachusetts Continentals marched silently back in the light of the rising moon, reaching their tents an hour before midnight.[120]

Out on the battlefield the muffled groans of the badly wounded mixed with the shuffling sounds of the wives of missing British and German soldiers and the human vultures that follow armies. A few dead men would be found by weeping women, now widows. Many of the dead and not a few of the wounded would be stripped of clothing and equipment by morning. Wolves, too, caught the scent of death and began to gather around the fringes of the battlefield.

The exaggeration of enemy losses and the minimization of one's own began even before the last shot was fired. In the British camp Burgoyne claimed that his men had counted five hundred American dead on the field. On the American side Wilkinson estimated eighty Americans killed and two hundred wounded or missing. Meanwhile, prisoners and deserters told Scammell that Burgoyne had lost fifteen hundred or two thousand men. At the end of the day Gates had a hundred prisoners, but he had lost twenty of his own captured. No American regiment had suffered more than Cilley's 1st New Hampshire. He had lost one out of every seven of his men killed or wounded. Cook's Connecticut militiamen were also badly hurt, but the regiment remained intact. Two of Morgan's officers and one of Cilley's had been taken prisoner.[121]

Rumors still circulated that Colonel Scammell had been wounded, but later in the evening he could be seen walking around the American camp. Scammell was well, but like Cilley's his regiment had taken significant losses.[122]

8:30 PM, Benjamin Warren, the American Camp at Bemis Heights

Benjamin Warren was a captain in the 7th Massachusetts Regiment of the Continental Line, one of four in Nixon's brigade. He had only heard the battle in the distance through the course of the afternoon. The noise of battle had died at dusk and exhausted American troops streamed back to camp. Warren heard accounts passed up the line from Arnold's division off to the west. According to the reports he heard it had been a hard day for both sides. At eight o'clock Warren had been called out and ordered to take two dozen men from his regiment and combine them with equal numbers from the other three regiments in Nixon's brigade to form a picket in the woods north of the American line. Each army thought the other might attack during the night, neither fully convinced that the enemy was exhausted, too.

Warren's detachment moved so close that they were within earshot of the British line and the scene of the day's battle. All night long they heard the cries and groans of wounded men still lying on the field, but they were too near the British to attempt to carry the poor, desperate men off. A few of the Massachusetts men went on the field without orders and took arms and equipment from some of the dead. A horrified Colonel Putnam spread word that he would shoot the next man caught doing such a thing. Warren would get no sleep at all that night.[123]

9:00 PM, Horatio Gates, American Headquarters

Gates consulted with his generals in the evening. What might happen next? Would Burgoyne attack tomorrow? Gates knew that his army lacked the ammunition to counter such an attack, but he kept the information to himself for the time being. If Burgoyne were sensible and did not attack either frontally or along the river road, where might he move instead? What if he retreated? What if he recrossed the Hudson and drove south along the east bank? The generals considered these and other possibilities. After a tense discussion they all agreed. The best thing was for the main army to stay put for the time being. Burgoyne could claim a technical victory, but the Northern Army held the strongest possible position in front of him. It made no sense to alter the current deployment of the army. On the other hand, Lincoln's troops were still not in a position to contribute effectively. Everyone agreed that Gates needed to write to Lincoln immediately. Lincoln should bring his forces to the camp Gates's army had so recently occupied at Stillwater. Five or six hundred men should be moved to the heights on the east side of the river, just in case. There, straddling the Hudson, Lincoln's forces could serve as an effective reserve. Gates sat down and wrote the letter, urging Lincoln to get to Stillwater as quickly as possible. Provisions would be made available to him there.[124]

10:00 PM, Richard Varick, the American Camp at Bemis Heights

It had been a long day, but Richard Varick was still energized by the action. He sat down to write another long letter to General Philip Schuyler in Albany, having detained the latest express rider in order to have it delivered quickly. He lamented that Lincoln had still not arrived but he was sure that Burgoyne's army had been badly crippled by the fighting. He laid out the sequence of the battle as best he could from what he had been able to see himself or learn from others in the evening. He was close enough now to the American hospital in the barn to be haunted by the groans and cries of the wounded there.

He could not sleep. He begged Schuyler to send more wagons to take the wounded to Albany for treatment, and while he was at it, to first make sure the same wagons carried rum to camp for the men. He had heard Gates's orders that all tents would be struck and wagons loaded by three the next morning and was sure it meant that they would be renewing the battle at first light. What else could it mean? Surely they would have Burgoyne on the run by noon Saturday and the Northern Army would be on its way to Saratoga.

At eleven, another express rider arrived with a letter from Schuyler, so Varick resumed writing. Washington was having success off to the south, according to Schuyler. Varick was pleased to read this, but he was soon grumbling again about Lincoln's protracted and probably fruitless "airy scheme" to capture British positions at Lake George and Ticonderoga. He decided to keep one of the express riders with him until Saturday evening, in case there was additional good news to send back to Albany at that time.[125]

Meanwhile, British prisoners told Gates that Burgoyne might launch a desperate attack again in the morning. Supplies of shot and powder were nearly exhausted for several American regiments, and half of Gates's army clearly needed more than a few hours' rest. The tents would be struck and the wagons loaded well before dawn, but the immediate goal was not to strike for Saratoga. No, the immediate goal was to save the army from disaster, by pulling back south of the Mohawk River if necessary.

The day had ended in a stalemate. Parts of both armies were exhausted, some regiments badly bloodied. The Americans had returned to their lines; the British and German troops made camp more or less on the ground they held at the end of the day. Burgoyne worried as Gates did. His regiments were camped on open ground and thus vulnerable to an attack. His British and German troops needed time to dig in. Both commanders had regiments that were still fresh and ready to continue the action. Both expected help to arrive soon. But both also had good reasons to pause and regroup. In fact, the hoped for arrival of help would lead both Gates and Burgoyne to delay. While Washington struggled to avoid defeat in the fighting around Philadelphia, the commanders north of Albany settled into a protracted middle game that would lead to a decisive final battle in the northern theater of the war.

3

The Middle Game

SATURDAY, SEPTEMBER 20, 1777

6:00 AM, Burial Parties, No Man's Land

The British morning gun fired into a thick fog.[1] Soldiers of both armies who had lain on their guns in uniform all night moved stiff joints and creaked slowly out of their tents. Fires were lit because everyone felt nearly frozen from the cold. Indians from the British camp moved silently across the battered landscape and scalped the dead Americans who had fallen the day before.[2] While the Americans reluctantly tolerated this tradition, the British encouraged it by paying scalp bounties to their Indian allies. Scalping was an ancient tradition in North America, and the English had long since found it expedient to pay for the scalps brought in by their Indian allies.[3] Gates and the Americans had staked out a position on higher moral ground by allowing but not rewarding the taking of scalps by their own Indian allies. The Americans let the pro-independence press exploit the contrasting policies by painting Burgoyne and his allies as monsters, and it was working.

American camp followers moved from one body to the next, stripping them of clothing and valuables. Unarmed parties from both sides began to bury their dead and bring off the wounded, ignoring each other as best they could in an undeclared truce.[4] The wounded had lain all night in subfreezing weather. Some were found still alive, but begged to be left to die rather than suffer the agony of being carried back to the hospital. Some were unconscious or nearly so, numb from the cold and weak from loss of blood. Others had barely survived the night, and sighed away just as help arrived.[5]

Even now, the British burial parties were careful about social standing. Dead officers were granted individual shallow graves. The American riflemen had sought them out and there were many of them. Three subalterns of the 20th Regiment, the oldest not more than seventeen, were buried together. Enlisted men were buried together in larger but still shallow graves.[6] Some common graves were dug for fifteen or twenty men. Some officers worked their burial detachments hard, insisting that each of their dead comrades have something approaching a decent burial. Other burial parties were not so respectful, leaving arms, legs, and even heads protruding from shallow graves. It was tough going because the soil of Freeman's farm was heavy and hard with cold clay.

Young British Ensign Charles Phillips of the decimated 62nd Foot still lay where he had fallen, a ball in his leg and stiff from the wound and the cold. Before the burial parties reached him, one of the human vultures scouring the field came up to him and, seeing that he was not yet dead, helped him along with a shot through the chest. An hour later American soldiers sent to bring in the wounded and bury the dead found him still alive and took him back to the American hospital. He appeared to be no more than sixteen years old.[7]

British baggage and ammunition wagons were unloaded and used to carry the wounded from the battlefield. British and German officers alike groused that the wagons had to pass by most of the long encampment that was strung out for a mile and a half along the line from Freeman's farm to the hospital near the river. Soldiers who had survived the fighting without becoming casualties themselves now had to see up close what might happen to them in a future engagement.

It was an agonizing trip to the hospital for the British wounded, a jarring wagon ride across rough ground. For many it was nothing more than an hour of fruitless torture; they died as soon as they reached the hospital at the riverside. Leaving them on the field would have at least spared them the final agony.[8] It was a time when medicine still knew little about the prevention of infection, and even a minor wound could lead to death. Perhaps twenty of the wounded who did reach the hospital would die by the end of the day. Another twenty would die tomorrow, and the next day.[9] The few small houses and barns in the area were soon overflowing with the wounded; tents were pitched for the rest.

The British counted fewer than a hundred American dead on the field. They were sure that the rebels had taken many more casualties the day before.

How could it have been otherwise? Burgoyne blustered, "The enemy gave ground on all sides with the loss of about five hundred men and thrice that number wounded."[10] But nothing like those numbers could be seen lying on the field. The explanation they favored was that every time the Americans pushed across the battlefield against the British line, rescue parties had moved in behind them to carry off the dead and wounded. The lower-than-expected body count must have come from just the last American charge. To the British it seemed like the only possible explanation.[11]

Joshua Pell was a Loyalist officer with Burgoyne who encouraged this view of American losses. "They carried off as many of their killed and wounded as they could. They left about three hundred dead in the field." It was clear to him too that Americans killed had to have been over five hundred. Even worse, he sniffed, "The rebels were in general drunk, a piece of policy of their general in order to make them fight." Pell knew that Burgoyne's army had lost over two hundred killed, two dozen of them officers, and another four hundred rank and file wounded. It was simply not possible for American losses to have been fewer than that; it was simply not possible that American courage came from anywhere but a bottle.[12]

Most of the British soldiers knew that they had gained nothing from their nominal victory. The fighting had left them with no advantage. There was still no forage to be had. They still had no intelligence, no knowledge of the terrain or roads lying before them, no good prospects for reaching Albany without many more days like yesterday. Their Indian allies were quick to perceive that they could expect little plunder but increasing hardship from now on.[13] The remaining Indians began to gather in small groups to discuss the situation in their own languages. Little by little, they too began to disappear.[14]

Scouting parties were sent out and the foragers got ready to follow them. But the woods were alive with American scouts and skirmishers. It was impossible to forage without sending out large detachments to protect the foragers, and the horses were suffering from a lack of feed. The men were starting to feel the pinch as well. Already there were no vegetables, no brandy, and no tobacco to be had.[15]

6:30 AM, Benjamin Warren, No Man's Land

Captain Benjamin Warren of the 7th Massachusetts was still at his advanced post at the southern edge of the battlefield. No one had slept. No picket had had to fight off sleep, not with the constant, agonizing sound of wounded men on the dark battlefield just north of them. The moon had come up around eight o'clock the night before. It was only a few days past full, and there had been sufficient light to allow the American pickets to see well enough to go to the rescue of the wounded if that had been possible. But the proximity of British pickets would not allow it. Instead they could only wait and listen.

Sunrise came at just after six. Tomorrow would be the autumnal equinox; they could count on a few minutes more than twelve hours of sunlight for only a few days. A wounded American militiaman stumbled in just after first light. He had been shot in the head and had spent the whole night wandering blindly in the woods. A deserter came through the line as well, with news that Burgoyne had been mortally wounded and General Phillips killed the previous afternoon. At least part of this was consistent with rumors circulating among the Americans. The British soldier was from the 62nd Foot, a regiment that was now almost nonexistent. He said that most of the officers and men of his regiment had been killed or wounded; he saw desertion as his best option.[16] Warren detailed a couple of men to escort the deserter back to headquarters.

7:00 AM, Horatio Gates, American Headquarters on Bemis Heights

Horatio Gates had a big problem. The British had been stopped, but not beaten back. Arnold was arguing forcefully that the Americans should not waste time but should renew the attack immediately. Gates was temperamentally inclined to wait in any case, but this time he had a reason that even Arnold would accept. After Friday's fighting the American regiments that had been engaged were down to only a few cartridges per man, and there were no more to be had until the army was resupplied from Albany. Gates had kept the secret to himself as long as he could, hoping that Burgoyne would not renew the fighting until the critical supplies arrived. There was nothing to be done about it in the meantime, and no good reason to risk morale by informing his officers of the potential danger.

Gates had ordered everyone to strike their tents and pack their gear by three o'clock in the morning in case there was action. He thought he would do this every day from now on, at least until more ammunition came in.[17] A lot of baggage was sent back to Stillwater as a precaution.

Some of Glover's brigade were marched off in the fog to reinforce the right wing of the army.

The returns were coming in. Three hundred fifteen had been killed, wounded, or were missing. Two-thirds of them were wounded and accounted for; the remaining third were either known dead or missing. Lieutenant Colonel Colburn of the 3rd New Hampshire was dead. So was Lieutenant Colonel Adams of the 2nd. Both had been able men. Their deaths meant that Henry Dearborn now automatically rose to their rank, but he remained in command of his battalion of select light infantrymen.[18]

The officers of the 2nd New Hampshire had been particularly unlucky. Their commander had been captured in July. Their major had been wounded earlier and was on furlough. Five of the regiment's company captains had been captured or wounded. Gates found himself left with a captain to command the entire regiment. The captain was a good man and he seemed up to the task, but Gates hoped he would not have to make many more battlefield promotions.[19]

Morgan had lost as prisoners both Captain Van Swearingen and a lieutenant from Henderson's company. A captain of Cilley's 1st New Hampshire was also taken prisoner.[20] It could have been worse. Meanwhile, the wounded who could travel were put on boats and eased down the river to Stillwater. There they would be transferred to wagons that had been sent up by the Committee of Correspondence in Albany. From Stillwater the injured men would have to be bounced along rough roads to the hospital in Albany, where many of them would lose limbs and lives over the next several days. There were about 160 of them, and at least another thirty more British and German soldiers.[21]

The British deserter standing before Gates still had smudges on his face from tearing open cartridges with his teeth all the previous afternoon. Warren had sent the man back under guard. He was from the British 62nd Regiment of Foot, and he had had enough fighting. His information was not encouraging. He had been in the British camp just minutes earlier, stealing away with the excuse that he needed to find a latrine. The British Army had lain on its arms all night. Earlier today the mutiny act had been read to each corps and they were preparing to attack the Americans again. Saying this the desperate deserter suddenly realized that he was in even greater trouble. If he were caught by the British, he would be hanged on the spot. He begged for a pass to move to the rear of the American lines.

"You should have the grenadiers at your lines on the left in fifteen minutes!" the terrified soldier said.[22]

Gates had no sympathy for the deserter, but he believed what the man had told him. Word was passed up and down the American line to be ready. The drums stayed silent, but everywhere men were sent to the line and told to be ready for an attack. The men were tired, and the units on the left wing were particularly low on ammunition. In all there were only enough bayonets for a third of the muskets. The fog limited visibility to no more than twenty yards. The time passed slowly. But then the sun burned off the mist and the landscape was revealed to have not a single redcoat upon it.[23]

8:00 AM, John Burgoyne, British Headquarters

Burgoyne was ready to finish yesterday's work. The baggage, the women, and the wounded were gathered on the river flats. The regiments had slept on their arms in their lines and he was sure that most of them still had plenty of fight left. They had been roused and needed only to be fed and formed in their ranks. Apart from that, it was a simple matter of waiting for the fog to lift and they could advance on the lines of the wounded American Army. Or so he thought.

Burgoyne dashed off a short note to General Powell at Ticonderoga, asking him to forward the news on to Sir Guy Carleton in Montreal that British arms had been very successful the previous day. He promised to forward a more detailed report when a safe conveyance could be found. He knew what his losses had been the day before. They approached six hundred. He hoped that the Americans had suffered more, but he also knew that the American dead on the field numbered many fewer than his own. He hedged in his message to Powell. "The loss on either side cannot be particularly ascertained."[24]

Burgoyne brooded over the toll the American riflemen had taken on his officers. He had been so sure that his Indian allies would counter Morgan's men, but nothing like that had happened. What few were left of his Indian allies had performed poorly, if at all. To an aide he muttered, "There was seldom a minute's interval of smoke in any part of our line without officers being taken off by single shot. It will naturally be supposed that the Indians would be of great use against this mode of fighting. Not a man of them was to be brought within the sound of a rifle shot."[25]

10:00 AM, Friedrich Riedesel, the Hudson River Flats

The Hessen-Hanau Regiment had arrived to relieve the Regiment von Specht at two in the morning. Everyone was in uniform and armed all night. Riedesel had carried on with his usual fussing, shuffling units through the night, making sure that the three rebuilt bridges were all covered, that there were plenty of men on the heights above the camp, and so forth.[26]

The Regiment von Rhetz took up a new position in line with the second bridge on the river flat. The two companies that had fought on Friday rejoined the regiment in the evening. Päusch's artillery, four 6-pounders, were placed ahead of that position and near the hill slope.[27] The Regiment von Specht anchored the end of the line on the heights above, with the Regiment von Riedesel and a British artillery brigade to its right. Beyond was another Royal Artillery brigade, and the four British regiments took up the ground east of what they had held at the close of the battle: the 9th, 21st, 62nd, and 20th in order. Two more Royal Artillery brigades separated the last three. At last, after what seemed to the men like endless hours of constant redeployment, it was a solid front.

Riedesel had pulled most of his units back to the top of the hill they had first ascended the day before. None of them could see the American lines through the dense woods, but scouts confirmed that the plain narrowed to the south, forcing the road into a narrow funnel between the river and the bluffs. Behind them, the 47th and the Hessen-Hanau Regiments were still assigned to cover the hospital, the artillery park, and bateaux on the plain next to the Hudson. What Indians remained camped north of them. On the bluffs above, men renewed work on what would become the Great Redoubt (Figure 3.1).

10:30 AM, Simon Fraser, the Western Flank of the British Lines

Fraser's brigade occupied the battleground on the cleared fields around Freeman's farmstead. The farmstead itself was occupied by the light infantry battalion and cannons of Royal Artillery. This was the strong right end of the British line, soon to be named the Balcarres Redoubt in honor of Alexander Lindsay, Lord Balcarres. The officers made sure that four cannons were dragged southwestward across Freeman's farm and set up almost at the southern edge of the clearing. The Balcarres Redoubt would have a salient that protruded more than two hundred yards southward to

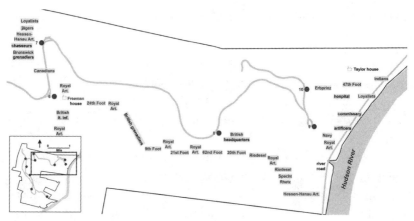

Figure 3.1 Burgoyne's camp from September 20 until noon, October 7, 1777.

include these forward cannons, even though this made no sense from a defensive standpoint. American snipers could easily fire on three sides of the
salient; if and when fighting broke out again it would be hopelessly vulnerable rather than the strong apex of the British line it should have been.
Although it made no military sense, this had been the killing ground all
through the battle of Freeman's farm, and the British Army had to occupy
it now whatever the danger in order to claim its technical victory.

The British grenadiers camped on the eastern end of the Freeman clearing, almost touching the 9th Regiment on the other side of a small stream.
Another Royal Artillery brigade separated the grenadiers from the 24th
Regiment camped just east of the Balcarres Redoubt. If the Americans
attacked it would be these men who would have to defend the salient,
or more likely, it would be these men who would cover the artillerymen
while they pulled their guns back to more sensible emplacements around
Freeman's house and farm buildings.

Von Breymann's German grenadiers dug in on a hill northwest of the
Balcarres Redoubt, a position that formed an angle with the main line
and was there to protect the British western flank. Two of Päusch's Hesse-
Hanau artillery pieces anchored the middle of von Breymann's position,
which was already being called the Breymann Redoubt.[28] With him now
were the chasseur battalion and what was left of the jägers. American
Loyalist volunteers camped at the very end of the long British line.
Canadian provincials fortified two small cabins between the Breymann
and Balcarres Redoubts. But the cabins were isolated and forlorn in the

broad gap between the two redoubts, a gap that was inexplicably left without any other defensive works.

Between ten and eleven the fog burned off and the sun began to bake the men under a bright clear sky.[29] The heat was rising quickly by midday. The Germans could not understand a climate in which men froze at night but were hot enough to melt on the following afternoon.[30] Rumors were spreading among the men, both German and British, that the American Army arrayed before them had twelve thousand men and was still growing. The Americans, it was said, were dug in behind strong abatis and showed no inclination to do anything but wait for Burgoyne to attack.[31]

12:00 Noon, John Burgoyne, British Headquarters

General Fraser was not convinced that his men could fight again so soon, and he made his case to Burgoyne. The grenadiers and light infantry of the Advanced Corps, who had been in the thick of it the day before, were still fatigued. Perhaps they should wait another day, until Sunday the twenty-first. The men would be ready then. Fraser's words calmed Burgoyne's enthusiasm and brought a sense of measured rationality to the discussion. Burgoyne depended on Fraser's wisdom in such things. The more he thought about it, the more it appeared that Fraser was right. At last Burgoyne yielded and countermanded his initial orders. They would wait.[32]

Then Phillips and Fraser began to argue that they should renew the attack as soon as possible, but Burgoyne decided against it. The generals had changed sides in the debate. Now it was Burgoyne who was being cautious. The hospital was full and the magazines were not properly secured. Burgoyne reconnoitered the British positions before noon and ordered some straightening and contraction while he made up his mind. The British soldiers began to dig in. At noon he finally issued his orders for the day. The whole army would attack again at three o'clock.[33]

A captured American soldier was brought into camp and questioned by some of the officers. The man seemed crestfallen when he saw Burgoyne. He explained that there was jubilation in the American camp because everyone there was convinced that Burgoyne had been wounded or killed in the previous day's fighting. The rumor had started when a rifleman shot Captain Green, thinking that an officer with such a fancy saddle cloth had to be Burgoyne.[34] The soldier could see now that it had been a false rumor; his captivity was probably going to be longer than he had hoped.

The work of entrenching continued through the heat of the day. The first of thousands of trees were felled. Those far enough forward were dropped toward the American lines and their branches sharpened to create an abatis. Others were trimmed to become logs for redoubt walls. Trenches were dug, logs laid up, earth piled. In addition to the Breymann and Balcarres Redoubts at the western end of the British line, fortifications that would make up the Great Redoubt were rising on the river bluffs above the hospital and artillery park.[35]

The British lines began to take on the standard characteristics of a fortified encampment, and units arranged themselves according to well-practiced rules and procedures. It was far from the thin red line that the regiments had presented the day before. From the quarter guard posted farthest into no man's land to the rear guard was ideally a zone more than three hundred yards deep. The forest and terrain forced deviations from the ideal layout, but the British and German officers did their best to impose regularity. There was a thirty-yard-wide parade ground behind the quarter guard. Tents for the storage of muskets and colors came next, and behind them were the tents of the enlisted men. Still farther back were guns, wagons, and gunners' tents, and behind these the subaltern tents, field officer tents, staff officer tents, dining tents, and kitchens, in that order. Horses were picketed here and there, along with other livestock that would be butchered for meat as needed. Camp followers fit in where they could. It was a long sinuous tent city of mostly men that could be packed up and mobilized in a matter of minutes.[36] But its temporary nature did nothing to discourage military order and neatness.

2:00 PM, Daniel Taylor, British Headquarters

Burgoyne had set up his headquarters behind the gap between the Regiment von Riedesel's hilltop position and the 20th Regiment of Foot.[37] Burgoyne dined with his commanders at two o'clock. It was their first opportunity for a full discussion of Friday's battle at Freeman's farm. Burgoyne was largely pleased with his officers, if not entirely so with the performance of their men. "We have had a smart and very honorable action, and we are now encamped in the front of the field, which must demonstrate our victory beyond the power of even an American news writer to explain away."[38]

Outside, Daniel Taylor was making his way into the British camp. It had been a harrowing trip northward up the Hudson Valley. Taylor was a Loyalist. He spoke with an American accent and wore standard American clothing, but he was a messenger carrying a cipher for Burgoyne from General Henry Clinton, who was far down the Hudson at Fort Montgomery. Had Taylor been caught by the rebels and had they known what the cypher contained he would most likely have been quickly hanged as a spy. Even without deciphering it they would certainly know that it was a letter from one British officer to another.

Burgoyne excused himself to receive the report and decipher the written portion. Daniel Taylor was the only one who had managed to get through to Burgoyne since the beginning of August. The message looked banal and harmless, but Burgoyne's secretary had a paper mask to place over the message. When he did he saw only the words that were intended to be read in an hourglass-shaped portion of the letter (Figure 3.2). The rest was obfuscation, words used to obscure the true meaning and content of the letter.[39]

Taylor said that Clinton intended to attack Fort Montgomery in about ten days. The cipher was dated September 10. That meant that Clinton might even now be attacking; certainly he would be in a few days.

> You will have heard D' Sir I doubt not long before this
> can have reached you that **Sr. W. Howe** is gone from hence. The
> Rebels imagine that he **is gone to the** Eastward, but this time
> however he has filled **Cheasapeak bay with** surprise and terror
> Washington marched **the greatest part of the** Rebels to Philadelphia
> in order to oppose Sir W^{ms} **army. I hear he is** now returned upon
> finding none of our troops **landed but am not** sure of this, great part
> of his troops are returned for **certain. I am** sure this [illegible]
> must be ruin to them. I am **left to Command** here, half of my force may
> I am sure defend every thing **here with** as much safety I shall therefore
> send Sir W. 4 or 5 Bat^n. I have **too small a force** to invade the New England provinces,
> they are too weak **to make any effectual** efforts against me and
> you do not want any **diversion in your favor.** I can therefore very well
> spare him 1500 men. **I shall try something** certainly towards the close
> of the year not until then **at any rate. It may be of use** to inform you that
> report says all yields **to you. I own to you I think** the business will
> quickly be over now. **Sr Ws' move just at this time** has been Capital.
> Washingtons have been **the worst he could take** in every respect. I
> sincerely give you much joy on your success and am with
> great Sincerity your hbl obt st   HC

Figure 3.2 The cipher sent to Burgoyne by General Henry Clinton. A mask was intended to reveal the true message, shown here in bold. Replica by the author.

Burgoyne did not hesitate. Taylor was ordered to wait until dark and then head back south with a briefing of the current situation for Clinton and Howe and carrying a brief written message concealed in a small hollow silver ball. In it Burgoyne again begged for an attack up the Hudson so that Gates would be forced to split the Northern Army, sending some of it south of Albany to counter the threat from that direction. Burgoyne estimated that he could hold out where he was until October 12. Two more messengers were then scheduled to be dispatched with the same message over the next two days. They would take different routes and carry only unwritten memorized messages.[40] Taylor steeled himself and waited; it would be another 150-mile trek, every mile of it as dangerous as the ones just completed.

Burgoyne returned to brief his generals. Yesterday had been a technical British victory, for they had held the ground they had contested, but they all knew they were in trouble. Yet Burgoyne brightened as he informed them of the news. "I have received intelligence from Sir Henry Clinton of his intention to attack the highlands. That measure may operate to dislodge Mr. Gates entirely, or to oblige him to detach a large portion of this force. Either of these cases will open our way to Albany."[41] It was good news to be sure.

The conversation then turned lighter. Burgoyne told them that his Sunday orders would include dividing 120 men from the ranks of the provincials and Canadians between the six regiments of British regulars. They would each receive a stipend when assigned and another when they were discharged in December. He explained that the incorporation of twenty of these men into each of the regular regiments would make up for recent casualties while at the same time stiffening what were otherwise undependable militiamen. Someone raised the question of whether the new recruits would be counted toward the recruiting goals of the regiments. Burgoyne assured them that they would be.

That settled, Burgoyne steered the discussion to the problem of random gunfire in camp. The men, particularly the irregulars, were accustomed to clearing their weapons by simply firing them in the air, but the practice was particularly dangerous in their current situation. "Discharging the arms in camp, which would be at all times irregular, is particularly so when near the enemy, as it occasions false alarms," said Burgoyne. The generals discussed the dangerous business of drawing unfired shot from musket barrels and considered various options. At length, Burgoyne spoke for the consensus and said that he would resolve the matter in his orders Sunday morning.[42]

Burgoyne and his officers were no longer feeling quite so abandoned. Yet it was still the case that they had all expected Howe to send significant forces up the Hudson to carry out a coordinated attack on Albany. Instead Howe had gone off to chase Washington around Philadelphia, leaving Burgoyne's force at hazard, devoted merely to drawing Gates and the American Northern Army away from Howe's primary objective.[43] Such a secondary role for the army from Canada had never been previously mentioned, not even implied.

The extent of Burgoyne's losses became clear as new returns came in from the regiments. There had been eleven hundred men engaged in the four regiments that had borne the brunt of the battle. So far the reports indicated that seventy-six rank and file had been killed and nearly 250 had been wounded. About thirty were missing and presumed taken prisoner. Ten officers were dead and another twenty-five were wounded or missing. The 62nd Regiment was particularly mauled. Colonel Anstruther and Major Harnage were both wounded, not to mention several more junior officers. The four guns in the action had been manned by forty-eight men, of whom thirty-six had been killed or wounded. As the day passed the overall casualties grew to 577, one more than the number still fit for duty in the units that had fought yesterday.[44]

Burgoyne summed up the losses of the previous day. "Few actions have been characterized by more obstinacy in attack or defense. The British bayonet was repeatedly tried ineffectually. Eleven hundred British soldiers bore incessant fire from a succession of fresh troops in superior numbers for above four hours. After a loss of above a third of their numbers (and in one of the regiments above two-thirds) [they] forced the enemy at last." Such things were to be expected, but some deaths seemed more poignant than others. The Canadians had lost their captain, whose eleven-year-old son had been at his side when he died.[45]

"It will be observable from the accounts of the killed and wounded that the loss of officers was proportionally much greater than that of the private men. The enemy had great number of marksmen armed with rifle-barrel pieces. These hovered upon the flanks in small detachments, and were very expert in securing themselves and in shifting their ground. Many placed themselves in high trees in the rear of their own line, and there was seldom a minute's interval of smoke in any part of our line without officers being taken off by a single shot. Captain Green, aide-de-camp to Major General Philips [sic], was shot through the arm by one of these marksmen as he was delivering me a message."[46] Somehow Burgoyne's order that the army would march at three o'clock was set aside and forgotten, cleared away like the dirty dishes by the servants.

Scouts came in with news that the American lines were nearly within cannon shot of the line the British now held. The Americans were working hard to strengthen their left. They confirmed that the American right flank on Bemis Heights overlooking the river and the road to Albany was already too strong to be attacked. That night the British Army would rotate men so that half stood ready for action while the other half slept. In the distance they could hear the Americans felling trees to further fortify their already formidable defenses.[47]

6:00 PM, *Horatio Gates, American Headquarters on Bemis Heights*

The vital powder and shot had arrived during the day and the critical ammunition shortage passed. Only then did Gates tell his officers about it. Arnold was filled with reproach. Why had Gates not told him of this problem? Gates had only a gruff dismissal. "It was bad enough for me to know it myself."[48] Most of the officers thought that they would have had different opinions about Gates's decisions of the previous day had they known about the shortage. Now they were uncertain how to gauge Gates's secrecy. Did it increase or decrease their confidence in him? For that matter, what did it say about his confidence in them?

Wilkinson made the rounds of the American hospital, looking over the moaning wounded of both armies. Among the captured British wounded he saw one who stood out. It was a young man, no more than sixteen, in a well-tailored officer's uniform. He turned out to be Ensign Charles Phillips. The wound in his thigh was bad enough, but he explained to Wilkinson that while lying on the ground one of the looters that followed the American Army came up and shot him through. Now he was lying stiff, faint, and pale, his uniform soaked with dried blood. Wilkinson was so overcome with rage and pity that he carried Phillips to his own tent where his still undressed wounds could be cared for. When he mentioned this to Gates, the general was taken aback. "Just Heaven! He may be the nephew of my wife."[49] Gates went to look closer at the young man's face and was relieved to see that it was not *that* Charles Phillips. Gates made a note to tell Dr. Potts to look in on the lad.[50]

The news of British deserters coming in had a positive effect on the American militia. Gates might believe the desperate stories about imminent attack, but the rank and file were hearing something else. The British Army was in confusion and supplies were short. If Burgoyne were strong enough to attack today, why would any of his men be deserting? Word spread among both the militiamen and regulars that the British were like militia without commanders, in other words not like an army at all.[51]

The Americans did not know it, but Burgoyne was at that moment losing most of what was left of his Indian irregulars. Meanwhile, fresh Indian supporters of the revolution started to arrive in the American camp. About a hundred Oneida Indians had joined the Northern Army by the end of the day. The scales were shifting and everyone was beginning to notice it.[52]

Gates began a letter to Betsy and his son Bob. The face of young Ensign Phillips nagged at him. He did not date the letter because he knew he would not have time to finish it tonight. Then he told Wilkinson to write a short report on the battle to Colonel Vischer in Albany. Wilkinson did as he was instructed, describing the action as accurately as he could, but including the false rumor that Burgoyne had been wounded. Wilkinson went on to say that several prisoners had corroborated a preliminary report that General Lincoln's men had successfully retaken Fort Ticonderoga, and that he was inclined to believe it.[53]

7:00 PM, Alexander Scammell, the American Lines on Bemis Heights

The newspapers in Albany were already reporting the battle. Readers wondered at the terrific speed of modern communication. According to the papers, Burgoyne had led the attack in person and had nearly been wounded. Colonel Alexander Scammell had fought like a hero until he was wounded and carried from the field. The ever-impetuous Arnold had rushed into the thickest fighting with his usual recklessness, seizing rifles and firing at British targets himself. A soldier in a Massachusetts regiment claimed he had killed or injured two British officers. With a few horses the Americans might have captured British cannons. And so forth. The breathless report was brief, but apart from the Scammell claim it was surprisingly accurate.[54]

Alexander Scammell seemed unaware of his reported injury. He mended the hole in his coat and went looking for a fusil to replace the one that had been ruined yesterday. As a regimental commander he could not be sure what was going on between the general officers, and he did not know about the temporary shortage of ammunition. Scammell thought that an opportunity had been lost, and he said so to his peers. "Not more than a fourth of our army engaged. Had General Gates known their disposition he would have ordered out a great part of the army, which probably would have totally defeated Burgoyne." Other colonels agree with this rueful appraisal, but yesterday was done and gone.[55]

8:00 PM, Benedict Arnold, the American Lines on Bemis Heights

The jubilant Americans were sure that Burgoyne had lost more than a thousand men. Arnold came back from Gates's headquarters to find his aide-de-camp, Matthew Clarkson, still excited and ready for renewed action. Like Scammell, Clarkson was convinced they should have attacked in the morning. It was Gates's fault that they had not, further evidence in Clarkson's mind that Arnold, not Gates, should be commanding this army. Arnold did not mention the close call with the late arrival of ammunition and allowed his aide to think what he wanted. Clarkson jabbered on, furious that they had not followed up with an attack in the morning. "The flower of their whole army was opposed to us and they were made to believe that on the first onset we would give way." Arnold said nothing. "We should in all probability have entirely destroyed their whole army."[56]

9:00 PM, Benjamin Warren, the American Lines on Bemis Heights

In the afternoon Warren's men had ventured far enough forward to retrieve the body of a sergeant from Marshall's regiment of Massachusetts Continentals, one of four such regiments in Paterson's brigade. Another party had brought in a captain in the Massachusetts militia. He had been stripped naked by camp followers and left to die of a head wound. He had been rendered speechless by the wound, but he was alert. Warren found out that a captain of his own regiment was dead on the field, and he heard about the losses among the New Hampshire officers. The American losses were painful to recount, but Warren had been able to see from his picket line that acres of Freeman's fields were still covered with more British than American fallen. It appeared that the dispirited deserter who had passed through early on had been correct. Most of the British 62nd seemed to have been left lying silently on the field. Through the day British burial parties had moved about in the distance, burying British and Americans where they had fallen. The sun had set on the dreary scene just after six. At nine o'clock Warren and his detachment were at last ordered back to camp, where they all fell instantly asleep in their tents.[57]

11:45 PM, Daniel Taylor, the British Lines

Taylor had eaten, rested, and relaxed as best he could, but he was once again facing a long, dangerous journey back southward to the British Army headquarters on the lower Hudson. This time his only written message was concealed in a small silver ball. If he was stopped perhaps it would not be noticed. He silently rehearsed the stories that had served him well on previous trips, all of them plausible answers to such questions as "where are you going?" "why are you not serving in the militia?" "where do you live?" It was hard to be convincing and terrified at the same time, but he had managed it so far and he would manage it again. General Clinton by this time had probably captured Fort Montgomery as he had promised to do by now back on September 10. That's where Taylor would go, and by the end of the month he would be safe. At midnight he set off alone into the darkness once again.

SUNDAY, SEPTEMBER 21, 1777

5:00 AM, Simon Fraser, the Balcarres Redoubt

The nights following the battle of September 19 were long, dark, and frightening, especially for the men camped around the strong fortifications that anchored and protected the right flank of the British line a mile and two-thirds west of the Hudson. There the hills and uncleared forest lay close to the encampments. Each night brought a chorus of howling from the forests to the west. For the first two nights everyone thought that dogs were to blame for the disturbance. Many officers had dogs with them, and the men grumbled that their masters needed to take them in hand. Sleep had been hard enough to come by the night after the battle, but the next night had been just as bad what with all the howling. General Fraser had ordered all dogs to be confined to their masters' tents; if any were seen running around the camp the provost had orders to hang them.[58] But now, like just about everyone else, he knew that dogs were not to blame for the howling. It was wolves, and when daylight came his men would see what had been done to the shallow graves scattered across the battlefield.

At dawn the American morning gun had sounded alarmingly close. The Americans had brought up a gun and posted it as close as they dared to the British line. They did not bother to waste a cannonball in this show of bravado, but the American piece was so close that over the coming days the wadding from the gun would sometimes hit the British advanced works. Farther away the British and German soldiers could also hear the Americans still felling trees to create abatis.[59] American drums beat out orders from time to time, and these too could be heard through the fog. It all had the desired effect on Burgoyne's men. The Americans were numerous and close, and these constant reminders wore on their nerves.

6:00 AM, *John Burgoyne, British Headquarters*

Burgoyne had awakened in the early morning hours. Now the idea of a renewed attack on the Americans later in the morning seemed unnecessary. It could be postponed. It would be better to wait until Gates was forced to divide his army and send brigades to oppose Clinton south of Albany. At dawn Burgoyne rose for the day in his camp at Freeman's farm and wrote his morning orders: "As parties are to be employed making roads this day in order to advance towards the Enemy, it's the General's Orders that the Corps encamp on their present Ground immediately."

That was it then. Dig in and wait for Clinton to advance. Surely this would draw strength away from Gates's army just beyond the woods to the south. Surely it was better to do that than to attack now. Burgoyne checked with his commissary. There were twenty-five days' worth of provisions left. Surely Clinton would do something before provisions were exhausted. Then, Burgoyne thought, he could continue his own push toward Albany with a much smaller American Army in his way.

Burgoyne worked with Robert Kingston to produce a statement evaluating what had occurred on the nineteenth. The statement then went on to assign some new recruits and volunteers to regiments. Burgoyne had their officers select 120 men from their corps of Loyalists and Canadians to replace men lost from the English regiments in Friday's battle. They should all be men picked for their demonstrated courage and loyalty. The 62nd and the 20th were in particular need, but some of the men balked at the idea of making an open-ended commitment to the regular British Army. Burgoyne responded by giving each of them a certificate stating that he was not obliged to serve past Christmas of 1777. Burgoyne knew that one way or another he was not going to need these soldiers even that long.[60] Finally, Burgoyne issued an order that followed up on the discussion of the previous day about how to deal with the frequent firing of guns in camp, which with the Americans so close kept everyone unnecessarily on edge.

Burgoyne also wrote a second letter to General Powell at Ticonderoga. This time he decided to stretch the truth a bit more. "I hear the enemy is not a little disconcerted with the reception they met with in the action of the 19th. We found five hundred of their bodies the morning after." He boasted that had the battle taken place closer to the river, where he could have brought all of his forces to bear, not a single American would have escaped. With that, he handed both letters over to an Indian courier and sent him on his way north. The man put the two letters in his shot pouch and got ready to leave for Ticonderoga.

7:00 AM, Friedrich Riedesel, the German Camp on the River Flats

Riedesel sent a construction party out into the foggy morning. The working detachment was made up of a hundred men drawn from the four German regiments. Another hundred armed men were sent along to protect them. Their task was to clear a road southward along the top of the river bluffs toward the American lines to at least as far as the Mill Creek ravine that lay close to the American lines. Riedesel already had pickets and minor entrenchments overlooking the ravine from the north side. If Burgoyne's forces could not advance along the river road because of the American batteries on Bemis Heights, maybe they could cut a new road along the top of the bluffs and attack that way. Of course, getting across the ravine would not be easy, but if a decent road could be cut as far as its north side, then Riedesel would be ready to move if Burgoyne decided to strike there.

Meanwhile a party of about 150 Americans had decided to move up from the south to the same Mill Creek ravine from their forward position on the river flats. They had been up since four again today, and to them it seemed like another good way to maintain pressure on Burgoyne's left flank. A sudden rain shower drenched them as they climbed the slope on the north side of the ravine, not knowing how close they were to Riedesel's pickets. At nine o'clock, as the rain reached its heaviest, the American and German detachments ran into each other. There was some shouting and firing but with little effect.

The Germans decided to pull back, but now Riedesel's entire command was alerted to the possibility of an American attack.[61] The Americans also thought the action presaged an attack. The American detachment fell back to the south side of the ravine, slipping and sliding down the north slope, then scrambling through the wet brush back up the south slope. There the Americans did their best to make ready. As drums rattled down the line, the Americans all along it braced for the expected attack. As the rainstorm passed, the entire American line was ready, muskets primed with dry powder. But of course neither side had any intention of attacking the other here. The two armies slowly relaxed as the morning wore on.

Burgoyne's men were feeling the pinch of short supplies. Wine was in short supply, low quality, and expensive. The Germans complained that a bottle cost over two reichthalers. The cost of things like coffee and sugar was also climbing quickly. They could not get replacement clothing for torn uniforms or find ways to wash soiled ones. It was increasingly difficult for Riedesel's officers to put a good face on the situation.[62]

9:00 AM, Horatio Gates, American Headquarters on Bemis Heights

Gates was content to wait, but Arnold was not, certainly not now that adequate ammunition and other supplies were in hand. A whole day had passed without a renewal of fighting. Gates had an excuse on Saturday; there had been, after all, a serious shortage of shot and powder following the battle of the day before. But that danger had passed and the army was ready. Arnold argued that every day of delay was another day for Burgoyne to gather his wits and launch a new attack. Gates saw it otherwise, of course. More men and supplies were expected daily on the American side, and Burgoyne could no longer expect either of them. To Gates it made sense to wait while the scale tipped more and more in his favor.

With every day that passed, Gates was more convinced that he had to be rid of Arnold. The man had been out of control on the nineteenth. Something had to be done. Gates opted for a characteristically passive approach to the problem. Lincoln would arrive sooner or later, and when that happened Arnold would be displaced. Both Arnold and Lincoln were major generals, but because of Congress's fumbling, Lincoln was senior to Arnold. Gates was convinced that as soon as the gentle and compliant Lincoln arrived, his troubles with Arnold would be over.

Cook's Connecticut militia and other units were ordered to strike their tents and parade in preparation for battle. Arnold appeared before the regiment and announced that word had reached him that General Lincoln had moved north over the previous days to retake Skenesborough and to cut British communications with Canada. Fort George had been retaken and American troops had moved undetected northward on Lake George. An attack on Fort Ticonderoga three days ago had freed a hundred American prisoners, had taken many more British prisoners, and had seized three hundred baggage bateaux. There was some exaggeration, of course. The Americans had been unable to retake Ticonderoga, and they had destroyed only two hundred bateaux and seventeen sloops. Still, Colonel Brown, the man who had accused Arnold of malfeasance in Montreal, had captured over three hundred men, most of them from the 53rd Regiment. Brown had captured an armed vessel with several officers as well.

The men cheered wildly. Arnold moved on to the next regiment with the news, getting the same response. When the good news had been fully broadcast, the artillery used some of their new powder to fire a *feu de joi* of thirteen guns in celebration, one for each of the thirteen United States. With John Stark and his men long gone, no one bothered to recognize Vermont as a fourteenth state. A mile and a half to the north the British and German soldiers heard the thirteen-gun salute, taking it as further evidence that they were about to be attacked. They waited for a tense hour in the intermittent rain before deciding that the Americans had given them merely another false alarm.[63]

10:00 AM, James Wilkinson, American Headquarters on Bemis Heights

Young British Ensign Phillips quietly died in Wilkinson's tent near Gates's headquarters.[64] He was not Gates's nephew after all, but Wilkinson had taken a liking to him. Wilkinson lamented the loss of life on both sides, but not for too long. He sat down to write a letter to General Arthur St. Clair, a friend of Gates but a man disliked by Arnold ever since St. Clair had been promoted over him. At the age of twenty the sly and scheming Wilkinson was already a master at pitting his superiors against each other. He briefly described the fighting on the nineteenth, then got to the meat of his message.

General Arnold was not out of camp during the whole action. Pray, my dear General, read the inclosed, and let the amiable object know, the first opportunity, what was accomplished by our troops. General Gates despises a certain pompous little fellow as much as you can, and tells me, confidentially, that nothing could give him so much satisfaction as your presence here, though I find his supporters are, unfortunately, your enemies; hence his silence.

Sly, obtuse, and courting favor with Washington through St. Clair on behalf of Gates, Wilkinson was doing his best to undercut Arnold's standing. The ambitious young lieutenant colonel would be too clever for his own good in the long run, but for the moment, his scheming was working. St. Clair was under censure for having abandoned Fort Ticonderoga to Burgoyne in July and was facing a court-martial. But Wilkinson was sure there was no harm in currying favor with a man who was himself well out of it just in case St. Clair recovered his reputation and was inclined to reward those who had stayed with him.[65]

3:00 PM, Horatio Gates, American Headquarters on Bemis Heights

During the afternoon, the fresh Oneida scouts brought in a pair of Loyalists they had caught behind the British lines. The captured men had painted themselves, thinking that they could pass for Indians. The amused Oneidas brought the two men before Gates, who shared their mirth. Arnold and Gates questioned the terrified men for a while, then handed them back to the Oneidas for their entertainment.[66]

The Indians knew what the poor men expected, but these American allies were not unschooled warriors of the western nation from which Burgoyne had recruited. These were not anything like the killers of the unfortunate Miss McCrae. Most of the Oneidas were bilingual, and some were reasonably well educated. The Oneidas had for decades enjoyed easy economic, political, and religious connections with Albany. Death by torture was a thing of the past for them and they scalped only those enemies who had already been killed in battle. They had played a major role, some of it theatrical, in the defeat of the British at Fort Stanwix. But the Oneidas knew what to do to extract the most information from their Loyalist captives. It was once again time for their theatrics.

The Oneidas dug holes five feet deep and buried the Loyalists up to their necks. There they had the best seats in the house for the powwow that played out into the night. When the Oneidas tired of this sport they pulled the men out of their confinements, bound them, and alternated heating their heads and feet near their fire, hooting and hollering all the while. The terrified Loyalists told the Oneidas everything they knew, which was not much. When morning came, the chastised captives were handcuffed and sent to the Albany jail, where the stories of their supposed near-death experiences at the hands of the Oneidas would be told over and over.[67]

6:00 PM, *John Burgoyne, British Headquarters*

The British settled down in camp by six in the evening. By sundown the British engineers completed working on the new bridge of boats across the Hudson and its *tête de pont* on the opposite bank. The bridge had been constructed just south of the stream that flowed out of the Great Ravine. Lieutenant John Schank and his sailors had once again managed what the infantrymen thought was a prodigious accomplishment. But they all knew that the far shore of the Hudson was infested with Americans. It was a bridge it would be best not to cross, but now it was completed and ready should they need it.[68]

Later in the evening the second express message was sent to Clinton saying that if he could not advance nearer to Albany, Burgoyne would have to return to Ticonderoga. This would have to occur by October 12 at the latest. There would be no provisions left after that. This was not entirely true. By his commissary's calculations Burgoyne would still have four more days' provisions on the twelfth, more if they went to half rations before then. But Clinton needed to be aware of the urgency of Burgoyne's situation, so a little exaggeration was allowed. The messenger left in civilian clothes, making his way across the new bridge of boats as a heavy rain began to fall. It was a hazardous assignment. He would have to avoid settlements and sleep alone in the cold damp New York forest every night. If the Americans caught him making his way south along the east side of the Hudson, he would be hanged. If they did not catch him he might still succumb to pneumonia. Either way he would be doing his duty as he saw it. It rained heavily and constantly all through the night.[69]

9:00 PM *American Soldiers, the American Line on Bemis Heights*

Many of the American soldiers were nervous and inexperienced, and it showed. Late in the day a sentry on the picket line shot and killed an intruder. The dead man turned out to be another sentry from the same unit who had wandered out of position.[70] It was another life lost unnecessarily.

A dim moon rose behind the thick clouds, making the cold wet landscape barely visible to the nervous pickets. It would be another long night on the American side too.

MONDAY, SEPTEMBER 22, 1777

4:00 AM, Horatio Gates, American Headquarters on Bemis Heights

It was another cold and foggy morning. Gates was up at four o'clock again. He had postponed writing a report about Friday's battle, but now he could delay it no longer. Sending a letter to George Washington would acknowledge that Washington was his superior; indeed that seemed to be what the title Commander in Chief should imply. But Congress, not Washington, had put Gates in command of the Northern Army. So instead John Hancock and Congress would receive his report. It was a snub that Washington would pretend to ignore.

Gates started writing, using the language drafted two days earlier by Wilkinson. Then he expanded on it.

> Friday morning I was informed by my reconnoitring parties, that the enemy had struck their camp, and were moving towards our left. I immediately detached Colonel Morgan's corps, consisting of the rifle regiment and the light infantry of the army, to observe their direction, and harass their advance.
>
> At this instant, hearing from prisoners that the whole British force and a division of foreigners, had engaged our party, I reinforced with four more regiments. This continued the action till the close of day, when both armies retired from the field.

Well, the number of American regiments that had been engaged was in fact more than twice that number, but Gates chose to ignore the actions Arnold had taken on his own. He did remember to mention the report that Burgoyne had been on the field and had received a wound in his left shoulder. He noted the deaths of two New Hampshire officers, but did not mention any other officers by name, writing only, "They all deserve the honour and applause of Congress."

The armies were still within two miles of each other. Gates pointed out that he had asked the neighboring states to send militia as soon as possible back on the seventeenth. He then gave Hancock a quick accounting of men taken prisoner.[71]

Gates closed his letter to Hancock and turned to other tasks on his desk. Among them were letters from General Lincoln and Colonel John Brown detailing American successes at Ticonderoga and elsewhere northward in Burgoyne's rear. There was no time to rewrite the letter to Hancock so Gates simply attached the two new pieces of good news and added a second note of his own.

> I congratulate You, Sir, & the Congress, upon the remarkable good success of the armies of the United States. I think there is now a fair prospect of the Northern department being soon freed from these violent enemies, who from the sudden eruption & rapidity of their attack, threatened no less than the entire conquest of this state.

It was a moment of triumph for Gates, although the dangerous enemy he was writing about was still within earshot. Most satisfying was that he had managed to get through his report and its codicil without ever mentioning Benedict Arnold.[72]

Arnold had persuaded Gates against his better judgment to take the battle to Burgoyne on Friday. First Morgan and Dearborn, then gradually Poor's entire brigade, then part of Learned's. He had even ordered out a regiment from Paterson's brigade. Arnold himself had left his side precipitously to display his heroics and had to be ordered back. Then he had done it again, riding off without leave near the end of the day. The man was erratic, undependable, impetuous, reckless—all the things Gates prided himself in not being. They had been fortunate that Burgoyne had not attacked the next day, or the day after, or today for that matter.

Gates knew he had to make changes. He had to do what was necessary to prevent the headstrong, reckless Arnold from risking everything in the new battle that was almost certain to come. The arrival of General Lincoln would settle the matter, but Gates might have to take some more pointed action sooner than that.

Gates drafted his orders for the day. He had made sure that each man had been fortified with a little rum on Friday morning, and that had been a fortunate decision in light of the fighting that had gone on later that day. But he had not ordered a ration of rum since then. Gates was convinced of the medicinal value of rum and was sure that his men would benefit from it. He wrote a standing order for his commissaries to provide every man with a half gill of rum every morning until further notice. Then he slipped in the item that he expected to have an immediate effect. In a single sentence he stripped Arnold of his command of Morgan's rifle corps and Dearborn's light infantry by pretending that they had never been assigned to Arnold's division in the first place.

6:00 AM, *John Burgoyne, British Headquarters*

Burgoyne was up early again, as was the whole camp. The regiments had stood to arms every morning an hour before dawn for days, and Burgoyne had extended the order for as long as the army was in its current camp. But he issued no additional orders this day.

The autumnal equinox passed during the course of the day. There were twelve hours between sunrise and sunset, more from the top of a hill but less in the valley. The men set their watches by the sun, fixing noon midway between the rising and setting of the sun by marking it at its noon highpoint. Every day was three minutes shorter than the last. Hard frosts were already biting the sleeping army at night. The sumac was already red and in the forest turkeys were beginning to gather in flocks of hundreds. Burgoyne's men could hear them in the forest, but none but the Indians dared go after them. The Indians liked to hunt the turkeys with dogs, knowing that the big birds would regroup in the same gathering places if they were scattered, but there would be none of that sport with American patrols this close.

The new bridge of boats across the Hudson was open, and everyone knew that they would be exposed to fire of all kinds if they tried to take the army across. But this morning there was a surprise. Fifty Albany men came across the new bridge from the other side. Some of them were sincere Loyalists, others merely debtors, criminals, or men pressed by personal circumstances to opt for alligiance to the king. Burgoyne tried to be positive, but the truth was that these were fifty more mouths to feed and he was down to twenty-four days of provisions for his army, with no new supplies expected. The volunteers were posted to the Breymann Redoubt, where they joined German jägers, Canadians, Indians, and some other Loyalists at the far western end of the main line.[73]

12:00 Noon, *Horatio Gates, American Headquarters*

The American soldiers had turned out early again, struck their tents, and packed up their baggage, just as they had been doing for days. Whether they would suddenly advance or retreat was anyone's guess. Either way, they were ready. They had paraded and marched off to man their posts on the breastworks and to build more of them where there were still gaps. A steady fall rain started around noon. It was clear that there would be no action today, so Gates ordered the tents set up again so that the men could get some shelter from the cold rain.[74]

The Oneidas were once again making sport around the two immobile armies. A scouting party of them worked close enough to the British line to capture two of their pickets without being detected. A less fortunate man was killed and scalped. The two prisoners were brought back to the American camp. The Indians removed the men's hats and painted their faces in the traditional Iroquois fashion, red or black depending on the fate the Oneidas had decided upon. It was all for show, of course, and the terrified prisoners were turned over to Gates with a laugh at noon. Later another party of Oneidas brought in eight prisoners who had been caught far behind the British lines while trying to make their way to Montreal. One turned out to be an American deserter.[75]

Lieutenant Hardin finally brought his detachment of riflemen back. They had been gone since Thursday, the day before the battle, scouting behind the British lines even as the battle had raged on Freeman's farm. Over the last four days they had circled around to the west and north, eventually coming back at Saratoga from the north. They had been trotting down a path along the top of a ridge when Hardin met an Indian courier headed north. The two men had seen each other in the same instant, just yards from each other. Both had raised their guns and fired simultaneously, as if in a duel. Hardin's rifle had found its mark and the courier fell. The Indian's musket ball had grazed Hardin's left side. The dead man's shot pouch had contained letters, one of them being Burgoyne's letter of Saturday to General Powell at Ticonderoga.[76] Things were looking up.

Gates had scanned Burgoyne's note to Powell. It was a smug appraisal of British military prowess in "a smart and very honorable engagement." Then he had added that "the loss on either side cannot be particularly ascertained."[77] Burgoyne's losses were greater than Gates's had been, and the man had to know it. Lieutenant Hardin knew what he was about. Gates would let him rest and heal a few days then send him out again.

12:00 Noon, John Burgoyne, British Headquarters

An officer arrived from Clinton's brigade, far to the south near the mouth of the Hudson. It seemed a miracle that he had made it through. The

Americans were swarming over the hills and valleys to the south and hanging every British spy they caught. The man's arrival immediately sparked rumors that Clinton was coming up the river. Burgoyne made a comment to Riedesel that seemed to confirm it. A shiver of hope spread through all ranks.[78]

Scouts from Fraser's Advanced Corps were particularly excited. They had reports that the Americans had thrown their own bridge of boats across the Hudson just below Bemis Tavern. They predicted that if Clinton approached Albany, Gates would have to abandon Bemis Heights altogether, sending part of his force south to defend Albany and pulling the rest across the bridge of boats toward New England. But this gush of optimism found little support among Burgoyne's officers.[79]

British pickets brought in an American prisoner and the man was grilled about the cheering and the *feu de joi* heard Sunday. He told his interrogators that they had news that Ticonderoga had been attacked by the Americans, who had freed at least a hundred prisoners of war.[80] In their exuberance over the rumors about Clinton's intentions most men chose not to believe the American's story. The rumors continued. Clinton was moving north. Surely he was sailing, not marching, up the Hudson Valley. He would disembark north of Albany and attack the city from the rear. It was all quite exciting—and dead wrong.

The captured American also told his British captors that the Americans still thought that Burgoyne had been killed on the nineteenth. Like the other American captured on Saturday, the prisoner seemed crestfallen when he realized that Burgoyne was alive and well.[81] Better and better; things were truly looking up for Burgoyne.

4:00 PM, *Benedict Arnold, the Neilson House on Bemis Heights*

Arnold had sent his aides over to hear Wilkinson read out the orders of the day, but it was not until Varick and Livingston came back to the little outbuilding near the Neilson house Arnold used as his quarters did he know their contents.[82] Now they all knew about Gates's preemptive decision to remove Morgan and Dearborn from Arnold's divisional command. Worse yet, they all now knew that Gates had sent a letter to Hancock in which Arnold's role in the fighting on Friday was not even mentioned. Meanwhile, Wilkinson was busy spreading the story that neither Arnold nor any other general officer had been in the thick of the fighting on Friday.[83]

Arnold was not the kind of man who could tolerate such treatment. Almost two weeks ago Gates had told him to annex the New York and Connecticut militias to his division as he saw fit, then behaved as if he had never mentioned it. After Arnold had assigned them Gates reassigned the same regiments differently, making Arnold look like a fool. Now, after all his exertions on the battlefield, Gates was dismantling Arnold's divisional command. Worse, Gates did not even have the courage to reassign Morgan's corps; instead he pretended that they had never been assigned to Arnold in the first place.

Arnold stormed into Gates's headquarters in a fury. "When I joined the army at Van Schaick's Island you were pleased to order me to Loudon's ferry to command of General Poor's and Learned's brigades and Colonel Morgan's corps of riflemen and light infantry. Your commands were immediately obeyed. I have repeatedly since received your orders respecting the corps as belonging to my division. This has often been mentioned in general orders. The gentlemen commanding those corps have understood themselves as my division."

Arnold pressed on. "On the ninth you desired me to annex the New York and Connecticut militia to such brigades as I thought proper in my division, which I accordingly did. I ordered the New York militia to join Poor's Brigade and the Connecticut to Learned's. The next day you placed me in the ridiculous light of presuming to give orders I had no right to do and having them publicly contradicted." Arnold was just getting warmed up. "On the nineteenth you desired me to send Morgan and the light infantry. I obeyed your orders. Before the action was over I found it necessary to send out the whole of my division to support the attack."

Arnold knew that he had not been mentioned at all in Gates's report to Hancock. He could see that Gates was removing him from divisional command. "I have ever supposed a Major General's command of four thousand men a proper division! And no detachment when composed of whole brigades! Forming one wing of the army!"

Gates tried to remain bland. "I do not know you are a major general or have any command in the army. I expect General Lincoln in a day or two, at which time you will have no command of a division. You are of little consequence to the army, and with all my heart I will give you a pass to leave it whenever you think proper." Arnold stormed back to his quarters.[84]

5:00 PM, Horatio Gates, American Headquarters

At five o'clock General Lincoln arrived at the American camp sooner than expected, a day or two ahead of most of his two thousand New England soldiers. Benjamin Lincoln (Figure 3.3) was a forty-four-year-old farmer from Massachusetts. Two years ago he was a lieutenant colonel of the local militia, and he had never aspired to more than that. But the rebellion had revealed him to be a natural leader. A member of the Committee of Correspondence and an elected member of the Massachusetts Provincial Congress, by 1776 he had found himself appointed brigadier general. Then in February 1777, on Washington's recommendation Congress made him a major general. Washington had assigned Lincoln and his troops to the Northern Army in July. He had taken his station at Manchester and from there had directed the operations against Fort George and Fort Ticonderoga, behind Burgoyne's advancing main army. Today he had brought his command across the Hudson on the American floating bridge

Figure 3.3 Benjamin Lincoln by Charles Willson Peale, from life, ca. 1781–1783. Courtesy of Independence National Historical Park.

to support Gates on Bemis Heights. Now Lincoln found himself Gates's second in command, replacing the mercurial Arnold.[85]

With Lincoln were his bodyguards, the mounted dragoons of the 2nd Regiment of Connecticut Light Horse. This was a militia unit made up of men who had horses and could find uniforms. They wore blue coats with buff facings, but their hats were what made them unique. These were actually iron helmets camouflaged by plain brown felt hats with crowns and brims but decorated with fancy yellow lace trim. Like proper dragoons they carried heavy sabers and needed at least a little armor in case they ran into Burgoyne's German dragoons. But that had seemed unlikely since Stark and his men had all but wiped them out at Bennington, and for the last few weeks the Connecticut Light Horse had been escorting and protecting General Lincoln as he moved around the country east of the Hudson.[86]

Here at last was the major general who was senior to Arnold, the solution to what had become Gates's biggest command problem. Lincoln found Gates, the commander still worried that Burgoyne would attack again and shaken by his confrontation with Arnold.

Gates was relieved to see Lincoln now that the rupture with Arnold was complete. Gates had been commanding the right division himself up to now, but having taken command away from Arnold he could now make the left division his own and give the right to Lincoln. Gates and Lincoln ordered Glover's brigade to relocate from the ground just east of Nielson's house to positions closer to other brigades in the right wing. Some of Glover's regiments made a new camp just south of Nixon's brigade atop the bluffs while the rest made camp behind the log ramparts built on the plain between the bottom of the bluff and the Hudson River. Lincoln's regiments would replace Glover's as they came into camp (Figure 3.4).[87]

Orders were issued to strike the tents yet again, pack up, and man the lines in preparation for an assault. The 7th Massachusetts Continentals from Nixon's brigade were moved west to the vicinity of Gates's headquarters. There they were held in reserve for the expected attack, which of course did not come.[88]

7:00 PM, *Benedict Arnold, the Neilson House on Bemis Heights*

Benedict Arnold composed a long letter to Gates detailing the arguments he had just made in his defense. In two long paragraphs Arnold detailed

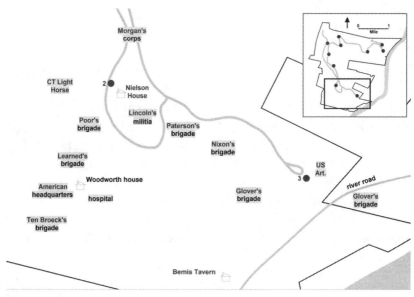

Figure 3.4 Gates rearranges his forces in the American camp as new units arrive.

both his own contributions and Gates's several offenses. He concluded with a final paragraph in which he displayed his wounded pride as clearly as anyone could, taking Gates up on his offer to provide him with a pass out of the Northern Army.

From what reason I know not as I am Conscious of no Offense or Neglect of Duty but I have lately Observed little or no Attention paid to any Proposals I have thought it my Duty to make for the Public Service, and when a measure I have proposed has been agreed to It has immediately been contradicted. I have been received with the greatest coolness at Head Quarters, and often huffed in such a manner as must mortify a Person with less Pride than I have & in my station in the Army. You Observed you expected General Lincoln in a day or two, when I should have no Command of a Division, that you thought me of little Consequence to the Army, and that you would with all your heart give me a pass to leave it, whenever I thought Proper. As I find your observation very Just that I am not or that you wish me of little Consequence in the Army, and as I have the Interest & safety of my Country at heart I wish to be where I can be of the most Service to Her. I therefore as General Lincoln is arrived have to request your Pass to Philada. with

*my two Aid-de-Camps, & their servants, where I propose to join General
Washington, and may possibly have it in my power to service my country, although I am thought of no consequence in this department.*

I am with due respect

Sir

Your Hb^l. Servt.

B Arnold

Hon^bl. Major Genl. Gates[89]

Not far away, Arnold's aide, Richard Varick, wrote his own account of
events in his latest letter to Philip Schuyler.

> This I am certain of, that Arnold has all the credit of the action on
> the 19th, for he was ordering out troops to it while the ——— Other
> was in Dr. Potts hut backbiting his righteousness ... Had Gates
> complied with Arnold's repeated desires, he would have gained a
> general and complete victory over the enemy.[90]

Varick was just getting warmed up. The letter went on in that vein, itemizing Arnold's virtues and Gates's offenses. There was flattery for Schuyler
and hints that James Wilkinson was a false friend who had done much to
engineer the confrontation between the two generals.

8:00 PM, *Frederika Riedesel, the German Camp*

Frederika Riedesel nursed Ensign Henry Young as well as she could, but
infection from the ball in his leg soon proved the surgeons right. The leg
was gangrenous. Frederika had spent the last three nights listening to the
young man's groans through the thin partition that separated her room
from his. The surgeons undertook amputation earlier in the day, but it
was too late. Ensign Young died despite her efforts and those of the over-
worked surgeons.[91] Lieutenant Reynals turned out not to have been shot
dead after all, to the great relief of the man's wife.

10:30 PM *American Soldiers, the American Camp on Bemis Heights*

Elsewhere in the American camp the effects of Gates's generous morning orders were still being felt. Noise still filled the air and rum was still
flowing. A half-moon rose just after ten, dimly lighting the landscape and

tempting the revelers into the night despite the rain. Twenty young farmers temporarily turned warriors who had drunk more rum than necessary to ward off the wet chill decided to undertake an unauthorized raid on the British pickets and bring back as many captives as possible. Like anything any human being does, it seemed like a good idea at the time. But rum has the effect of increasing the fraction of ideas that seem like good ones to dangerously high levels. This time there were no sober officers near enough to head off disaster.

The militiamen elected officers from their number with inebriated formality. The man elected captain put on an old powdered wig and topped it with a huge tricorn hat trimmed with threadbare fragments of discarded gold lace. To this was added a faded long-waisted blue coat with buff facings and a black silk neck scarf. Buckskin knee breeches, a pair of dragoon boots, and a heavy saber in a leather scabbard completed the outfit. The other elected officers in the self-appointed drunken detachment did their best to equal their leader with what they had at hand.

Like many militiamen they were armed only with fowling pieces, but they set out with rum-fortified determination, skulking as silently as drunken men could across no man's land. It was still wet and rainy, but the waning gibbous moon provided enough gray glow through the clouds to let the men find their way forward. When they got to within a few yards of the British pickets their leader blew an old horse trumpet and they charged forward yelling, stumbling, and laughing. "Ground your arms or you are all dead men," shouted the group's leader at an unexpectedly large number of British pickets. The astonished regular British soldiers could only conclude that they were facing a large American raiding party, so they complied, dropping their muskets and raising their arms in surrender. The drunken militiamen paraded over thirty humiliated British captives back to the American lines in their clownish gear, lucky that they had not all been killed.[92]

11:45 PM, John Burgoyne, British Headquarters

It continued raining into the night, another seemingly endless soaking autumn rain.[93] Burgoyne had let the disguised officer from Clinton rest during the afternoon. Now he roused him and told him that it was time to risk his life yet again. No one knew if the previous messengers had got through, and everyone had to assume the worst. The man made ready to leave camp at midnight, crossing the river over the bridge of boats in the steady rain and taking to the woods on the other side. The intended third messenger who had been selected on Saturday was made ready as well. He too would try to run the gauntlet down to Fort Montgomery. Both men had to know that their chances were slim. The message was the same as the one sent Sunday. They were to plead for help from Clinton. Without it Burgoyne would have to retreat by October 12.

Burgoyne ordered the artillery to fire eight rounds around midnight to make the Americans think an attack might be coming. This, everyone hoped, would cause the Americans to pull back their pickets. The ruse was intended to provide an opportunity for the two officers to slip through the American lines across the river in their disguises.[94] They had each memorized the same short desperate message.

> Have lost the old cipher, but being sure from the tenor of your letter what you meant it so to read, I have made it out—An attack, or the menace of an attack, upon Montgomery, must be of great use, as it will draw away a part of this force, and I will follow them close. Do it my dear friend directly. Yours ever faithfully. J. B.[95]

TUESDAY, SEPTEMBER 23, 1777

6:00 AM, Horatio Gates, American Headquarters on Bemis Heights

Gates read Arnold's letter, which he had left unread since receiving it at bedtime on Monday. Gates was convinced the man was daft. Not only was he getting rid of Arnold, the man would be taking his Schuyler supporters with him. So much the better. Gates dashed off a brief reply, edited it, and handed it to Wilkinson so that a clean version could be written out.

> *Sir*
> *I did not receive your Letter until I was going into to Bed last Night. This pass permission you request for yourself and Aides de Camp to go to Philad^a* ~~shall be~~ *is Inclosed.*
> > *I am Sir*
> > > *Your most Ob^d S.*
> > > > *Horatio Gates*
>
> *Hn^{ble} Maj. Genl. Arnold*[96]

To his letter to Arnold, Gates attached a pass, addressed to John Hancock, to allow Arnold to go to Philadelphia.[97] Gates then turned to dictating his orders for the day. On top of all the consequences of the confrontation with Arnold, Wilkinson now informed Gates of the drunken escapade carried out by some of the militiamen the night before. It was bad enough that the Oneida Indians were now putting on almost daily shows for the rest of the army; the lack of overall discipline had reached a new low last night, even if the band of drunken soldiers had managed to bring back more than two dozen prisoners. Gates had to get better control of his army. The rum allotment was revoked, and there would be no more theatrical performances by the Oneidas. The men would have to find diversion elsewhere. The standing order for a half gill of rum for every man first thing in the morning until further notice had lasted only a day. The men would have to find another remedy for their stiff joints.[98]

8:00 AM, John Burgoyne, British Headquarters

It had rained all night again.[99] Burgoyne sat in his tent listening to the incessant patter of raindrops while he wrote out his orders for the day. In the British and German camps the cold rain had dampened Monday's euphoria. Everyone was wet and cold. They could see their breath. Fingers were numb and clumsy. The British and Germans had heard several cannon shots between three and four o'clock in the morning. Like everyone else Päusch let his imagination run out of control. Could it be the approach of Clinton's relief corps from the south? Could it be St. Leger coming to their rescue from the north? It was, of course, neither of those happy possibilities. The guns were just cover for the messengers Burgoyne was trying to send south past the Americans. The grim truth was that the expedition was no longer receiving anything from the north, not even messages. Messages from the south were rare and only temporarily encouraging. The weather turned pleasant later in the day, but it did not help the mood.[100]

Some of the men thought the army might be ordered to retreat under cover of night, but others argued that Burgoyne would never abandon the sick and wounded, which a nighttime retreat would require. Most were convinced that Burgoyne would fight again before resorting to retreat. Others argued that Burgoyne was waiting for reinforcements, either from Clinton or from Ticonderoga, but they all agreed that reinforcement from the north was unlikely and would not be sufficient in any case. Even if Clinton came up the river in force, the numbers of Americans who would be drawn off to stop him would still leave Gates with superior numbers north of Albany. Burgoyne's junior officers listened to all of this with growing despondency. The men increasingly argued more from hope than reason. In the afternoon the possessions of deceased officers were auctioned off. This did nothing to improve morale.[101]

The British continued to strengthen their lines while they waited to hear from Clinton. More trees were felled to build breastworks and abatis. By now the army had also dug small entrenchments at the advanced picket locations, so the pickets were relatively safe from American attack. At dawn a detachment of two hundred men mounted the heights overlooking the Hudson south of the Great Ravine and began constructing two major gun emplacements to cover the hospital, baggage park, and artillery park below. The Hessen-Hanau Regiment held this position, and now they were joined by a total of six cannons crewed by the Hanau artillerymen. Four of the guns were put in the larger emplacement and two were put in the smaller one. Together the two hilltop fortifications had come to be called the Great Redoubt.

The *tête de pont* was strengthened on the end of the bridge of boats that lay on the opposite shore. The grenadier company of the Hessen-Hanau Regiment moved to an advance position south of the third bridge and dug in. It was exhausting work, but the camp began to take on some of the more permanent characteristics of a garrison. Burgoyne was clearly waiting, but for what? For the Americans to attack? For St. Leger to come down from Lake George? For Clinton to come up the Hudson? No one was quite sure. Everyone hoped that whatever they were waiting for would arrive in a few days. It was getting colder at night, the soaking rains were ever harder to endure, and there was no sign of resupply from any direction.[102] The few remaining Indians still with Burgoyne appeared to shy away from going out on any scouting parties, and who could blame them?[103]

Kingston reported out the results of a court-martial, which had found Private Philip Skene guilty of desertion from the 62nd Regiment on September 9. Skeene had been caught, but had been kept under guard ever since. The man had escaped the fighting on the nineteenth and the high probability of death or injury with his decimated regiment, but now, like another private, he faced a thousand lashes.[104]

10:00 AM, Benedict Arnold, the Neilson House on Bemis Heights

Arnold read through Gates's brief note (Figure 3.5). Then he examined the pass. Gates had had the gall to address the pass to Hancock. Arnold had asked for a pass and Gates had sent him what was actually a note to Hancock. If Gates wanted to send a sealed letter to Hancock Arnold would be happy to take it to him, but this nonsense was unacceptable. Arnold wrote another letter to Gates. He asked again for a proper pass for himself and his aides.[105]

12:00 Noon, Horatio Gates, American Headquarters on Bemis Heights

Gates read Arnold's latest tirade and answered with a dismissive response that admitted nothing, conceded nothing, this time with a standard pass attached. Arnold had his pass. Gates hoped he would take advantage of it and leave.[106]

Figure 3.5 Benedict Arnold Reading a Letter from Gates, 1777. After Du Simitiere. Courtesy of the artist Ruth Major.

The Americans heard firing in the British camp and raised the alarm, but as usual it turned out to be nothing.[107] Regiments of Warner's brigade of Massachusetts militia were starting to arrive. They camped on part of the ground vacated by Glover's brigade.[108] Gates enjoyed moving the new regiments into places along the American line and finding new and better deployments for the regiments that were already there. It was rare that even a master at chess gained pieces through the course of a match, but that was the advantage Gates now had over his opponent. With Arnold on his way south Gates could now settle into the ever-strengthening defensive posture he preferred, and wait for Burgoyne to make his last desperate move.

8:00 PM, John Burgoyne, British Headquarters

After dark Burgoyne sent yet another well-disguised messenger to Clinton, not knowing if the four he had sent yesterday and the days before had any chance of getting through. Burgoyne was still willing to express a little bravado to his generals from time to time. "Should Gates be rash and ignorant enough to detach to support Putnam he will give me very fair game," he quipped.[109] But they all had to know their chances were decreasing. The leaves were beginning to turn yellow and red. The nights were increasingly cold and damp. The clock was ticking and their options seemed to be falling away with each passing day.

WEDNESDAY, SEPTEMBER 24, 1777

8:00 AM, John Burgoyne, British Headquarters

There were no written orders again Wednesday, but Burgoyne kept his men busy reinforcing their entrenchments. Parties of American riflemen worked their way close enough to the British lines to fire on unwary pickets. At dawn one such party had managed to kill three German pickets without being caught. Work continued on the redoubts, more freshly cut logs were laid, more earth was piled up. Batteries were positioned and re-positioned, but for the most part quiet prevailed between the two armies. The British and German troops persuaded themselves that the deaths of a few unfortunate pickets were no cause for alarm.[110]

Burgoyne and his generals still did not know exactly where the Americans were and what they were about. The woods seemed to be filled with American scouting parties, and the British were going to have to take a few chances if they were going to gain the information they needed. At length, they agreed, and Fraser ordered his nephew, Captain Fraser, to take a detachment of ten of his rangers, forty light infantry, a few officers, and whatever remaining Indian allies he could find to scout the forest and fields to the west and south of their position. They could take the whole day, but staying out overnight seemed inadvisable.

Captain Fraser was trying to pull his party together when he discovered that the Indians had already left on their own initiative. He reported back to his uncle and his orders were countermanded. The rangers and light infantry detachment stayed in camp. Burgoyne was not pleased. The incident revealed the difficulties Burgoyne had working with irregulars, particularly the Indians. These were not men accustomed to following orders.[111]

Several times during the day British or German pickets sounded the alarm when American scouting parties pushed close. The Americans seemed to be everywhere. For an army that presumably intended to attack Albany soon, this one was in a very defensive posture. The point was not lost on the men, who were busy enough to avoid depression but smart enough to perceive the reality of their situation.[112]

*12:00 Noon, Horatio Gates, American Headquarters
on Bemis Heights*

The bulk of Lincoln's troops finally arrived, as did militia from Berkshire County. The army was in high spirits, and Gates once again set about the happy task of finding more space for the new units to camp. Even better, regiments of the Albany militia were arriving in larger numbers.[113]

Two regiments of Albany County militia were already present and attached to Glover's brigade, as was a combined regiment known as Graham's battalion of Dutchess and Ulster County militia. Fourteen more regiments of Albany militia had been called into service on the eighteenth of the month and put under the command of Abraham Ten Broeck. Ten Broeck had shown up the day before the battle, along with a few men of his militia brigade. But at first Ten Broeck had been a commander with few men to command, and his militia had not taken part in the battle. Now men of the Albany regiments were appearing in numbers sufficient to require a major expansion of the American camp. Gates temporarily assigned Ten Broeck's brigade to the space recently vacated by Glover's brigade.[114]

More Massachusetts militia battalions of Jonathan Warner's brigade arrived in camp too, but it was still a piecemeal arrival. One of the brigade's five battalions, the Hampshire County unit, was still at a distance, and it could be a week or more before it joined the army. Other battalions were missing officers and enlisted men. Only one colonel was present so far, and no one seemed to know when the strays might appear.[115]

Deserters were also coming in from the British lines every day. Three had come in during the morning and said that there were rumors in the British camp that Burgoyne would attack today. They said the British general had harangued his officers yesterday, telling them that he would either force his way to Albany or leave his bones on the field.

Later in the day the Oneidas brought in another three prisoners, this time Loyalists. These men said that Burgoyne had lost seven hundred killed and wounded on and since the nineteenth, but the British had persuaded themselves that the American losses must have been twice that many. In fact, American losses had been more like half those of the British. The Oneidas paraded the morose men with ropes around their necks before they were sent back to Albany for imprisonment.[116]

The imbroglio between Gates and Arnold was now widely known and a source of agitation among the rank and file.[117] Arnold was expected to depart any day, but so far he and his aides had not moved. General Poor suggested that the senior officers should make a presentation to Arnold thanking him for his past services and urging him to stay. Poor's officers even drafted the document. But Learned and his officers declined to endorse it. Learned said that he and his officers agreed with the sentiments in the document but they feared that signing would not go down well with Gates. By this time Lincoln had come around and was supporting the idea of trying to mollify Arnold. It was Lincoln's style, always calm and cooperative, always trying to find mutual accommodation. Henry Brockholst Livingston held out hope that Lincoln carried enough weight with Gates to make it happen, but those closer to Gates knew that it would not.

Gates also received news that Howe had lost three thousand men fighting against Washington at Brandywine Creek in Pennsylvania on September 11, while Washington had lost only a thousand. This was good news if it could be believed, but Gates worried that Washington would want him to send regiments south before his business with Burgoyne was finished. Word of Washington's action far to the south circulated among the men, sometimes represented as good news, sometimes as bad. That night another American sentry would be shot by friendly fire, killed by one of his own comrades by mistake.[118]

2:00 PM, *George Washington, near Philadelphia*

Far to the south in eastern Pennsylvania, George Washington was doing exactly what Gates feared. Washington was pleased to read the results of September 19 at Saratoga but annoyed that Gates had reported directly to Hancock rather than go through the commander in chief. Washington was also anxious about his own circumstances. Today he was sure that Gates had checked the British advance, but he did not know if Burgoyne had been turned back. What was clear to him was that he needed Gates to send him reinforcements as soon as the northern threat eased. Congress had evacuated Philadelphia in order to move to Lancaster on the eighteenth. Washington's losses at Brandywine had been twice those of the British, not a third, as friendly newspaper propaganda was saying, and he was in trouble. Washington wrote to Gates.

> *Sir*
> *This army has not been able to oppose General Howe with the success that was wished, and needs a reinforcement. I therefore request, if you have been so fortunate as to oblige General Burgoyne to retreat to Ticonderoga, and if you have not, and circumstances will admit, that you will order Colonel Morgan to join me again with his corps. I sent him up when I thought you materially wanted him, and if his services can be dispensed with now, you will direct him to return immediately. You will perceive I do not mention this in way of command, but leave you to determine upon it according to your situation; if they come they should proceed by way of water from Albany as low down as Peekskill; in such case you will give Colonel Morgan the necessary order to join me with dispatch.*
>
> *I am Sir, your most obedient servant*
Go. Washington[119]

If Washington was uncertain about the outcome of fighting in the north, he was just as uncertain regarding his authority. Congress had appointed

Gates, and Gates was under their direct orders, not Washington's. Washington was not quite commander in chief under these circumstances, and he knew that he could not pretend otherwise, particularly as Gates seemed to think himself equal to and qualified to replace Washington. The letter was as close to obsequious as Washington's sense of dignity would allow it to be.

8:00 PM, *John Burgoyne, British Headquarters*

The Americans fired a cannonball as they pulled back to their line. The shot soared over the Regiment von Riedesel, reminding everyone of the close proximity of the enemy. They hardly needed reminding. The Indian scouts came back. They had ranged westward as far as Saratoga Lake and returned to report that they had seen only the tracks of small parties here and there. Burgoyne now knew no more than he had known before the scouts went out. As if to emphasize the gloom of the current stalemate, it rained heavily that night.[120]

THURSDAY, SEPTEMBER 25, 1777

5:00 AM, *Friedrich Riedesel, the German Camp on the River Flats*

The Americans were becoming bolder. There was gunfire every night, usually American sharpshooters targeting British pickets. Sometime after two o'clock in the morning the Hessen-Hanau outpost at the third bridge on the river flat was attacked by an American patrol that appeared to be three times as strong. The German troops were driven back to the officers' quarters with two wounded and one taken prisoner. Quiet fell again after the Americans made off with their prisoner. The Germans consoled themselves with the report that seven of the Americans had been wounded in the action. But of course no one could verify the claim.[121]

5:30 AM, *Ebenezer Wild, No Man's Land*

Ebenezer Wild was a Massachusetts man. He had enlisted at the rank of corporal and had seen action at Bunker Hill and Ticonderoga. Now, at barely nineteen years of age, he was already a sergeant in Captain Hancock's company of the 1st Massachusetts, one of the regiments in General Glover's brigade.

Wild's regiment had been here for two weeks. They had camped first just east of Fort Neilson at the apex of the American line. Now they were camped close to Nixon's brigade overlooking the Hudson River. It was becoming part of the routine for American scouting parties to disappear into the woods in the early morning hours and come back a few hours later with a new batch of prisoners. Today it was at last Ebenezer's turn to be part of one of these detachments from Glover's brigade.

The late quarter moon had come up just before midnight, but it gave little light in the nighttime fog. The scouting party had left camp at one o'clock, but they were unable to do much until dawn approached and the sky began to lighten. They crept forward through the soggy darkness, the spongy wet forest litter underfoot compressing with soft squishes rather than the snap and crackle of drier days. One of the advantages of wet conditions was that it had allowed them to sneak almost silently to within a quarter mile of the German pickets. There they had stopped and waited for the first glow of daylight to penetrate the dripping forest canopy.

The false dawn revealed the profiles of German pickets ahead, men spaced close enough to each other to stay in contact through the night, men shifting their weight silently from left to right to keep off the cold, stiffness, and boredom of sentry duty. The Americans rushed at them as quietly as they could. What the startled pickets saw were black phantoms flying silently at them out of the dark. One sentry fired, then the others followed. The Americans stopped and fired too. The noise exploded the silence of the sleeping camp and flashed on for two or three minutes. The German pickets had fired wildly when surprised, but the Americans had seized the advantage and taken deadly aim at the silhouettes. Eight of the Germans were dead or wounded. One, a German officer, was captured. The Americans gathered up what equipment they could carry and fell back with their prisoner as silently as they had come, leaving an unnerved German line behind them. On the way back, four men of the detachment disappeared. All of them were recent immigrants and a rumor quickly spread among Ebenezer and his friends that they might have gone over to the enemy.[122]

10:00 AM, Horatio Gates, American Headquarters on Bemis Heights

Gates announced to his officers that the American Army had grown by three thousand in the last three days.[123] The core of Lincoln's new command was made up of Paterson's, Nixon's, and Glover's brigades, which had been present since before the battle of the nineteenth. To these Gates had added Warner's brigade of Massachusetts militia regiments and Wolcott's much smaller militia brigade from Connecticut, units of which had been coming in during recent days. Lincoln also took over the two cavalry units, which had mostly been performing messenger duty. One of these, Hyde's Connecticut Light Horse, he had brought with him, and continued to use mainly for security and courier service.[124] His orders for the day again focused mainly on where the newly arriving units would be stationed.

The Oneidas brought in another twenty-seven British and German regulars, along with two Loyalists. The latter got their usual attention and abuse, much to the amusement of the American soldiers.[125] The soldiers' fascination with the Oneida Indians and their almost daily entertainments at the expense of hapless Loyalist prisoners was turning dark. Some of the soldiers were now mocking the Indians and Gates knew that for the sake of morale he had to put an end to it.

Gates still kept for himself the units of the left wing that had once been under Arnold's command, but he had still not formally relieved Arnold. Poor's and Learned's brigades were now supported by Ten Broeck's brigade of Albany County militiamen. Arnold still sulked in his hut next to Neilson's house, his pass to Philadelphia unused.

Gates sent a letter to Burgoyne, along with a list of prisoners currently in American hands as a result of the action on the nineteenth. He mentioned that there were about thirty more in the American hospital and that Dr. Potts would provide a list of their names. Gates then mentioned twenty-seven British and German prisoners taken before the nineteenth, along with the late Lieutenant Colonel Baum's servant and his wife, who had taken baggage to prisoners captured at Bennington. Gates went on to lament that despite all efforts to save the young officer's life, Ensign Phillips had died of his wounds last Sunday morning.

Dr. Potts and Dr. Wood on the British side had been exchanging messages on the care of the wounded. Gates inquired about Burgoyne's sentiments in that regard. He asked Burgoyne for a list of the American prisoners taken on the nineteenth, if it would not be too much trouble. He invited Burgoyne to send over clothing, money, and anything else he thought his imprisoned officers might need. To this general accommodation he specifically added an invitation to the wife of one of the British officers. Finally, Gates sent back General Fraser's servant and the two horses Burgoyne had lent to the Americans he had sent over back on Tuesday the sixteenth. It was all very civilized. Amid death and despair both men thought it important to keep a tidy accounting of such things and to be polite about it.[126]

12:00 Noon, John Burgoyne, British Headquarters

Two American drummers approached some German pickets with a flag of truce. Von Geismar was sent to meet them. They handed him the letter from General Gates addressed to General Burgoyne. They also passed along a packet of letters to other officers from men now held prisoner, mostly officers who had been captured on August 16.[127] The truce party also returned the carts and horses that the British had used to send baggage to the captives. No general wanted to be indebted to his opponent.

Colonel Baum's servant also came back in the exchange. From him Burgoyne learned that the men captured at Bennington were now being held in Massachusetts. The officers were still in Springfield, but the rest had been sent to Boston. All of them were sheltered and well fed, according to what the man said.[128]

The general quartermaster and captain of engineers for the Brunswick infantry, Captain Gerlach, was sent with a small party of provincials across the floating bridge to scout the American lines from that side of the river. But even with the help of the local Loyalists in his party Gerlach was unable to discover much that was not already known. They found the Americans there drawn up in two lines. To the south, below Bemis Heights, the Americans were found to have constructed their own bridge of boats across the Hudson. Gerlach saw only a few small parties of Americans and houses occupied by pacifist Quakers before he rushed his patrol back across the British bridge to safety.[129]

Three men arrived from Albany with good news. General Howe had defeated Washington in a battle near Philadelphia, a place called Brandywine. The men said that morale had declined in the American Army in the wake of Washington's loss. Perhaps now Clinton or even Howe himself would make good on their promise to push up the Hudson and help Burgoyne's forces.[130]

Burgoyne ordered most of the regiments to construct more new defensive trenches and ramparts a little ahead of their present positions. Men were sent even farther forward with axes to clear away trees and brush so that the army would have clear lines of fire in case of attack. Burgoyne was particularly concerned about the possibility of a night attack and wanted his regiments to have ease of movement were one to occur. From this day forward the army would be protected by logs, trenches, and earthen mounds. Even the bateaux men, sailors not soldiers, were pressed into service. The men were required to drill daily so that they could be used as replacements in the infantry companies. Small artillery pieces were put on some of the bateaux, and rafts were constructed to carry larger ones if that became necessary.[131]

1:00 PM, *William Wilkinson, British Headquarters*

Lieutenant William Wilkinson was an engineer who had been initially assigned to the badly wounded 62nd Foot. In August he had been reassigned to act as an assistant engineer under Lieutenant William Twiss, the commanding engineer. Twiss was responsible for bridge repairs, the bridge of boats, and the designs of fortifications that the British and German troops were now building all along the line that extended from the Hudson to just past Freeman's farm. Twiss had lost one engineer when the man was assigned to remain at Fort Ticonderoga; another was captured at Bennington. The latter loss deprived Twiss of the man he had depended on to draft reliable maps, and to replace him he needed a draftsman having the same talents. Lieutenant Wilkinson was perfect for the job.

Wilkinson was a twenty-one-year-old Irishman from Meath. He had the mapping skills Twiss was looking for, and Burgoyne had been easily persuaded that his transfer was a good idea. As the days following the battle of September 19 stretched out and the army settled into a defensive posture Wilkinson had more and more time to move around the British and German camps, sketching positions from a series of vantage points. He found that he could draw fortifications and place units accurately from each of the several vantage points, but he could not as easily map the vantage points relative to each other on the broader landscape. He lacked both the surveying equipment and the staff to accurately map the bigger picture, but he did the best he could with what he had. The Americans had no one like him (Figure 3.6).

Burgoyne's aide, Sir Francis Clerke, made similar good use of his spare time. One day he made his way across the new bridge of boats to the east

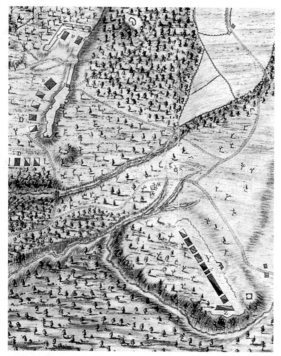

Figure 3.6 Detail from the Wilkinson 1777 map (south is up) showing the Balcarres Redoubt on the upper left and the Breymann Redoubt on the lower right. Courtesy of the Library of Congress.

bank of the Hudson. There he had an excellent view of the army's positions on the river flats as well as the emplacements of the Great Redoubt on the bluffs above. What Wilkinson saw and drew as a cartographer, Clerke saw and sketched as a landscape artist. Neither man knew that his work would illuminate a singular moment in history. Neither knew that one of them would survive the battle they were sure was coming while the other would not.[132]

4:00 PM, Benedict Arnold, Neilson's House

Varick and Livingston both wrote to Philip Schuyler. The dispute between Arnold and Gates was still at a boil. An antagonism had also grown up between Livingston and a Major Chester, and this added to the atmosphere of animosity. By now it was obvious to all from side conversations that Livingston's departure was a precondition for any rapprochement between Gates and Arnold. But that this could happen was a false hope. The dispute between Gates and Arnold was not the result of some petty dispute between a couple of junior officers. It could not be solved by simply sending away a subordinate or two. Arnold would not agree to send Livingston away, even though Livingston was ready to leave on Friday. Varick thought that if there were no likelihood of battle by Saturday or Sunday he would go to Albany as well. Varick and Livingston were both convinced that if Gates had listened to Arnold on the nineteenth they would have seen a British retreat by now.[133] Neither man had much interest in staying. They were still in camp only because they were devoted to Arnold and Arnold stubbornly refused to leave.

FRIDAY, SEPTEMBER 26, 1777

8:00 AM, John Burgoyne, British Headquarters

Burgoyne continued to busy himself with the management of his defenses and the well-being of his troops. He buried himself in minutia. His orders for the day reflected his concern—and his increasing focus on trivia.

Burgoyne fretted over the rising stench of the dead now lying in and around their expanding camp. Many of the bodies that had not been buried deeply enough were now exposed because of the rain. It had been either impossible to dig deeply enough in the heavy clay soil or difficult to keep bodies covered where the soil was too sandy to remain in place when it rained. He fretted when a party of Indians came in with two scalps and an American prisoner half dead from fright. The Indians had managed to slip past the rear of the American camp. It was clear that Gates was making political hay in the Albany press over the conduct of Burgoyne's Indian allies, and this was not helping. Burgoyne fretted more when a report circulated that Ticonderoga had been taken by the Americans. The report was not generally believed, but just the possibility that it might be true eroded morale. Burgoyne fretted again when more men were captured while foraging. He issued yet another order forbidding foraging by small unprotected parties, but it was like trying to keep control over rambunctious children. The attrition resulting from careless foraging and desertion was beginning to look like the early stages of an epidemic.[134]

Reports came in that an American rifleman and his Indian allies had captured three German soldiers and two sailors early in the day. Around noon the they would kill and scalp another man and capture one of the Loyalists. All told, Burgoyne's army would lose twenty more captured by the end of the day.[135]

10:00 AM, *Horatio Gates, American Headquarters on Bemis Heights*

Gates was especially careful in writing up his orders for the day. He wanted his officers and men to be fully aware of the praise they deserved. Just as important, a copy of his carefully worded statement was being sent to the Albany press as soon as it was read out at the daily briefing. With any luck it would be widely available in print in a day or two. He was again careful to make no mention of Benedict Arnold.

Both sides were claiming victory on the nineteenth, but the Americans were deriving more benefit than Burgoyne was from the good press. Regiments of fresh militia were still making their way toward Bemis Heights. Militiamen from the Albany regiments were still arriving in especially large numbers.[136] Where to post them he left to a deputy quartermaster general. Fresh supplies were also coming in as fast as Gates's staff could accommodate them. These were the kinds of problems that Gates relished.

The resourceful Oneidas brought in eleven more captured British regulars and two scalps taken from men they had killed. Among the prisoners had been an officer to whom the Indians had offered quarter. The man had refused it and had been promptly killed. His men had then watched the Indians scalp the officer. The shaken prisoners were delivered along with the scalps to headquarters.[137]

2:00 PM, *Henry Brockholst Livingston, the Neilson House on Bemis Heights*

Henry Brockholst Livingston and Richard Varick were working hard to persuade Arnold to do what he was already doing. Arnold had requested and received a pass from Gates to travel to Philadelphia and place himself under Washington's command, but now, days later, he was still in camp. Livingston and Varick had made a show of preparing to return to service under Philip Schuyler in Albany, but they were still in camp as well.

On Wednesday the two aides had helped orchestrate General Poor's effort to persuade Gates to keep Arnold, circulating Poor's petition among the senior officers. Most of them agreed and signed the petition. It was not in Lincoln's interest to sign because he and Arnold were both major generals and Lincoln was not about to give up command of the right division. That left the brigadier generals—Poor, Learned, Paterson, Nixon, and Glover—supporting the idea. This was a bigger consensus than they had been able to muster a few days ago.

A junior officer had made his own attempt to bring about reconciliation, without result. It seemed clear to most that Arnold would have to make the first gesture if Gates were to be persuaded. Getting rid of the principal aides whose loyalties were with Philip Schuyler, Livingston and Varick, might suffice. The junior officer, Major Chester, thought so. He approached James Wilkinson to see if he thought the attempt might work. Livingston's reaction was, of course, that Chester was an impertinent pedant. He made sure that Arnold heard about Chester's proposal, and Arnold responded just as Livingston hoped and expected. "My judgment has never been influenced by any man, and I will not sacrifice a friend to please the face of clay," his new epithet for Gates.[138]

But Livingston knew that his presence was a growing problem for Arnold, and he decided to leave the next day, Saturday the twenty-seventh. Livingston then wrote to Philip Schuyler to tell him that Arnold had been persuaded to remain with the army, even though Gates had not yet been persuaded to employ him again.

> It gives me pleasure to assure you that General Arnold intends to stay. When the general officers found him determined to go, they thought it necessary to take some measures to induce him to continue with the army. They have accordingly wrote him a letter (signed by all but Lincoln), requesting him not to quit the service at this critical time. He has consented, though no accommodation has taken place.[139]

4:00 PM, Alexander Scammell, the American Camp on Bemis Heights

Colonel Alexander Scammell of the 3rd New Hampshire Continentals wrote to his friend Jonathan Chadbourn, giving his return address as "Camp Now or Never." He described the battle of the nineteenth in as much detail as he could remember and fit on the single sheet of paper he had available at the moment. Now, a week after the battle, Scammell was as optimistic as anyone else in the American encampment. More men and supplies were arriving daily. It was clear that Burgoyne was beyond any hope of receiving either kind of fresh support. Scammell scribbled a second quick postscript to his friend.

> We expect another severe Battle every Hour. Within two miles of the enemy, and they're drove to Desperation. Not more than ¼ of our army engaged. Had Gen¹ Gates known their Disposition he would have ordered out great part of Army, which probably would have totally defeated Burgoyne.[140]

SATURDAY, SEPTEMBER 27, 1777

8:00 AM, John Glover, the American Camp on Bemis Heights

It was a cool day. Autumn had clearly arrived, and the maple trees were turning scarlet.[141] Brigadier General John Glover now commanded a brigade of four Massachusetts regiments of Continental regulars and three New York militia battalions. Because his brigade had been moved to a new posting on the right wing of the army he now found himself in a division under the command of Major General Benjamin Lincoln.

Like many American officers, Glover came from modest beginnings and found himself caught up in the long series of events that had gradually led the colonies into this revolution. He had been born in Salem, Massachusetts, nearly forty-five years ago, and seemed destined for a life as a merchant and shipowner. He had become a militia officer in the early months of fighting. Washington had chartered Glover's schooner *Hannah* as the first of the privateers that eventually became the United States Navy. The men of his regiment were almost all fishermen, and in the early battles on Long Island and Manhattan they used their amphibious skills to extricate the army more than once. Last winter, just before their enlistments expired and the regiment was disbanded, they had ferried Washington across the Delaware for the successful surprise attack on Trenton.

Glover had gone home to tend his sick wife after that. Congress had awarded him a promotion to brigadier general in February, but he had declined it. He relented when Washington pleaded with him to return, and now here he was, a brigade commander. Glover assessed the condition of the army. The current count of casualties from the battle on September

19 was sobering, but it was good news compared to what he was learning about Burgoyne's losses. The count now stood at 81 American officers and men killed that day and 202 wounded. Twenty Americans had been taken prisoner, seven of whom were wounded. Many of the wounded had since died, and a few more had been killed in skirmishing, bringing the total to 303. There had been two flags of truce that he knew about, and under one of them Glover had been told that Burgoyne had lost 746 killed and wounded in the battle. Worse for Burgoyne was the high proportion of officers among them, evidence of the skill of Morgan's riflemen, Glover thought. Glover and his fellow officers were sure that this number actually underestimated Burgoyne's losses, just as the British officers were convinced that the Americans had lost many more than they were admitting.[142]

9:00 AM, John Burgoyne, British Headquarters

According to his commissaries, Burgoyne's expedition had provisions remaining for only nineteen days. There was no word from General Clinton. It was a week since Burgoyne had received the cipher from Clinton, days since he had sent back a series of messengers in disguise. It seemed unlikely that they had all been caught and hanged by the Americans, and just as unlikely that they had all managed to get through. Enough time had passed. Surely one or two of the men had reached Clinton. By now Clinton might even be pushing up the Hudson toward Albany. Who could say?

Fortunately, Burgoyne had distractions to lighten his evenings. The wife of one of the commissaries was a pretty and obliging companion to Burgoyne.[143] Various officers were ever ready to indulge Burgoyne's love of song, wine, and cards. He still had an ample supply of drink, especially champagne; the trash pits around his headquarters were starting to fill up with empty bottles.[144] But morning always brought a return to reality. In no more than two or three weeks it would surely be do or die.

Burgoyne continued to busy himself with the minutia of managing a military encampment. The horses needed forage and his biggest task for the day still was to keep soldiers from foraging on their own, where they might be shot, captured, or lured into desertion. A major foraging party was organized, along with a covering escort to protect both men and horses. Provisions were distributed, bakers assigned, and vacancies filled. Leading his list of things to do was the search for the owner of an errant cask of wine. Burgoyne handed off his orders for the day.

He wrote on, assigning Canadian officers, moving them up the chain of command to fill gaps left by casualties. He took great pains to detail the way in which foraging would be undertaken. There had to be a covering force of 150 men, properly officered and committed to a rigid schedule if they were to pull it off without losing more to capture and desertion. Satisfied that he had done as much as he could to provide forage for the animals, Burgoyne finished with an order that two days' provisions be issued to every man on Sunday morning. Tuesday would be the last day of September and he would decide then about further provisioning.

Burgoyne also answered Gates's letter sent two days ago. He provided a list of thirty American prisoners now in his hands, thirteen of whom were wounded and in the British hospital. There were three officers, including Captain Van Swearingen from Morgan's corps. He went on to mention the exchanges between Drs. Potts and Wood, and he endorsed their proposal that physicians from each side be allowed to pass through the lines and visit wounded men after an action. Burgoyne then thanked Gates for sending back the servant and his wife. He did not mention the returned horses, mounts lent by Burgoyne to the two ailing American officers back on the sixteenth of the month. With forage in short supply Burgoyne might have preferred not to have them back. Like Gates's letter, this one was very civil.[145]

2:00 PM, Horatio Gates, American Headquarters on Bemis Heights

Arnold was still in camp, and Gates was still mostly ignoring him. Gates administered the occasional barb to try to get the man moving toward Philadelphia. A payment of fifty dollars that Arnold had authorized was disputed; the predictably angry retort came back from Arnold in writing. Gates replied in kind, pointing out that although the amount was small the expenditure had been against established policy. Arnold was unmoved. He stayed, nursing his humiliation.[146]

3:00 PM, Ludwig Gräfe, the American Lines on Bemis Heights

Gates had decided that he would agree to send Dr. Potts over to check on the American wounded. Burgoyne would in turn send over his Dr. Wood to look at the British and German wounded. Gates was more concerned about American officers currently held as prisoners by the British than he was with Arnold. Ethan Allen was being held somewhere; Gates was not sure where. Captain Van Swearingen and two other officers taken on the nineteenth were in Burgoyne's hands. Gates wondered if he might find a way to exchange them for some of the German officers who had been captured at Bennington. Gone was Gates's earlier concern that there was no cartel in effect for the exchange of prisoners. Eleven days ago he had rebuked Burgoyne for presuming to exchange prisoners, but things had changed. Gone too was Gates's earlier belief that Washington would have to negotiate such an exchange as commander in chief. Gates could and would make his own exchange arrangements with Burgoyne.

Gates consulted with his generals. A young cornet named Ludwig Gräfe was selected from the German officers captured at Bennington and brought to Bemis Heights for the purpose of communicating with Burgoyne. Gates gave Cornet Gräfe a pass to cross over to the British camp and remain for up to five days, in exchange for Gräfe's promise as a German officer to return to the American lines at the end of that time.[147] The young Gräfe eagerly agreed, and he set off with an escort under a flag of truce.

Other former prisoners of the British were already returning. Some of the hundred men rescued from imprisonment at Fort Ticonderoga over a week ago rejoined the army. There was food, clothing, and equipment for all of them, and their arrival boosted spirits throughout the camp. Gates issued orders for everyone to cook three days' provisions and be ready to march at a moment's notice.[148]

6:00 PM, John Burgoyne, British Headquarters

For days Burgoyne's officers had been promoting the rumor that General Howe had decisively beaten Washington in Pennsylvania. Today the rumor was confirmed by another party of Loyalist refugees from Albany, but it was still widely disbelieved in the ranks.[149]

Other good news was that the British pickets had turned the tables on the Americans for a change. A few American soldiers were caught by British pickets while foraging for potatoes in no man's land. It was small satisfaction, and the score in this game still favored the Americans, but Burgoyne took what good news he could get.[150]

Burgoyne was heartened by the news of Howe's victory, but sobered by the continuing silence from Clinton. He sent yet another messenger to Clinton, the fifth in a week, again in disguise, still not knowing if any of the previous ones had got through. This time the officer sent was

Captain Thomas Scott of the 24th Regiment. Scott knew that he would be hanged as a spy if he were caught, of course, but the growing desperation of Burgoyne's situation made the risk worth taking. He carried a brief letter from Burgoyne:

> *Sir, Captain Scott of the 24th regiment is entrusted with the fullest dispatches and communications necessary to be known by your Excellency. He is an officer of great merit and entitled to the fullest confidence. I request you to return your orders by triplicates by different routes, reckoning that your own cipher subsists. I am etc. J. Burgoyne.*

The urgency of Burgoyne's tone increased with every new message. This time, added to the desperation of his tone was the request for three separate replies and a sly request that they take the form of orders. Burgoyne was trying to put himself under Henry Clinton's command. There it was in writing. If his friend took the bait and the expedition ended in disaster, Burgoyne would have someone to at least share the blame. Scott prepared to leave at midnight.

Clinton, the Loyalists had said, would surely march north soon. But, they added, a letter Clinton had sent to Burgoyne had been intercepted. The probable fate of the messenger did not have to be discussed. They added that there were American forces in the mountains near the middle course of the Hudson whose aim it was to impede Clinton any way they could. These were the same stalling tactics that had delayed for weeks Burgoyne's efforts to get his army from Skenesborough to its present location. There were also reports that the Americans had retaken Skenesborough, Hubbardton, and Ticonderoga, bits of bad news that the rank-and-file soldiers were inclined to believe. As dark settled on the army, most of what was left of Burgoyne's Indian allies quietly left camp and disappeared into the northern woods.[151]

7:00 PM, *Ludwig Gräfe, the German Camp*

In the evening some Americans moved up river in bateaux, tempting them, annoying them, embarrassing them just a little. The Hessen-Hanau and 47th Regiments rechecked their defenses along the river and the bateaux bridge. Burgoyne's pickets later brought in three American captives, all of whom claimed to be officers. This assertion brought snorts of derision from the junior officers and soldiers who were within earshot. Not one of them was in anything like a uniform.[152]

A bit later a ghost came up the river road through the fog, striding along between a drummer and an American officer carrying a white flag of truce. The young Ludwig Gräfe had been in Baum's dragoon regiment. No one in camp had seen him since the disaster at Bennington a month and a half earlier. Yet now here he was, healthy, well fed, and delighted to be chatting in German with the Hessen-Hanau men at their outpost near the third bridge. As night fell the paroled young officer bedded down with the German troops. In the morning he would go to Burgoyne's headquarters, where he would put Gates's exchange proposals before the British commander.

8:00 PM, *John Glover, the American Camp on Bemis Heights*

General Glover was pleased that the Americans had taken another thirty prisoners since the battle and that a similar number of deserters had come in. It was a week since his men had seen any real action and he decided that it was time to get a little exercise. His scouts had detected a party of about sixty British or German pickets about a half mile to the north on the river road. Glover proposed to Gates that he send a hundred men from his brigade and another two hundred to cover them in an attempt to capture the enemy pickets. Gates had agreed. It was the first time such a large cutting-out party had been sent out, and Glover was eager for it to succeed. So anxious was he that he went along himself, not something Gates would have sanctioned had he known of it. The sun had set two hours ago. There was no moon, and there would not be until nearly three hours after midnight. Even then it would be only a faint sliver. They would have to move carefully through the dark woods, and they would probably not find their quarry until the gray false dawn brightened enough to show them the way.[153]

SUNDAY, SEPTEMBER 28, 1777

5:30 AM, *John Glover, No Man's Land*

The hours before dawn were dark and foggy, but the ground was not wet enough to cover the sound of their movements. The waning crescent moon provided almost no light at all through the thick fog. Glover's detachment found it hard to move, and they did not find any pickets to seize until the twilight of morning. The men picked their way forward, trying to step without crackling the dry autumn leaves underfoot. They were out beyond the line of two hundred men that was covering them. It had been a long night. There were no fires, no cover, not even conversation out here in no man's land on the river flats.

The scouts had been right. There were dozens of them, but they were more than just a line of pickets. This was a German outpost with gear and supplies. It was more than Glover had bargained for, but he knew that surprise is always a huge advantage. No soldier can stay at the peak of readiness for hours on end. Even a wide-awake sentry needs time to react to an attack. It began all at once at Glover's signal. The Americans rushed the outpost, ducking the wildly inaccurate fire of the sentries, stopping to fire their own muskets, and rushing on. The outpost was quickly abandoned as the enemy soldiers sprinted back toward their own lines, most of them with empty guns or no guns at all.

In the end the detachment found that they had killed three and wounded many more as they drove them back into their lines. The Americans picked up packs, blankets, guns, and a sword that had been left behind. Glover was pleased that he had lost not a man. The smiling Continentals from Massachusetts lugged their prizes back to the American lines, where the officers would auction them off for revolutionary paper scrip that now seemed not quite as worthless as it did yesterday.[154]

7:00 AM, *Ludwig Gräfe, the German Lines*

Cornet Gräfe had passed through the lines safely the night before. Now he reported to Riedesel and Burgoyne that most of the men who had been captured at Bennington were in Massachusetts. But those were just the healthy ones. The officers and men who had been wounded were still being tended to in Bennington. Their quarters there were confining, but they had no reason to complain about the food. Burgoyne and everyone around him had to know that the fare in Bennington was better than what the men were currently getting here in camp. Gräfe said the captive officers were free to roam about, and it was clear from his enthusiasm that he and many of his comrades were increasingly taken with life in America.[155]

Gräfe handed Burgoyne the letter from Gates. Gates was proposing that Colonel Ethan Allen be exchanged for two officers the Americans were holding in Bennington now that their wounds were healing. Allen was a prize captive, but as it happened he was being held in New York City and not available for exchange. Burgoyne and Riedesel decided to take the days left on Gräfe's pass to think about how to respond.[156]

It was still foggy. Gräfe had been able to see little the previous evening, and he would probably see little more on his return trip to American lines. He was unable to answer most of the generals' probing questions about the size and disposition of the American Army. But he was able to clarify what had happened at Ticonderoga on the eighteenth of the month. The Americans had freed all of the American prisoners held outside Ticonderoga but they had not been able to recapture the fort. Although the attack had been repulsed, many men of the 53rd Regiment had been captured by the Americans, and dozens of bateaux had been lost. It was hard to find a way to turn this into good news. A hundred freed American prisoners Powell no longer had to feed? Well, that was one way to make this into good news. The survival of a reduced garrison that could neither send forward supplies nor contribute men to the march on Albany? That was the news as Burgoyne heard it, and it did not seem like good news at all. Burgoyne had not yet issued his orders for the day. Now at least he had something to report, even if it was little more than an object lesson for his officers and men.

Foraging had been forbidden for days. There was no grass left and some of the horses were dying for lack of it. Burgoyne ordered that a large armed detachment be sent out behind the British lines to forage in the fog. The horses needed twenty tons of the stuff a day. Even a thousand foragers would need to carry back forty pounds every day if the horses were to be fed only their basic needs.

A staff officer took 250 men to protect the foragers. They foraged on the height above Dovegat, well to the rear, but everyone knew that American scouting parties were everywhere. Another 250 soldiers moved north along the river road below them, just in case they were needed. This detachment kept in communication with the main camp. They expected every minute to be attacked but they were not. They expected to be recalled to camp by the prearranged signal of three cannon shots if the Americans attacked from a different direction, but they were not. In the end they brought in some hay for the starving horses. But there were many hundreds of horses, and they would be hungry again soon.[157]

8:00 AM, Horatio Gates, American Headquarters

Two miles away to the southwest Horatio Gates issued his own orders for the day. They were typical of Gates, Gates the adjutant, Gates the fussy detail man, Gates the organizer. He ended with a reward for a missing horse. Men's lives could be spent with a word or two to a subordinate, but an officer's missing horse, now that was something that demanded the full attention of a commander.

At ten in the morning the camp was alarmed by a discharge of cannon in the British camp. The men were sent to their posts and remained there all day.[158] Meanwhile Gates sent another letter to Arnold, an answer to Arnold's peevish note on Saturday. Gates managed to make his letter just as peevish.

The shortage of supplies on the British side was confirmed for Gates by two prisoners brought in by an Oneida scouting party. They said that provisions were very short in Burgoyne's army, and it occurred to Gates and his officers that the British pickets seemed almost eager to be captured. If it was so easy to snatch Burgoyne's pickets, why not oblige them? The Americans sent out another large party to sweep up as many advanced British pickets as possible, but this time they found that the British had taken steps to stop the bleeding. The pickets were reinforced and ready when the Americans came through the woods and there was a sharp firefight. The Americans returned to camp without prisoners, having lost one man killed and three or four wounded.[159]

12:00 Noon, Alexander Campbell, British Headquarters

Around noon the Americans to the south along the road and across the Hudson began a game of harassing the German pickets. They did no damage, but they made their point, as they had so often on previous days. Burgoyne responded by ordering hundreds more trees felled and their branches sharpened into abatis ahead of the main British and German lines. The order had the additional benefit of getting the soldiers to focus on productive labor instead of their deteriorating fortunes.

It was difficult for anyone to imagine that the Americans could attack through the bristling hedge of timber. But it was equally difficult for anyone to imagine why the Americans would bother to try such an attack. The obvious went unspoken. If Gräfe and wounded dragoons in Bennington were happy and well fed, then so were the Americans. The American Army was clearly well supplied and probably growing. Meanwhile Burgoyne's army was shrinking and receiving no supplies at all. If this contest was settling into a waiting game, the Americans had a decided advantage.

Burgoyne readied a sixth disguised messenger to Clinton, not knowing if the first five had got or would ever get through. The urgency of the message increased yet again. The officer sent was Captain Alexander Campbell of the decimated 62nd Regiment. Like Scott and every man who went south before him, Campbell knew that he could be hanged as a spy if caught.

> *The bearer, Captain Campbell, an officer of great merit and full confidence, is charged with an exact duplicate of my message to your Excellency dispatched yesterday by another officer. I request the most speedy answer by triplicates. Believe me, &c. J. Burgoyne.*[160]

The note was nothing more than a letter of introduction to establish Campbell's authenticity. Campbell would relay the rest of the message orally. During the afternoon Burgoyne briefed Campbell on what he should say to Clinton. "My whole army does not exceed 5000 men. The consequence of the battle on the nineteenth was the loss of between five and six hundred men. The enemy is within a mile and a half of me. I do not know their certain numbers, but I believe them to be twelve or fourteen thousand men. There are besides a considerable body in my rear. I wish to receive his orders whether I should attack or retreat to the lakes."

Burgoyne had already tried to subordinate himself to Clinton in the note Scott had carried south yesterday. Burgoyne was independent of Clinton, not under his command. They were to cooperate, yes, but now Burgoyne was again implicitly trying to put himself under Clinton's orders.

> I have but provisions to the twentieth of the month and I would not have given up my communications with Ticonderoga had I not expected a cooperating army at Albany. I wish to know General Clinton's positive answer as soon as possible, whether I can open a communication with Albany when I should be there, and when there keep my communication with New York. If I do not hear from General Clinton by the fifteenth instant I shall retire.[161]

The truth was that at the current rate of consumption his army would be out of provisions by the eighteenth of October. He could stretch what was left by going to half rations, but even that would not suffice for long.

That night Campbell left across the bridge of boats and disappeared. At nine o'clock Burgoyne could hear new firing around the advanced outpost of Hessen-Hanau at the third bridge. The men had to fall back. Riedesel was weary of the constant harassment of this forward position. It was too close to the Americans and too vulnerable to random attacks. He ordered the sergeant and fifteen Hessen-Hanau men to reposition the post a hundred paces closer to their main camp.[162]

9:00 PM, *Ebenezer Wild, No Man's Land*

It was the dark of the moon. Ebenezer Wild was out again, this time to help man the defensive line in front of the camp. It had been a long and confusing day, the kind of day that soldiers come to expect when action is at hand but not quite ready to commence. About eight in the morning he had heard a cannon fired in the enemy camp. Two or three hours later an alarm had been raised and they had all rushed to their places in the defensive line. Tents were struck, equipment was loaded, and everything was readied for an expected attack. And once again it did not come. Ebenezer and his platoon had been ready with their muskets loaded until two in the afternoon, then they walked back to camp, unloaded everything, and pitched their tents all over again. They cooked all the provisions they had, drew another day's allowance of pork and hard bread, just in case an attack came. Now it was well past dark. Another alarm sounded and they were all once again in their defensive lines, waiting for an attack.

This time the alarm was the result of real action. American scouting parties were now out every night, thirty or forty men in each. It was becoming so routine, and Burgoyne was so reluctant to do the same, that the principal danger was that the scouts would run into each other and mistake friend for enemy. A skirmish in the dark between an American scouting party and some errant British soldiers had alarmed the whole army. Drums rolled and the whole American Army turned out to man the lines in the moonless dark. But only a fool would attack at this hour, and Burgoyne was no fool. The two armies did what armies do most of the time. They waited.[163]

MONDAY, SEPTEMBER 29, 1777

8:00 AM, *Ebenezer Wild, the American Lines*

The clumsy skirmish that had led to the alarm last night had got three men of the 1st Massachusetts wounded. A scouting party of thirty-four officers and men from Ebenezer's regiment had spent the night in no man's land, most of it in inky darkness, with no moon at all, and now they were coming back into camp. They had been out since midnight. They were exhausted and took to their tents.

10:00 AM, *Burgoyne, the British Lines*

About a thousand men were busy all across the front of the British and German lines felling trees toward the American line and sharpening their branches.[164] Foraging was still a problem. Burgoyne had to once again issue strict orders forbidding any soldier to go beyond the advanced guards to forage or on any other pretext. He was worried for their safety, but there was a darker reason. Some men did not come back and there was no evidence that they had been captured unwillingly. The desertions were sapping the morale of those still in camp.

2:00 PM, *Daniel Morgan, No Man's Land*

The hemorrhaging of British strength resumed. A party of Morgan's riflemen, bored with the interminable wait, prowled no man's land looking for unwary Brunswickers. They found and captured five of them, along with an American Loyalist. In addition to these, a German sergeant, a corporal, and a drummer had deserted to the Americans, bringing horses with them. The sergeant told American interrogators that an entire company of Brunswickers was ready to defect, but they had been found out and prevented from deserting.[165]

4:00 PM, *John Glover, the American Lines*

From the deserters' reports and Glover's own calculations, it appeared that Burgoyne had provisions left for about twenty days. This too was not bad news, and the American troops seemed to be in good spirits. More units were coming in every day. There were now at least ten thousand men in camp, or maybe a thousand more than that. Things were changing so rapidly that he could not keep an accurate tally.[166]

10:00 PM, *Ebenezer Wild, No Man's Land*

It was the dark of the moon for the second night. Tonight it was again Ebenezer Wild's turn to go out on a scout. He was one of forty-six men from his regiment sent out—a colonel, two lieutenants, and another sergeant in addition to Ebenezer also being among them. They left in the fog before midnight with provisions for three days. They were not alone. Other regiments sent detachments as well, over a hundred men just from Glover's brigade. They moved northwest from the American lines, reaching the thin line of American advanced pickets and stopping there for the night. The fog lifted and the sky filled with a dazzling display of stars made brighter by the near absence of a moon. What there was of it did not rise until almost three in the morning. The men built big fires to keep themselves warm and to annoy the British pickets that they assumed were shivering in the dark somewhere to the north, but within earshot.[167]

One American soldier, separated from his scouting party, lost in the fog between the lines, wandered into the British camp by mistake. When the British sentry challenged him, he paused, realized where he was, and said, "I believe I am wrong and may as well stay where I am." For the British it was another mouth to feed.[168]

TUESDAY, SEPTEMBER 30, 1777

8:00 AM, Ebenezer Wild, No Man's Land

The bonfires had kept them warm through the night, and the men of Ebenezer's scouting detachment were eager to get moving. The problem was that one of the captains had sprained his ankle. Getting him to the rear had taken time, and now at eight o'clock they were finally ready to set out. Saratoga Lake was about eight miles to the west, and if the officers could keep their wits and their footing they could get there by noon.[169] (See Figure 3.7.)

Prisoners and deserters continued to pass by them and move back through the American lines. The American who had blundered into the British camp and had been taken prisoner managed to escape back to American lines with the trickle of British and German deserters.[170]

There was an alarm later in the morning back in camp. Burgoyne was coming at them in three columns again it was said. The 1st Massachusetts detachment was already moving toward Saratoga Lake on its scouting mission, but the men who had been left behind and were still in the American line braced for an attack. The Americans in camp hoped against hope, but once again the attack failed to materialize.[171]

Figure 3.7 Key locations in the actions and decisions of the middle game. SNHP = Saratoga National Historical Park.

9:00 AM, John Burgoyne, British Headquarters

The British sentries reported seeing the bonfires set by the scouts of the 1st Massachusetts; they speculated that the Americans might be preparing to set up a battery on the British right. They also pointed out that the Americans had fired three morning guns rather than the usual two. This prompted the British field officers to conclude that more reinforcements might be arriving on the American side.[172]

An American deserter came into camp and was brought before Burgoyne. The news he provided was not good. Gates's Northern Army was now up to fourteen thousand strong. Fresh militia regiments were still coming in from New England and New York. Even the detachment that had been sent to Ticonderoga was now back with the army. The deserter confirmed the suspicions of Burgoyne's field officers, but Burgoyne was uncertain how much of what the American was saying could be believed. If American strength was growing, the man standing before him must have had powerful personal reasons for deserting. Either that or he was a lunatic.

The deserter had a copy of an Albany newspaper on him. It contained an article based on Gates's press release of Friday the twenty-sixth. For Burgoyne and his staff it made for sobering reading. American propaganda was effective; Gates clearly knew how to use the press.[173]

Burgoyne again turned to the task of finding more food for the vast herd of British and German horses. He sent out another major foraging party, this time covered by two hundred armed men. The foragers could be forgiven for wondering if the guards were more to keep them from deserting than to protect them from the Americans. The party crossed the bridge of boats and foraged on the east side of the Hudson downstream from the bridge. Burgoyne ordered cannons to be positioned along to the west bank so that they could fire across the river on any Americans who might attempt to attack or capture the foragers. It was a worrisome undertaking. The party was too exposed, too far from camp, and too dependent on a frail bridge of boats. But there was no forage left anywhere closer to camp and the horses would be useless or worse if they were not fed better. Burgoyne turned to his written orders for the day.

> All the drivers are to be assembled this evening at their different departments at the time of roll calling, and are to be informed that seven men of those who deserted have been scalped by the enemy's Indians, and that the Indians belonging to our camp are in pursuit of the rest. They are also to be informed that the first deserter taken belonging to them will be hanged up immediately.[174]

Burgoyne could not in fact be sure what had happened to the deserters, of course. Nor could he even be sure that his Indian allies, what was left of them, were in pursuit of anything other than getting home. The threat to hang deserters if they were caught was real enough, but the officers who would have to pass the message along down the line of command had to know that it was mostly bluster.

6:00 PM, Ebenezer Wild, Saratoga Lake

The scouting party from Glover's brigade had been sent on a long loop around the western flank of the British Army to Saratoga to see what was going on in that quarter. Ebenezer and his detachment had reached the east side of Saratoga Lake around noon, as predicted. To reach the village of Saratoga they would have to go around the southern end of the lake and strike north, then northeast, and finally east from there. It could take them all of tomorrow to accomplish that.

They had stopped at Saratoga Lake and settled down to eat some of their provisions. After resting they set off again, scouting the forest around the east and south sides of the lake. Just as it was starting to darken they ran across three men. They turned out to be Loyalists. The captain decided to send them back to Gates under guard, and a sergeant and small party of men were detached to make sure they got there.

The rest of the scouting party continued up the west side of the lake past its mouth. It was now eight o'clock, and a dense cold fog began forming in the dark woods. The men found what shelter they could and settled in for the night. The heavy fog blanketed the land and would have blinded the moon had there been any.[175]

8:00 PM, John Burgoyne, the British Camp

The foragers had returned with what seemed like with a good supply of forage. But as much as they had gathered it was only enough to save the situation for another day or two. The need for forage would continue to grow; rations for the horses were cut.[176]

In the evening a courier arrived from Lieutenant Colonel St. Leger, protected by a party of twenty Mohawks who had come to join Burgoyne's forces. Burgoyne was glad to have them. St. Leger said that he would do his best to join Burgoyne by coming south from Ticonderoga over Lake George. Fort George at the southern end of the lake was held by only a single British officer and thirty men, but there was a larger British force on Diamond Island, about halfway down the lake to the north. The little garrison at Fort George could fall back to the island in bateaux if attacked. The courier also had the good news that new Brunswicker recruits had arrived. But the courier went on to explain that Brigadier Powell had ordered that the recruits go no farther than Ticonderoga and to remain there to bolster the garrison. At least Burgoyne had the twenty Mohawks.

If the Americans could threaten Ticonderoga severely enough to have nearly taken it back, they could surely prevent St. Leger from reaching Burgoyne. With the strength he now had, Gates could send another detachment for that purpose whenever he pleased. Given the size of his force it was surprising that he had not bothered to snatch Fort George away from the British already, or for that matter Fort Edward. To Burgoyne it seemed that Gates probably thought it not worth the effort at this stage. It was all very discouraging for Burgoyne.[177]

WEDNESDAY, OCTOBER 1, 1777

6:00 AM, Ebenezer Wild, Saratoga Lake

The new moon rose unnoticed just before sunrise. The weather was fine.[178] The forests of upstate New York were full of color; the crimson sugar maples were the brightest of all. Occasional frosts would soon be followed by incessant freezing, and still the two armies waited mostly in silent antipathy.

The scouting detachment shook off the heavy dew and started off, following Fish Kill from its source at the mouth of Saratoga Lake northeastward toward its lower course to the Hudson at Saratoga. It was October 1, and no matter what astronomers said, everyone with any sense knew that it was already the second month of autumn. The men made their way through the woods, staying away from the main road, knowing they were now well to the rear of the British lines. They went seven miles, coming up on the high ground west of the village. The landscape was empty and quiet, but that was about to change.

9:00 AM, John Burgoyne, British Headquarters

Dispatches came in to Burgoyne from Brigadier General Powell at Ticonderoga. He described the American attack, which had been repulsed after some losses, the Americans retreating over the mountains. This at last provided some detail regarding the events around Ticonderoga that had so energized the American camp days earlier. It was not good news for Burgoyne by any means, but it was not all bad either. Burgoyne announced what he knew with the daily order.

> In consequence of authentic Letters received by the Lieutenant General from Brigadier General Powel at Ticonderoga, and Captain Aubrey of the 47th Regiment commanding at Diamond Island in Lake George. The Army is informed that the Enemy having found means to cross the Mountains between Skenesborough, and Lake

George, and having marched with another Corps from Hubbardtown, a sudden and general Attack was made in the morning of the 18th upon the carrying Place at Lake George, Sugar Hill, Ticonderoga, and Mount Independence.[179]

10:00 AM, Benedict Arnold, the American Camp on Bemis Heights

Benedict Arnold was still in camp and still brooding. He tried another long message to Gates as part of his ongoing letter-writing campaign. Arnold was mortified, filled with self-pity and self-righteous nobility, but unable to quit the scene. He spent the morning penning the new letter to Gates. Arnold warned Gates that if he did not take action against Burgoyne soon the militia would start going home. It had been a mistake to not press their advantage on September 20. It would be another mistake not to do so now. Arnold finished with what was the closest thing to an olive branch he could manage to offer. "I hope you will not impute this hint to a wish to command the army, or to outshine you when I assure you it proceeds from my zeal for the cause of my country in which I expect to rise or fall."[180]

Two more British deserters arrived at the American camp in the morning. They said that provisions were critically scarce in Burgoyne's camp. Bread in particular was almost impossible to find.[181] Everyone in the American camp was beginning to see how this would end. If they simply waited Burgoyne's army would starve before winter set in.

American newspapers were already relishing the view that Burgoyne's situation was hopeless. They were reporting that an advance to Albany was impracticable and that a retreat to Canada was now all but impossible. Everyone knew that Burgoyne was counting on Henry Clinton to send a force upriver from New York City to at least draw off a portion of the Northern Army facing the British advance southward. British messengers were being routinely intercepted and executed as spies. A man named Nathan Palmer was just the latest such unfortunate. Loyalist leaders had tried to intervene in some of these cases. The rebels hanged them anyway.[182]

12:00 Noon, John Hardin, Near Saratoga

Lieutenant Hardin was out with his riflemen again, having mostly recovered from the wound he had suffered on the previous scout. They were scouting to the rear of the British and looking to intercept messengers. Luck was with him again. They intercepted two British officers who were with a party on its way from Ticonderoga to Burgoyne's camp. One of them carried a letter from the hapless Barry St. Leger to Burgoyne. Having retreated all the way from Fort Stanwix to Montreal, St. Leger was now at Ticonderoga, feeling abused and unappreciated. As he had passed through Quebec, Governor Guy Carleton had taken a hundred of his men before sending him on his way. Now he needed guides and more than a little luck to find his way to Burgoyne.

Hardin smiled at the discovery. The British officer and his party would not be reaching Burgoyne's camp. St. Leger was not going to get an answer to his letter. St. Leger and his men would stay shut up in their fort, no use to Burgoyne or anyone else. Gates was going to enjoy this news and the arrival of his new British guests.[183]

1:00 PM, Ebenezer Wild, Saratoga Lake

The two American scouting parties never ran into each other. Hardin and Wild might as well have been in different armies. Ebenezer went with a captain and two men and moved as quietly as they could to within a stone's throw of the barracks on the north side of the village of Saratoga. The captain climbed to the top of a tall tree, but he could see or hear nobody in the village. They found their way back to the rest of the detachment by the middle of the afternoon. They discovered to their delight that the men they had left behind had captured two Loyalist boys and some cows.

The village of Saratoga had been abandoned by Burgoyne's army; every man of it had moved forward to the line of new fortifications between Freeman's farm and the Hudson River. But the still-lucky scouts discovered and caught five Canadians and two Germans who had deserted and were trying to make their way back to Montreal. How they thought they would get there without supplies was a mystery. How they imagined they might avoid being shot or hanged as deserters when they got there was an even bigger one. But life in the Burgoyne expedition had become too hard, and the expected outcome was too bleak for these men. A sergeant and some of the American scouts took them all back to the American lines.[184]

Ebenezer's detachment circled around the village to Schuyler's mills on the south side, still seeing no one. There they discovered that the British had repaired the bridge over Fish Kill, so they set aside their arms and found axes to destroy it again. They did as much damage as they could in the time they had available, then set the ruined bridge on fire. Surely in the end Burgoyne would find himself retreating up this road. Wild thought the Americans would enjoy watching him try to get his artillery across Fish Kill and back into Saratoga when that time came. The scouting party left the bonfire once it was burning well, striking two miles westward before camping for what turned out to be another pleasant starry night. The Americans owned the woods all around Burgoyne's army, and in Wild's case they still had not fired a shot.[185]

2:00 PM, John Burgoyne, British Headquarters

Still no word from Howe or Clinton. It was the middle of autumn and once again the army found itself shrouded in a heavy morning fog. Burgoyne was still requiring the men to stand to arms an hour before dawn every day in case the Americans opened a surprise attack through the thick fog. It was an irrational fear and they all knew it, but it lasted every day until the fog lifted at about nine o'clock. If they could not see twenty yards neither could the Americans, and the thicket of the abatis in front of the line made a stealthy approach by the Americans ludicrously unlikely to happen.

As if to mark the beginning of the month, earlier in the day a heavy hoarfrost had covered everything at first light. The cold penetrated the tents, the damp uniforms, and the men's flesh to their bones. But then, astonishingly, the sun burned off the fog and heated the scarlet landscape to afternoon temperatures that the men remembered experiencing at home only in the heat of late summer. Maples and sumacs were redder than the British uniforms. The Loyalists called it "Indian summer," a reference to the paints the Mohawks wore into battle. It was yet another strange feature of this foreign American landscape, something to add to the descriptions of rattlesnakes, turkeys, hummingbirds, and other exotic Americana in their letters home.

The incidence of sickness increased as time went on. Ague, camp fever, and all the other maladies that afflict men in close quarters came visiting with a vengeance. The doctors said that bad night air was surely the cause of much of it. There were more than seven hundred in the hospital now, the wounded joined by the increasing legion of the sick. There were deaths every day.

Everything was getting more expensive. The amount of money in circulation remained the same in this closed society of soldiers, but the inputs of new supplies had stopped. With the same numbers of shillings and thalers chasing ever smaller quantities of rum, sugar, coffee, and tea, the prices inevitably spiraled upward. Enterprising brewers made spruce beer every day, boiling spruce and pine needles in water, adding a little maple sugar, and letting it ferment for a day or two. Though it lacked more than a little of the alcohol that made rum such a treat, the men became accustomed to it.[186]

Word came in that a man had deserted from the picket line after the daily parole and countersign had been issued. The man was probably already behind the American lines telling Gates everything he knew or suspected. Burgoyne ordered both words changed, and the new ones were passed down the chain of command.[187] He disliked having to do it. A change in passwords was a clear signal to all the men that security had been breached, and the only conclusion the common soldiers could come to was that one of their own had deserted. It was not a message that Burgoyne wanted to send, but he had no choice.

Another party of British soldiers went out foraging behind their own lines not far from Burgoyne's headquarters and were surprised by an American patrol while digging potatoes. Yet again some unwary British soldiers had been picked off by the Americans. The men were acting against Burgoyne's standing orders, but they had been so close to camp that they thought they were in compliance. Who could imagine that the Americans would approach so near to the British lines, or behave so audaciously when they did? Thirty British soldiers were killed or captured, and morale slumped a little more.[188]

7:00 PM, Alexander Fraser, Fish Kill

Captain Fraser took some of his British rangers out on an evening scout around seven o'clock, guided by a Loyalist named Jones. Perhaps they could give the Americans a taste of their own medicine. The moon was new and the night as black as pitch, but Jones knew the ground. They picked their way northward toward Saratoga. Then around midnight they turned west and followed Fish Kill up to the higher ground above the village. Jones owned a mill and a home there, and he was more than a little worried about his family and his buildings. There were rebel scouting parties everywhere. Jones wondered whether his mill was still standing, whether his family was safe at home. By dawn he would know the answers to these and a dozen other questions. What none of the men in Fraser's detachment knew was that Ebenezer Wild's scouting detachment from the 1st Massachusetts was already between them and the mill.

8:00 PM, Horatio Gates, American Headquarters on Bemis Heights

Everyone in the American camp wondered what Burgoyne was waiting for. Perhaps he thought St. Leger could assist him from the north. Maybe he was waiting for Clinton to come up from the south. Neither prospect seemed likely to the Americans. Patrols were out in all directions and the news was all good. Lieutenant Hardin came in with his prisoners and the letter for Burgoyne from St. Leger, who was now at Ticonderoga. The letter was so discouraging for the British that Gates wondered briefly if it might have been a fake message intended for interception by his scouts. The message said that St. Leger had lost men from his already depleted 8th Regiment for other purposes in Canada. He was undermanned and uncertain how to find Burgoyne. He was awaiting orders, seemingly with the hope that they would not actually find him. Gates decided that the letter was authentic. Having it meant that he knew more than Burgoyne did regarding St. Leger and his diminished capabilities. Perhaps they should have let the bad news reach Burgoyne.[189]

THURSDAY, OCTOBER 2, 1777

6:00 AM, American and British Scouting Parties, West of Saratoga

Ebenezer Wild and the rest of the American scouting party were up early. Before dawn they continued working upstream along Fish Kill, back toward Saratoga Lake. They found a mill and a cluster of houses at a place called Jonesville. The houses were inhabited, but everyone seemed to still be asleep. The men checked the mill and discovered that it held a large quantity of grain. They were behind the British lines so the only reasonable conclusion was that the people still remaining in this little community were Loyalists and that the grain was destined for Burgoyne's army. Without hesitating they moved in quickly. Doors were broken down; terrified women and children were roused and pushed outdoors. They took seven more prisoners. The women pleaded but the rebels set the mill ablaze and went back inside the houses to see what things of value they could find.[190]

Around first light, while the Americans were looting the houses and barns, Alexander Fraser's British detachment of rangers suddenly appeared on the other side of the stream, guided by Jones, who instantly took in the whole scene. The distraught Jones could see his mill in flames, his family and friends in a tight group and under guard. Without thinking he crossed the creek to try to save his family and his mill, injuring himself as he scrambled across. The Massachusetts men abandoned their looting and turned toward the new threat across the stream. Jones came straight at them, ignoring the danger. The miserable Jones was captured almost willingly. Fraser and his rangers simply stared after him. The Massachusetts men did the same. The men on each side of Fish Kill worried that their enemies across the way were just the advanced guard of a larger force not far away. Neither could see much reason to risk attacking. On both sides of the water men slowly backed away, the Americans taking their captives with them. If there was to be a new battle it would not begin here.

Not a single shot was fired across the stream by either side. The American scouts slowly backed out of the little settlement, moving back upstream on the north bank of Fish Kill. Fraser and his rangers moved just as quietly downstream along the south bank toward Saratoga, and the confrontation was over. The Massachusetts men picked up speed and began circling back toward the American camp on Bemis Heights as quickly as they could. Abandoned by both detachments, Jones's home and mill burned to the ground.[191]

2:00 PM, John Burgoyne, British Headquarters

The men needed good news. Burgoyne had reliable reports from Brigadier General Powell at Ticonderoga and Captain Aubrey of the 47th Regiment on Diamond Island. Although he could not know it, Burgoyne was fortunate in not having St. Leger's report. The American scouts had done him a favor by intercepting it. Burgoyne sent out another large, armed foraging party. They again crossed the bridge of boats, but this time they went even farther inland to the east in search of food for the men and forage for the livestock.[192]

3:00 PM, Christopher Fisher, No Man's Land

Private Christopher Fisher came from the Schoharie Valley, from one of the Palatine German families that had lived there for decades. Christopher spoke fluent German, so it was no surprise when he received a message from John Tillman, Gates's German translator. Tillman and Gates were looking for a German-speaking soldier who could infiltrate the British camp and try to persuade the Brunswickers to desert. Tillman and Gates thought Fisher could pull off this dangerous mission if they could persuade him to take it on. Tillman offered Fisher a purse of gold coins and an immediate discharge if he was successful.

Fisher had decided to think about it. He went to see his friend Jacob Van Alstyne. Jacob reminded Christopher of what he could expect to happen if he were caught as a spy but refused to advise him one way or the other. "Well, if you will not advise me how to proceed, then I must act on my own judgment." Fisher was a man with no shortage of self-confidence, so he went back to Tillman and accepted the assignment.

Morgan's riflemen had been scouring the woods in front of the British positions every day, and they knew the ground well, right up to the edge of Burgoyne's tent city. They also knew from information acquired from deserters that the redoubt that protected the right flank of the British line was manned primarily by Brunswick troops. Fisher would try his hand at turning a few coats in and around the Breymann Redoubt.

Earlier in the day Morgan's men had been treated to an odd sight when Fisher walked up through their pickets with a dead sheep on his shoulders. He stopped long enough to brief them on his mission and what he expected them to do. Then he left again, headed toward the British lines with his dead sheep.

A German sentry hailed Fisher as he approached, demanding to know where he was from and the reason for his visit. Fisher replied in German: "I live a few miles back in the country. The damned Yankees have destroyed all my property but one sheep, which I have killed and am bringing to my friends." The sentry was impressed, and probably hungry. He escorted Fisher into the camp and turned him over to an officer. Soon there were other officers and some tough questioning. How could they be sure he was not a spy? Fisher was ready with an answer. "The rebels are preparing to give you battle, and if you will go with me, I will convince you of its truth." The senior officer followed Fisher to a spot from which they could see the woods that concealed Morgan's advanced pickets. The riflemen had been waiting for this and put on a good show of skulking about in their distinctive hunting frocks. Fisher pointed, "There, there, don't you see them devils of Morgan's dodging about among the trees?"

It was enough for the officer. Fisher found himself able to move freely about the camp. While the British and German officers intermittently tried in English or German to convince him to enlist, Fisher demurred, claiming an aversion to fighting and the need to get home to protect his family against the wicked rebels. Fisher spent the day sidling up to Brunswicker enlisted men quietly urging them to desert while they still could. He stayed for several hours, playing his double game. Eventually the German officers attempted to dislodge the riflemen Fisher had pointed out; he used this as a diversion so that he could sneak back across no man's land to the American side.[193]

The charade did not end there. In the evening a report was sent to Burgoyne from his pickets saying that the Americans had marched a brigade to a position possibly threatening not just the western flank but the entire rear of the army. Burgoyne immediately ordered Indians, Canadians, and Loyalists out to reconnoiter at night.[194] While this was going on, Christopher Fisher, who had engineered the whole alarm almost singlehandedly, reported back to Tillman and received both his coins and a discharge. But he did not go home. It was a story he would want to tell his grandchildren, and the story was not yet finished.

4:00 PM, Simon Fraser, the Breymann and Balcarres Redoubts

Fisher and his rifleman friends had done their acting jobs well. Simon Fraser fretted over the placement of his units on the right flank. He issued orders for their dispositions should the Americans attack the Balcarres Redoubt and other emplacements on that wing. Troops manning outposts were expected to hold their ground. The 20th Regiment from the grenadier battalion was posted to the left of the rest and expected to hold it, come what may. The light infantry battalion was ordered to man the works on the right and protect the artillery posted there. Other grenadier companies and the 24th Regiment were told that they would be pulled back behind the ravine in the woods north of the redoubt and held there in reserve. The women, children, horses, and carts would also be moved back behind the ravine for their protection.[195] While some saw these contingent orders as reasonable precautions, others could not help but notice a certain implied fatalism. But most of the men followed the orders with precision, bracing for the impending attack predicted by the Americans' theatrical performance in and around the Breymann Redoubt.

5:00 PM, Horatio Gates, American Headquarters

Meanwhile the Americans welcomed a major, a captain, and a lieutenant, along with several private soldiers who had been captured by American scouting parties that were growing in size and confidence every day. Along with them the Americans had taken cattle, sheep, and horses that Burgoyne army desperately needed but now would have to do without. Counting those who had come into the American camp during the night, the day produced thirty-six British and German deserters. At the same time the American Army received another infusion of fresh militia. Best of all, Schuyler's efforts back in Albany were ensuring that there was enough food to feed all of these mouths. Movements ahead of the British lines raised alarms and sent men to their battle stations, but for the time being nothing more than skirmishing came of it. Whereas the alarms debilitated the British and German troops, they seemed to energize the Americans, each new alarm raising their confidence rather than diminishing it.[196]

6:00 PM, Ludwig Gräfe, British Headquarters

General Riedesel wrote a letter for Cornet Gräfe to take back to Gates. Gräfe's pass was about to expire and he was honor bound to make his way back through the American lines and into captivity once again. It was a pleasant prospect, now that Gräfe had experienced the depleted comforts of Burgoyne's encampment. The quarters the Americans had found for their prisoners and the food they were feeding them were better than anything Burgoyne could offer the men still under his command.

Burgoyne was not willing to consider an exchange of Ethan Allen for two officers who were Gates's prisoners. Riedesel's letter was polite and careful. Colonel Allen, as it turned out, was officially a prisoner of state, not a prisoner of war, and he was in any case under the purview of Sir William Howe. Lieutenant General Burgoyne could not pretend to dispose of such a prisoner, but he could probably be persuaded to entertain the possibility of an exchange of equal numbers of other officers as long as all of them were prisoners of war.

Riedesel then added a proposal that from his point of view as commander of the German troops was more urgent. Would Gates consider allowing a certain captain of the German dragoons and a lieutenant of the German grenadiers to return to Riedesel's service for a month? They were both paymasters for their respective units and the accounts were a mess without their services. With that Riedesel sent Gräfe off with his best wishes and instructions to thank Gates for taking such good care of his wounded prisoners.[197]

9:00 PM, *Ebenezer Wild, the American Lines*

Ebenezer Wild's scouting party had its hands full. They had ten prisoners, three of them commissioned officers, a dozen horses, and eighteen cattle. It had taken them all day to herd them all back to American lines. Gates was happy to see them. After delivering their prisoners and livestock they marched happily off to the brigade commissary, where each man received a hard biscuit and a gill of rum. When they were done they marched back to their tents. It had been a good three days' work, and now they were dismissed. Ebenezer could hardly believe their good fortune, and he said so. "What is very remarkable is we never exchanged a shot the whole scout."[198]

FRIDAY, OCTOBER 3, 1777

5:00 AM, *John Burgoyne, British Headquarters*

It was nearly an hour and a half before sunrise. The moon was still new and the night was as dark as dark could be. Captain Alexander Fraser readied his company of rangers for another quiet departure. The moment the sky lightened enough to allow them to move out they would begin exploring the countryside behind and to the west of the sprawling camp. Burgoyne had ordered Fraser to cover the ground to a distance of four miles and determine whether the Americans really were closing in on their rear. Over two hundred Indians, Canadians, and Loyalists were already out, but Burgoyne wanted more intelligence.[199] Meanwhile, Christopher Fisher, the American who had triggered all this commotion, slept on in his tent in the American camp.

Burgoyne set the password and the countersign for the day. Then he issued his daily order.

> There is reason to be assured that other powerful armies of the King are actually in cooperation with these Troops. Although the present supply of provisions is ample, it is highly desirable to prepare for any continuance in the Field that the King's Service may require, without the delay of bringing forward further Stores for those purposes. The ration of Bread or Flour is, for the present, fixed at one Pound.
>
> The Lieutenant General is confident he shall meet with universal and cheerful Obedience to this Order, and as a testimony of his Attention to the Spirit and good will of the Troops upon all occasions, and confident of his Majesty's Grace toward such merit, the Lieutenant General will take upon himself to suspend the usual Stoppages during the Diminution of the ration, or for one Month, and the Soldier will be accounted with for his whole pay during that time, the Stoppages then to take place again in their usual Course.
>
> With the same Confidence in the King's Grace, the Lieutenant General has ventured to order the Deputy Pay Master General to issue One Hundred and Sixty five Days Forage Money to the Officers of the Army.[200]

The ration of flour or bread had been cut by a third.[201] Burgoyne had ordered the deputy paymaster general to issue 165 days' forage money to the officers, hoping but not expecting that this might enable the army to obtain more supplies from the locals. Then he ordered the provost to go around the camp in the afternoon to try to determine where fresh meat was coming from. There was too much of it. Either the men were acquiring it privately from local farmers or the army's dwindling herds were being pilfered.

Other daily problems facing Burgoyne and his staff were multiplying. There was a sobering new report regarding the rise in desertions. The prohibition against straying beyond the pickets to forage was still being violated. Men who said they were going to the latrine left and were never seen again. Pickets disappeared from their posts. Some officers tried to convince themselves that the disappearing men were being taken by Oneidas, Stockbridge Indians, and other Indians allied with the rebels, but the truth was that most were simply deserting.[202] So many men had already disappeared this morning that Burgoyne again changed the parole and countersign for the day. The original passwords were by this time probably as well known to the rebels as they were to Burgoyne's own troops.

Dispatches from Ticonderoga were clearly being intercepted by the Americans.[203] Burgoyne would have received more of them were this not the case. In addition to this problem, guns, shot, and powder assigned to men killed or currently unfit for duty were scattered around the camp. There was no hope of replacing guns or ammunition if they were lost. Burgoyne ordered the deputy quartermaster general to collect all the arms assigned to men in the hospital and to store them until such time as the regiments needed them.

The troops appeared to be taking the cut in rations in stride, but Burgoyne knew that the additional steps he was now forced to take could shift from merely worrisome to truly ominous in a few days. American strength was growing. Every bit of intelligence coming to him pointed to it. Privately, and against his own temperament, he was beginning to contemplate a retreat to Canada.[204]

12:00 Noon, Horatio Gates, American Headquarters

Gates was fretting again. Morgan and Dearborn were scouting the country between the Hudson and Saratoga Lake six miles to the west almost every day. But what if Burgoyne tried swinging even farther to the west, moving around far to the west of the lake and striking south along roads there leading through Ballston and Burnt Hills to the fords at Rexford or Schenectady? The possibility kept Gates awake at night. It made little sense to anyone else, but a vision of himself sitting like a fool in his camp on Bemis Heights while Burgoyne evaded detection with a wide detour around to the west plagued him. It made no difference to Gates that the ponderous British war machine had been clanking along for months and had not once shown any ability to move either quickly or quietly. Burgoyne had not managed to move a mile without making such a commotion that no one could fail to notice it, but Gates still worried that it might be possible. Gates could not in good conscience send Morgan or Dearborn farther afield; he needed them close so that they could take the lead when the almost inevitable attack came. But in Gates's mind Burgoyne might use such an attack as a diversion to mask a western detour by Fraser's Advanced Corps.

Gates came nervously to a conclusion, albeit one that might last only a day or two. He scrawled a new general order. He ordered his seven brigades to take turns readying detachments of 150 men and a sufficient number of officers, with provisions for three days in case fighting began. The New York militia should be ready to send a detachment west of Saratoga Lake to intercept any British detachment there tomorrow, Saturday, October 4. It would be the turn of Poor's brigade to be on alert on Sunday if nothing happened Saturday. Nixon would have his turn on Monday, and so forth, through the seven brigades.[205] The ridiculous precaution would carry them through to Friday, October 10. Still apprehensive, Gates once again ordered all men in all brigades to draw three days' provisions, cook them immediately, and be prepared to march at a minute's warning. On Bemis Heights the battalions of the South Berkshire County and York County, Massachusetts, militias appeared in camp. Gates assigned them to John Paterson's brigade, bringing it up to six regimental-strength units.[206]

1:00 PM, James Wilkinson, East Side of the Hudson

Lieutenant Colonel Wilkinson had wondered if Burgoyne might try a fast movement down the Hudson by bateaux in a flanking move to take the batteries at Bemis Heights from the rear. Raising this possibility with Gates had only heightened his commander's anxieties. Here was yet another possibility that threatened the ruin of the Northern Army. Wilkinson knew his commander and the man's weaknesses well. It had been easy to persuade Gates to let Wilkinson lead a reconnaissance expedition of seven hundred men on the east side of the Hudson, just to make sure Burgoyne was not undertaking this absurd option.

It had been an easy march across the American bridge of boats near Bemis Tavern. Now Wilkinson was almost three miles north, within view of the British bridge of boats. They found only that the British had constructed a *tête de pont* on the east side of the river to protect their own bridge of boats. There were no signs of any preparations for a British advance either on the river or along the main road that paralleled it on the east side. It was satisfying in a way, but there was nothing to do but return to camp and report that no news was good news.

On the way back Wilkinson's detachment ran into an armed party of British seamen. The men had decided to take a break from tending the British bateaux and go out on a raid for food and supplies, just the sort of initiative that was currently driving Burgoyne to distraction. The British sailors were hopelessly outnumbered and easily captured.[207] They had about twenty horses with them and these too were taken back to the American camp. To a man they all reported that provisions were desperately short on the British side.[208]

Wilkinson later estimated that he had captured forty-five sailors. Meanwhile the British recorded that nineteen sailors had left camp without orders in search of food and loot, and had been captured by the rebels. Sentries reported hearing some gunfire later in the day and everyone concluded that they had all been killed or captured. Such are the games of numbers played in war.[209]

6:00 PM, John Burgoyne, British Headquarters

The Canadians and Loyalists straggled back into camp as night fell, leaving as many as fifty Indians still out for the night. Fraser's Rangers were not far behind. None of them had found any evidence of American troops in their rear. There were no rebel units within four miles of the British camp, and there would be no attack from that direction. Burgoyne considered that he still had the option of retreating northward back to Fort Edward or Fort George. But at the same time one of the Loyalists reported that he had found out that a party of thirty Americans had intercepted a courier coming from Governor Carleton in Canada to Burgoyne. That meant that while the rebels did not know everything they certainly knew most of what they needed to know about Burgoyne's strength and his intentions. The scouts had also picked up rumors that General Clinton was still trying to move up the Hudson to support Burgoyne.[210]

Burgoyne still had to stem desertions and stop losses that came as a consequence of foraging too far from camp. The problem simply would not go away. Burgoyne came to a decision and Kingston drafted new orders requiring sentries to light fires a hundred yards in advance of their positions so that they could more easily see anyone advancing toward the British lines in the darkness. At least that was the official explanation. Kingston was careful not to mention that it would also allow easier detection of deserters and foragers leaving camp.[211]

SATURDAY, OCTOBER 4, 1777

6:00 AM, British Troops, the British Camp

American skirmishers attacked the British pickets near dawn. As usual, the British were sleeping with their arms and in their uniforms, and they were on their feet in seconds. Irritating as it was, the feint led to nothing.[212] Just the same, the British soldiers were reminded that the rebels owned the woods and were increasingly bold. Everyone was on edge, and everyone had to know that this was precisely what the Americans were hoping for.

Burgoyne was still determined to wait for Clinton before moving up the Hudson. The whole army was on short rations. The officers, for whom the deprivation was not so severe, assured each other that this was accepted with the utmost cheerfulness by the troops.[213] What else could the rank-and-file soldiers say to their officers?

The Indians who had stayed out overnight came in bearing gifts for Burgoyne. They had five American prisoners and four scalps. The Indians were dutifully paid for both. It could have been worse. There might have been nine more mouths to feed instead of five.[214]

10:00 AM, Horatio Gates, American Headquarters

Horatio Gates had enough food supplies for the time being. If action were imminent, he might do well to distribute a few days' rations to his army. But if he distributed too much it might be wasted or spoiled. He came again to his usual conclusion; then he wrote out the order. "The whole army to be immediately victualled to the 7th inst. inclusive, with two-thirds fresh and one-third salt provisions, which is to be cooked as soon as possible." Provisions through the seventh, three days' worth; that should be enough. He could order another three days' worth on Tuesday the seventh.[215]

Gates wrote a letter to General and former governor George Clinton on October 4, repeating some of the same words he had used on September 17. He wrote about the other General Clinton, Burgoyne's friend and colleague Henry Clinton, who seemed to be busy doing as little as possible far to the south near the mouth of the Hudson.

Camp Behmus's Heights 4th Octo^r:1777
Dear General,

I have the Satisfaction to Acquaint Your Excellency, that the public Affairs in the Northern Department have a pleasing appearance. By a variety of Intelligence, such as Intercepted Letters, the Information of Deserters and Spies, I have good reason to believe, that Genl. Burgoyne has only three Weeks provissions in his Magazine, it will take him Ten Days to make anything like a Regular Retreat, and even in that case he must Abandon some precious Articles to those from whom he would wish to withhold them. Perhaps his Despair may dictate to him, to risque all upon One Throw. He is an Old Gamester, and in his Time, has seen all Chances. I will endeavour to be ready to prevent his Good Fortune, and, if possible, Secure my Own.

By accounts received from Deserters, and others, I am Confident Genl Burgoyne expects a great Effort will be made by Genl Clinton, to Open a passage through the Highlands, to facilitate his (General Burgoyne's) approach to Albany. Your Excellency, and General Putnam, will be prepared to defeat that Attempt. I desire Your Excellency will be so Obliging, as to forward the packet to Congress by a Trusty Courier.

I am, Sir,
Your Excellency's
Most Obedient
Humble Servant
Horatio Gates

His Excellency Governo^r:_ Clinton.[216]

He also wrote a letter to John Hancock, enclosing a third letter addressed to George Washington. He reported that a British deserter who had come in this morning had told him that Burgoyne had provisions for only fifteen more days. His worries about an attack down the river road, a flanking attack from the east side of the Hudson, or even a flanking attack around Saratoga Lake to the west were slowly dissipating. Now he told Hancock that he was ready not just to stop Burgoyne but to cut off a British retreat northward back to Canada.[217]

12:00 Noon, Council of War, British Headquarters

The army had awoken again to hoarfrost from the frozen fog. Yet by afternoon it was hot again.[218] Surely this was unhealthy. The bad night air undoubtedly accounted for the spread of ague and camp fever. The surgeons were busy bleeding the men to counteract the sicknesses, bleeding even healthy men as a precaution.

Burgoyne's army followed the orders he had issued Friday. He had ordered that the entire army would forage today, with large covering parties for both the British and German troops. The exception would be a reserve of three hundred men held back under the command of Brigadier General Specht, and kept at a high state of readiness with two 6-pounders close at hand. Some of the foragers went across the bridge of boats and ranged farther downstream and back away from the Hudson on that side. Everyone expected them to be attacked as the sailors had been yesterday, but the expedition went well. Now there were some vegetables for the men and the horses could be fed for another day.

Loyalists from Albany came in carrying local newspapers with reports of Washington's loss to Howe in New Jersey. The officers read the accounts avidly, astonished at their apparent candor. One would think the Americans would censor them, or at least try to restrain their excessive honesty. Washington's army had been so dispersed that it had taken days to get it back together. They had lost twelve cannon. And so forth. It was all very gratifying.[219]

But Burgoyne himself was not gratified. The situation here was getting critical. He could take no comfort in Washington's temporary disarray. Burgoyne summoned Generals Fraser, Phillips, and Riedesel to his tent. This was not another pleasant dinner meeting of his senior officers; it was his first council of war. There were no other officers, no aides, and no servants, just the lieutenant general and his major generals. Simon Fraser, a brigadier, was included, but Hamilton was not, despite being at the same rank. Burgoyne spoke first and proposed what he had in mind. "We should completely abandon the supplies and bateaux on the flats near the river for a few days, leaving about eight hundred men for their cover in the retrenchments. The army should march off to the right, turn the left flank and the back of the enemy around, and attack them."

To Riedesel and Phillips it was inspired, audacious, bold, insane, impossible. The two men began to go through the problems with the idea. "Nobody is familiar with the roads or with the position of the enemy's left wing." It was a good point. British scouts had not been able to get close enough to the American lines to be sure of their strengths or even their locations. The woods were simply too full of rebel bands to allow it. "Such an expedition could easily take three or four days. It is too dangerous to abandon our last depot for such a long time, especially since the redoubts for covering our supplies are already spread much too far apart. They defend each other quite badly." This was especially true on the right flank around Freeman's farm and northwestward. "The enemy can penetrate the ravines in between the hills without having to attack the hills on which the redoubts have been built." And so forth. Burgoyne knew all the negatives before he had uttered his proposal, but he had needed confirmation from his two highest ranking advisers. He was also laying the groundwork for his future defense of his actions in case all of this turned out badly. He could later say that he had wanted to take the initiative but that his senior officers had argued against it.

Burgoyne thanked the generals and asked them to return the next day for another consultation. Perhaps another day of hard thinking would produce some new ideas.[220] The four generals debated the proposal and agreed that it would take three or four days to organize such an attempt, and they finally agreed to hold another conference on the evening of the next day, Sunday.

2:00 PM, *Abraham Ten Broeck, the American Camp on Bemis Heights*

It had taken two weeks and they had missed the first battle in September, but General Ten Broeck's militia brigade was now almost entirely in camp with the Northern Army and he had about as many men as he could hope for. Bits and pieces of the sixteen Albany militia regiments from which his men were drafted had been arriving daily. There were now about thirteen hundred of them in his brigade, not as many as in the other brigades, but enough to be creditable when the time came to fight. He had Gilbert Livingston as his aide, and similarly suitable colonels from good families to lead each of his regiments.

The Albany militiamen brought with them copies of their local newspapers. They ran exciting stories about what might or might not occur to break the stalemate north of Stillwater. They said Burgoyne had dug in and was making every effort to brace for another battle. Burgoyne's Canadian and Indian allies were deserting him in droves. The accounts gushed with patriotic fervor of the sort that can only be written by those who have not personally faced the awful realities of battle.

The advantages obtained over the enemy on this occasion, excites the greatest exultation and rejoicing throughout our army and country. It is indeed a remarkable fact, which must animate the heart of every friend to the cause of America, that our troops, so little accustomed to encounter the prowess of European veterans, and the peculiar warfare of the savages, should face these enemies with such undaunted courage and intrepidity. Sanguine hopes are now entertained, that we shall, by the help of Providence, be finally enabled to destroy or capture the whole British army. Our troops are panting for another opportunity of displaying their valor, and another dreadful conflict is daily expected; alternate hopes and fears continually agitate our minds and create the greatest anxiety and solicitude. What can excite ideas more noble and sublime, than impending military events, on which depend the destiny of a nation?[221]

Meanwhile Wolcott's brigade of Connecticut militia also arrived in the American camp. This top-heavy brigade was actually made up of just a single battalion of only 250 enlisted men. Its commander, Brigadier General Oliver Wolcott, was assisted by no fewer than two colonels, two lieutenant colonels, two majors, and thirty-four company-level officers. It was surely the most elaborately officered unit in the burgeoning Northern Army. They were the opposite of Ten Broeck's growing horde of Albany militiamen. Gates must have hoped the effectiveness of the new Connecticut regiment would rise to the level of its organizational complexity.

The Hampshire County Massachusetts militia under Colonel Benjamin Woodbridge also arrived. Somehow the more than five hundred men in this battalion managed to get along under the leadership of a single colonel, a lieutenant colonel, and a handful of staff officers.[222] Such were the workings of the improvised American Army.

SUNDAY, OCTOBER 5, 1777

10:00 AM, John Burgoyne, British Headquarters

It was Sunday. Anglican religious services were available for those who desired them. Burgoyne fretted over the dwindling supplies, the inaction of the army, and the bored indiscipline they were causing. The provost had reported back that cattle had been stolen and slaughtered, the source of the fresh meat the men had been eating. Burgoyne issued a new order requiring written permission from the quartermaster general for any further slaughtering, which would be granted only if the ownership of the beast could be demonstrated.

Once again he had to change the parole and countersign again during the day as reports of new desertions came in. Such changes were becoming frequent. Burgoyne did not mention the reasons for them, but the men had to know. Healthy soldiers went missing and only a fool could not guess what had happened to them.[223]

The camp was starting to take on the look of a frontier town. Huts began to appear, some of them for sleeping, others used as little kitchens. Men worked to improve entrenchments every day, and even these started to acquire small comforts.[224] The weather had been fair and dry for over a week, but this failed to brighten the general mood very much.

2:00 PM, Benedict Arnold, the American Camp on Bemis Heights

The confidence of the Americans was growing every day. Arnold was still sulking in his cramped quarters, resisting the efforts of Matthew Clarkson to cheer him up. After all, Burgoyne had to be desperate. Clarkson tried a pep talk. "His provisions must almost be consumed, which will render it absolutely necessary for him to attempt something." Clarkson pressed on. "If he attacks us, certain ruin attends him. If he retreats the spirits of his soldiers are at once depressed."

Arnold was unmoved, so Clarkson tried another tack. "The flower of their whole army was opposed to us and when they were made to believe that on the first onset we would give way we should in all probability have entirely destroyed their whole army." But regret for what happened in the past worked no better than optimism about the future. Clarkson's general was inconsolable.[225]

3:00 PM, Horatio Gates, American Headquarters

Gates disliked having to write Washington as if they were anything but equals. Congress had appointed both of them, and it was still not entirely clear to Gates whether he should report to Washington as his commander in chief or report directly to Congress. Washington had lent him Morgan and his regiment of riflemen. Now he wanted them back. Washington's letter of September 24 making that request had just arrived. It was a request between equals, not an order from a superior.

Being a request and not an order meant that Gates could politely decline to send Morgan and his men back to Washington. It was another moment to be relished. Another battle could not be very far in the future, and Gates would need Morgan's rifles when it came. Gates also wrote another letter to John Hancock. In this one he urged Congress to be mindful of the importance of securing the Hudson Highlands so that Henry Clinton would not be able to press northward toward Albany and support Burgoyne from that direction. Other threats were of less consequence. And of course he felt compelled to add that he was nearly out of money.[226]

4:00 PM, Enos Hitchcock, the American Camp on Bemis Heights

It was Sunday, a fair day, and some of the men marched to the meeting at four in the afternoon. They heard the Reverend Enos Hitchcock deliver a sermon based on the theme "Return to the stronghold ye prisoners of hope." This was accompanied by a reading of scripture, Matthew 5:32: "But I say unto you, That whosoever shall put away his wife, saving for the cause of fornication, causeth her to commit adultery: and whosoever shall marry her that is divorced committeth adultery."

Some of the men wondered where, under their current circumstances, Hitchcock's scripture was supposed to be taking them. Their wonder increased when he reached verse 39, which advised them to turn the other cheek, and then verse 44, which urged them to love their enemies. Hitchcock ended with the flourish, admonishing all those who were listening to seek perfection. As they all returned to their duties, Hitchcock was satisfied and most of his congregation was bewildered, not an unusual Sunday service outcome.[227]

5:00 PM, Council of War, British Headquarters

The four generals met again late Sunday afternoon. This time Burgoyne waited for them to come up with alternative proposals. Riedesel's frustration was near boiling. "Our situation is of such a nature that if we do not march against the enemy within one day, to attack him and bring affairs to a crisis, it would be expedient to move back again to the Battenkill. After having passed the Hudson in the rear of the Battenkill, where we cannot again be cut off from Fort George, we should await General Clinton's movements in opening communication." Fraser agreed. Phillips offered no opinion.[228]

Burgoyne thought about this. It was not in his nature to make retrograde movements. As previously at Skenesborough, he could not countenance backward movement. He had given the matter considerable thought; the generals could see that he was about to give them full benefit of his deliberations and his wisdom.

> Suppose the British army that invaded Britany in 1758 had gained a complete victory over the Duke d'Aiguillor, to have marched rapidly towards Paris, abandoning the communication with the fleet, exposing the army possibly to great want of provision and to the impracticability of retreat. It would certainly have been a measure consummately desperate and unjustifiable if tried up on military system. Yet will any man say that if that measure must evidently have produced such alarm and confusion in the heart of France as to have compelled the recall of her whole force from Germany, or such part of it as would have given uncontrolled scope to the armies under the King of Prussia and Prince Ferdinand, that the minister of England would not have been judicious (though at the palpable risk of the army as far as capture was concerned) in ordering the general to proceed by the most vigorous exertions and force his way to Paris?[229]

Burgoyne's love of the theater was never more evident. "On the seventh I want to reconnoiter the enemy's left wing as closely as possible in order to see whether it can be attacked or not. If it can be I will then attack the enemy in one day, that is, on the eighth. If not I will start to retreat behind the Battenkill on the eleventh."[230]

So there it was. Burgoyne would take Riedesel's advice, but not immediately. First there would be a probe of the American left to see if it could be forced. Riedesel saw this as wasted effort, but he silently accepted half a loaf. Their army was clearly outnumbered: two to one, three to one, perhaps even four to one. If Burgoyne had to see for himself to be convinced of the futility of their current situation, then so be it. So long as they could get back north beyond the mouth of Batten Kill and reestablish a supply line through Fort George and Fort Edward. They had been in a position that was strategically offensive but tactically defensive for over two weeks. It was a good position to be in, so long as the enemy was compelled, or at least thought he was compelled, to attack. So long as the expedition could be adequately supplied. But it was clear by now that Gates felt under no compulsion to attack. It was just as clear that there would be no more supplies. It was time. There was more discussion, but Burgoyne remained determined that this was the best course. In two days they would probe the Americans to see if there was a way to force the issue. There was nothing for the other generals to do but submit.

5:30 PM, Alexander Campbell, the Lower Hudson

Far to the south, near New York City, Captain Campbell of the ravaged 62nd Foot completed his hazardous journey. Burgoyne had sent him off on Tuesday, September 28. It had taken him a week and who knew how many close calls to reach Henry Clinton. He handed Clinton the notes from Burgoyne, which because the cipher had been lost were terse. The real content had been committed to Campbell's memory.

> The General's army does not exceed five thousand men. The consequences of the battle on the nineteenth was the loss of between five and six hundred men. The enemy is within a mile and a half of him. We know not their certain numbers but believe them to be twelve or fourteen thousand men. There is besides a considerable body in his rear. He wishes to receive your orders whether he should attack or retreat to the lakes. He has provisions to the twentieth of this month. He would not have given up his communications with Ticonderoga had he not expected a cooperating army at Albany. He wishes to know your positive answer as soon as possible whether you can open a communication with Albany, when you should be there, and when there you should keep your communication with New York. If he does not hear from you by the fifteenth he shall retire.[231]

Clinton was taken aback, especially by Burgoyne's proposal that he become Clinton's subordinate. Burgoyne wishes to receive his orders? This honor Clinton promptly declined. Burgoyne would not be able to hide his impending defeat by placing himself under Clinton's command. Clinton gave Campbell his reply, then he repeated it. Then he had Campbell repeat it back to him until they were both satisfied that he had accurately committed it to memory. With that Campbell was sent off again to run the lethal American gauntlet that lay along both sides of the Hudson between the two British Armies.

That night, not far from Burgoyne's lines, rebel patrols probed twice at pickets of the Regiment von Rhetz.[232] Perhaps their Indian allies had gone home, but rebels raised on the frontier seemed no less able or willing to skulk about in the darkness. The moon was still crescent and did not rise until near morning. By then the fog obscured everything. Yet the Americans were still out there someplace, waiting.

MONDAY, OCTOBER 6, 1777

9:00 PM, Friedrich Riedesel, the German Camp

Now there was grumbling from the German ranks too. German recruits in the British regiments had been annoyed by the Sunday Anglican services. Burgoyne scribbled an order telling British regimental commanders to allow those Germans requesting it to attend Lutheran services. British officers could later be seen marching small groups of German troops to the place selected for this purpose. Other men spent Monday foraging as best they could. Rations were distributed for four days; Riedesel told the men that they were expected to subsist on what they carried until the end of the week.[233]

They sent out another large detachment to forage close to the American lines. The horses were still near starving, and Burgoyne thought it was worth the risk. They encountered no Americans, but on their way back to camp they heard firing that resulted from a unit of British rangers running into an American party near the Regiment von Rhetz. About sixty Indians heard the commotion and immediately ran toward the firing. No one had ordered them forward, but in a half hour they were engaged with the Americans. A couple of them were wounded and they came back to report that the Americans had also suffered several killed or wounded. The foraging continued during the firefight, which lasted an hour and a half. By three o'clock the foragers were safely back in camp.[234]

10:00 AM, Horatio Gates, American Headquarters

The newspapers in Albany had picked up news of a message that passed through on its way to Gates. Four thousand British troops under Clinton and Vaughan were advancing up the Hudson. Their objectives were Fort Montgomery and Fort Clinton in the Highlands, an action that they hoped would force Gates to detach some units to defend Albany from that direction.

Closer to Bemis Heights, American pickets and scouts across the Hudson noticed unusual movement in the British camp during the day, especially in the part of it that was stationed down by the river. Gates formed the impression that Burgoyne might be preparing to retreat. He ordered detachments from Glover's brigade on the American right to augment the units manning the forward line at Mill Creek, and to be ready to advance quickly up the river road in pursuit if the British started to withdraw. But it became apparent that Burgoyne was only rearranging his forces for reasons that Gates could not yet fathom.[235]

Gates was now the de facto mayor of what was probably the fourth largest city in the colonies. New York, Philadelphia, and Boston were surely larger, but there had to be more men under his command here than there were people in cities such as Baltimore and Charleston. Supplies and more men kept streaming in. Latrines were dug, tents pitched, spirits consumed. But unlike the cities this temporary metropolis rivaled, one way or another it would all be farmland again in a matter of weeks. This was surely no place for winter quarters. The Continentals would move south by then. The militias would go home. The crimson leaves would soon fall here as winter overtook autumn. This was not a place where he would be staying much longer.

12:00 Noon, John Burgoyne, British Headquarters

At some point, probably more than once, Fraser had said, "Let us do or die." This was it then. The wait was over; all other options were gone. Gates knew Burgoyne's provisions were short, and he was playing the waiting game from a stronger position. Gates would stay in his lines and fight a defensive battle. He would not allow his officers and men, least of all himself, to advance beyond those lines. Burgoyne had to probe for weaknesses in the American entrenchments. That was the way out of this stalemate.

The more Burgoyne thought about it, the clearer it became to him that his best option was to detach a force of his fittest to take up a flanking position on rising ground to the American left around midday tomorrow, Tuesday the seventh. If the Americans stayed within their lines, as the timid Gates was inclined to do, and if the American line appeared vulnerable to an attack, the main British forces could be moved up with artillery to the flanking position during the night. From there they could pound and then storm the American left flank with everything he had left on Wednesday. Meanwhile the excursion would also give his men a new opportunity to forage for food for both themselves and the livestock.[236]

Burgoyne knew that he had to conceal the desperation of the plan. He would lead the force himself, with his best senior officers, with the best units of the best army on earth. The best of the best would rally as they always had, and in two days' time they would break through to Albany, Howe and Clinton be damned.

They all knew that it was a desperate plan. Burgoyne had only about five thousand effective rank and file left. There were probably no more than three thousand healthy British regulars left, perhaps a few hundred less than that. If Riedesel had managed to stem German desertions, there were likely still only about twenty-two hundred German rank and file remaining. To these they could count on additional help from only about a hundred Canadians, perhaps 450 Loyalists, and maybe up to fifty Indians.[237] Burgoyne had given up the idea of taking as many as four thousand men on the flanking attack on the American right. His generals had persuaded him to pare it to less than half that. Even so, there were barely enough men left to guard the main camp around the Great Redoubt. Meanwhile, the American Army had grown, and was continuing to grow each day. But Burgoyne and his advisers could only guess at its size.

Burgoyne was happier to order two-day distributions of meat and spirits, more to the point and more likely to instill goodwill and discipline. The men would need it for what was planned for tomorrow, but his written orders of the day contained no other hint of what might be coming on Tuesday. Even most of the brigadiers were still in the dark. Each man received a pound of meat for each day, and a dozen barrels of rum were sent off to the brigades. Four went to Riedesel's regiments, four to Fraser's, three to the British, and one to the auxiliaries. By nightfall Lutherans and Anglicans alike had recovered their spiritual lives and thought they were ready for whatever Tuesday might bring.[238]

9:00 PM, Ebenezer Wild, the American Lines

Colonel Joseph Vose had taken five hundred of his Massachusetts Continentals out on a scout at two in the morning and had enjoyed another successful foray. Ebenezer Wild had remained in camp all day, wishing he was with them. Vose and his detachment got back at dusk, just as the rain was starting. In all, almost two dozen British and German soldiers deserted to the Americans during the day. One Loyalist was captured as well. Meanwhile, the last of Lincoln's militia came in. Best of all, four more Americans who had been prisoners escaped and made their way back through the lines.[239]

American patrols engaged the British and German pickets again in the evening. This time the pickets could see American officers using the probes to assess the placement and strengths of the British and German troops. Both the Regiment von Rhetz on the bluffs and the Hessen-Hanau Regiment down on the flats were engaged by them, and once again the Indians went spontaneously forward to fire at the American interlopers. They found a house and some sheds that the Americans had repeatedly used as a forward position and from which they had harassed the Hessen-Hanau Germans. The Indians burned all the structures to the ground. They came back to report finding a dead American officer.[240]

A couple miles west Morgan and Dearborn headed out on a scout with eight hundred men. The size of the scout was another measure of their still growing confidence. This time it grew dark early as another long, soaking autumn rain began. They blundered about in the sodden dark, lost their bearings, and ended up spending the entire night out. They had to lie quietly in the rain, not knowing how close they were to the enemy.[241]

12:00 Midnight, John Burgoyne, British Headquarters

The British fired a single shot from a 12-pounder at midnight. This was followed by three rockets. No one ever found out why Burgoyne had ordered these signals. The usual reason, communication between close allied armies, did not seem to apply. The men in both armies speculated that Burgoyne might have thought that Clinton was near enough to see and hear the signals, or he wanted Gates to think so, or he wanted his own men to think so. Perhaps it was a ruse intended to make the Americans complacent about signals they might see or hear the next day.

There were several alarms and occasional small arms fire from sentries during the night.[242] Something was afoot, but only at Burgoyne's headquarters was anything but speculation to be had. Yet even most brigade commanders could detect nothing. Burgoyne and his war council were tight lipped. A light supper and a few cups of champagne had seemed called for. After that Burgoyne played cards into the night with the Earl of Balcarres, a diversion for Burgoyne from what was coming tomorrow.[243]

4

The Battle of Bemis Heights

TUESDAY, OCTOBER 7, 1777

6:00 AM, Ebenezer Wild, the American Camp

It was a beautiful morning, warm, clear, and quiet.[1] Before the first gray rind of light began to show on the eastern horizon, anyone who looked could see the Big Dipper standing on its handle in the northern sky. The sky had begun to lighten before five-thirty, and by six it was light enough for those who could to read.[2] The first sliver of sun appeared over the hills to the east of the Hudson at twelve minutes past six. By then the sounds of quarreling crows and army camp life filled the morning air. Vees of migrating geese passed overhead, heading southward for warmer waters.

8:00 AM, John Burgoyne, the British Camp

No field officers were assigned; there were no written orders at all. There would be desertions and Burgoyne wanted nothing to leak into American intelligence.[3] All the regiments stood to arms an hour before sunrise as usual. On this day that was at a quarter past five. The morning patrols were back and the regiments returned to their daily positions by eight. Only then did Burgoyne issue his orders for the detachments he intended to use to probe the American left flank.

Burgoyne and his generals met for breakfast in Fraser's tents while companies from German regiments brought from the riverside waited with the men his officers had assembled from the British line. Phillips and Riedesel would be with them. Some German units remained behind to guard the camp and protect the left flank should the Americans surprise them along the river road.

Fraser tried to be optimistic. He knew well how much trouble they were in, but Burgoyne was at last taking action and Fraser wanted to be supportive. "I expect in a day or two to be in Albany." Burgoyne appreciated the gesture, but he wanted no smooth talk. "Hold," he said, "the owners of the land are come out against us. We cannot proceed any farther so fast as we have done."[4] As painfully slow as progress had been up to this point, Fraser knew his commander was right. They would not succeed today by simply willing it.

They certainly had to do something; if anything they had waited too long to make a move. Given the impossibility of advancing southward along the river road, they had to see if a way could be forced around the American left. If they could find high ground overlooking the American lines they would bring up more artillery to pound their way into the American left flank. Failing that they could try to dislodge and confuse the Americans sufficiently to facilitate their own retreat back toward Canada. At the very least a probe toward the American lines would make it possible for his men to gather desperately needed forage for the horses and cattle.[5]

To do it Burgoyne decided to take the healthiest men he could find and detach them from their units rather than take a half dozen complete but unevenly manned battalions. It was a fragmented assortment. Though each man was individually strong and skilled, as a group they were wearing no fewer than two dozen different regimental uniforms. Men who had grown accustomed to serving in larger close-knit units looked around and saw too many strange faces to instill confidence. Burgoyne saw it too. He had troops who were uniformly healthy, but to get them he had sacrificed unit coherence. He could only hope that discipline and experience would be enough to unify them when they went into action.

9:00 AM, Horatio Gates, American Headquarters at Bemis Heights

The American Army was in position and deployed as well as Gates could make it (Figure 4.1). The mass of men, haphazard uniforms, makeshift tents, and random equipment looked more like a refugee camp than a military one. Latrine trenches were dug and re-covered every day, but it was still a stinking squalor to anyone downwind. The New Englanders

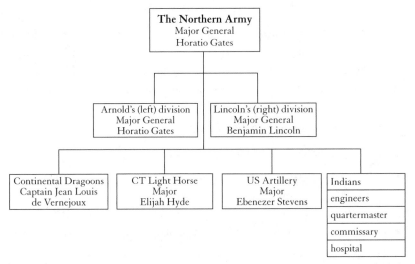

Figure 4.1 Organization of the Northern Army on October 7, 1777. Chart by the author based on Schnitzer (2016).

preferred to bake food, but ovens were makeshift and hard to find. Yankee food was far from tasty as a result, and the men poured molasses on everything to make it palatable. The Virginians tended to prefer fried food, but here too the ingredients were often barely palatable. But it was a huge force, still growing, and morale was correspondingly high despite poor food and cold nights.[6]

Fortunately, he also had the Continentals, twenty-one regiments of them from New York, New Hampshire, and Massachusetts. They were still green, lacking in proper training, but at least they were regulars who had enlisted for longer terms than the militiamen. Of course, that meant also that they were largely men who lacked other prospects, something that made these recruits only slightly better than the soldiers who made up Burgoyne's regular units.[7]

Captain Jean Louis de Vernejoux was the commander of the detached 2nd Troop of the 2nd Continental Light Dragoons. The French were not yet officially committed to the American cause, but a few volunteer officers had come over to serve in the American Army. The Marquis de Lafayette would eventually become the most famous of these, but there were many others. Vernejoux and his dragoons had done the cause good service in the Schoharie Valley back in August, when they had prevented one of the Albany County militiamen from persuading his regiment to go over to the British side.[8] The dragoon's uniform was indisputably pretty. His trim blue jacket with white facings and tails was topped off by a French-style brass helmet with a horsehair crest and a light blue turban. Vernejoux wore high black boots, and a red sash signaled his rank. The contrast between this and Gates's ragtag militiamen could not have been greater.

10:00 AM, Thomas Anburey, the British Camp

Anburey and a few other British artillery officers were playing cards when the orders arrived. One of them thought the day had arrived at last. They were finally going to take action. He said, "God bless you, Anburey. Farewell, for I know not how it is, but I have strange presentiment that I shall either be killed or wounded." With that he left to set his artillery brigade in motion.

Anburey was then ordered to take a sergeant and some men forward beyond the guards to reconnoiter across two ravines. His commanders were particularly concerned that the Americans might be advancing in that quarter, or so they said. The real plan for the day was still under wraps. Anburey still did not know it but he and his men were actually part of the advanced probe of a much larger force.

They explored the ravines, but Anburey's reconnaissance detected no American movements in either of them. He did see Americans, but they were unburied dead who had lain there since September 19. Three who were lying close to each other were two men and a woman. The woman's arms were flung out and her dead hands still grasped cartridges. Like the British Army, the American Army had women in its ranks, and like the wives and other anonymous women supporting the British soldiers, the American women clearly could be counted on to participate in the fighting.[9]

10:00 AM, John Burgoyne, the British Camp

After breakfast Burgoyne emerged and walked to where the Indians were waiting, and addressed them in the long-winded fashion that was customary between British and Indian officials. Most of the men watching could neither understand nor believe what they were seeing. The Indians were a combination of the tiny remnant of the larger numbers that had been with the army previously and the more recently arrived Mohawks, no more than 180 in all. The Mohawks were mostly from a community not far from Montreal, men from families that had been Catholic for generations. These were not brutes who were likely to repeat the McCrae atrocity, yet Burgoyne was spending time and energy on traditional warrior formalities. It took two hours.[10]

While this was going on British and German detachments moved toward the assembly point at the western end of the British line. There they added the men from von Breymann's battalion of German grenadiers and seven of the ten companies of Lindsay's 53rd Light Infantry Battalion. The detachments left Lindsay's Balcarres Redoubt defended by only three companies.[11] The Breymann Redoubt was almost unmanned; only eighty German grenadiers and fifty jägers remained there to defend the redoubt against any flanking attack by the Americans. But Burgoyne was not worried. He was sure the Americans would stay within their lines and fight defensively. There was little risk here at the far right flank of the British line.

Burgoyne did not expect the German units by the river to be attacked in their current strong positions either, but there had been much about this adventure that he had not expected. For all he knew, Gates was planning an attack on the German left just as Burgoyne was leading his own against the American left. Just in case, he had ordered the generals who remained behind to defend their positions near the river to the last man if fighting came to their quarter. "The part remaining in camp will operate to keep the enemy's right wing in check, from supporting their left. It prevents the danger of their advancing by the plain near the river and falling upon our rear. Mr. Gates has determined to receive the attack in his lines."[12] Or so Burgoyne thought. It would turn out to be a fatal miscalculation for many of Burgoyne's men.

12:00 Noon, John Burgoyne, the Balcarres Redoubt

The morning was long gone before the force started to move again, joined now by a hundred jägers, Canadians, American Loyalists, and Indians. The detachment was supported by two 12-pounders, six 6-pounders, and two 8-inch howitzers. Two of the 6-pounders were under the command of Captain Georg Päusch of the Hessen-Hanau artillery.[13] The rest were under the command of Burgoyne's amiably gruff Major Griffith Williams. Burgoyne brought along the howitzers in the hopes that he would have occasion to lob their explosive shells into the American lines. Unlike mortars, the howitzers were mobile and effective field pieces that could be handled like light cannons, and this was the first time the expedition had brought them into action.

Burgoyne exuded confidence, which was not generally shared by his senior officers. "I should in a few hours gain a position that in spite of the enemy's numbers will put them in my power." Gates had his own bridge of boats across the Hudson near Bemis Heights. Burgoyne still believed that it was meant to give the Americans an escape route across the river and eastward toward New England. Gates would not, could not, send his army out to meet him in battle on the open field. It simply was not in the man's nature.[14]

1:00 PM, *Oliver Boardman, the Wheat Field*

The morning had seemed to Oliver Boardman to be a monotonous repeat of all the others that had passed since September 19. Scouting parties had grabbed another five prisoners, along with some sheep and cattle. Boardman and fifty other Connecticut militiamen were posted to a hill in advance of the American line, in a spot overlooking a wheat field in no man's land. It was far from the river, and west of them there was only forest. For much of the day it had seemed like a quiet place to be.[15] It was pleasant and warm. The boredom of routine military duties was tolerable in such nice weather, and the minutes slipped past easily. It seemed like it was going to be another long afternoon with little of interest for Oliver to note in his journal. Then Boardman saw the first of the irregulars from Burgoyne's expedition appear along the edge of the woods north of his position.

1:30 PM, *John Burgoyne, No Man's Land*

Burgoyne's detachment moved forward in three columns, spreading out before the Balcarres Redoubt, on the Freeman and Coulter farm clearings where so much blood had been lost on September 19. Farthest to the west Lindsay's light infantry, the 24th Regiment, von Breymann's German grenadiers, and British artillerymen with two 6-pounders moved southward through the woods under the command of Simon Fraser. Ahead of them were the scattered skirmishers, jägers, Indians, Canadians, and Loyalists. The irregulars trotted south through the woods just beyond the clearings. Burgoyne had ordered them to circle around by way of secret paths that he presumed existed to the west of the American line, and to attack the rebel flank from the woods, keeping them in check there. The problem was that the woods paths were not secret. The Americans knew them well and had pickets posted there. Burgoyne's men knew neither the ground nor the supposed secret paths at all. They had to learn what they could about them on the fly.[16]

The center column was made up of the German grenadiers and companies of other German regiments, supported by the two 12-pounders and the two 8-inch howitzers. This column moved along a rough road and across cleared fields. The left column, made up mainly of the British battalion of grenadiers under John Acland, moved forward to cover the left flank of the force.

The three columns marched for half an hour, passing outposts of von Breymann's grenadiers and squalid abandoned farmsteads. Päusch paused anxiously with his big guns so that some of the grenadiers could return and let the artillerymen know where the ground was firm and passable. At length the left and center columns emerged into the wheat field. It seemed likely that the American entrenchments were not far away, but no one could see them through the dense woods that lay on the other side of the wheat field.[17]

Burgoyne had Phillips and Riedesel riding with him. There was a small house on the north side of the wheat field. The lead troops found American pickets quartered there and quickly expelled them. The Americans ran back to their lines with the news of the British advance. British engineers did the best they could to convert the roof of the house into an observation platform.[18]

Soon there was a crowd of adjutants, engineers, and quartermasters on top of the house, peering toward the American lines through their glasses. Hamilton ordered his units to deploy in a long line in front of the house. Acland's grenadier battalion formed along the top of a slope that angled back northeastward on the left side of the wheat field, so that his men were covering the left flank.

The heavy British artillery was put in the middle, two 12-pounders set a few yards in advance. These were Williams's guns, the man known by the British and German soldiers alike as himself an old 12-pounder. He was an "old wolf" who knew better how to lay and fire a medium 12-pounder than anyone else on the field, and everyone knew it. Williams did not like taking his beloved 12-pounders on this adventure, and he said so. "Once a 12-pounder is removed from the Park of artillery in America it is gone," he grumbled. But Williams was a professional soldier and he followed orders.[19]

The artillerymen knew that one of their number had deserted earlier in the morning. The man had gone over to the Americans, taking what he knew of this action with him. Many of the artillerymen had the impression that the Americans were ready and waiting as a result. They were sure the deserter had tipped the Americans off.[20]

Westward beyond the British artillery were more companies of German grenadiers, the two British howitzers, and beyond them a long thin deployment of jägers and chasseurs. Even farther to their right, on a hill beyond the German irregulars, was Fraser's third column, made up of Alexander Fraser's rangers, the 24th Regiment and the British light infantry battalion under Alexander Lindsay, and the last two 6-pounders. The single company of rangers and the 24th were positioned around the small hilltop facing west so as to protect the right flank. It was a long thin line, two ranks drawn up almost shoulder to shoulder for more than a half mile.[21] It was made up of seventeen hundred proud men who were elegantly arrayed, highly trained, battle hardened, and pathetically insufficient to oppose what was about to come at them.

1:30 PM, Georg Päusch, the German Line on the Wheat Field

Foragers started cutting wheat in the field. Other men stood battle ready without completely knowing why. Suddenly a British officer rode up to Päusch. "There are no cannon on the flank of the left wing. You must immediately send one of yours." Päusch was dumbfounded. He had only two 6-pounders. The British had six guns, four of them 6-pounders and two more big 12-pounders. Now here was someone demanding that he split his little battery to cover an exposed left flank. Päusch refused. He would either respond to a direct order from a superior and move both guns to the left flank or he would stay where he was.[22] The frantic British officer rode off, and the waiting continued. It was not a good sign. If there was already confusion in the detachments, what would it be like if the Americans attacked? Päusch waited, his guns loaded, slow matches smoldering and ready.

1:30 PM, Horatio Gates, American Headquarters

Gates was dining with several of his officers. Colonel Brooks was there in place of his ailing regimental commander. Arnold was also at the table. They were both uncomfortable, letting the formality of the occasion provide a formula for civility. Protocol had required Gates to invite Arnold, and protocol had required Arnold to accept. Fortunately, the other officers knew how to keep the conversation moving, and more importantly how to keep the two major generals from going after each other across the dinner table.[23]

Gates's officers kept the conversation focused on the question that was foremost in every mind. Should the Americans continue to wait for Burgoyne to attack or should they use their growing superiority and launch a preemptory attack themselves? It was no surprise to anyone when Arnold argued they should attack. "The assailant has the advantage for he can always take his own time and choose the point of attack. If repulsed, he has only to retreat behind his own lines and form again."

Gates continued to favor defensive tactics. "If undisciplined militia were repulsed on the open field and the enemy pressed upon them in their retreat, it would be difficult to form them again, even behind their own breastworks. For if they were under a panic they would keep on retreating, even after they had passed their own lines." At the moment it was all hypothetical, but the situation could change at any time, and Gates was clearly worried about what Arnold might do when that time came.[24]

The Americans had heard two signal guns fired in the British camp at about one o'clock. There had been a signal cannon and rockets last night that had come to nothing, but this time would prove to be different. Now, at one-thirty, the advanced pickets reported back that they could see troops advancing. The drums of the advanced American units rattled to arms. This was caught up and repeated by each succeeding unit until in a matter of seconds the alarm reached Gates's ears at his headquarters in the rear.

Days ago James Wilkinson had prevailed upon Gates to limit the use of the beat to arms. The drummers had caused too many false alarms, and every time the drums rolled there was a great expenditure of energy as men rushed to assemble and deploy. The drums were more often silent now, so there was surprise around the table when the officers heard them. It could be a false alarm, but a betting man would wager that it was not. Regiment after regiment of Continentals and militia formed up or ran to their assigned posts as the drumming rippled down the American line.[25]

Predictably, Arnold spoke first. "Shall I go out and see what is the matter?" The question could not be ignored. All eyes were on Gates. "I am afraid to trust you, Arnold," he finally said.

Arnold was as close to contrite as any of them had ever seen him. Even though Gates had not formally removed him, he had no command and no respect for Gates, but still he knew that his only chance to play a part in what was coming was to be a dutiful subordinate. "Pray let me go. I will be careful, and if our advance does not need support I will promise not to commit you." Gates relented and allowed Arnold to go out and see what was happening, but he shot a meaningful look at Lincoln when he did. Arnold quickly disappeared, with Lincoln right behind him. Gates thought he could count on Lincoln to keep Arnold from doing anything rash.

Gates also sent Wilkinson out to discover what was going on. Wilkinson was on his horse and riding north within moments. When he reached the post of the first drummer he was told only that someone unnamed had reported the enemy to be advancing on the American left. Wilkinson spurred his horse past the pickets and into no man's land. On a rise a half mile from the American lines he saw several British and German units advancing, perhaps 350 yards distant on the wheat field. They were out of musket range. Wilkinson might have been a target if Burgoyne had a few of Morgan's riflemen, but he did not and Wilkinson knew he was safe at this distance.

Burgoyne's troops were wading across the uncut wheat field. There was a little stream on Wilkinson's side of the field. He watched the British troops deploy into a long double line that stretched across the field. Most of the soldiers sat down with their guns between their legs. Some foraged, cutting the wheat as quickly as they could for transportation back to their lines. Beyond the field Wilkinson could see officers with their glasses observing him and trying to see the American lines from a perch on top of a small house. There were British grenadiers on his right. West of them were some German units and four regiments of foot. Still farther west were green-uniformed jägers and some other German units. There were still more units even farther west on a hill, apparently the right flank of Burgoyne's line. Even without a glass Wilkinson could see parts of at least eight battalions, probably more. This was no simple foraging party. Burgoyne had sent out his crack troops. Wilkinson watched for fifteen minutes, then turned and spurred his horse back to headquarters.[26]

When Wilkinson got back he described the situation to Gates. "They are foraging, and endeavoring to reconnoiter your left, and I think sir they offer you battle." Gates thought about this. "What is the nature of the ground and what is your opinion?" Wilkinson replied, "Their front is open and their flanks rest on woods under cover of which they may be attacked. Their right is skirted by a lofty height. I would indulge them."

No one was quite sure where Arnold was at the moment. Had he been there, Arnold would have been shouting, demanding an immediate attack, pressing Gates hard. That would probably prompt the commander to dig in his heels and resist sending battalions forward to attack, even when Gates knew it was probably the right thing to do. But Wilkinson was not Arnold. He was a twenty-year-old adjutant, not a major general. It was Gates's decision and his young adjutant had presented him with advice, not demands. "Well then, order on Morgan to begin the game." It was as simple as that.[27] The Americans were going to leave their entrenchments and go on the attack.

If anyone remembered the preposterous general order of October 3, it was not mentioned. According to Gates's standing orders that day, today it was the turn of the Massachusetts militia brigade to have 150 men ready to draw three days provisions and race westward past Saratoga Lake to cut off Burgoyne's imaginary flanking move there.[28] But that was forgotten. The focus was here and now. The threat was within earshot, almost within sight.

Off to the east, German pickets began engaging Americans along the river road. Word of it was relayed back to headquarters in a matter of a few minutes. In Gates's mind the discredited fear of a distant flanking move west of Saratoga Lake was instantly replaced by a new fear of an attack on his eastern flank. It seemed like what he had expected all along, a direct attack southward along the river road.

Wilkinson rode off to find Morgan. The colonel was formed and ready with nearly his entire corps in front of Fort Neilson. Apart from those already out on picket duty the riflemen were all there, as organized as they could be made to be, which for the irregular riflemen was less so than a green militia regiment. Morgan's subordinate Henry Dearborn was also there with his light infantry battalion, strapping young men with speed and just enough equipment for the task of providing musketry to support the riflemen. This time they would stay in close contact.

Wilkinson rode up to Morgan and used Gates's exact words. Morgan knew the ground. He had ridden and walked it over and over again since the armies had settled into their current positions eighteen days ago.

"What is the position of the enemy?" Wilkinson briefed him as well as he could. "They are formed across a newly cultivated field. Their grenadiers with several field pieces on the left border on a wood and a small ravine formed by the rivulet. Their light infantry is on our right, covered by a worm fence at the foot of the hill, thickly covered with wood. Their center is composed of British and German battalions."[29]

Morgan thought about this and said, "My corps will make a circuit by our left and under cover of the wood to gain the height on the right of the enemy. From there I will commence my attack so soon as our fire is opened against their left." Wilkinson thought it was the best plan that could be devised. He spun his horse to carry it back to Gates.[30]

Lincoln and Arnold had been off checking with regiments posted closer to the river. There was action there, but not much. Information being relayed from the west indicated that it was there where the main threat was focused. They returned to headquarters together and rode up to Gates, who was standing in the door waiting for news. Lincoln said, "General Gates, the firing at the river is merely a feint. Their object is your left. A strong force of fifteen hundred men are marching circuitously to plant themselves on yonder height. That point must be defended or your camp is in danger."[31]

Immediately Gates responded: "I have sent Morgan with his riflemen and Dearborn's infantry."

"That is nothing," Arnold said. "You must send a strong force."

"General Arnold, I have nothing for you to do. You have no business here," said Gates.

Arnold said nothing.

Lincoln spoke up again. "You must send a strong force to support Morgan and Dearborn, at least three regiments."

The generals had gathered around, waiting. The plan all along had been to fight only defensively from well-constructed entrenchments. This was the best ground Kościuszko could find. Burgoyne would destroy his army trying to take it. But now even the easygoing Lincoln was urging Gates to meet Burgoyne outside the fortifications. Gates could see nothing in the faces of the other generals to contradict Lincoln. Gates ordered General Learned to send out two of his New England regiments. He ordered General Nixon to send one of his as well. Fine, there were the three regiments Lincoln wanted him to commit. The rest would stay in their lines for now.[32] It was the least Gates could do.

Lincoln and Arnold remounted their horses and left. The remaining generals worked on Gates. More troops had to be committed. Three regiments would not be enough. If they waited in their lines they risked letting the British turn their left flank. At last Gates yielded. Morgan's rifles and Dearborn's light infantry were already on their way. Gates countermanded his previous orders to Learned and Nixon. Now instead he ordered forward General Poor's brigade of five Continental and two militia regiments to attack the left of the British line on the wheat field while Morgan and Dearborn engaged from the woods on the British right. General Learned's brigade of three Continental and three militia regiments was redirected to attack the British center. Instead of three regiments Gates had now committed thirteen of them, not counting Morgan's corps, all from the left wing he had taken away from Arnold (Figure 4.2).

Wilkinson rode up to headquarters to report Morgan's intentions to Gates. Gates approved it and decided to send word to Poor and Learned to wait long enough to allow Morgan to move off to the west and get in position against the British right flank. Gates needed time to put his revised orders into effect. He ordered Wilkinson to instruct General Poor to position his brigade to attack the British grenadiers and others on the British left flank. Wilkinson rode off again.

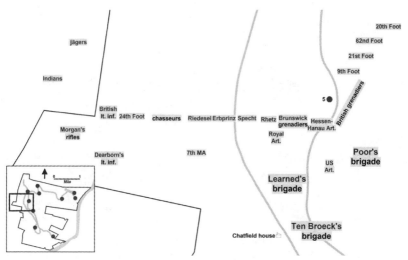

Figure 4.2 Battle of Bemis Heights, 2:00 p.m., October 7, 1777.

No sooner had Wilkinson delivered these orders to Poor than a rider came up, calling him back to headquarters to receive new instructions from Gates. This time he was sent to the rear to order Brigadier General Abraham Ten Broeck to bring up his Albany militia in support of Learned's brigade. By now it was a massive brigade, fourteen regiments and over three thousand men. Gates knew that the militiamen had more enthusiasm than discipline, but he also knew that he could depend on them to back up the Continental regiments, giving the Americans weight in the attack. Few men would break knowing they had that much support both in front and behind them (Figure 4.3).

Gate's also ordered the 7th Massachusetts Continentals forward to support Morgan's and Learned's units. They had been detached from Nixon's brigade on September 22 and held in reserve at Gate's headquarters ever since. Now they marched out to take up a position on Morgan's right.[33]

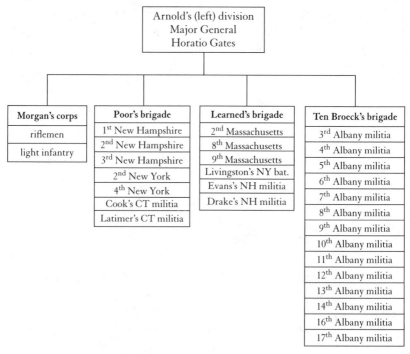

Figure 4.3 Left Division of the Northern Army on October 7, 1777. It was still technically under Arnold's command but had been assumed by Gates. Chart by the author based on Schnitzer (2016).

Gates was fully committed to battle now. On September 19 he had concentrated the available American artillery on the bluffs overlooking the river road, thinking that Burgoyne would attack there. Today he had some artillery available on the left flank. The Northern Army had two detachments of the 3rd Regiment of Continental Artillery, a total of only twenty-two cannons, a majority of them 4-pounders. With only a single 9-pounder and twenty-one lighter pieces, the Americans had nothing like the weight of artillery that Burgoyne had dragged all the way from Canada, but today some of it would see action. Gates ordered two gun crews forward with their cannons. One of the crews was commanded by young Lieutenant Ebenezer Mattoon, who was about to see his first action, and record the incident that would change the course of the war.

2:00 PM, *Benedict Arnold, Fort Neilson*

The great climactic battle was finally beginning and Arnold was acting like a caged lion. They could all hear the firing as the lead units started to engage. Arnold had not been able to follow the confusion of commands, countermands, and new orders that Gates had issued since he had left headquarters, but men were moving forward. At last he said to Clarkson, "No man shall keep me in my tent today. If I am without command, I will fight in the ranks. But the soldiers, God bless them, will follow my lead. Come on, victory or death."[34] Arnold's dark bay was the best of his mounts, a Spanish horse named "Warren" after an old friend who had died a hero at Bunker Hill. Strictly speaking, Warren was not his; he had generously been lent to him by a friend in Connecticut.[35] No matter. Arnold spotted Dr. Chadwick, surgeon to Scammell's 3rd New Hampshire. He spurred the horse over to the surgeon's tent where the good doctor had an open hogshead of medicinal rum. "Give me a dipperful of that rum!" Arnold gulped a half pint of encouragement and raced off into the fight.[36]

Arnold's departure could hardly go unnoticed. Gates was furious. He sent Armstrong, his aide-de-camp, after Arnold to order him back to camp.[37] It was no use; Arnold outdistanced the messenger on the big bay.

2:00 PM, *Daniel Morgan and Henry Dearborn, West of the Wheat Field*

Morgan's men had scampered through the woods like released hounds, keeping far enough from the edge of the wheat field to screen their movements from the British observers. This time, Morgan's men moved to the left at the fork in the road. Dearborn's light infantry were right behind them, moving just as fast. This time Dearborn did not veer farther to the west as he had on September 19, and the light infantry was in position to support Morgan's rifles. All of them were farther west than they had been at the beginning of the first battle, yet not as far from the American lines today as they had been on the nineteenth (Figure 4.2).

Once he was in place Morgan could see two battalions of the British left on the hill in front of him. One unit appeared to be the 24th Regiment, Simon Fraser's own. The second was the British light infantry battalion commanded by Major Lindsay, the Earl of Balcarres, or at least parts of it. Mounted behind them was their brigade commander, a portly officer who had to be Simon Fraser. Dearborn and his light infantry had followed Morgan through the woods until they, too, overlooked the British right flank. Out ahead of the two British battalions Morgan and Dearborn could both see another smaller unit. This had to be some of Alexander Fraser's Rangers.

Arnold was suddenly there amid the light infantry, and Dearborn assumed that he was in command of this division, just as he had been on September 19. Wilkinson had passed along orders to Morgan, and there was no reason for Dearborn to believe that they had come from anyone but Arnold. John Armstrong caught up with Arnold and told him that Gates had ordered him to return to camp. Arnold wheeled and shouted at him, his eyes wild. "I promised Morgan to support him, and support him I will by God."[38] He tore off, leaving a speechless Armstrong to wonder what he should do next. Dearborn had no advice.

2:00 PM, *Joseph Cilley, East of the Wheat Field*

After receiving Gates's orders from Wilkinson, Poor had immediately started deploying his five Continental regiments, three from New Hampshire and two from New York. Colonel Joseph Cilley led the 1st New Hampshire at the point of attack on the British left. Cilley's regiment had led the way on September 19 and they would do so again today. They had earned it. This time they were facing portions of John Acland's battalion of British grenadiers.

The Americans, Continentals and militia alike, were loading their muskets with both a ball and two to four buckshot.[39] The combination, called buck and ball, would make for horrible wounds, another affront to the British sense of fair play. Poor drew his regiments up in two ranks facing the British grenadiers on their left flank and the eastern portion of their main line. There was a long, heavy pause. Poor had given orders to wait for Burgoyne's troops to fire the first volley.[40] At last the grenadiers opened up with muskets, followed by canister from their supporting artillery. Virtually all of it flew over the heads of Poor's men. Now it was the Americans' turn.

Enoch Poor had deployed his brigade with Cilley and the 1st New Hampshire at the far right of the American line. A British unit was sent out to try to turn the flank of Cilley's regiment, and thus the entire American line. They appeared suddenly from behind a brush fence, rising and firing, but almost without effect. Once again most of their balls passed harmlessly over the Americans' heads. They were so close that Cilley could hear the British colonel order his men to "fix bayonets and charge the damned rebels." Cilley shouted back, as much at his own men as at the British, "That is a game two can play at. Charge, by God, and we will try it." The Americans charged before the British could, then discharged a volley at close range before the British had finished reloading. The British flankers broke and ran, leaving several dead and wounded.[41]

The rest of Poor's brigade surged forward in support of the 1st New Hampshire. Alexander Scammell's regiment advanced beside Cilley's, just as it had on September 19. The other New Hampshire regiments advanced as well.[42] The British had more artillery in position than the Americans, but the infantrymen were hopelessly outnumbered. Poor's seven regiments threw themselves at Acland's grenadier detachment of only 266 officers and men.

2:30 PM, Daniel Morgan and Henry Dearborn,
West of the Wheat Field

Morgan heard the firing erupt on the American right wing as Poor's brigade engaged. The firing was Morgan's signal to "begin the game," as Gates had put it. But Dearborn was still getting organized and Morgan's men were not yet fully deployed.[43] Morgan yelled and his riflemen opened fire on both Fraser's front and his flank from the cover of trees. Lindsay's light infantrymen were taking fire from two sides and he began trying to change his front to deal with both threats at the same time. Morgan's rifles were doing damage, but Lindsay's men would be able to hold them off if he could get them properly positioned, so long as Morgan was not reinforced. But this time Dearborn was right behind Morgan, and the light infantry would be ready in a few minutes.

Arnold moved past the light infantry, spotted Morgan, and shouted at him, pointing toward Fraser. "That officer upon a gray horse is of himself a host and must be disposed of. Direct the attention of some of the sharpshooters among your riflemen to him." Morgan urged his men forward.[44]

Dearborn could see the British officers scrambling to reset their line as Morgan came at them from both their front and their right flank. For the moment, like Gates, Dearborn was convinced that the British advance here on the American left had to be a feint. The main attack would surely come along the main road near the Hudson. Why else would the British attack with such a small force? There had to be a total of fewer than two thousand British and Germans facing the Americans here. The main attack had to be somewhere else. Nothing else made sense to him.[45]

The British units in front of Dearborn numbered only a few hundred, separated from the main British line by about five hundred yards. Like Morgan, Dearborn was now in the woods, only 150 yards from the enemy. Morgan's rifles were taking a deadly toll on the redcoats, picking them off one by one. All the British could do at this range was return volleys of ineffectual musket fire. Dearborn's light infantrymen were ready. They had superior numbers, and Dearborn could feel nothing but confidence. It was time to see what they could do.

2:30 PM, American Soldiers, the South Side of the Wheat Field

The fighting roared for thirty minutes, during which time Learned's brigade came up beside Poor's.[46] There was scarcely room for them all. Men were falling, but more moved up behind to take their places. Each would have his own story to tell. A young soldier from Massachusetts took a ball in his shoulder and dropped to his knees. The ball lodged under his shoulder blade and would remain there for the rest of his life. The man next to him was shot through and fell dead. The wounded soldier left the field and staggered back toward the American hospital.[47]

Even through the dense smoke everyone could see that Burgoyne's troops were hopelessly outnumbered. Some of the cannons supporting the British and German troops were taken, lost, and retaken five times. With each volley the soldiers of one side would surge forward, only to fall back when the other side fired and surged in turn. The dense clouds of gunsmoke forced both sides to fire almost blindly but nothing suppressed the crash of the American muskets. The grenadiers wavered, then broke, leaving much of the flower of the King's army behind on the field.

3:00 PM, Benedict Arnold, the South Side of the Wheat Field

Arnold appeared among Learned's regiments of Massachusetts Continentals as they pressed the attack on Burgoyne's center. He behaved as if he were in command, and the men began following him without regard to their regimental commanders or other officers. Arnold was riding back and forth like a lunatic, screaming and swinging his sword over his head in his efforts to animate the officers and men around him.

Arnold raced up to one of Poor's militia regiments, leaving Clarkson far behind, Armstrong even farther. "Whose regiment is this?" A young Private Foster replied, "Colonel Latimer's, sir." Arnold grinned. "Ah, my old Norwich and New London friends. God bless you! I am glad to see you. Now come on, boys, if the day is long enough we'll have them all in hell before night."[48]

Arnold wheeled his horse again and rode back and forth across the field encouraging men he could not order, looking for opportunities the British might offer. Arnold urged them, accompanied them, and led them in a ferocious attack on the German grenadiers. The Germans held against the first charge, but the Americans steadied and tried again. This time the Germans broke and fell back.[49] Arnold spun on his horse and saw the reason why. General Ten Broeck was now in position with his three thousand Albany militiamen. It had to be an awful sight to the Germans. It was too much for the center of Burgoyne's line.

3:00 PM, Henry Dearborn, West of the Wheat Field

Dearborn was worried. The firing far off at the other end of the American line was intense, and in his imagination it sounded like the Americans were getting the worst of it. He refocused on what was in front of him. The British officers closest to him seemed to still be having trouble resetting their line and Dearborn decided to take advantage of the confusion and try to get behind the British. How better to take advantage of the light weight and speed of the men in his command? Dearborn put it to his men and found them eager to give it a try. The American light infantry leapt the fence separating the woods from the open field and dashed at full speed at the British right flank. They had Morgan's rifles for covering fire and made the most of it by yelling as they ran forward. Fraser's men were clearly outnumbered. They gave way in confusion without firing a shot.[50]

3:00 PM, *John Burgoyne, the North Side of the Wheat Field*

Burgoyne watched with his aides from behind the center of the British line. The Americans were out of their camp. This was a surprise; it was not what was supposed to happen; it was not what Burgoyne had expected of Gates. Burgoyne had enough artillery to turn the American flank and tear up the American camp, but if the American infantry numbers were too great he would not be able to get the guns into position. He might be stuck here in no man's land, or worse. He glanced around for Charles Stanhope. He sent Stanhope off to the 20th Foot detachment, one of four partial regiments he had left positioned in reserve behind and to the northeast on or near the fields of Coulter's farm. The orders were to post fifty men under a captain on the left flank to cover a retreat to Fraser's camp should that become necessary.[51]

3:00 PM, *Ebenezer Wild, the American Entrenchments by the Hudson*

Most of Brigadier General John Glover's brigade had been marched forward of the lines they held on the river flats until they came up with their own advance pickets. It was the most they were expected to do. The brigade was being held back, and Glover had no orders to join in the fighting. Ebenezer Wild was there with the 1st Massachusetts, listening to the distant firing off to the west and wondering if they would engage here on the far right by the river. There they stood for the afternoon, waiting for an attack that never came but hearing the roar of action off to their left.[52] Glover himself could not stay that far from the action. He probed out ahead of his brigade with a few aides. By the end of the day he would have three horses shot out from under him[53] (See Figure 4.4.).

A quarter of Nixon's brigade had been detached to serve as a reserve force on the left. Gates had thrown them into the fight, but Nixon's other three Continental regiments now waited near the Hudson, far from the current action. John Nixon rode forward on the left to see how the 7th

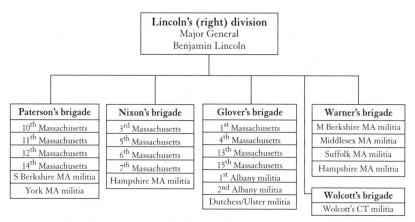

Figure 4.4 Right Division of the Northern Army on October 7, 1777, by then assigned to Lincoln. Chart by the author based on Schnitzer (2016).

Massachusetts from his brigade was doing. This put him within range of Päusch's German artillery on the wheat field, which were now in action.[54] Nixon, now fifty-two years old, had fought in the French and Indian War. He had been a minuteman at Lexington. He had led a regiment at Bunker Hill. Without warning, a random German cannonball passed over his shoulder, within a few inches of his head. The concussion deafened the ear and injured the eye on that side of his head. After decades of risky combat Nixon was finally injured and nearly killed.[55]

Behind the reserve brigades and closer to American headquarters also waited hundreds of women whose husbands were forward who knew where. Many were wringing their hands with worry. More than a few were weeping, and jumping at the roar of the big guns. "Och, my husband! My poor husband! Lord Jesus, spare my poor husband," came one cry. Others were harder women, or women whose marital investments were less precious to them. "Damn your poor husband; you can get another!"[56] And so it went as the afternoon progressed.

3:00 PM, *John Acland, the British Line, the Wheat Field*

Major John Dyke Acland had led his Grenadier detachment as he had since the expedition began. Acland's grenadiers were all big men, gifted with equal measures of courage and strength. But they were facing a sea of Americans. Acland could see five regiments. The American front seemed unfazed by the grenadiers' initial volley. His men reloaded and fired again. Now the rebels were nearly on top of them and there was nothing to it but to fall back. Some of the men panicked; the retreat was becoming chaotic. Acland's aides shouted "for shame" at men who were fleeing rather than retiring, and that caused them to recover some order.[57] But they were too few.

Musket balls seemed to come in clouds. Acland was shot through both legs. He dragged himself far enough to sit back against a tree and waited for help. The British and German troops were retreating steadily now and he faced imprisonment or worse if he could not find help to get back to camp. Suddenly there was his old friend Captain Shrimpton of the 31st. Shrimpton was a big man and with some effort and after discarding some equipment he hoisted Acland onto his back. They were halfway to the Balcarres Redoubt when it became clear that the Americans were gaining on them. Shrimpton had no choice but to abandon his friend to the enemy and save himself.[58]

Acland cried out to the panicked men rushing by him. "Fifty guineas to any soldier who will convey me into camp." A big grenadier stopped to take up the challenge, but it was too late. Both men were overtaken by the Americans.[59] Acland was lying propped up in the angle of a worm fence. He squirmed as a teenage American militiaman glared at him down the barrel of his musket. James Wilkinson rode up and Acland entreated him. "Protect me, sir, against this boy." The young militiaman relaxed as Wilkinson assumed control of the situation.

Wilkinson asked, "What is your rank, sir?" Acland responded, "I had the honor to command the grenadiers." Wilkinson knew him immediately by reputation. Acland quickly told him the story of Shrimpton's effort to save him. Wilkinson dismounted and shook his hand. "I hope that you are not badly wounded." "Not badly," said Acland, "but very inconveniently. I am shot through both legs. Will you, sir, have the goodness to have me conveyed to your camp?" Wilkinson motioned his trailing servant forward. The man dismounted and helped Wilkinson lift Acland on the horse. Wilkinson instructed the man to take Acland back to headquarters; the wounded officer was led slowly into a painful captivity.[60] In less than a half hour he reached the Neilson house at the apex of the American line, and some Americans carried him to a bed inside.[61]

It had taken less than an hour from the first shot. Where Acland had posted his grenadiers, in a space scarcely more than a dozen yards square lay eighteen grenadiers dead or close to it. Every British officer's horse lay dead or dying. Three more British officers lay wounded, probably fatally, propped up against tree stumps. Poor's Continentals and Ten Broeck's militia had swept past, and Wilkinson could see an American surgeon tending to one of the wounded officers as the battle roared on ahead of them. The surgeon looked up with a grin and yelled, "Wilkinson, I have dipped my hands in British blood." It was a brutal joke immediately regretted. The man saw the hard look on Wilkinson's face and knew that he would regret it even more later. Wilkinson rode on toward the roar.[62] Here and there American soldiers were escorting British and German prisoners to the rear. There were already at least fifty of them.[63] Others helped the wounded or tended the dead. The New Hampshire regiments secured the part of the field they had taken as other troops rushed past them toward the fighting.

3:05 PM, Georg Päusch, the German Line, the Wheat Field

The American regiments began a concerted assault against the center of the British line as well. There were thousands of them. From where he stood Päusch could see at least four regiments, and they looked like Continentals. Päusch's German crews loaded and fired as rapidly as possible. The American advance on the center held back even as other American units appeared to be overwhelming the British left, kept at bay by the murderous fire of British and German artillery.

The German grenadiers in the center saw British grenadiers on their left reeling and began falling back themselves. Päusch turned around to see men who had formed the line not fifty paces behind him suddenly leave without a word. To his left the Americans were now no more than three hundred paces from his position. Acland's British grenadiers were in disarray, dead on the field or running for their lives. He looked behind him again. The German grenadiers were gone. His servant and his personal horses were gone. His battery was alone, facing thousands of mad Americans.

3:10 PM, Simon Fraser, British Line, the Wheat Field

General Fraser was mounted on his favorite horse, a big gray gelding. The portly Fraser had been particularly well fed this day. It might have been only a twelve-minute quick march from his position to that of Acland's grenadiers on the far left, but the line was thin in places. He was on a strong position with steep slopes down to the front and left of him, but he was vulnerable just the same.

It was not a sustainable arrangement. Lindsay had tried resetting his men to face firing from both the south and on his flank to the west. Then there had been the rippling roar of voices from the woods. A battalion of American light infantry emerged from the woods, vaulted the worm fence, and came uphill straight at them. The noise had grown and men had begun to fall. Flashes from rifle muzzles in the trees were still picking off Lindsay's men.

Fraser had ordered Lindsay's light infantry and part of the 24th Regiment to refuse the line by pulling back and facing west to prevent the expected American flanking attack. While Fraser was trying to complete that move, noise in the distance told him that the Americans had thrown fresh units at the British grenadiers and Germans far off to the left. Fraser could see even at this distance that the left end of the long line was giving way.

The Mohawks and the other irregulars were supposed to have cleared the woods off to his own end of the line, but it was plain to Fraser that this had not happened. They were overmatched.[64] It was too much for Fraser's right wing. The woods offered too much cover for the Americans. There was too much distance between Fraser's undermanned brigade and Riedesel's brigade at the center of the line. The chasseur and jäger units in the long gap between them were too thinly deployed. Fraser's brigade was becoming isolated, unsupported, and in danger of being enveloped. The Americans were coming on at a dead run; Lindsay's men were starting to break.

It suddenly became clear to Fraser that Lindsay had misunderstood his order. Instead of forming a line that angled back from the main line in a way that would cover its right flank, Lindsay was moving his men rapidly to the left to a new position behind the German regiments and was forming a second line parallel to them. He was in position to cover a retreat, but not to hold off a renewed American attack from the right. Fraser saw the mistake through the clouds of gunsmoke when he got close, but it was too late to reverse the redeployment. The Americans were coming on too fast. The whole right flank was in danger of collapse.[65]

Seconds dragged on. Fraser knew that he had no choice but to have the rest of his brigade retreat behind Riedesel's units still holding the center and redeploy his men in the new line, turning them if possible to face the flanking American attack. Fraser shouted orders and drums began to roll. He rode among men who were on the edge of panic, their military order close to breaking. The men of Dearborn's light infantry were advancing relentlessly. Somehow Fraser got the men of his corps away, moving northeast at the double quick to the open space behind the German brigade.

Fraser and his officers were now protected to their front behind the German troops that had been on his left just minutes earlier, but firing was still coming from the American flankers. Dearborn's light infantrymen were re-forming in the field in front of the trees and again threatening to fall on Fraser's right. Meanwhile Morgan's riflemen were also repositioning themselves in trees closer to Fraser's new position. They could still hit mounted officers at this distance, but it was slow work. Many of the riflemen had to climb down from their perches to complete the arduous process of reloading their rifles each time they fired, moving to different trees as the British fell back.

3:20 PM, Simon Fraser, the British Line on the Wheat Field

Fraser needed to re-form his brigade so that it faced the American threat from the right, protecting the flank of Riedesel's brigade. He was just beginning to get control through his officers when a rider came up with fresh orders from Burgoyne. The British left wing had collapsed and now the front was in trouble as well. Burgoyne ordered Fraser to hold his new line to the rear of Riedesel's and Hamilton's brigades and parallel to the original line so that he could cover their impending retreat. Fraser hurried to get control of his regiments, pressing their commanders to move at the double quick. Back and forth he rode, pointing, gesturing, shouting to be heard over the noise of battle, letting the men see him on the big gray. Clouds of gunsmoke drifted around him. (See Figure 4.5.)

The crupper strap on the rump of Fraser's gray snapped, cut by a ball from an American rifle, and the horse pranced, tucking its hind quarters away from the blow. Fraser reined the gray to a halt and squinted through the smoke ahead of him. Seconds later a second rifle ball tugged at the horse's mane just behind its ears.[66] This time Fraser glanced in the direction of the shots and saw a sharpshooter in a tree two hundred yards off to his right.

Fraser's aides were anxious. Two shots had nearly found their mark, and it was obvious to them that Fraser was targeted. "It is evident that you are marked out for particular aim. Would it not be prudent for you to retire from this place?" asked one. Fraser would have none of it. He

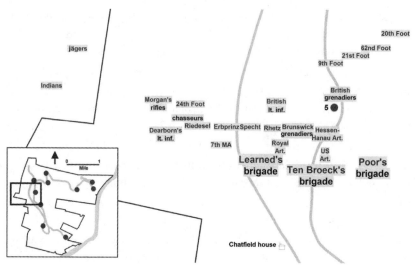

Figure 4.5 Battle of Bemis Heights, 3:20 p.m., October 7, 1777.

still affected the much-practiced detachment of a proper British officer in battle. If he was anxious it would be for the success of his command, not for his personal safety. "My duty forbids me to fly from danger." With that Fraser once more spurred his big gray horse toward the fighting, with his worried aides in pursuit.[67]

3:20 PM, Ebenezer Mattoon, American Artillery on the Wheat Field

Ebenezer Mattoon was twenty-two years old and from Amherst, Massachusetts. He had joined the Continental artillery shortly after graduating from Dartmouth in 1776. Now he was in the thick of it, managing the crew of one of the cannons. The American guns were finally in action, firing canister at the German lines as fast as they could.[68]

They had first positioned the two guns on a rise, where they had a good field of fire over the heads of the American infantry. But they appeared to be facing bigger guns across the wheat field. The bigger British and German guns targeted the two smaller American ones and made their positions untenable, so both were ordered to move up with the American infantry. There the gun crews had some protection and cover behind clouds of gunsmoke.

The smoke from muskets and artillery was so thick that neither side could make out the other much of the time. Ebenezer caught a glimpse of the German troops through a break in the smoke and could see that they were advancing slowly, urged on by their officers. Now the American Continental infantrymen seemed to be retreating slowly past his gun.[69]

Ten Broeck's Albany militiamen were behind them all for support. They could not be restrained, and many started to move up among the Continentals on the front line. The flow of militiamen forward counteracted the slow retreat and steadied the American line. Next to Mattoon an artilleryman fell, severely wound. Mattoon dragged the wounded man to the rear of their position then moved forward again to direct his crew.

To Mattoon's surprise an elderly militiaman suddenly appeared at his side carrying a long hunting gun. Mattoon yelled at the old man, "Daddy, the infantry mustn't leave. I shall be cut to pieces." The old man said, "I'll give them another gun."

Just then the smoke rose a little and Mattoon could see a group of British officers moving across the field behind the Brunswickers. The mounted British officers were doing what they could to steady their men; they were less than seventy yards from Mattoon and the old militiaman. The senior officer among them was conspicuous on a big, gray horse. The old man steadied himself and fired. Fraser was a mere sixty-six yards away, just passing under the branches of a basswood tree. The ball pierced Fraser's left side, ravaging his gut. Fraser slumped forward on to the neck of his gray. The old militiaman said, "I have killed that officer, let him be who he will." Mattoon answered, "You have, and it is a general officer, and by his dress I believe it is Fraser." He saw consternation as Fraser's aides moved in to support him. Three of the horses fell. Then the smoke closed in again and they disappeared. It was the tipping point.[70]

3:30 PM, Simon Fraser, the British Line on the Wheat Field

Fraser began to slide from his saddle into the arms of an aide-de-camp.[71] Men were dismounting, some of them from horses that had been shot out from under them. With Fraser fallen, his command devolved to Alexander Lindsay, the Earl of Balcarres.[72] Officers who still had mounts converged on Fraser and steadied him on the big gray. Two of them escorted him off the field as quickly as they could, using the gunsmoke as cover, keeping the wounded general from falling off his horse as they made their way back to the British hospital. As Fraser was being taken from the field, Lindsay looked up. Through the smoke he could see the swarming advance of Ten Broeck's militia.

3:35 PM, John Burgoyne, the British Line on the Wheat Field

Burgoyne sat, scarcely moving, on his mount, his face set, impassive, impossible to read. Men glanced at their general and saw what they wanted to see. To some he was more than a man, unperturbed by his own danger, anxious for the fate of so many that was at stake.[73] Others would describe Burgoyne's mask differently. Courage, fate, determination, despair lurked behind it. It was do or die, the last throw of the dice. The Americans had not stayed within their lines as predicted. They had come out, and there seemed to be no stopping them.

Burgoyne saw Fraser slump. The British and German lines rallied one more time, firing and driving the Americans back, but another American surge was on the way. Burgoyne knew that retreat was the only thing left to them.

What was left of the artillery had thrown canister shot at the Americans for a quarter of an hour, firing without swabbing, which made the guns too hot to touch and rendered their crews temporarily deaf. After all this abuse the American regiments still advanced on Burgoyne's position.[74]

It was a disaster. The Americans had turned both flanks of Burgoyne's outnumbered and fragmented force. The roar of fire was incessant; everywhere his units were breaking or on the verge of it. Burgoyne shouted again for Charles Stanhope, who was poised on his flank. Burgoyne sent him off with orders for Phillips. "Draw as soon as possible back to the camp." Burgoyne wheeled his horse and led his party back to the British lines to organize a defense against the renewed attack he was sure would come soon. A ball made a hole in Burgoyne's hat and nearly pulled it off. Another tore his waistcoat. He looked around for another aide to carry orders to cover the retreat to Riedesel.[75]

Stanhope galloped off to find Phillips, lost in the smoke, woods, and confusion of battle. He found Francis Clerke. Stanhope tried to enlist Clerke's help finding Phillips. They set off again in different directions with Burgoyne's orders to Phillips. The two friends would never see each other again.

Major Griffith Williams kept his battery of 12-pounders firing, his men loading, dragging lines, and firing without pause. His men began to fall around him, either dead or badly wounded. Twenty minutes into the fighting Captain Blomefield turned his head yelling and took a shot that passed through both cheeks, shattering several teeth. A lieutenant took a shot to the knee.[76] The infantry around them broke. The number of Americans before him seemed to multiply without limit. At last Williams, the old curmudgeon himself, took a ball and sank to the ground. He watched and wept as the Americans overran his beloved guns and took him prisoner. The British artillery horses were all down. Most of his artillerymen appeared to be dead or close to it. In minutes the situation would turn into a rout. There was no choice. Except for the howitzers, the artillery was surrounded and taken, and the Americans seeing this came on shouting loudly.[77]

3:40 PM, Ebenezer Mattoon, American Artillery on the Wheat Field

A British gun was seized by the Americans, then recaptured, then seized again and recaptured again before the Americans finally secured it. Colonel Cilley of the 1st New Hampshire came up. A jubilant soldier said, "Colonel, we have taken this piece, and now we want you to swear it true to America." Cilley dismounted and vaulted to the top of the hot cannon, declaring it "sworn true to America." Unlike what happened on September 19, this time the artillerymen had also abandoned the limber and ammunition with the gun, so the New Hampshire infantrymen turned the gun around and began firing canister at the retreating British and German troops.[78]

More Americans began appearing around Ebenezer Mattoon and the American guns. They sent the Brunswickers in front of them into retreat with a heavy volley, then began running forward, a screaming bayonet charge with empty muskets. Mattoon helped his gun crew to move forward with the Americans. They came up on British brass cannons surrounded by dead and dying men and horses. A little farther on they found two more pieces. It seemed to Mattoon that this was all or most of the artillery the British had brought up for action.[79]

The battalion of Brunswickers to one side of the British artillery had broken as soon as American firing began, falling back before taking any casualties. German officers rallied and re-formed them in a ragged line behind the artillery. For the time being, the Brunswickers to the other side of the British artillery held their ground under the direct command of Riedesel.[80]

Now there seemed to be a new line of infantry ahead of the Americans. A volley from the re-formed line killed or wounded thirty-six of one

American regiment. Mattoon's gun answered with canister, firing as fast as the men could load, not bothering to sponge. The Germans ceased firing. Mattoon saw them advance with trailed arms. He thought that next they would be ordered to quick, and then to double quick, and there was little left to slow them. The American advance was about to tip back into a retreat, and Mattoon thought he would soon lose either his gun or his life. Then he heard Arnold's frenzied voice. Arnold had Colonel Brooks and part of the 8th Massachusetts with him. The fresh Continentals fired a volley into the advancing Germans, and the tide turned again.[81]

3:40 PM, Francis Clerke, in the Wheat Field

Clerke encountered Robert Kingston as both British and German units were breaking and falling back around him. Clerke shouted over the noise to his friend, "Have you given any orders to the artillery?" It was a simple question. Kingston said, "I will not take on myself as adjutant general to give orders to any part of the artillery." Clerke was dumbfounded. The army was collapsing and Kingston was both misunderstanding the intent of Clerke's question and invoking procedural excuses. Clerke wheeled his mount and shouted, "There is a general retreat and I'm going with orders from General Burgoyne to bring off the artillery." But most of the British guns were already gone, their crews dead, the guns in American hands. Just then, the fire from the American side intensified, and Clerke disappeared in the smoke.[82]

3:45 PM, Georg Päusch, the German Line, the Wheat Field

Some of the German grenadiers turned and formed a new line in front of the house. British grenadiers were also there, but there was confusion as officers rode back and forth trying to gain control of the situation and men who were unsure whom to follow. Päusch had his guns hooked to their limbers and pulled his battery off the field. His teams pulled his two 6-pounders past the abandoned English 12-pounders to a spot near the house and the rallying grenadiers. He found a small earthen mound that the Americans had thrown up over the last week or two and repositioned his cannons behind it. A British artillery lieutenant and his sergeant were trying to find a crew to get at least one of the 12-pounders back into action. The lieutenant asked Päusch for some of his crew, but it was hopeless. Päusch had already lost two dead, four wounded, and several missing. All he had left were four or five men and a subaltern, not enough to serve a single slow-firing 12-pounder, barely enough to keep his 6-pounders in action.

Päusch's short-handed crews went through three wagons of ammunition. The guns were now too hot to touch; the men risked losing their limbs just loading them. Päusch's canister shot had cleared a wide killing zone in front of his new position, but it did not last. Americans were flanking both sides of his position and small arms fire behind them was getting closer. The collapse of the re-formed line was certain, but it was a less precipitous retreat than had been the case with the left wing. Päusch had a chance to save his guns.[83]

Päusch and three of his crew struggled to drag one of the guns toward the road. A junior officer and some additional men dragged the second piece in the same direction and hooked it to a limber. The second limber was brought up and hooked to the other gun. Päusch and one of his men jumped aboard the last remaining ammunition wagon. They were moving now, the horses by some miracle still alive and the road back to British lines apparently open. All around them terrified men seemed to be running in all directions. There was no chance they would be able to form and hold a new line. Now the Americans were everywhere: in front of them, behind them, in the woods all around them. Musket balls seemed to come at Päusch and his men from all directions. He yelled, "Save yourselves," to the men he had left and drove his ammunition wagon through a fence and into the comparative safety of the underbrush.[84]

3:50 PM, Henry Dearborn, West of the Wheat Field

Henry Dearborn drove his light infantry hard at the exposed British right. They fell in with Americans who were overrunning some of the British artillery and taking prisoners. It took them only two or three minutes to secure the guns and send the prisoners back. Then Dearborn formed his men again to deliver flanking fire into the second line that Fraser had hoped would cover Burgoyne's retreat. The German and British troops had been so focused on the horde of Americans in front of them that they had no idea that Dearborn's light infantry was on their flank until the murderous fire erupted. The last of them broke and headed for the Balcarres Redoubt. Dearborn found Francis Clerke severely wounded and lying on the ground near his horse, which was also wounded. Dearborn had Clerke taken back to Gates's headquarters.[85]

William Hull of the 8th Massachusetts Continentals was again in command of a picket stationed north of the main line of Learned's brigade on the left wing of the American Army. He had about 250 men in his detachment, as he had on September 19. Hull's detachment got caught up in the confusion of the American attack on the wheat field. As soon as the German grenadiers broke, Hull was ordered to fall back to his original picket position and prepare to receive prisoners and wounded Americans. Hull's men moved on to the field gathering the wounded and taking charge of abandoned British and German artillery. Hull lost count. There must have been between two hundred and three hundred prisoners escorted to the rear. A similar number of British and German dead littered the field. Fifty minutes after the fighting had begun, what was left of the British and German forces were gone from the wheat field.[86]

3:55 PM, Benedict Arnold, the Balcarres Redoubt

Arnold wheeled his horse, still shouting at anyone who could hear him over the din, hatless and whipping his sword in the air around him. Mounted officers, Continentals, and militia were all racing about in the chaos and noise as Arnold tried to rally them and get them all moving in the same direction. The tip of his sword hit two captains, wounding one of them in the head. The wounded officer's first impulse was to shoot Arnold, but he recovered enough to lower his weapon to simply scream at the deranged general. But Arnold had already charged off into the noise.[87]

The British and German troops were in full retreat. Phillips and Riedesel had been ordered to provide covering fire so that the bulk of the troops could be pulled back to defend the Balcarres Redoubt. It did not matter that the orders were never received; the troops knew that the redoubt was the closest safe haven and they headed straight for it. The first of them reached the ramparts, tumbled in, caught their breath, and then turned to reinforce the soldiers manning the walls. The men who made it to the redoubt had barely reached it when the Americans launched a ferocious but uncoordinated attack on the position.[88] The Americans quickly overran an outwork southwest of the main redoubt and continued running across low wet ground toward the main fortification.[89] The Balcarres Redoubt was now full of British grenadiers and men from other units who had been detached for Burgoyne's reconnaissance in force. The Balcarres Redoubt was now the strongest point on the long British line, but the Americans rushed it anyway, heedless of their own officers.

The flank of the British line just north of the Balcarres Redoubt, the Breymann Redoubt, was now the weakest part of all. Many of the German grenadiers, chasseurs, and jägers who had been detached from their units in the Breymann Redoubt earlier in the day were now in the Balcarres, leaving von Breymann's position severely undermanned. These men knew that von Breymann needed them, but few showed any inclination to sprint across the four-hundred-yard gap between the two redoubts. There were Americans swarming everywhere and covering fire in the huge gap was available only from a few Canadians holed up in two cabins there.

Inside the Balcarres Redoubt everyone was focused on the tide of Americans rushing straight at them. Burgoyne had come and gone, shouting at John Lindsay to defend the redoubt to the last extremity as he rushed by, then galloped off to his headquarters nearer the Hudson.[90] Men stood at the parapets, firing, handing their muskets back and receiving loaded ones in exchange. Behind them everyone who was not engaged in firing was busy loading weapons and handing them back forward as rapidly as they could. Many were women, some of the hundreds who had followed their men into war. One was small and elderly, but she was doing as much as she could to help ensure that her husband would not be one of those left behind in a shallow grave. As she handed a musket forward she could not resist a quick peek over the top of the rampart to see for herself how much danger they were all in. The charge from an American musket struck her full in the face, the ball and buckshot doing their brutal work. The slight old woman was dead before her body fell into the foot trench.[91]

The American pursuit of the retreating British and Germans was enthusiastic but utterly disorganized. The men of dozens of regiments were mixed together in what seemed more like a rioting mob than an army. Arnold was charging about, inspiring many but controlling few. More Americans poured into the hollow between the outwork and the main Balcarres Redoubt, stopping to fire, reload, and in many cases, to fall. Some reached the abatis; some found their marks among the heads visible over the ramparts. But the attack stalled.[92]

Arnold could see the headstrong Americans starting to fall before the redoubt, victims of their own enthusiasm. He surveyed the confusion and sent one of his aides to the right with orders for General Poor, who had no reason to obey them but seemed inclined to do so just the same. "Bring your men into better order." Poor looked around for subordinate officers to help him get control of the exuberant men. They did so, after a fashion, but the delay allowed most of the last straggling British grenadiers to reach the Balcarres Redoubt. Had Poor's men simply been allowed to continue their headlong attack they might have carried the redoubt before the reinforcements were able to get organized inside it. Now, however, the defenders of the redoubt were cutting Poor's units to pieces on the ground close to the rampart walls.[93]

4:00 PM, John Brooks, the Balcarres Redoubt

Arnold was now in the Balcarres outwork with the men who had overrun it. He looked back and saw John Brooks again. Behind the colonel he could see the Continentals of the 8th Massachusetts, ready for action. "Let's attack Balcarres's works," Arnold said. Brooks glanced at the redoubt and back again. He could see what was happening to other units of Poor's brigade. "No! Lord Acland's detachment has retired there. We can't carry them." Another man came back from checking in with Morgan in front of the Breymann Redoubt. The British line appeared to be vulnerable there. Arnold heard the news and said, "Well, then let's attack the Hessian lines." To this Brooks shouted, "With all my heart," and was off. The hapless Armstrong was still pursuing Arnold with Gates's orders to return to camp.[94] (See Figure 4.6.)

Brooks ordered the seven companies of his regiment forward, leading them and some other men from Learned's brigade northward in a westward detour away from the Balcarres Redoubt and through the cover of woods so that they came up to the northwest of the Breymann Redoubt. With them came the 5th and 6th Massachusetts, two more regiments from Nixon's brigade now joining the action.[95] The move took less than fifteen minutes and left Arnold still rallying men in front of the Balcarres Redoubt. If the Breymann Redoubt could be taken, the whole of the British line could be flanked and rolled up. The redoubt was on a hill that faced west. There was boggy ground between the main redoubt and an outwork that the Germans had built on a lower ridge there. The Germans manning the outwork fell back to the redoubt as the Massachusetts Continentals approached. Beyond the outwork on the lower ridge and about a hundred yards from the main log fortification, the slope dropped sharply; this gave the Massachusetts men splendid cover for the time being. The Germans could not see them, let alone fire on them. Officers climbed high enough to allow them to see the redoubt over the brow of the hill.

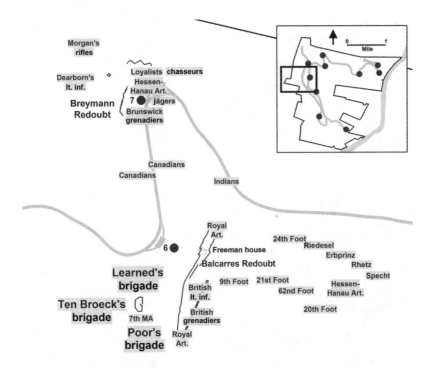

Figure 4.6 Battle of Bemis Heights, 4:00 p.m., October 7, 1777.

There was an artillery battery with two guns in the center of the fortified line. Hats and uniform colors indicated that it was thinly manned
by German grenadiers, chasseurs, jägers, and apparently some Loyalists.
The Loyalists would probably run. The chasseurs and jägers probably had
rifles. They might pick off a few of his men, but if they moved fast enough
the defenders would have no chance to reload. The grenadiers would be
tough to dislodge, but the Americans thought they had them badly outnumbered. There was no musket fire from the Germans; it was too far
for that to be very effective even if the Americans were exposed, and the
Brunswick grenadiers appeared to be saving their ammunition. But the
German cannons threw canister at the Americans as fast as the gunners
could load, keeping them below the break in the slope.[96]

The Americans formed up raggedly behind the ridge, 120 yards in
front of the Breymann Redoubt. Continentals and militia from several
regiments lined up as best they could and got ready to push toward the defensive wall the Germans had constructed. The breastwork was about 250
yards long and made up of rails and logs that had been stacked between

pairs of posts. The Americans waited, protected from fire by the hillcrest so long as they did not advance.

The Massachusetts men had the afternoon sun behind them as they peeked eastward over the crest of the hill at the Breymann Redoubt. Off to their right they could see the huge four-hundred-yard gap between the Breymann Redoubt and the Balcarres Redoubt. It was a hole in the British right flank that was manned only by Canadians stationed in a pair of small cabins. The Canadian contingent was a ridiculously small plug for such a large gap.

General Learned came up to discuss options with Colonel Brooks as Arnold continued to charge about off closer to the Balcarres Redoubt. James Wilkinson rode up to Learned and heard him ask, "Where can I put in with most advantage?" Wilkinson pointed at the cabins lying between the two redoubts. Not much fire was coming from that part of the line, which appeared to be loosely held. "Incline to your right and attack that point," Wilkinson recommended.[97]

It seemed obvious that the weakest point was the lightly manned gap, so they began to concentrate their forces in that direction. Some of the Massachusetts men deployed and attacked toward the south end of the Breymann Redoubt and the cabins. The Canadians fled, leaving the left flank of the German redoubt uncovered. At almost the same moment Benedict Arnold appeared from their right on his big bay, having galloped between the firing lines of the units still contesting for the Balcarres Redoubt. He charged past the cabins and the men of Learned's brigade surged forward to follow him toward the rear of the Breymann Redoubt.[98] (See Figure 4.7.)

It was chaotic. Most of the American units were not properly formed up. Off to the American left, Brooks saw the movement and ordered his Massachusetts men to charge the redoubt as well from their position. In the center the men of the 5th and 6th Massachusetts moved out as well, these two regiments as least having some semblance of order. The Germans were surprised when the front ranks emerged from the woods and became visible above the edge of the hill. Von Breymann's grenadiers leveled their muskets over the top of their fortification and the Americans could all see that a volley was coming. The company at the extreme left of Brooks's line seemed the most exposed. Brooks saw the men fall as the volley came and the air filled with gunsmoke. Brooks and the captain of the exposed company both rushed in its direction to assess the extent of

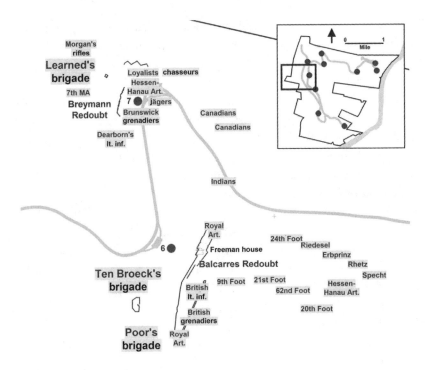

Figure 4.7 Battle of Bemis Heights, 4:30 p.m., October 7, 1777.

their losses. It turned out that the entire company had seen the muskets leveled atop the redoubt wall and had dropped to the ground just as the volley was fired. Now they rose up again. Not a man had been hit. Brooks was still agitated by the disorder, and took it out on the captain. "What business have you here, sir?" "I came to see what had happened to the company on the left," came the captain's reply. "You are out of place, sir," said Brooks. The captain was a good enough soldier to know not to argue with a superior even when the superior was mistaken. "I am ready to obey your orders, Colonel." Brooks was not mollified. "My orders are that you advance and enter those lines, sir." The captain turned without any hesitation, shouting, "Come on, my boys, and enter that fort." The whole regiment surged forward with the captain and his men leading the way.[99]

The men advanced quickly up the slope to where they were exposed to musket fire, cringing and ducking when the cannons fired, waiting for the shock of the inevitable musket volley. A hundred yards, seventy-five yards, fifty yards. Wet ground was pulling at the feet of some of the men. When the Americans had closed to forty-four yards the entire Brunswicker line fired again. A few Americans fell, but most of the thin volley again passed overhead. The advancing line faltered momentarily, then began advancing again. There was time enough for another partial volley from the Germans; again, only a few Americans fell.

The Americans were beginning to understand. The redoubt was severely undermanned. Now von Breymann had to try to defend the right flank of the whole British line with at best half the men he had started the day with, hardly two hundred of them. The rest had been sent out to the wheat field. Who knew where they were now? Worse for him, the rear of the redoubt was open and vulnerable.[100]

Dearborn's light infantry fell in behind Arnold, along with men from several Continental regiments. These included Harry Livingston and others from the 4th New York, part of Poor's scattered brigade. There were a good two hundred of them. Arnold was pounding ahead on his big dark bay, galloping past the abandoned cabins. He yelled at a dozen and a half riflemen near him, seeing that they could cut through into the back of the Breymann Redoubt while the Germans were occupied with the frontal attack being pressed by the Massachusetts regiments.[101]

Von Breymann turned and saw Arnold lunging through the sally port on the big bay, followed by soldiers who appeared to be American. Von Breymann yelled, demanding to know if they were the enemy. "Naw," came the answer in a thundering voice from one of the men contriving to sound German.[102] Some of von Breymann's men at the rampart turned and fired at the Americans. Arnold shouted at them to lay down their arms.

Arnold felt a numbing blow to his left thigh, the same leg that had been wounded at Quebec late in 1775. A wounded German soldier had fired at him from the ground. The ball hit Arnold in the left leg, passed through it, then apparently hit his mount's heart. The big horse slumped to the ground, pinning Arnold's good right leg. Arnold yelled, "Rush on, my brave boys," to the men pushing past him. At Quebec the ball had passed between the tibia and fibula before lodging in muscle, not a terrible wound as wounds went. This time the ball shattered Arnold's femur. The wound was much worse, and Arnold began to writhe in pain as he lay pinned by his right leg under his dying horse.[103]

By this time the men of the Massachusetts regiments from Learned's and Nixon's brigades had reached the front wall. The Americans poured over and through the redoubt. Von Breymann lay dead alongside several of his men. What was left of the four companies of Brunswick grenadiers fell back through their camp toward the cover of the woods, some wheeling to fire wild shots as they left. The jägers fell back with them, recoiling before the swarm of Americans flowing into the redoubt from both the sides and the front. Tents, knapsacks, supplies, the dead, the wounded, everything was left behind as the Germans retreated into the woods with empty muskets. The Hessen-Hanau cannons in the redoubt were quickly taken. Two of the artillerymen had been killed and most of the others were wounded. Now they were all captives.[104]

Men rushed to roll the dead horse off Arnold's good leg. Armstrong finally caught up with him again. Arnold looked back and saw a young soldier running at the wounded German who had shot him, his bayonet leveled. Arnold yelled, "He's a fine fellow. He did but his duty. Don't hurt him." The American soldier stopped. The German soldier and Arnold both lay back and let the pain overtake them. Dearborn had seen it happen. "Are you badly wounded?" he asked. Arnold grimaced and said, "In the same leg." Then he said, "I wish the ball had passed my heart." The sun was setting as they got the dead horse off him and began to carry him back to the American line.[105]

Back in camp the surgeon there would look at the leg. It was a compound fracture of the femur, and he thought the leg might have to be amputated. Arnold would growl, "No such damned nonsense. If that is all the surgeon has to say, the men should lift me upon my horse and I will see the action through." The leg would stay on, but Arnold would stay in bed.[106]

4:30 PM, Frederika Riedesel, the Taylor House in the British Camp

Frederika had invited British and German officers to dinner, and the table in the Taylor house was already set.[107] She kept it that way, displaying as best she could a calm certainty that dinner would move ahead as planned. At four-thirty the first of Frederika's guests arrived. It was General Fraser, riding in supported on each side by two mounted junior officers (Figure 4.8). Frederika could see that he had been shot in the abdomen. The servants cleared the table of china and silver and set up a bed for Fraser. Frederika sat in the corner trembling as the noise of battle continued to increase, getting closer. The house filled with more sick and wounded soldiers. Beaten men continued to stream into camp. Anxious officers asked about the seriousness of Fraser's wound. Officers, soldiers, and women gathered around the popular general, and all of them soon

Figure 4.8 Simon Fraser, mortally wounded, is received by Frederika Riedesel. The unknown artist incorrectly placed the wound on his right side. Courtesy of Library and Archives of Canada.

knew that there was no hope. The ball had entered his left side, a little below his chest.[108]

Fraser was faint from the loss of blood. When he had recovered a little he said, "I saw the man who shot me. He was a rifleman and up in a tree."[109] If anyone realized that Fraser was mistaken they let it pass. The surgeon did his best to dress the wound. When he was finished Fraser asked, "Tell me, son, to the best of your skill and judgment, if you think my wound is mortal?" The surgeon replied, "I am sorry, sir, to inform you that it is and that you cannot possibly live four and twenty hours." A shot through the abdomen was almost invariably fatal. Fraser had only a few hours of clarity left to him before toxins and fever overtook him. Fraser asked for pen, ink, and paper so that he could write his will. After that, he gave a few tokens to his officers and asked to be taken to the hospital, where he would not burden Frederika and her children. But they left him where he was.[110]

Burgoyne, Phillips, and Riedesel rode in. Everyone expected the Americans to pursue and continue the attack. The camp, hospital, and even the artillery park were in jeopardy. Burgoyne rode up to an officer and said, "Sir, you must defend this post to the very last man."[111] Burgoyne saw no choice but to abandon his headquarters near the center of the British line and to pull back all regiments to the heights overlooking the Hudson during the night. They could hear the American artillery being brought closer.

5:45 PM, John Brooks, the Breymann Redoubt

At dusk General Learned gathered the regimental commanders of his brigade around him for a council. John Brooks was there for the 8th Massachusetts, as were the other five colonels. Learned was dithering, and Brooks glowered at the man for his indecision and fecklessness. Brooks was appalled when Learned brought up the main question within earshot of the enlisted men. "I have called you together, gentlemen, to see whether you agree with me in opinion that it is best to return to our position. I am clearly of opinion that we cannot hold this place till morning. We may all fall a sacrifice in making the attempt." Most of the officers present agreed with this weak assessment. Brooks and the other officers of the 8th Massachusetts, who felt they had taken the brunt of the fighting, were the only ones to dissent. Brooks spoke for them: "I think there will be time enough to retreat when the enemy appears. If he does not attempt to retake the fort it will be an everlasting disgrace for us to abandon it, and if he does and we cannot defend it there will be no dishonor in retreating. At any rate, my men are fatigued and want rest and refreshment before then can move anywhere." The men of the 8th had heard it all, and they cheered Brooks as he walked back from the council.

Learned dithered again for a while. Then he called his officers back. This time, Brooks's men had plenty to say as he passed by. "For God's sake, Colonel, don't retreat. We have taken the work and we are able to keep it." There was more cheering and encouragement from men who had risked their lives to take this redoubt and were damned now if they would just walk away from it. But the collective mood of Learned's officers had not changed much. Only one other officer now supported Brooks's view that they should stay and hold the redoubt overnight.

Just then, a man rode up on a foaming horse. It was one of Gates's aides-de-camp. "Who commands here?" "Brigadier General Learned," came the reply. As Learned came forward the aide said, "My orders from General Gates are that you should retain the possession of this fort at all hazards." With that he wheeled his horse and galloped off.

Learned turned to Brooks. "There now, Colonel Brooks, I dare say you like that. And as your regiment had a principal hand in taking the work I will commit to them the defense of it." The 8th Massachusetts Continentals could not have been more pleased.[112]

6:00 PM, *Ernst von Speth, the Breymann Redoubt*

The sun had set and it was getting dark under lowering clouds. Lieutenant Colonel von Speth found some men from his part of the fragmented detachment and decided to do what he could to help bolster the defense of the Breymann Redoubt. He knew that a large fraction of von Breymann's grenadiers had fallen back into the Balcarres Redoubt and that the Breymann Redoubt had to be severely undermanned. What he did not know was that it had already fallen. In the failing light von Speth led his men through the woods behind the Balcarres Redoubt and into the rear of the Breymann Redoubt, expecting a warm reception. He got one, but his hosts were American. Von Speth and his men were instantly disarmed and made prisoners. Von Breymann and many of his men lay dead in the redoubt and the Americans were busy gathering up what supplies they could and converting the rail defenses to their own purposes.

Back at the river Burgoyne sent Stanhope to tell Hamilton to defend the rear of the camp the best he could. Like von Speth's Germans, the British troops Hamilton sent out in response approached the Breymann Redoubt unknowingly from the rear. This time the Americans instantly fired on them, scattering them back toward the main British camp. As night closed in, some Americans gathered up weapons, loot, and prisoners and started back for the American lines. Brooks and the 8th Massachusetts stayed put.

More accurate reports started to come in to the British camp. The Americans had made a ferocious attack on the redoubt commanded by Lord Balcarres, nearly taking it despite furious application of grape and small arms fire. It was said that Arnold had led the assault and was wounded. But the redoubt manned by von Breymann's Germans had fallen. Survivors said that von Breymann's men had managed to fire only a single effective volley before they were overrun by superior numbers, many of them pouring in from a breach left open by fleeing provincials. Von Breymann himself was cut down while trying to rally his troops.

Now it was clear to nearly everyone. Burgoyne's flank had been turned. The kind of action Burgoyne had hoped to carry out against the Americans was now being carried out against his own line. Burgoyne ordered the army to stand to arms throughout the night, to strike their tents and send them to the baggage depot on the flats.[113] Few doubted that British artillery was the only thing that had prevented an even worse rout. As day grayed into night British anxiety only deepened. Fraser was certain to die. Francis Clerke was probably dead on the field. Colonel Acland was wounded and taken prisoner. The artillery officers were nearly all prisoners, at least two of them wounded. Blomefield had escaped back to the Great Redoubt, but he had been shot through the mouth and was not fit for service.

It was as dark a night as any of them had known. The sun had set at a quarter to six and the crescent moon would not be up for another three and a half hours. An ashen-faced officer came to Burgoyne's headquarters to say that he had gone to what he had taken to be German campfires only to be fired at by the Americans who were now camped around them. Burgoyne impulsively ordered Riedesel to try to retake the camp behind the Breymann Redoubt; but it was hopeless, and they all knew it. Riedesel's troops were dispersed, many of the men from his own regiment were missing, the woods were black, and there was nothing to be done about it.[114]

Surviving German grenadiers from the Breymann Redoubt were straggling in, most of them without packs, tents, or equipment. Nearly all of it had been left to the Americans. Nasty rumors were spreading through and beyond the Regiment von Rhetz. Von Breymann had stabbed at least four of his own men with his sword in an effort to make them hold their positions, they said. One captain even claimed that it was one of von Breymann's own men who had shot him, just before the redoubt fell.[115]

6:30 PM, *Horatio Gates, American Headquarters*

Gates was at his headquarters in the Woodworth house, where he had stayed all day.[116] Express riders from Hyde's Light Horse cantered back and forth between his headquarters in the Woodworth house and various

American positions, reporting on the action. Early returns indicated that the British forces had been more numerous than expected. Gates thought about this. Ever ready to entertain the possibility of defeat, he ordered the teamsters to prepare to move out in case the American Army had to retire. He worried about Learned's brigade, which he had ordered to maintain possession of Burgoyne's right flank through the night. Then came a rumor that the British right wing had pulled back. Gates countermanded the order to the teamsters, then countermanded it again. For nearly an hour of uncertainty the wagons alternately began moving and then stopped again as the order was reinstated and countermanded. Finally, a dragoon pounded up and yelled, "The British have retreated." Gates at last ordered the teamsters to stand down.[117]

Regiments were starting to return to camp. Morgan was back with most of his riflemen, exhausted, shaken, but proud of themselves. It was six hours since Gates had ordered Morgan to begin the game. Now the colonel stood before him to report that the day had been a success. Gates embraced him, saying, "Morgan, you have done wonders." To others he would later say that "too much praise cannot be given to the corps commanded by Colonel Morgan."[118] There would be, as usual, no mention of Benedict Arnold.

7:00 PM, Francis Clerke, American Headquarters

Francis Clerke was lying wounded on Gates's bed in the general's headquarters when Wilkinson returned from the battlefield. Clerke and Gates were having a spirited debate on the merits of the American rebellion. Clerke was actually sympathetic, but only to a point. "Every procedure on your part, short of the declaration of independence, is warranted by the conduct of the British administration. But the sudden act of severance convinces me that the contest originated in a premeditated view to independence." Clerke went on, arguing that the New England Puritans had been behind it all and that this had altered his pro-American opinion sufficiently to prompt him to join Burgoyne's expedition.

Gates had a different view. "On the other hand, the idea of disunion never entered into the head of any American until the menaces of the parliament, the repeated oppressive acts of the British government, and the manifest vindictive resentment of the sovereign left the colonists no alternative between abject vassalage and self-government."[119] This had some weight coming from a man who had once served in the British military.

The discussion went on in that vein. At length, Gates left the room in a huff with Wilkinson trailing him. Gates was indignant. "Have you ever heard so impudent a son-of-a-bitch?"

Wilkinson went back in, taken by Clerke's frank and fearless personality. The political debate went on, then Clerke suddenly changed the subject. "Are your surgeons good for anything? I do not like the direction of my wound and I am desirous to know whether it is mortal or not." One of the American doctors attended Clerke that night and said it was hopeless. Another abdominal wound; death seemed certain.[120] Clerke was convinced that the order he had been conveying from Burgoyne would have changed the outcome of the fighting had he been able to deliver it. But now he was mortally wounded and the day had been lost. Clerke lay back and accepted the inevitable.

About two hundred wounded men from both armies had been brought back to the American camp in wagons through the course of the afternoon and evening. The sky was clear but there was going to be a hard frost tonight. There was not enough space in Potts's improvised hospital. Many men were laid out in a vast circle on bare ground. Exhausted but unwounded men found it impossible to sleep amid the groans and cries. They would spend the night bringing water, blankets, whatever they could, to help the wounded lying in the cold. Doctors moved from one to the next, doing what little they could. By morning over a third of them would be gone.[121]

7:30 PM, Frederika Riedesel, the Taylor House

Friedrich Riedesel returned after dark, to Frederika's intense relief. He wolfed down a quick meal outside the house with Frederika and his adjutant. They exchanged brave words and reassurances, but their faces betrayed something else. When they had finished eating, Riedesel drew Frederika aside for a private word and said, "Everything might go very badly. You must keep yourself in constant readiness for departure, but by no means give anyone the least inkling of what you are doing." Frederika pretended to prepare for a move to her new log house the next day, packing everything for that happy occasion, but knowing that she would probably be heading north with her servants and children instead, retreating toward Canada with the beaten army.[122]

Lady Harriet Acland was living in a tent very close to the Taylor house. Word came that her husband John had been wounded and taken prisoner. His men had tried to save him but he had fallen into American hands. Frederika did her best to comfort the young woman. "It is only a slight wound. No one can nurse him as well as yourself. You should go at once to him. You can certainly obtain permission." Frederika thought John Acland to be a plain, rough drunk, but she knew that Lady Acland loved him, and that was enough for Frederika. Like virtually everyone else in the British camp, Frederika regarded Harriet as the loveliest of women.

Fraser was in agony through the night, rambling on from time to time. "Oh fatal ambition! Poor General Burgoyne! My poor wife!" Before lapsing into unconsciousness Fraser sent a message to Burgoyne. "Have me buried at six o'clock in the evening on the top of the hill in the Great Redoubt." He asked to be buried without any elaborate parade and by the soldiers of his own corps. The hours dragged on. Fraser apologized from time to time for being such a burden.[123] As Fraser lay dying, Frederika spent the night comforting her children and her friends, and sleeping not at all. She worried that the children might cry and disturb the miserable people around her and she turned all of her efforts to preventing it.

Two miles away the muffled sounds and smells of death began to creep over the battlefield. The horde of American camp followers tended the wounded in their camps. Others shuffled through the lines toward the wheat field, where the dead offered enough plunder to keep them busy through much of the night. Their British counterparts would not venture out this night. It was too risky. By morning there would be little for the Americans' burial details to identify.[124] Tomorrow the men assigned the grim task would dig graves for the dead and the near dead, friend and enemy no longer distinguishable. One grave near where Fraser fell would contain forty men, none covered by more than a thin layer of dirt.[125]

About an hour before midnight it began to rain, and it was soon a soaking downpour. Both sides could hear the moans and cries of the wounded on the field, men who would soon die of the wet and cold even if their wounds were not mortal.[126]

5

The End Game

WEDNESDAY, OCTOBER 8, 1777

5:00 AM, John Burgoyne, the British Camp

It had rained overnight and many of the men got little or no sleep. In the hour before dawn Burgoyne ordered Fraser's brigade, now under Lindsay's command, to the top of the bluff overlooking the second bridge. The remnants of Breymann's command took a position just to the west of the other units of Fraser's brigade. Riedesel's regiments camped in the hilltop fortifications of the Great Redoubt. Their immediate task for the day was to clear brush and create a new line of abatis so that they would have a field of fire if the Americans were able to penetrate this far.[1] At this time yesterday Burgoyne's army held fortified positions extending two miles inland from the river. Today they were confined to the bluffs and flats near the river in a disorganized and vulnerable camp not much more than a half mile across (Figure 5.1).

The regiments of Hamilton's brigade pulled back closer to the Great Redoubt and turned to protect the northwest side of the army. Every regiment was required to send out patrols of about two dozen men to ensure that the Americans could not approach undetected. The 47th Regiment dug in at their previous location on the river flats and a hundred bateaux men were assigned the task of holding the western end of the bridge of boats. The remaining Indians, Canadians, and Loyalists had camped along the river road toward the north. They would soon be sent southward on the river flats to serve as the advanced corps there, in case the Americans attacked from that direction. The Indians were ordered to dismantle the bridge of boats.[2]

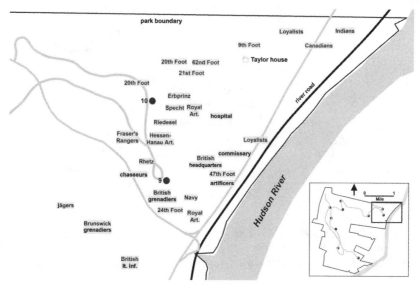

Figure 5.1 British Camp around the Great Redoubt, October 8, 1777.

Breymann was dead and Fraser would be soon if he was not already. Acland, Clerke, and Williams were prisoners and possibly dead. So were two more captains, seven subalterns, sixteen sergeants, and seven drummers. As for the rank and file, there were at least 160 dead and thirty-four taken prisoner. There were hundreds wounded. Their prospects were not good, and everyone knew it.[3]

Burgoyne worked on how best to redeploy his sick and wounded army. He wanted to move the hospital farther to the rear because it was exposed to American cannon fire. But the squalid facility was so swamped with the sick and wounded that moving it was impossible. For now, that was the vulnerable core of his encampment. All other units had to be deployed to protect it.

Burgoyne shared his glum assessment with his generals: "If there can be any persons who, after considering the movement of the enemy under General Arnold in the attack upon the post of Lord Balcarres and various other actions of the day, continue to doubt that the Americans possess the quality and faculty of fighting, they are of a prejudice that it would be very absurd longer to contend with." No one could disagree with him on this point. They had been surprised by the steadiness of the American Continentals. Even the militia had impressed them. Burgoyne was not finished with his assessment of the American Northern Army. "The standing corps are disciplined. The militia are inferior in method and movement, but not a jot less serviceable in woods. The panic of the rebel troops is confined and of short duration; the enthusiasm is extensive and permanent."[4]

The behavior of the Canadians had been distressing by comparison. Burgoyne's assessment was a glum one. "The Canadians were officered by gentlemen of great condition in their country, but were not to be depended upon." American militiamen could be counted upon to fight well when they were defending hearth and home, but while the New Yorkers were so motivated, the Canadians clearly were not. The American Loyalists were even less dependable than the Canadians. They seemed to Burgoyne to be motivated by profit, personal security, or revenge, and few seemed ready to subordinate themselves to his officers. Burgoyne had to admit that Morgan's corps might be the best of its kind anywhere.[5]

Burgoyne was unusually expressive regarding the loss of some of his most valued officers. He did not know yet, but he assumed that Clerke was probably dead.

> The losses in the action were uncommonly severe. Sir Francis Clerke originally recommended himself to my attention by his talents and diligence. As service and intimacy opened his character more he became endeared to me by every quality that can create esteem. I lost in him a useful assistant, an amiable companion, an attached friend. The state is deprived by his death of one of the fairest promises of an able general. The fate of Colonel Acland, taken prisoner is a second source of anxiety. General Fraser is expiring.[6]

A messenger came from the Taylor house (Figure 5.2) at eight with a report from Fraser's staff. Burgoyne passed the news on to his staff. "General Fraser has breathed his last, and with the kindest expressions of his affection, his last request has been brought to me, that he might be carried without parade by the soldiers of his corps to the Great Redoubt and buried there."[7]

Burgoyne dithered. Retreat to Batten Kill was the only reasonable option left open to him, but he could not bring himself to it yet. Riedesel pressed for an immediate retreat. Burgoyne needed Fraser's opinion, but it was gone forever. The hospital was swelling with the wounded. There were hundreds of them. How could he move them? It seemed impossible. They needed a day to get the wounded ready to move if they were to do it

Figure 5.2 The Taylor House, after Lossing (1851: 66).

at all. In death Fraser gave him the last excuse he needed to postpone the inevitable decision. The general had asked to be buried at the evening gun in the Great Redoubt. Surely that request had to be honored.[8]

8:00 AM, John Nixon, American Lines on the River Road

The morning was foggy but warm. Most of the regiments that had seen action the day before had come back to the American camp. General Nixon was impatient. He had spent the whole previous day waiting with the bulk of his brigade, hearing the action in the distance but not participating in any meaningful way apart from having a cannonball nearly take his head off. Today he was deaf in the ear that had been just missed by the ball. The eye on that side of his head was also giving him trouble. Nevertheless, Nixon had requested and received permission from Gates to advance northward along the river road to apply pressure on the German positions. Nixon had eagerly ordered drummers to beat his brigade to their alarm posts at first light. Then he had paraded them and marched them up the road to within three hundred yards of Burgoyne's camp. The

German units that had been closer to the American positions had already fallen back to the flats below the Great Redoubt.

Nixon had artillery, several 6- and 12-pounders, and he was eager to use them. The British had brought artillery to both of the major actions, but up to now the Americans had not used their cannons as much on this campaign. Until yesterday most of the big guns had been positioned mainly to prevent Burgoyne's advance down the river road. Today would be different. The guns had been brought down from the bluffs and pulled northward to be within range of Burgoyne's shrunken camp. At eight o'clock Nixon's artillery began their harassment of the British and German lines, firing into their camp and pounding the bluffs of their Great Redoubt. Burgoyne's men fired back with both cannon and musket fire, but without much effect.

Nixon could see that Burgoyne's Indian auxiliaries had been sent to dismantle the British bridge of boats. There were sixty bateaux filled with provisions and doing double duty as a floating bridge, lashed side by side across the Hudson. Nixon's artillery harassed them too. The bridge was torn up and the bateaux were dragged back one by one to relative safety upstream.

On the bluffs above Nixon's brigade, and to the west along Bemis Heights, the entire American Army moved forward, leaving behind only camp guards. Glover's brigade moved out with the rest, the 1st Massachusetts relieving Brooks and his 8th Massachusetts and moving on to take possession of the abandoned western and central British works, tightening the noose around the Great Redoubt at the eastern end. They marched along inside the lines the British had held just hours earlier. The British fired cannons at them as they advanced, and it was clear that they were not yet ready to give up. A regimental commander had his horse shot out from under him. But the American troops pressed on, full of grim confidence in the wake of yesterday's victory.[9]

9:00 AM, *Ebenezer Mattoon, the American Floating Bridge*

Gates realized that with his bridge of boats broken up and dismantled Burgoyne had no option but to retreat northward along the river road toward Saratoga. The east side of the Hudson was wide open for whatever use he wished. That meant that Gates could send fresh American units across his own bridge of boats and have them move quickly to positions opposite Saratoga and northward as far as Fort Edward, all without the least fear of resistance. That way they could prevent Burgoyne from cross-ing to the east side of the river at any of the handful of fords available. They could also easily prevent Burgoyne from constructing a new bridge of boats. Gates could see that retreat to the mouth of Batten Kill on the east side of the Hudson was no longer an option for Burgoyne.

The captain of Ebenezer Mattoon's artillery unit was ordered to be among the first to cross the floating bridge and head north. He was told to advance his pair of guns along the east side of the Hudson as quickly as he could in order to position them to control the ford just above Saratoga. This was the crossing point where Burgoyne had positioned the earlier bridge that had allowed his army to cross over into Saratoga in the first place. Gates also sent General Fellows with a detachment of thirteen hun-dred militiamen to supplement troops already moving to cover the east bank of the Hudson opposite Saratoga. These tactical moves ensured that Burgoyne's army would remain on the west side of the Hudson.[10]

9:30 AM, James Wilkinson, American Forward Positions

Gates found the mortally wounded Francis Clerke to be impudent, and had said so. By comparison, Wilkinson had found John Acland to be quite amiable. Yesterday Wilkinson had arranged for Acland to be conveyed to the rear and made comfortable in the Neilson house. He looked in on him in the morning. The two men found that they liked each other. Acland had asked for paper, pen, and ink to write a letter to his wife, Harriet, who he knew would be worried about him back in the British camp. Wilkinson was happy to comply.

Acland gave the letter to Wilkinson, who was reasonably sure Gates would send him out toward the shrinking British lines to assess the cur-rent situation. Wilkinson had promised to try to deliver the letter under a flag of truce, but at every point along the British line he was turned back. The British sentries imagined that he was carrying an ultimatum from Gates and they would have none of it. Meanwhile, deserters came over to the Americans in increasing numbers. A chaplain counted at least thirty deserters coming across as he went over the ground where the fighting had taken place. He found dead soldiers already stripped of their clothes and equipment.[11]

Wilkinson could see that the British Army was now concentrated around the Great Redoubt on the bluffs overlooking the Hudson and on the flats below. Men were positioned at points where ravines started at the edges of the bluffs, points at which the British feared the American irregulars would try to infiltrate their fortifications. The heavy artillery provided cover to the concentrated units. At eight in the morning the British had been able to see the American units marching toward them. Their numbers were huge. The fields were blackened by their dark clothing. They brought up cannon and attempted to throw up emplacements for them, but the heavy British guns demolished the works as soon as they were built. The Americans would bring up a 12-pounder, and the howitzers would take it out, sometimes before the Americans could fire a shot. With this much heavy artillery the British Army was safe for the moment in this stronghold, but it could not last, and every soldier knew it.[12]

10:00 AM, Daniel Taylor, Fort Montgomery on the Lower Hudson

Far to the south on the lower Hudson River, Daniel Taylor was ready to make another long trek northward with a new message for Burgoyne from General Henry Clinton. It was good news. Clinton had taken Fort Montgomery on Monday, October 6. Taylor had expected this, but it had taken a week longer than Clinton had predicted in his previous message to Burgoyne.

Although the season was late, Clinton was now in a better situation to support Burgoyne by undertaking movements that would probably draw some of Gates's forces southward to protect Albany. The problem for Clinton was that though Howe had taken Philadelphia, Howe was much too far away to contribute to the effort on the Hudson; without help Clinton had too few men to push through the rebel resistance he expected to encounter between Fort Montgomery and Albany.

Taylor had made his way through to the British camp after several days' travel south along the Hudson, getting his message to Clinton. Today Captain Campbell made his way in as well. Clinton had been nonplussed by Burgoyne's request in the written and oral messages the men carried that Burgoyne and his entire army be put under Clinton's command. When he recovered he wrote a brief note back to Burgoyne and gave both Taylor and Campbell copies to take back north. Taylor's was concealed in the same small silver ball he had brought south from Burgoyne. In both messages Clinton promised little and sidestepped Burgoyne's request to be taken under Clinton's command.

Nous y voice, and nothing now between us but Gates. I sincerely hope this little success of ours may facilitate your operations. In answer to your letter of the 20th Sept. by C. C., I shall only say I cannot presume to order or even advise, for reasons obvious. I heartily wish you success.
 Faithfully yours,
 H. Clinton

11:00 AM, John Henry, the Wheat Field

It is not easy to be the son of a national hero. Patrick Henry had spoken eloquently in favor of mobilization against the British back at the beginning of all this in 1775. He might have even said most of the stirring words that many admirers now attributed to him. The revolutionary legislature of Virginia had made him governor the year before. John Henry was left with little choice but to join the cause. Now here he was, a junior officer in the artillery of the Northern Army. The awful battle was over and the burial parties were out on the field, doing their best to dig graves in the hard clay. Everywhere John looked he saw only the tragedy of war.

People expected John to have his father's eloquence and fortitude, and he did his best to measure up; but he also had his mother Sarah's fatal sensitivity. Sarah had died privately, confined at home in the throes of insanity even as her husband was demanding liberty or death in the public world of politics. The family had looked after her through her final tormented months. Now, more than two years later, they still grieved for her. The pain had been made worse by the refusal of the church to provide her with a proper funeral. This was on the appalling grounds that she had been possessed by the devil and consequently could not be buried in consecrated ground.

Like so many men in this army, twenty-year-old John left a sweetheart behind in order to do his duty. He had met young Dolly Dandridge at school and soon fell in love with her. But the war had separated them. Worse, back in Virginia, John Henry's widowed father was now courting Dolly himself, unaware of John's attachment to her. In fact, Patrick, who already had six children, two of them older than Dolly, was on the verge of marrying the young woman his son adored. John was spared this knowledge for the time being. What he saw strewn on the wheat field had his full attention at the moment.

John had done his duty well yesterday, but now he wandered in anguish, back and forth across a field dotted with the bodies of men who had been given death. He stepped from one to the next, seeing faces of men he did not know and wondering who they had been, pausing longer to look at the few faces he recognized. At last he came to the body of a friend and stopped. He stood looking at the lifeless face for a long time. Then he drew his sword, snapped it into pieces and threw it on the ground. Sanity had abandoned him, as it had his mother, and John began raving. He was still raving as other men brought him back into camp, and he would never again be the son his father remembered.[13]

12:00 Noon, Harriet Acland, the British Hospital

At noon the American cannons began to bombard the camp. Places hit included the hospital tents, which were pitched on the river flats below the Great Redoubt. The hospital had to be moved out of range. Some of the more severely wounded died as their attendants tried to move them to safety. The firing continued through the afternoon. Harriet Acland and Frederika Riedesel spent the day among the wounded in the hospital tents, doing what they could. Neither of them had any idea that James Wilkinson or anyone else might be trying to deliver a letter from Harriet's husband, John.

Frederika urged Harriet to ask Burgoyne for permission to pass through the lines and join her husband in captivity. A lady could expect such special treatment, but for now it did not seem to Harriet to be the appropriate thing to do. They both went back to tending the sick and wounded.[14]

1:00 PM, Benedict Arnold, the Neilson House

Arnold was glad when Colonel Brooks came by his quarters to see him. He was ready to hear Brooks's congratulations on the outcome of yesterday's assault on the Breymann Redoubt. But there was another reason for the visit. Behind Brooks were two captains, one with a bandage on his head. Brooks said that an explanation was required for Arnold having struck both men with his sword the day before. It was the kind of offense that could easily lead to a duel, and they all knew it. Arnold was twice appalled, first that he was accused. Then later, when Brooks had convinced him of the truth of it, he was appalled that he had unknowingly done it. Arnold quickly offered the required apology and all four men relaxed into a discussion of the battle, the crisis of honor averted.[15]

3:00 PM, John Burgoyne, British Headquarters

The Americans were pounding at the British positions from three sides. The Advanced Corps was particularly exposed, and it took casualties throughout the day. The patrols found Americans everywhere they looked. Everyone expected a general attack at any time. Even wounded officers, some on crutches, others in wheelbarrows pushed by their servants, left the hospital and moved up the river bluff to the Great Redoubt to get a better view of the action. American cannons that had been moved to the river flats continued to duel with the British guns. The hospital was still exposed to the American artillery; the struggle to move the wounded farther back continued.[16]

A veteran sergeant watched the British troops dig in around the Great Redoubt. It was his task to keep up the courage of the men under him and it seemed to come to him easily. As the men labored he commented upon the cleverness of Burgoyne's judicious maneuver. "By this entire change of front the American Army is under the necessity of forming a new disposition." Yes, that was it, they had forced the American Army to undertake a laborious redeployment. They had the Americans right where they wanted them.

Burgoyne expected an all-out American attack all day, but it did not come. Burgoyne and his officers were at a loss. The German troops were still reasonably fresh, and many of the men thought there was no way the Americans could not be beaten or at least stalled in a set piece fight on the river plain. Of course, the Americans would have none of it. Nearly everyone on both sides knew the Americans had time on their side.[17]

4:00 PM, Benjamin Lincoln, No Man's Land

Lincoln's men were rested but still feeling restless. They had listened to the distant roar of battle all the previous day, waiting in reserve to be called out. But it had not happened. Gates had later ordered Lincoln to take his troops forward to relieve the men who had fought yesterday and were now in need of rest. They had left at one o'clock in the morning. Lincoln had some of the men of the Connecticut Light Horse with him as bodyguards.

Lincoln's men had moved slowly and carefully forward in the darkness. The moon had long since set and it was as dark as ink. They could see the fallen from both armies from time to time as they passed by. They had followed the interior road that led to the Balcarres Redoubt, now deserted, and moved eastward toward the river along the abandoned lines the British regiments had built over the last two weeks.

At dawn they had been close to the new British and German lines, too close as it happened. The new British lines were strong and covered by thick forest, making it difficult for Lincoln's men to approach quietly without exposing themselves. Burgoyne had stationed his Canadians and Loyalist sharpshooters at the heads of springs and ravines that fed the Great Ravine, and they shot at anyone who crossed their line of vision. Lincoln's party of officers and Connecticut Light Horse guards got a taste of it when they came within range.

Lincoln and his detachment were exploring the woods roads just west of the British Great Redoubt, the same ones that Burgoyne had used to advance on Freeman's farm back on September 19. Lincoln rode around a sharp bend in the road and could see soldiers not far ahead. They looked like the usual motley American troops, a few red uniforms, several blue ones, and several more militiamen in hunting clothes. He was only a few yards away when he realized that they were British, Brunswickers, and Loyalists, mostly not Americans at all. The British soldiers raised their muskets and fired, one of them hitting Lincoln in the right leg before he could escape. The rest of them also opened fire as Lincoln cantered back around the sharp bend to safety. It was a bad fracture; both bones of his lower leg appeared shattered. He had to be carried from the field by the men who had failed in their assignment to protect him.[18]

Of the three major generals in the Northern Army two were now wounded and out of action. Arnold and Lincoln both had severe leg wounds and were unable to serve. Gates himself, the only major general left, now directly commanded a set of brigadier generals. His burgeoning army, which needed to be organized into divisions, had no divisional commanders at all.

5:40 PM, Simon Fraser, the Great Redoubt

Fraser had not wanted an elaborate funeral, so his body was carried up to the Great Redoubt attended only by the officers who were his closest

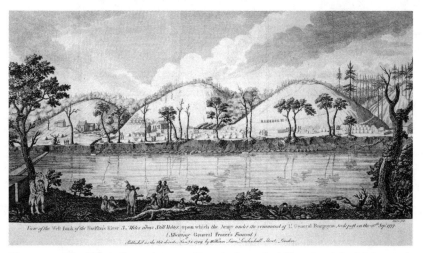

View of the West Bank of the Hudson's River 3 Miles above Still Water, upon which the Army under the command of Lt. General Burgoyne took post on the 20th Sep. 1777 (Shewing General Fraser's Funeral) Published as the Act directs, Jan 31 1789, by William Lane, Leadenhall Street, London.

Figure 5.3 The Fraser funeral procession winds up the hill to the right. Lithograph by Lane based on a sketch by Francis Clerke, 1777. Courtesy of the National Archives.

aides and subordinates. But as his body passed, Burgoyne, Phillips, and Riedesel fell in behind. Soon all the generals and their aides were with them, except those who were posted to specific duties elsewhere (Figure 5.3). The solemn procession curved its way up to the top of the bluff above the Taylor house. The men of the Advanced Corps had dug a shallow but neat rectangular grave where two cannons of the Royal Artillery stood silent. Each officer did his best to avoid flinching as the American cannonade continued through the funeral service. American artillerymen, oblivious to the meaning of the occasion, continued to bombard them, even as the graveside service was going on, to the general resentment and indignation of the discouraged British.[19]

Chaplain Brudenel droned on, not rushing even as the American balls tried to scatter the funeral party. The assembled generals did their parts, uttering the responses they had said hundreds of times. The minutes dragged on, but he was not yet done. Balls struck nearby trees, thudded into the ground around them, whistled overhead, but Brudenel stuck to his script and the mourners refused to flinch. There were two more standard, lengthy prayers.[20]

6:00 PM, Ebenezer Mattoon, Opposite Saratoga

Mattoon's artillery battery of two guns was in place above the ford on the east bank of the Hudson opposite Saratoga by dusk. There they found about nine hundred New Hampshire militiamen busy building a large number of fires as darkness fell. These, they hoped, would convince British scouts that the east bank of the Hudson was swarming with American troops. There was in fact not yet a big enough force to prevent Burgoyne from using the ford, but more units were on the way.[21]

6:00 PM, John Fellows, Opposite Saratoga

Brigadier General John Fellows had led Massachusetts militiamen north to disrupt Burgoyne's progress way back in July. Philip Schuyler had still been in command at the time; Gates had not yet replaced Schuyler. Fellows and his men had been lurking east of the Hudson ever since. Now, along with several other New England regiments, they had converged on the approaches to Saratoga in order to make themselves more directly available to Lincoln and Gates.

Fellows had already reached Saratoga with his militia detachment. They had made good time, starting out at Bemis Heights and reaching a point on the east bank opposite Saratoga before noon. Fellows did not know it, but men from the 1st Massachusetts Continentals were not far away, across the river in the woods west of the same village. Like Fellows, the men west of Saratoga thought the village looked like it was theirs for the taking. Surely the Massachusetts men could take Saratoga easily and cut off Burgoyne's retreat. They considered it, but in the end they decided that the 1st Massachusetts was not strong enough to hold the village, and at the end of the day they marched back to their camp.[22]

Fellows was less cautious. Instead of remaining on the east bank his detachment had forded the Hudson into the village of Saratoga and moved into the empty barracks there. This had seemed like a reasonable idea at the time; after all, the village was deserted. But Fellows knew that he was now behind Burgoyne and that it was only a matter of time before he would be defending the village from the entire retreating British and German Army. He had sent an express rider off with a letter to General Lincoln. In it he politely suggested that it would take at least four thousand to defend Saratoga if and when Burgoyne began his retreat. Fellows did not know that Lincoln was already wounded and out of action.

8:00 PM, John Burgoyne, the British Camp

The retreat began at eight o'clock. The four companies of the 47th Regiment had already pulled back from their garrison duty around the baggage to open the way back to Saratoga. The Loyalists and the Canadians had been pulled back, and the bridge of boats had been broken up, the bateaux from the bridge collected with others already loaded with supplies and baggage. Burgoyne sent orders to Major General Phillips to use what had been Fraser's Advanced Corps as the rear guard. If he was attacked he was to pay attention to the main objective, which was to cover the retreating troops.[23] Phillips was going to have to issue orders of his own to infantry in order to comply with Burgoyne's orders, and they both knew that this was against regulations. But now was not the time for military niceties; the fate of the expedition was at stake.

Riedesel left next with the German grenadiers, jägers, chasseurs, and the British 62nd. By nine o'clock the artillery, ammunition wagons, and equipment were also getting ready to move, pulled by horses that did not appear to have many miles left in them. The effort to get the artillery off dragged on to midnight. Burgoyne was, as always, concerned about the artillery. The infantry regiments were ordered to march in two files, one on either side of the road, so that wagons and artillery could be pulled more rapidly between them. When the guns eventually moved out they were followed by Hamilton's brigade and the German regiments. Major Lindsay fell in with the Advanced Corps, to guard the rear, leaving behind the camp and a hospital overflowing with seven hundred sick and wounded men. By eleven at night the whole army was on the move, with General Riedesel commanding the vanguard. General Phillips, commanding the rear, managed to get all the baggage away even though the Americans were within musket shot.[24]

Burgoyne scrawled a note to Gates or whatever other American officers might arrive first, and left it behind with some of his physicians and the overwhelming number of sick and wounded men in their care. The physicians compiled a list of officers in the hospital and waited for the Americans.[25]

Oct^ber^ 8 1777

Sirs

The state of my hospital makes it more adviseable to leave the wounded and sick officers whom you will find in my late camp than

to transport them with the army. I recommend them to the protection
which I feel I should show to an enemy in the same case.
> *I am Sir*
> > *Your most Humble Servant*
> > > *J. Burgoyne*
M. Genl Gates[26]

Frederika's calash was ready but she was reluctant to leave before her husband. Word spread that the hospital and wounded soldiers were to be left behind under protection of a flag of truce. Major Harnage, alive but badly wounded, dragged himself out of the place in order to accompany Frederika and avoid capture. He saw Frederika with her children and servants and immediately ordered them into their calash. Frederika begged to stay; she did not want to be separated from Friedrich. "Well, then your children at least must go that I may save them from the slightest danger," said the major. Harnage knew that Frederika would never agree to be separated from her children. It was a ploy to get her to leave. She gave up and climbed into the calash.

The little calash moved through a darkened, surreal landscape. Campfires were set and tents were left standing, all to convince the Americans that the army was not in retreat. They crept along through the night.[27]

8:00 PM, James Wilkinson, American Headquarters

Wilkinson had been hiding a persistent illness for weeks, the result of poor food and long hours, he thought. Like many others, he collapsed at the end of the day and put himself to bed. In the evening he received a note from General Fellows. It had been intended for Fellows's commander, General Lincoln, but because of Lincoln's injury it was delivered to Wilkinson instead.

The alarmed Wilkinson set his illness aside. Fellows had rushed up the east side of the Hudson so quickly that he had passed Burgoyne's army trudging along in the rain on the west side. Then he had somehow crossed to the west side ahead of the retreating British and was now at the Saratoga barracks. Good grief. Fellows was in Saratoga and facing Burgoyne with a paltry thirteen hundred men. He had carried out his orders too well.

Wilkinson thought about this. The army could not march until new provisions were drawn, and this would take all day tomorrow. Meanwhile, if Burgoyne were to reach Saratoga and cut off the fords north of it, he was still strong enough to cut Fellows to pieces. Wilkinson was convinced Burgoyne would try to do just that. After a quick consultation with Gates he dictated a warning letter to be sent to Fellows, with an identical copy to be sent up to the American units on the east side of the river.[28]

The rain continued through the night. One of Wilkinson's messengers somehow reached Fellows. But his men were exhausted, having crossed the Hudson River twice and marched ten miles in the rain. Fellows let them settle in for the night. Just to the south almost the entire British Army was headed straight for them.

10:00 PM, Horatio Gates, American Headquarters

At the end of the day Gates and his officers realized that the entire American Army had been running all day on little more than the excitement of victory. This included Gates himself, who had managed only to set a password and countersign for the day. All his other orders had been made on the fly, including granting permission to Nixon to press an attack up the river road.

Now, at the end of the day Gates was wondering what to do with his army. His major generals, Arnold and Lincoln, were both badly wounded, Arnold also being fired in any case. He had eight infantry brigades now, each commanded by a brigadier general. But unless he made a battlefield promotion of one or two of them, he had no way to divide the army into divisions as a means to organize his lines of command. Poor had done well yesterday and Nixon was showing initiative today despite having nearly lost his head to a cannonball. But Glover and Learned deserved consideration as well. The biggest problem was that Congress jealously guarded its prerogatives when it came to the promotion of general officers and Gates had no desire to risk damaging their current high opinion of his performance in the field. It was better to leave things as they were for the time being.

The men's field supplies were used up and wagons had not been sent forward from the old lines. He had ordered three days' rations to be distributed on Saturday the fourth. In the heat of yesterday's battle no one had thought to issue more. Everyone was hungry, wet, and cold. There had been no choice but for all units to retire to their tents, re-provision, and rest. The fatigue of the previous two days caught up with the wet and exhausted men, and the sodden tents left on Bemis Heights seemed to everyone like the warm hearth of home.[29]

American crews had brought in the artillery Burgoyne had left on the field the day before. Down on the river flats the two armies had traded cannon shots all day, one of the British balls eventually dismounting one of the American guns. At the end of the day Nixon pulled back along the river road, having lost two men killed and one wounded. For their part, they thought they had killed one artilleryman and a horse. An advance guard of fifty Americans was left behind in the positions previously manned by Riedesel's men.[30]

Unknown to Gates, far down the Hudson, Israel Putnam had written Washington to tell him that the British had landed about three thousand men at Tarrytown and were pressing northward. Putnam had warned of this possibility before and his tone was a bit peevish when he informed the general that he had been right to be concerned. Putnam also had written to Gates to let him know that the British were pressing northward with the apparent intention of relieving Burgoyne. Putnam had written Washington again in the afternoon, laying out his plans to harass and delay the British advance up the Hudson. The two armies had fought around Peekskill, and Putnam was pleased with the results. American losses were fewer than he had expected. Even better, nearly two hundred men that Putnam had thought had been captured had in fact escaped and reassembled.[31] Yet the threat remained. Gates would have to address it.

THURSDAY, OCTOBER 9, 1777

3:00 AM, John Burgoyne, Dovegat

They marched through the night. By three o'clock in the morning Burgoyne's sodden army had moved only as far as Dovegat, barely four miles (Figure 0.5). Nearly the entire army piled up there because Riedesel had been ordered to halt his brigade, which was immediately behind the leading 47th Regiment. The delay seemed inexplicable to Frederika, but Burgoyne said he was worried that units of the army could be picked off if they were too strung out along the road. Burgoyne also said that he wanted to wait while the supply bateaux came abreast of the lead units.

Provisions were being passed out from the bateaux in case the Americans should find a way to cut out or sink the boats.[32]

Burgoyne had to prepare for the worst as best he could. He ordered six days' provisions to be issued to every man. Von Breymann was dead and his battalion of grenadiers was in disarray, equipped only with what they wore or had carried away from the battlefield in Tuesday's rout. "Breymann's corps having by some mistake not drawn two days provisions on the last delivery will now receive eight days provisions." The truth was the Americans were now enjoying the provisions Von Breymann's corps had left behind in the German camp behind Breymann's Redoubt. But right now, honesty about this would do the army no good. British and German officers were ordered to take detachments to unload whatever carts they needed to fetch the provisions and get them distributed without delay. A flood of Americans was behind them, probably alongside them, perhaps even ahead of them. His army might be broken up, dispersed, or worse by tomorrow. Another scribbled order specified that each regiment would send four carts immediately to the bateaux to collect their provisions.[33]

3:30 AM, Nicholas Sutherland, Saratoga

Lieutenant-Colonel Nicholas Sutherland and his 47th Regiment had been sent forward by Burgoyne to reconnoiter the village of Saratoga. The regiment had been reduced to only six companies ever since two of them had been sent off to hold the fort at the southern end of Lake George. After that, what remained of the 47th had been mainly responsible for guarding the British camp. Now circumstances had put his short-handed regiment at the point of the army's retreat northward.

It was the middle of the night and still raining. The British column had still been stuck at Dovegat when Sutherland left. He passed Schuyler's country mansion and its nearby outbuildings, all empty. He crossed Fish Kill and saw dying fires through the gloom on the heights above the village. He dismounted and crept forward on foot toward them. Nothing. No pickets, no challenges came at him. These were not British or German troops. They had to be American militiamen. Sutherland made a circuit of the entire quiet camp, which to his astonishment appeared to be completely unguarded. He had stumbled on to John Fellows and his exhausted militiamen, every one of them sound asleep.

Sutherland found his horse and rode back to Burgoyne as quickly as he could in the sodden dark. The American camp at Saratoga was unguarded and he must have seen over a thousand men lying asleep and fatally vulnerable. Sutherland's six companies were fresh and eager to fight. Sutherland begged Burgoyne to let him attack the sleeping Americans, but the general refused. John Burgoyne was looking forward to the comforts of Philip Schuyler's home, not another round of battle. So they continued to plod along as General Fellows's American militiamen at Saratoga slept soundly, unprotected, and undisturbed.[34]

4:00 AM, William Digby, the British Camp

William Digby and the other British grenadiers had been left behind to cover the retreat. They spent the night breaking up bridges as best they could to delay the Americans. There were ironic comments among the men as they labored to wreck the bridges they had so recently built. Some argued that they should not have broken up the bridge of boats, which struck them as an unnecessary signal to the Americans that they would be retreating along the west bank only. Those making that argument seemed to be unaware that American artillerymen had made a good start at blowing the boats to pieces and would have finished the job easily had the bridge not been quickly dismantled. More than a few ventured that it would have been better to use the bridge and cross to the east side of the river immediately, a move that would put them on the same side as Fort Edward two dozen miles to the north, and make it unnecessary to cross the Hudson farther up in the face of American fire. But this argument failed to recognize that the eastern side of the Hudson was infested with thousands of American troops.

Finally, at about four in the morning, they finished up and left the camp to the Americans. The sick and wounded stayed behind in the hospital tents, with the letter to Gates from Burgoyne asking him to care for the men as well as British surgeons would care for American wounded if fortunes had been reversed. William Digby and the other departing grenadiers tried to put as good a face on it as they could, shaking the hands of surgeons left behind and displaying as much steady confidence as they could muster.[35]

6:00 AM, Friedrich Riedesel, Dovegat

Riedesel led the advanced guard. His optimistic orders were to cross the Hudson and post his corps behind Batten Kill. His units had left hours before midnight, but it had taken most of the night to travel just a few miles. When he had proceeded no farther than the Dovegat he had received new orders to halt.[36]

The retreating army still was immobile around Dovegat at six in the morning. Burgoyne now ordered that all the artillery should be lined up for an inventory. This, he said again, was to let the bateaux catch up. There were still twenty-nine pieces of artillery after the loss of four at Bennington and six more on Tuesday. The order of a few days ago to distribute the guns from the artillery park to positions along the British and German lines had never been carried out, so the army was still burdened by the heavy guns. The two remaining 12-pounders were dwarfed by the two 24-pounders that the army had dragged all the way from Skenesborough but had never used. Now the heavy cannons sat gloomy and impotent in the rain, sinking slowly into the mire. Their crews wondered how the weakening teams of horses and oxen were going to get them across Fish Kill, let alone the Hudson. In addition to the big guns there were a dozen 6-pounders, four 3-pounders, and seven howitzers. That was the lot. Now that a siege of Albany had clearly been abandoned many of the men wondered quietly why they were still dragging these beasts through the American wilderness; it was not an irrational question.

An exhausted General Riedesel squeezed himself into the overloaded calash with his wife and daughters and slept for three hours. While he slept Captain Willoe came to Frederika and asked her to take care of his pocketbook. Captain Geismar came around as well and gave her his watch, ring, and purse. Both men expected to be killed or taken prisoner and they wanted her to take care of their valuables. Frederika promised to do her best to preserve them, hoping that she would not get more such requests. The column got started again and after only an hour, they spotted a scouting force of about two hundred Americans. Frederika thought the Americans could have been easily captured and seethed silently at Burgoyne for passing up the opportunity. Instead the army simply halted again and did nothing. It was still raining heavily and they were still making almost no progress at all.[37]

Alexander Lindsay arrived to report that Fraser's brigade, the rear guard under his command, had nearly caught up with the column and that everything was secure. The last of the wagons and pack horses were expected to arrive by eight.

Burgoyne received a letter from an American surgeon. Somehow it had been passed through the moving lines of the two armies.

> I have seen Sir Francis Clark, and am sorry to inform you that I have some unfavorable opinion of his case. The ball entered his right flank, struck the two last of the false ribs, penetrated the cavity of the abdomen, and seems to run towards the spine; a tension of his belly, and involuntary discharges of urine are bad symptoms. He has been attended with great care and tenderness; I stay by him this night, and shall not omit any attention for his recovery. Major Ackland is wounded in the thick part of both legs. The left seems to have the bone touched, but of no consequence.[38]

He was going to lose Clerke, and the thought affected him deeply. Acland was another matter. It appeared that he would recover. Burgoyne sent a messenger off to Harriet Acland with this rare good news so that she might feel some relief.

6:00 AM, John Nixon, American Troops Enter the British Camp

Word came back from scouts that the British retreat had begun. At first light Nixon sent a fresh advance guard up the river road through the rain to relieve the fifty men who had spent the night there. The relieved men came back to confirm that the British and German troops were gone. They had left during the night. The fresh detachment from Nixon's brigade simply walked in and took possession of the abandoned camp.

Nixon estimated there were nearly four hundred sick and wounded men along with a few fit men who had stayed back to care for them when the rest of Burgoyne's army left. They were all scattered through a few barns and about twenty marquee tents. Apothecary drugs and other supplies had been left behind as well for the injured and ailing men. The senior British surgeon's mate had the note for General Gates from Burgoyne.[39]

7:00 AM, Daniel Taylor, along the Southern Hudson River

Daniel Taylor had found the British headquarters at Fort Montgomery, up the Hudson but still close to New York City. Now he was on another hazardous trip back northward with a message for Burgoyne, having left on Wednesday morning. This time he had a Loyalist companion, which was some comfort. They made their way north along the west bank of the Hudson, passing West Point, and now they found themselves at New Windsor, just south of Kingston. They began to see armed men, but it was not clear whether they were rebels or Loyalists. In this strange war many men lacked proper uniforms and it was never easy to distinguish friend from foe. It was not long before they were confronted, and the odd conversation of strangers trying to feel each other out began again, as it had so often over recent months.

Taylor recited his rehearsed answers to the usual questions, asking a few of his own and trying not to look as nervous as he felt. The men he was talking to said they were guards for General Clinton. Taylor relaxed a little. He had just left General Clinton at Fort Montgomery, not ten miles behind, the day before. It was amazing that Clinton had moved this far north so quickly, but with Loyalist supporters like the men before him it was clearly possible. Burgoyne would be delighted by this news. Given this happy turn of events perhaps Taylor should talk to Clinton again and see if he wanted to amend the message Taylor was carrying for Burgoyne. If a British advance up the Hudson was progressing this well Gates would surely have to send part of his Northern Army south to defend Albany.

Taylor asked to see General Clinton, and the guards were happy to comply. They all headed for the general's headquarters. On entering the general's tent, Taylor felt momentarily confused. With horror, he realized his mistake. The man seated before him was not British General Henry Clinton; it was the rebel General George Clinton. Taylor froze for a second, then he reached into a hidden pocket for the hollow silver ball, popped it into his mouth, and swallowed.[40]

Taylor was separated from his companion and a doctor was summoned. The Americans knew what to do about the silver ball. There would be no waiting about for nature to deliver it to a chamber pot. The American Clinton ordered his doctor to administer a strong tartar emetic. Before long the poison had Taylor retching uncontrollably, and the silver bullet reappeared. The Americans examined the message with unconcealed joy.

By the time Taylor recovered from the dose he was deflated in both body and mind. There was nothing left for him but to confess and hope for a quick outcome. The defeated Loyalist sullenly dictated his confession to an American aide.[41]

I left Fort Montgomery yesterday evening, with a charge from General Sr. Henry Clinton to go with all possible dispatch thru the Country on the West side of Hudsons River to General Burgoyne and acquaint him, that on Monday the 6th Instant he stormed and carried the Fort with the loss of Lt. Col. Grant Major Campbell Major Sela, one other Field & a number other Officers whose names he does not recollect, and upwards of 300 Rank and file killed, & to acquaint Genl. Burgoyne that the obstructions in the River are now nearly removed & that he might move forward as soon as he pleased. That General Howe had defeated the Rebels near Philadelphia, and that the two Frigates belonging to the Rebels in Hudsons River were both burnt.

A Captain Campbell of Burgoynes Army lately arrived with dispatches to General Clinton, and set off on his return yesterday morning with the news of the reduction of Fort Montgomery. & that a number of people are employed who go constantly from one Army to the other, and that Lt. General Clinton intended to push up the River.[42]

That was the end of Daniel Taylor's statement and of his career as a clandestine Loyalist messenger. He was a spy. He had no uniform and no hope at all for a future.

8:00 AM, John Burgoyne, Dovegat

The army got moving again around eight in the morning. Riedesel's brigade once more took the lead but Burgoyne ordered another halt after they had gone only a mile. Burgoyne fussed over the order of march, issuing orders and countermanding them, trying to move the army and keep it together at the same time. Regiments started and stopped in a chaotic series of lurching movements that did nothing to reassure the troops. Worst of all, a Loyalist arrived with the news that the Americans were rushing ahead of Burgoyne's army to cut off their intended route to safety north of Batten Kill.

The news of Gates's effort to trap them spread through the entire army in a matter of minutes. Nearly everyone but Burgoyne came to the instant conclusion that the only thing for it was to get the entire army moving quickly and without interruption, even if it meant leaving the baggage behind. This did not happen. Most units waited here and there, making short movements then being ordered to halt again. Some of the men filled the downtime and vented their anger by burning houses along the road.

8:00 AM, James Wilkinson, the Abandoned Great Redoubt

Wilkinson had been up at dawn and riding north. He had covered the ground between the American lines and the abandoned British camp quickly. Now ahead of the American advanced guard, Wilkinson was suddenly approached by a man riding at a full gallop, a white flag raised in his hand. He introduced himself as Dr. John Hayes and said that he had been left in charge of a great many sick and wounded officers and men below the Great Redoubt. Hayes was afraid that Indians and riflemen in the American Army would butcher them all if he could not persuade Wilkinson to protect them.

As it happened, Nixon's brigade was already there. Wilkinson assured the man he had nothing to fear from Americans. The man said that another nine wounded officers had been left behind in Sword's house, which had served for a time as Burgoyne's headquarters. Wilkinson rode on to Sword's house and met the wounded officers. Some of them had convinced themselves that their American enemies were barbarians from whom they could expect no quarter. The arrival of a gentleman officer did more than the surgeons could to restore their spirits, or so the twenty-year-old Wilkinson thought.[43]

Wilkinson sent word back to Gates recommending that the general send forward a detachment to take over supervision of the British hospital. But Nixon had already arrived at the hospital with men of his brigade and had sent Burgoyne's note back to Gates. When Gates received Burgoyne's message leaving his hospital in American care, he immediately ordered Dearborn to take his light infantry and a detachment of Morgan's riflemen forward to secure it. The rest of the army would follow, said Gates, but it was raining heavily now and Dearborn's light infantrymen quickly outdistanced the heavier units.

Dearborn reached the British hospital and counted 340 British and German wounded, six of them captains, attended by a few surgeons in the sodden and squalid hospital tents. Dearborn moved into a nearby house and sent out patrols to discover how close the retreating British Army was. They came back with the unsettling news that Burgoyne was only a few miles upriver, too close given Dearborn's exposed advance position.

Dearborn doubled the guard and waited for more support in the ceaseless cold rain. More than fifty German soldiers found their way back in the rain, deserters who had evaded Burgoyne's rear guard.[44]

Wilkinson returned to the American camp to find an army that had no interest in doing anything but resting for the remainder of the day. Gates had decided to indulge them. Most of the American Army spent the day staying reasonably dry in their tents.[45]

12:00 Noon, John Fellows, Saratoga

The morning had been cloudy and cold in the little village of Saratoga. It had been raining steadily since about ten in the morning. Wilkinson's letter had reached Fellows in the morning. By this time his men were wide awake and could see the lead units of Burgoyne's bedraggled army creeping toward Schuyler's house and the ruined bridge over Fish Creek. No additional American units appeared to be on their way. Fellows had made ready to evacuate his men across the fords north of the village. Now, as Burgoyne's army crossed Fish Kill into Saratoga, Fellows's thirteen hundred men forded the Hudson above the village and were clambering up the opposite bank of the river. None of them knew that a British detachment had circuited their camp while they slept the previous night. None of them knew how close they had come to disaster.[46]

2:00 PM, John Burgoyne, South of Saratoga

It had started to rain heavily again at ten in the morning. The sky was dark and the clouds thick and low. There seemed to be no prospect of it clearing. The army needed shelter, and yet they dithered. At two o'clock Burgoyne ordered each man to receive six days of food, which he was expected to carry along with the rest of his gear. This was taken as good news, because most men thought that it meant there would be no further interruptions of the march once they were all self-sufficient. The officers were also told to take their most valuable possessions into their personal care; the baggage train could no longer be guaranteed. This they did, and excess equipment and baggage piled up along the road. Some of the piles were burned. Phillips brought up the rear with the British light infantry, grenadiers, the 24th Foot, and their artillery. The two light 3-pounders became mired in the mud, their horses exhausted and dying. These too were abandoned.[47]

The army finally started to march in concert again at four o'clock in the afternoon. It moved forward in three columns, the artillery and baggage forming the center column on the road. Hamilton's brigade moved parallel to the road, across the fields to the right. The Advanced Corps and von Specht's brigade made their way through rough woods on the left. All of them slogged along in the continuing rain.

5:00 PM, *Ebenezer Mattoon, East Bank of the Hudson*

More Massachusetts militia appeared on the east bank of the Hudson. Everyone was aware that across the river the British and German troops were entering Saratoga and digging in. The Americans still did not have enough force to keep Burgoyne from pushing across the ford if he really set his mind to it, but they made as big a show as they could with what they had. The American artillery battery was repositioned so that it could be easily seen from the British positions. The American guns started firing, using the British and German fires as targets. This soon caused them to be extinguished.

As it grew darker, Mattoon's battery was ordered to cross Batten Kill and establish a new position on the long tongue of land that separated the main stream of the Hudson from the lower portion of its Batten Kill tributary. The move put them just opposite a house that the British had clearly decided to occupy. This would make for good target practice in the morning. For now, the battery settled in for the night.[48]

6:00 PM, *Friedrich Riedesel, Dovegat*

Riedesel was appalled. Most of Wednesday had been lost trying to manage the dead and dying. Now Thursday had been frittered away as well. "A day has been uselessly wasted," he grumbled.[49] His units had not marched again until evening, finally crossing Fish Kill into Saratoga at nightfall. By this time the Americans appeared to have occupied the entire opposite side of the Hudson, including the country above Batten Kill. Scouts reported that they were nearly surrounded by Americans on the western heights above Saratoga as well, everywhere except a possible escape route to the north of the village. They could have been here two days ago, but now everyone down to the lowest ranking private soldier knew that they were all but trapped. Riedesel could barely maintain civility with Burgoyne.

The torrential rain had continued all day. Except for the Mohawks, the last of the Indians had disappeared into the woods. Frederika's chambermaid was useless, spending her time cursing her situation and tearing at her hair. Frederika urged her to compose herself lest she be taken for a savage. The maid asked Frederika fiercely if that would trouble her and when Frederika said yes the frantic woman pulled off her bonnet, releasing her disheveled hair, and screamed, "You talk well! You have your husband! But we have nothing to look forward to except dying miserably on the one hand or losing all we possess on the other!" Lena, the other maid, said nothing, but Frederika tried to restore calm by promising to make good any losses either of them suffered.

They had at least reached Saratoga, only an hour from where they had squatted for most of the day. Everyone was soaked from the continuing rain. Frederika found a fire to warm the children, stripped off their wet clothes, and put them to sleep on some straw. Their old friend General Phillips came by and Frederika asked, "Why do we not continue our retreat while there is yet time? My husband has pledged himself to cover it and bring the army through." Phillips had to smile. "Poor woman, I am amazed at you. Completely wet through have you still the courage to wish to go farther in this weather. Would that you were only our commanding general. He halts because he is tired, and intends to spend the night here and give us a supper."

Frederika could not conceal her disgust. In her view Burgoyne spent half his nights singing, drinking, and dallying with one of the wives. Now Burgoyne had taken over Philip Schuyler's country home at Fish Kill and was diverting himself from the calamity facing his army by dining and drinking into the night. The general loved his champagne, and he still had an ample supply of it. The Riedesels and most of the other German officers thought the real reason for the day's delays had been to provide Burgoyne with comfortable lodging that night, and a chance for a final bout of revelry.[50]

7:30 PM, John Becker, American Bridge of Boats

Below Bemis Heights, just east of the American bridge of boats, John Becker and his father made their way back to his uncle's farm, hoping that it was still standing. What they found were a thousand militiamen in the house, barn, and outbuildings. The Beckers were dedicated to the cause of independence, but they had taken their family south to safety when Burgoyne's army had approached. Now the tide had turned and the adult men were back. John and his son wanted to see what could be salvaged from the family farms before winter set in. When the militiamen realized that the landowner had returned and that he was not a Loyalist they did everything to treat him decently as their host. But though they made space for him they did not leave.[51]

8:00 PM, William Digby, Saratoga

A hard rain had continued for the rest of the day and into the night. To William Digby's surprise the Americans had not appeared and fired down on them from the bluffs to their left as they retreated. He knew that it would have been hard going if they had. The reason was that the 9th and the 47th had been deployed on the heights above Dovegat to prevent the Americans from seizing those positions and firing on the retreating British Army.[52] There was a little more organization here than Digby realized.

They had slogged on for six hours in the rain, until around three in the afternoon when the retreat had been halted yet again. Digby could see masses of American soldiers advancing northward on the other side of the Hudson, paralleling the British retreat and moving fast enough to beat them to Fort Edward. Everyone was ordered to burn all unnecessary baggage and equipment to speed the retreat.[53]

Now it was eight o'clock at night, and it would be another hour before the bulk of the army made it to Saratoga. The regiments deployed and dug in around the vacant village as best they could. No one outside Burgoyne's inner circle expected that they would occupy the village for more than one night. Surely they would set out again in the morning. Nearly everyone thought that it would be the most temporary of camps.[54]

The trailing grenadiers waded across Fish Kill near Schuyler's house. The battalion was posted on the heights above Saratoga. There they remained through the night under the still steady rain, without fires or shelter, hearing occasional shots at the supply bateaux from the Americans across the river. No one slept or even had the inclination to.[55]

Burgoyne installed himself in Schuyler's house. There was great joy among the officers when it was made known that all the bateaux had been safely brought up the river and pulled up on the west bank next to the village. The supplies in the loaded bateaux were safe. The empty bateaux were available to build a new floating bridge across the Hudson. Everyone was also encouraged by the rumor that St. Leger was coming from the north with reinforcements, and that he might arrive as early as tomorrow. This would be sufficient for the army to hold out until Clinton arrived from the south. It was encouraging news, but few outside Burgoyne's headquarters believed a word of it.[56]

It had taken all day to reach Saratoga from Dovegot on the muddy road. Many of the British officers and wounded men took shelter in the barracks in the village. The bridge across Fish Kill had been destroyed by the Americans, so the troops had to ford the icy, swollen stream. They were up to their waists in the cold water, but they were already so soaked it hardly seemed to matter. The British artillery stalled on the south side of the kill. The artillerymen could see no good ford in the dark; the horses and oxen were so starved and exhausted they could not be sure fording was possible at all.[57] Most of the army stayed outside in the cold rain, which would turn to hoarfrost by morning.

8:00 PM, Harriet Acland, Saratoga

The distraught Lady Acland had her tent set up in the torrential rain. At least she knew her husband John was alive, but that only increased her desire to be with him. Frederika went to see her and urged her to find a way to go to him. Harriet finally agreed. She found Stanhope, one of Burgoyne's aides, and persuaded him to convey a message asking for permission to leave camp. The note begged, pleaded, and insisted. Burgoyne received it from Stanhope, and at length he agreed, knowing that the problem would not otherwise go away.

Even if her rank had not required special consideration, Burgoyne was as taken by Harriet Acland as any man under his command. He said so to his aides. "I am astonished at this proposal. After so long an agitation of the spirits, exhausted not only for want of rest, but absolutely for want of food, drenched in rains for twelve hours together, that a woman should be capable of such an undertaking, as delivering herself to the enemy, probably in the night and uncertain of what hands she might first fall into, appears an effort above human nature."[58] Burgoyne's weaknesses for both pretty ladies and bravery had combined to leave him with no option. He scribbled a few lines to Gates on dirty, damp paper. The handwriting was nearly illegible, his effort to write like a proper gentleman so stressed by his circumstances that he seemed to find it hard to be coherent.

> *Sir,*
>
> *Lady Harriet Ackland, a Lady of the first distinction by family rank & by personal virtue, is under such concern on account of Major Ackland, her husband, wounded & a prisoner in your hands, that I cannot refuse her request to commit her to your protection.*
>
> *Whatever general impropriety there may be in personal liking in your situation & mine to solicit favours, I cannot see the uncommon persuasion in every female grace & exaltation of character of this Lady, & her very hard fortune without testifying that your attentions to her will lay me under obligation.*
>
> > *I am, sir*
> > > *Your obedient servant,*
> > > *J. Burgoyne*
> > *Oct^ber 9 1777*
> > > *M. G. Gates*

Burgoyne noted Gates's rank this time but did not append his own rank to his name. He handed Harriet the pass and sent her off with two boats in the dark. Chaplain Brudenel chaperoned Harriet, along with one of her maids and John's wounded valet, while a drummer in one of the boats warned the Americans of their approach through the fog and darkness.[59]

8:30 PM, Horatio Gates, American Headquarters

Word reached headquarters that Henry Clinton had taken Fort Montgomery and was advancing up the Hudson. There was no time to lose; this business had to be settled soon or the Northern Army would find itself both chasing Burgoyne and defending Albany from an attack from the south. Gates ordered all units to draw and cook four days' provisions. It was time to pursue the enemy and the army needed to be able to sustain itself in motion for a few days without resupply. Morgan's riflemen would lead the pursuit. The steady rain would finally end after dark, but beneath the starry sky it would be cold and windy.[60]

9:00 PM, John Fellows, Saratoga

Gates had already sent Fellows's militia and artillery up along the east bank of the Hudson to prevent Burgoyne from crossing the river, but knew he needed to send more. The loss of Lincoln had been a blow to Gates. Before arriving at Bemis Heights Lincoln had ranged up and down the country east of the Hudson and he knew it well. Now Fellows would have to take on what might otherwise have been Lincoln's responsibility.

Fellows had pulled back to the east bank of the Hudson and was in position to block Burgoyne there, but he needed more troops. They were on their way, and Fellows waited for them. But Gates wanted Fellows to do more than that. Given the speed with which Fellows got his men to Saratoga in the first place Gates thought he seemed up to it.

Many of the militiamen who were going north to join Fellows had arrived from the south on horseback, so it made sense to mount all of them. Gates ordered that all extra horses be made available to Fellows's detachment. Most of the men doubled up on horses and started moving. Another battery was ordered to go along and position their artillery to help cover the fording place just above Saratoga. Each of the horses being used to pull the artillery also had a militiaman on its back. It was, as usual, an improvised solution, but it allowed the detachment to move quickly during the night.

The mounted detachment leapfrogged past the American militias and artillery already in place opposite Saratoga and continued on toward Fort Edward. It was a journey of over twenty miles, in the dark, and over barely passable roads, but they would make it there by dawn even without a moon to light the way.[61]

9:00 PM, Henry Dearborn, the Former British Camp

Dearborn was still awake at nine when his advanced picket reported that one or more boats were coming down the river. He could hear a drummer signaling the approach as he walked down to the river, but in the rainy gloom he could see nothing. Dearborn hailed the boats and a voice answered, "A flag of truce from General Burgoyne." The boats were guided to a landing and Dearborn was handed Burgoyne's note to Gates, along with the anguished but still beautiful Lady Acland. Dearborn went back to his quarters, in a house that had sheltered British or German officers just the night before. There Dearborn had light enough to read the note. He rushed back to the landing quickly as soon as he understood its contents. Lady Acland was invited to stay in the house until morning. Dearborn insisted that she not attempt to reach her husband in these awful conditions, assuring her that he knew Acland to have received only flesh wounds.

Within minutes the ever-winsome Lady Acland was in her own bedroom with a warm fire, two servants, and her baggage intact.[62] Brudenel was kept with the boats and crews so that they could take a reply from Gates back to Burgoyne when the commander had time to compose one.

Burgoyne's note was delayed by neither rain nor darkness. A messenger rode off immediately to deliver it to Gates. At about ten o'clock Wilkinson received word that the bateaux had arrived at Dearborn's camp under a flag of truce. Word was sent back to Dearborn by the same messenger. Dearborn was to make the lady comfortable for the night, it still being very wet and dark. By the time this unnecessary instruction arrived almost everyone was already comfortably asleep in Dearborn's quarters.

12:00 Midnight, John Burgoyne, Saratoga

Later that night more news came in, this time very discouraging news that everyone was willing to believe. The Americans were all over the far bank of the Hudson, firing at will on the bateaux and making it clear that British engineers would not be building a new floating bridge. They were also everywhere to the north along the eastern bank, making it just as clear that the route to Fort Edward or even just to Batten Kill on that side of the Hudson was now impossible even if Burgoyne's army found a way to cross over the river. Word also spread that the mired road from Dovegat had been too much for the big 12-pounders. The rumor was that both cannons had been left behind and that the men manning them had been captured. The hard new truth was that the good news emanating from headquarters had for weeks been largely contrived and almost immediately contradicted by reliable outside reports. Burgoyne had lost the faith and trust of his own army. The rain finally ended at midnight, pushed out by clear cold air. Without the rain a deep hard autumnal frost settled on Saratoga and its population of wet and largely unsheltered refugees.[63]

FRIDAY, OCTOBER 10, 1777

3:00 AM, British Soldiers, Saratoga

Some of the wet and exhausted British and German soldiers had found abandoned houses with fireplaces, but most had settled for temporary shelters and had warmed themselves as best they could. This was difficult in an abandoned village that was generally lacking in dry firewood

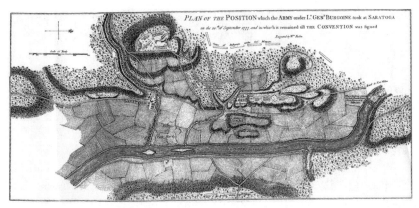

Figure 5.4 Historical map of Saratoga, now Schuylerville, New York, showing the disposition of Burgoyne's surrounded army.

and proper places to burn it. Desperate men built fires in buildings not designed for them, burning furniture and woodwork in open fires in an attempt to warm and dry themselves. (See Figure 5.4.)

Burgoyne and other British officers were better off in Philip Schuyler's mansion just south of Fish Kill. A few British soldiers had taken refuge in a henhouse that stood near the mansion. Other soaked soldiers filled up the empty barracks nearer the center of the village. They were for the most part sick and wounded men who were mobile enough to avoid being left behind in the abandoned British hospital. The Riedesel family found a house at the far northern end of the village.

Just when it seemed that conditions could not get worse, they did. The little henhouse caught fire during the night and the men who had found shelter in it were forced to join others on the exposed cold and wet landscape outside. During the early morning hours, the barracks in the village also caught fire and like the men in the henhouse the men there had to run for their lives. Many barely made it out. One sick soldier of the Regiment Riedesel did not escape.[64]

7:00 AM, Ebenezer Mattoon, Opposite Saratoga on the Bank of the Hudson

Mattoon's artillery unit had been ordered to cross the lower part of Batten Kill during the night. It was a move that repositioned them across the Hudson from the northern part of the village of Saratoga. In the morning they could see British officers on the porch and around the front of a prominent house that was within easy shot. Someone said that it was the Lansing house. Many of the British officers were apparently intent on surveying the American positions on Mattoon's side of the river. Captain Fernival was sick, and it fell to Mattoon to aim and level the guns. Soon his unit was throwing shot into and around the house, dispersing the British officers and disrupting activities inside what Ebenezer thought was probably now the British headquarters.[65]

For their part, the British finally got what was left of their artillery across Fish Kill. This included the two 12-pounders that many thought had been captured during Thursday's dark and soggy retreat.[66]

7:00 AM, Frederika Riedesel, Saratoga

Frederika drank some tea for breakfast at seven, and prepared her brood for renewed travel. An English officer gave her some broth. Frederika could see that the army was in disarray. Provisions had not been distributed. Cattle had not been slaughtered to provide the men with meat. Frederika used all the supplies she had left in her calash to feed the hungry officers and men camped around her. Her cook overcharged her, but he was a competent thief, and good at preparing what he stole. When it was all gone she stopped Captain Stanhope and gave him an earful. "Come and see for yourself these officers who have been wounded in the common cause and who are now in want of everything because they do not receive that which is due them. It is, therefore, your duty to make a representation of this to the general."

A quarter hour later Burgoyne himself came by to thank her for reminding him of his duty. He added lamely that "a general was much to be pitied when he was not properly served nor his commands obeyed." To this Frederika said, "I beg your pardon for having meddled with things which I well know a woman has no business with, but it was impossible to keep silent when I saw so many brave men in want of everything and had nothing more to give them." Burgoyne thanked her again. But Frederika knew that he would never forgive her for the affront. Burgoyne apologized to the English officers but peevishly asked why they had not come to him. Their response, which none would have risked a week ago, was that English officers were not accustomed to visit the kitchen of their general. Burgoyne then issued an order that all provisions be distributed. This, of course, further delayed everything else.[67]

Everywhere around the little village the British and German troops did their best to dig in and construct shelters and earthworks that would hold against the expected American attack. The main British encampment was placed on high ground above the southwestern side of the village near Fish Kill. There they were high enough and far enough from the Americans on the east side of the Hudson to be reasonably secure.

The positions facing southward along the western flats of the Hudson were strong. This was the direction from which an American attack was most likely to come. But the center facing the Americans on the heights to the westward and the units facing north were too weak to withstand even a modest attack. Strengthening them was going to take time and effort. On the north side of the village the soil was so rocky and tools were in such short supply that the trenches were barely a foot deep. The Hudson was to their backs on the east side of the village, a barrier for both armies because neither could cross it without risking huge losses. But the Americans were content to maintain their positions in the woods on the opposite side, their riflemen shooting with great skill at anyone who attempted to take drinking water from the river.[68]

7:00 AM, Harriet Acland, the Former British Camp

Harriet Acland was up at dawn and Dearborn's men were ready to take her to her husband. Aides had already appeared, sent by Gates to bring Harriet to his headquarters on Bemis Heights. They brought along a horse to take her there. Dearborn thought that she appeared pregnant, a condition that even if true would not be mentioned by Harriet, her servants, or any of the many perceptive and solicitous gentlemen who rushed to her assistance.[69]

John was already on his way to the hospital in Albany, along with other wounded officers from both armies. Harriet was momentarily crestfallen when she heard this, which elicited another tide of concern and recruited more men bent on helping her achieve her reunion with her wounded husband. At length she set off for Albany. She would eventually catch up with John at Stillwater.[70]

10:00 AM, John Becker, East of the Hudson

John Becker and his father awoke at home for the first time since Burgoynes' army had forced them to leave the area. They could see that the American troops were requisitioning shocks of wheat the local Loyalists had harvested from the Beckers' fields during their absence. The shocks were still stacked in the fields unthreshed. The wheat was probably no longer good for flour and the Beckers did not object when the soldiers began pitching the shocks into wagons to haul the grain across the bridge of boats for the benefit of American horses in the Northern Army.

The Beckers watched the wagons cross the bridge, proud that they could make a substantive contribution to the cause. They watched the wagons head northward toward the American camp that now nearly surrounded Saratoga, taking in the happy atmosphere of an army that thought it was on the verge of victory. But when the wagons began returning empty, the elder Becker suddenly feared that his rye was about to meet the same fate as his wheat. Generosity with wheat that was already partly spoiled was one thing, but the loss of his rye too might bring a long hungry winter to his family.

The Beckers sprinted back across the bridge of boats to stay ahead of the empty wagons. Back at the farm they dragged fence rails in place to bar access to the rye. An American commissary officer rode up and demanded the Beckers give the wagons access. Becker raised one of the rails as a long club and warned, "Touch those bars at your peril." The officer dismounted, drew his sword, and called on the wagoners to help him. The wagoners did not want any part of trouble and refused. At that the officer mounted his horse again and rode off, followed by the empty wagons.

The Beckers sprinted back to the bridge of boats again, and again they got ahead of the lumbering wagons. This time they positioned themselves at Gates's headquarters. Soon the commissary was there too, ready to complain to the general about the uncooperative Beckers. Gates came out. "Why have you returned empty?" The commissary was grumpy. "The owner forcibly resisted me." Gates studied the man. "Did you attempt to take lawfully? Did you take appraisers with you?" "No sir," came the reply.

It was the sort of thing that drives even the best administrators to drink. Gates was very good at supplying his army, better at that, in fact, than leading it, but he expected his subordinates to follow proper procedures. "You blockhead, he would have been justified had he resisted you to the last extremity," he fumed. The Beckers said nothing, but they were enjoying the moment. An aide nudged Gates and hinted that the elder Becker was the owner. Gates turned to the Beckers and did his best to sound reasonable. "We must have the grain for our horses." Becker replied, "My necessities are greater than yours, General. You have taken all my wheat. It is hard that my last grain should be taken from me."

Gates sighed. "My dear sir, I respect this necessity as much as you do, but it is easier for an individual to provide for his wants than me to manage for a whole army. This is the crisis of our fate. The salvation of this country rests on the issue of events now taking place, and in the result you and all of us are deeply interested." Becker thought about this. "Then take it, sir, but let it be done in the manner prescribed by law. My country demands the sacrifice and cheerfully will I make it." Appraisers were immediately appointed and they went off across the bridge to assess the contributions the Beckers were making to the war effort. But for the Beckers it would come to nothing. This was a war in which everything for the Americans was improvised. Like most people they would remain devoted to the effort to the end, and like so many others they would never receive any sort of receipt, never mind compensation, for their contributions. These were the costs of independence.[71]

11:00 AM, Nicholas Sutherland, North of Saratoga

The Americans had been close behind them, coming up from the south along the river road and smaller interior roads and trails. Some of them must be in positions west of them by now. The countryside east of the Hudson was clearly infested with them, as it had been for weeks. Burgoyne ordered Nicholas Sutherland of the 47th to take parts of two regiments to reconnoiter the road north from the village toward Fort Edward on the west side of the Hudson. It appeared that it was still open. If the detachment could clear the road and repair the bridges they might have a chance to escape this way.

Sutherland had men from his own regiment as well as some from the 62nd. He also had some of Fraser's Rangers, some Loyalists, and even some remaining Mohawks to help scout the route and protect the detachment. Captain Twiss and a party of engineers were sent along to repair bridges for the expected retreat. Maybe the army could reach Fort George at the southern end of Lake George. Maybe they could cross the main river well north of the mouth of Batten Kill and in that way avoid the Americans, who were everywhere along the east bank closer to Saratoga. Maybe they could reach Fort Edward.

Sutherland's detachment moved up the river road north of the village, bringing them within range of Ebenezer Mattoon's battery on the opposite side of the river. They provided the Americans with some target practice as they trundled north.[72] The detachment survived and got to work, but back in Saratoga Burgoyne was having second thoughts. By eleven o'clock messages came in that the Americans had moved around the army on the west side of Saratoga more quickly than anticipated. Burgoyne was now nearly surrounded and the Americans would probably cut off Sutherland's detachment soon. Burgoyne sent orders for the detachment to return quickly.

The messenger caught up with the detachment and delivered Burgoyne's order to return to the village. Sutherland was crestfallen. As nearly as he could determine there were no Americans along the road north of Saratoga. The men in his detachment were already working to repair bridges. With a little more time, the way would be clear for the army to escape northward. But it was no use. They had their orders. Most of the disheartened engineers retreated back to Saratoga.[73]

Captain Fraser left behind a few engineers and some provincials to protect them. Perhaps Burgoyne would change his mind again. Perhaps these few could make the vital repairs. It was their only hope for escape, and young Fraser could not bring himself to abandon it entirely. But the provincials soon fled when a small party of American scouts approached. They were too few. It was too late.

12:00 Noon, American Advance Guard, South of Saratoga

It cleared again by noon, but it was cold, and many in the American Army were still waiting for provisions. Nixon's and Learned's brigades had moved out at around nine o'clock. Glover's brigade was moving by eleven. Now the bulk of the army was finally marching in pursuit of the British. Poor's brigade would leave by one o'clock. Along the way they found burned houses and the discarded debris of the beaten army. Horse carcasses, baggage, and abandoned carts littered the side of the road. One abandoned wagon still contained three hundred pounds of gunpowder and other valuable supplies. In another wagon happy soldiers found heavy clothing that would come in handy as the weather got colder. Some other soldiers recovered a marquee tent that they were convinced had been Burgoyne's own.[74]

The lead elements of the advance guard reached Fish Kill just after noon and found the British and German troops setting up camp and transferring cannon, provisions, and baggage from their boats. Fellows's corps on the opposite side of the river started to harass the British positions at two o'clock and continued to do so for the rest of the afternoon. The bateaux at the mouth of Fish Kill were favorite targets as the British tried to unload and secure the supplies they contained. They hurried to move the supplies to safer ground in their main camp on the heights above the village.

One of the militiamen on the east bank of the Hudson noticed that some of the British officers' mounts were being allowed to graze on the hay surrounding Schuyler's mansion. Because of the deadly accuracy of American forces on the east side of the river there were no guards to be seen near the horses. The soldier asked permission from his captain to try to swim across the big river, steal one of the horses, and ride it back to the American side. It seemed like a good idea, so the captain agreed. The man succeeded in swimming through the cold water and was pounding back on a good-looking mount before the British were able to fire a volley in his direction. The British soldiers were too far away, and the horse was too fast. The American swam the horse back across the river and arrived beaming, without a scratch on either himself or the mount.

After a half hour's rest, the militiaman was so happy with his success that he smilingly suggested to his captain that it would not do for a common soldier to have a horse while a captain did not. The captain then cheerfully agreed that the militiaman could try the caper a second time. He did, and a while later he came back with a second horse for the captain.[75] They were well-fed horses that had belonged to senior British officers occupying Schuyler's mansion, perhaps two of Burgoyne's own mounts. The irony pleased the Americans as much as it must have annoyed the British.

2:00 PM, Frederika Riedesel, the Lansing House

Nearly everyone was eager to resume the retreat, convinced that calamity awaited them if they did not. Everyone but Burgoyne, who seated himself for dinner and waited for Howe to send him a miracle. Burgoyne and his officers were in a cluster of tents. Around two o'clock Mattoon's battery began to fire at the dinner gathering. In the general panic Riedesel sent a message to Frederika, telling her to take shelter in the nearby Lansing house. The calash was already loaded in the forlorn hope that they would be moving north soon. She did not get far when Americans across the river began firing directly at the calash as well. Frederika pushed her children to the floor and covered them with her body. A ball shattered the arm of an already wounded English soldier who was headed for the same house. As they reached it the American artillery made the house their primary target. Mattoon's battery was firing into the camp from a position only three hundred yards away on the opposite bank of the Hudson.

The Americans still thought that the Lansing house was Burgoyne's new headquarters and pounded at it without mercy.[76] Unknown to the Americans, the house was actually filled with the wounded. Frederika, her children, and her servants took refuge in its squalid cellar. The place had been used as a latrine by dozens of men during the day; for the moment there was little Frederika could do to clean the place up.

Frederika sent the terrified women and children out during a lull so that she could try to clean and fumigate the three bays of the cellar. Vinegar sprinkled on hot coals seemed to clear the air. Her servants scraped the dirt floor and carried out the filth as best they could.

Frederika proposed to the surgeons upstairs that one of the three sections of the cellar be used for the most seriously wounded men. The women and children could remain in a second section, and others who needed shelter could use the third. No sooner had women, children, and wounded soldiers moved back into the cellar but the American cannonade began anew. Eleven shots passed through the house above her; panicked soldiers tried to gain access to the cellar. Frederika braced herself against the door for fear that a suffocating crush would endanger everyone already sheltered there. Upstairs one poor man, a surgeon named Jones, was on a table; his fellow surgeons were in the middle of amputating his leg when a shot came through the wall and tore off the other leg. His colleagues ran for cover, and when they came back they found that Jones had managed to drag himself to a corner of the room. There he lay, scarcely breathing and near death.[77]

An officer appeared at the door. He looked stricken; there were nervous whispers. There were only three women left with Frederika apart from her maids: the wives of Major Harnage and Lieutenant Reynals, and Burgoyne's favorite, the commissary's wife. The messenger had bad news, and all three recoiled, each thinking she was to be the recipient. Reynals's wife had already been shocked by the false news that her husband had been shot dead back on September 19. Frederika shrieked, sure that it was terrible news about Friedrich, but after another whispered exchange the eyes of the messenger settled once again on Reynals's wife. This time the messenger said that a ball had taken off Lieutenant Reynals's arm at the shoulder. He was in a very bad way. His wife, who had already gone through the grief of a false report, now had to face it all over again. Frederika consoled her as best she could, battling with the mixture of grief, despair, relief, and guilt that it was her duty to bear. They all would spend the rest of the afternoon and the coming night in mud and stench, the children sleeping with their heads on Frederika's lap.[78]

4:00 PM, *Ebenezer Mattoon, East Bank of the Hudson*

The American battery pounded away at the Lansing house on the opposite bank. At last, some British artillerymen brought their own gun to bear on the American battery. Mattoon could no longer fire at the house without taking return fire. Before long the American artillerymen pulled back from their exposed position to a safer emplacement. As they did, new orders arrived. The battery was being sent another dozen miles farther north, to set up at Fort Edward and keep any British from fording the Hudson there. Massachusetts militia was ordered to accompany them. Mattoon could only conclude with some satisfaction that larger numbers were moving in behind them and that soon the whole east side of the Hudson would be so strongly held that Burgoyne would have no reasonable way to cross the river.[79]

4:00 PM, *American Main Forces, South of Saratoga*

By four o'clock the main force of the American Army had advanced to Fish Kill. Cannons were brought up to the south bank of the kill and these too were used to harass the British. Major Stevens drew up two small guns on the river flats below the Schuyler mansion and battered the British working party unloading the bateaux until they gave up and withdrew. With that the British artillery on the other side of Fish Kill opened up on Stevens's position and blew up one of his ammunition carts. Stevens withdrew amid cheers and catcalls from the British Army.[80]

On the south side of Fish Kill, Morgan's riflemen climbed into trees and sniped lethally at anyone who showed himself in the British camp.

A captain and six men were wounded. The Americans on the east bank of the Hudson continued firing at the British as well, focusing on the supply bateaux drawn up on the opposite shore. Some boats were lost and several men were killed or wounded in those that remained.[81]

Teams of Americans would use the covering fire from Morgan's rifles and Fellows's muskets across the river to dash in and draw off the occasional bateau. As soon as the Americans would capture a bateau their undisciplined militia and camp followers would descend upon it like vultures. Sacks were torn open and casks emptied as the looters made off with everything they found. Burgoyne had no choice but to order his men to unload the bateaux still holding supplies and move the stores to safer locations back away from the river. The Americans kept shooting at the boats, sinking them one by one, taking away the last remote possibility that the British might use them to build a new bridge of boats across the Hudson.[82]

5:00 PM, *William Digby, the Schuyler House*

The cordon of Americans around the south and west sides of Saratoga continued to tighten. The British pickets watched glumly as the rebels advanced toward the southern bank of Fish Kill. The henhouse on Schuyler's property was already gone, but the house still stood. The attacks forced Burgoyne to abandon his comfortable quarters in the exposed Schuyler mansion. Now Burgoyne feared that the mansion and the remaining outbuildings would be taken and used as cover by the Americans, so he ordered them all to be burned. Men set fire to the house, mill, and outbuildings, burning all the buildings to the ground. Only the privy was spared. Along with the house and outbuildings they burned most of their remaining baggage to keep it from falling into American hands. Burgoyne moved into tents on the Saratoga heights.[83]

The grumbling among the grenadiers, ever present, grew louder. Spike the artillery and make a dash for Fort George, they said. Forget Fort Edward. But even the grumblers knew that no fort south of Ticonderoga could be held for long and that a dash from Fort George to Ticonderoga would require boats they did not have. Retreat along the road between Fort Edward and Skenesborough that had been so hard to travel during the summer would be impossible now.[84]

Digby had noticed that when Burgoyne was successful the complainers were silent; it was another matter when fortune turned from good to bad.

The debate exhausted itself as the demoralized men gave up on futile complaining and came around to the reality of their current situation. Retreat was no longer a realistic option, and they gradually came to embrace the idea that they would rather fall together than disgrace the British Army. Orders came to shift their positions slightly and to dig defensive entrenchments. As night fell the men bent again to that grim task, many thinking that they were probably digging their own graves. Digby's low opinion of the German "foreigners" fighting with the British remained unchanged. "I have a poor opinion of their spirit since the night of the seventh." The recriminations were another sign of the declining morale in the hybrid army of British and German troops.[85]

7:00 PM, *Horatio Gates, American Headquarters*

As usual, Gates was uncertain. Burgoyne might keep moving or he might dig in at Saratoga. Gates worried that his exuberant forces might take chances against a wounded but still dangerous enemy. But he was just as worried that his army might fail to exploit the clear advantage it now had over Burgoyne. As nearly as Gates was able to determine, the way north along the west side of the Hudson was still open to Burgoyne. By evening Gates had convinced himself that Burgoyne would move north out of Saratoga as soon as he could. Gates decided that he needed to exploit his advantage and do whatever he could to keep Burgoyne off balance. He scribbled a new standing order: "That in case of an attack against any point, whether front, flank, or rear, the troops are to fall on the enemy at all quarters."[86]

This would be enough for Gates's brigadier generals. Unlike their commander they were, to a man, eager to finish the task at hand. As evening turned into night they convinced each other that Burgoyne would not stay long. He still had an escape route to the north and he would be crazy to not take it. He would accommodate the rebels. If and when Burgoyne did anything at all, they would follow Gates's new standing order. They would attack with everything they had.

11:00 PM, *James Wilkinson, American Headquarters*

James Wilkinson made it his new duty to review the posting of guards and pickets each night; it was a good excuse to get away from Gates and show himself to the officers and men. He completed his circuit and returned to

Gates's new headquarters around eleven o'clock. American headquarters was currently a dugout shack tucked into the base of a hill south of Fish Kill, a hovel no more than ten feet square. Gates and Wilkinson each had what passed for a bed, forked posts driven into the ground with a frame of saplings and boards. A pair of blankets and straw, a saddle for a pillow, and each bed was complete. As rude as they were, the quarters were the best any American enjoyed at Saratoga.

Wilkinson came in and found Gates already in bed. Gates showed Wilkinson a draft of an order he had written for the next morning: "The army will advance at reveille tomorrow morning, Morgan's corps to keep the heights on the left, and the main body to march on the great road near the river."

Wilkinson read it through. Then he read it again, not liking it any more the second time. "You would commit yourself to the enemy in their strong position," he said. Gates looked at him querulously. "They are already on the retreat, and will be miles ahead of us before morning."

Wilkinson was far from convinced and said so. "You have no assurance of this. I have just left their guards on post. With submission, I conceive we ought to reconnoiter before the army marches. Should we explore our way through a dense fog and fall in with the enemy posted behind their entrenchments, the consequences might be destructive."

Gates thought about this. It was true that every day so far this month had been foggy in the morning unless it was raining. Gates relented a little but would not concede the point. "Rise early to attend to the movement and report to me. It is natural that they should sacrifice guards to conceal their movements." That was it then. If Burgoyne was still in place in the morning Gates could countermand the order.[87] Otherwise, the American brigades would be nipping at Burgoyne's heels as he retreated north out of Saratoga. But Gates's brigadier generals had already seized on the standing order Gates had issued earlier. They were ready and eager to attack at first light. The Northern Army was already in motion.

SATURDAY, OCTOBER 11, 1777

6:15 AM, James Wilkinson, Fish Kill

To no one's surprise, it was another very foggy morning.[88] General Fellows and his men crossed the Hudson and seized a hundred British bateaux during the early morning hours. Burgoyne's men had still not been able to get all the supplies moved to safety on high ground; the incessant sniping by the Americans had made it too dangerous. The captured boats contained a hundred barrels of pork, some kegs of porter, and other supplies that the British clearly could not afford to lose. But the bateaux had been guarded by only a sergeant and fifteen men, and the Americans had their way almost without resistance.[89]

Gates and his generals had assumed that the British would resume their retreat early on Saturday. After all, the road north out of Saratoga could still be forced; there were not yet enough American troops there to prevent it. But the thick, cold fog over the damp landscape left the Americans unable to see whether their assumptions were correct or not. Their scouts could see little through it. The lead American units followed orders and began moving across Fish Kill at the southwest corner of the village at dawn. Upstream on the kill, Morgan and Dearborn were positioned to move in and take possession of the heights over Saratoga with four hundred of their men.[90]

The belief that Burgoyne was moving north appeared to be confirmed by a deserter who came in and told General Learned that Burgoyne's entire army was retreating to Fort Edward. Only a rear guard was still in position at Saratoga. Learned and the other generals were ready to believe such news, so they did not question it. They made ready to advance through the fog and seize the abandoned British camp.[91]

Wilkinson was on horseback before reveille. He rode up to Morgan's position, only to find the riflemen already decamped. Morgan and his men had crossed the upper Fish Kill on a raft of loose logs at the foot of a mill pond. Wilkinson forded the creek at a deep and rapid ford, and as his horse scrambled up the north bank, he heard several shots ahead. The fog was so thick that he could not see more than twenty paces; he wondered if Morgan's men could see what they were shooting at. Then it occurred to him that the shots might be coming from British sentries. It also occurred to him that this was no weather for riflemen untrained in close combat.

Wilkinson came up on Morgan and the colonel said, "I was advancing agreeably to orders. We fell in with a picket of the enemy. I have lost an officer and two privates." Morgan was now of the opinion that Burgoyne had not moved at all and that his riflemen were facing the entire British Army in the dense fog. Fish Kill was behind him; if the British charged, he would quickly be in a very serious situation. Wilkinson, who knew the stream, agreed. The situation could turn critical. Morgan and Dearborn fell back two hundred yards and waited for new orders.[92]

Wilkinson said, "I advise you to incline to your left and throw your corps into the air. I promise to support you with two brigades." With that, he turned his horse and reforded Fish Kill. He cantered back to head-quarters and informed Gates that the British were still in place and that Morgan and Dearborn were in trouble. Gates instructed Wilkinson to order up Paterson's and Learned's brigades to support Morgan.

Wilkinson rode off to find Paterson and Learned. He found Learned and showed him the ford he had used to cross Fish Creek. From there he doubled back to find the rest of the column and ran into Generals Nixon and Glover, halted in the road. Glover told him that they were waiting for guides to get them across Fish Kill. Wilkinson was offering his services for this purpose when an aide for Gates rode up and said that Gates had sent new orders. "The troops must immediately cross the creek or return to their camp." Wilkinson was confused by this contradictory order. What did it mean? Where the hell was Gates? Why was he not here himself? Wilkinson gave the messenger a new message for Gates. "Tell the general that his own fame and the interests of the cause are at hazard; that his presence is necessary with the troops." Here they were with an impossibly confusing order sent forward by an absentee commander, uncertain what to do, and lost in the fog. There were no American divisional command-ers; the brigades were in chaos.

The messenger sped off with the message. Wilkinson started to lead the column toward the ford over Fish Creek. Artillery Major Ebenezer Stevens offered to accompany him. They followed a different path to the kill, lower down than the one he had used earlier. The advanced guard of fifty men followed them into the fog. Wilkinson and Stevens guided their horses down to the stream, which was pleasantly noisy. Halfway across, the horses stopped to drink, as horses will. When Wilkinson looked up he could just barely see men moving in the fog. They were wearing red. He whispered to Stevens, and the two reined their horses around and back up the bank they had just descended. They realized with relief that the sound of the rapidly flowing water was masking their movements. At the top of the bank they encountered a captain of the 5th Massachusetts. Wilkinson ordered the captain to charge across the stream and seize the men he had seen, not knowing or much caring how many they might be.

The Massachusetts captain jumped at the chance for action and led his men quickly across the kill and up the slope into the fog. They found and seized a scouting party of thirty-five men led by a lieutenant of the 62nd Foot, taking them all without firing a shot. In almost no time the grinning captain was back with his captives.

Wilkinson quizzed the British captives and was appalled to find out that Burgoyne's entire force was still in place. Worse, the main British encampment was on the heights just across Fish Kill. The overenthusiastic American brigadier generals were about to blunder into a killing field. Morgan was already across Fish Kill. Learned probably was too. Gates was a mile away and Wilkinson had no authority to recall the dangerously exposed troops. And now, to make matters worse, the fog was lifting, leaving the American left nakedly exposed in front of the dug-in British force and its entire artillery park.

Small arms and artillery opened up on the suddenly exposed American troops. The shock broke the American units and the men began to fall back across Fish Kill in confusion. Now it was Wilkinson's turn to panic. He had no idea how far Learned had advanced, but his brigade had to be dangerously exposed as well. He found Learned at the front of two brigades on the top of a hill, still on the south side of Fish Kill. Fortunately, he was still about two hundred yards from Burgoyne's entrenched grenadiers and light infantry, who were also still protected by the stream. But Learned's units were just about to cross ground that the British had cleared to give themselves a free fire killing zone.

Wilkinson begged Learned to stop as his winded horse pulled up, gasping. "You must retreat." Learned signaled the advance to halt but asked Wilkinson, "Have you orders?" Wilkinson knew that he did not. "I have not, as the exigency of the case did not allow me time to see General Gates. Our troops on the right have retired, and the fire you hear is from the enemy. Although I have not orders for your retreat, I pledge my life for the general's approbation." Meanwhile, the phony British deserter, the man who had told them all that Burgoyne had pulled out of Saratoga, had disappeared.[93]

By this time several other officers had joined Wilkinson and Learned. The consensus among them was that Wilkinson was right and that they should pull back. They all agreed that the best course was to withdraw in a way that exposed them least, to come to the right about and march by the left. This they did, with the British watching. When it became clear that the Americans were disengaging, the British opened up with musketry and canister from their artillery. An officer and several men fell before the American troops found cover in the woods. Learned's brigade dropped back about a half mile and settled in. Morgan's men, who were also now back on the safe side of Fish Kill, positioned themselves on Learned's left. There were sighs of relief all around.

6:30 AM, *John Nixon and John Glover, the Lower Fish Kill*

The noise of musketry off to the west and upstream on Fish Kill was hard for Nixon and Glover to interpret. They concluded that Learned and Paterson were busy mopping up the rear guards of Burgoyne's retreating army on the high ground there. It was the signal they were waiting for to advance their own brigades, and "fall on the enemy at all quarters," as Gates had put it in his orders.

The Continental regiments in Nixon's brigade crossed Fish Kill close to its mouth on the Hudson. The leading regiments surprised British guards in the ruins of old Fort Hardy just as the fog was lifting. Glover's brigade was about to follow them across when a British soldier was seen frantically wading across the stream toward the advancing Americans. The man turned out to be another British deserter. Glover interrogated him and was surprised to hear that Burgoyne's entire army was still camped in and around the village. Not only that, they were deployed in order of battle and were well dug in. Glover could hardly believe it. He looked sideways at the terrified deserter. "If you are found attempting to deceive me, you shall be hung in half an hour; but if you speak nothing but the truth you shall be protected and meet with good usage." Never was an informant more inspired to be earnest and truthful. Glover pressed him. "Have not numbers been sent off to Fort Edward?" The deserter replied, "A small detachment was sent off a day or two ago, but are returned on finding the passes occupied by the Americans, and the whole army is now in camp."[94]

A German deserter was also brought in, and he told the same story. Then the entire reconnoitering party of thirty-five men from the 62nd Foot that had been captured upstream just minutes earlier was brought in. They too confirmed the story. The original deserter was sent back to Gates and a messenger was sent forward to warn the regiments that were by this time already across Fish Kill. Whispered countermands spread down the front line of Nixon's brigade; the men did their best to slip back across Fish Kill as quietly as they had come. The British artillery opened up with canister as they waded back across, and some of Nixon's men fell. Many men from Poor's brigade had to scramble too, but most of them made it back as well. The deserter had saved the two American brigades from disaster.

There were more deserters to come, and more prisoners as American skirmishers began picking off small parties that ventured too far from safety. For the rest of the day the American brigades would move around the western side of Saratoga, digging in on the heights over-looking the British camp, encircling their position, and settling in for the expected siege. Burgoyne kept his remaining artillery occupied with harassing fire intended to keep the Americans at bay. To counter this, the Americans simply dug deeper and laid up log fortifications. Seventy or eighty volunteers from Nixon's brigade focused on cutting out some of the British bateaux tied up near the mouth of Fish Kill, which they did without any losses. They had been very lucky. There was not a brigadier general left in the Northern Army that had any lingering enthusiasm for attacking the enemy in the fog.[95]

8:00 AM, Frederika Riedesel, the Lansing House

Through the early morning hours Frederika and the others in the cellar had lain awake listening to the moans of the unfortunate Lieutenant Reynals. He had died early in the morning. Frederika's companions, in-cluding even the new widow Reynals, made curtain partitions in their crude shared space. Frederika remained near the door, bringing in a little straw for the children and maids to sleep on. To her relief, Friedrich came by for a brief visit, giving Frederika and the children fresh courage.

Three wounded English officers shared space nearby. One of them was Captain Charles Green, aide-de-camp to General Phillips. It had been Green who had been mistaken for Burgoyne and wounded by an American rifleman on September 19. His shoulder was still shattered, but he could ride a horse. Green and the other two officers promised Frederika that if necessary they would each take one of her children on their horses and race to safety in Fort George or Fort Edward.

One of General Riedesel's horses was kept saddled at all times and ready for Frederika, so she too could escape when the time came, her maids to follow in the calash. From time to time, Friedrich would urge Frederika to take herself and the children and go over to the Americans for their protection. Frederika would have none of it. "To be with people whom I would be obliged to treat with courtesy while perhaps my husband was being killed by them would be even yet more painful than all I am now forced to suffer."[96] Friedrich understood. He promised to let Frederika and their daughters stay with the army.

The enemy seemed to be closing in. Three American brigades had crossed Fish Kill in full view of the British, taking up positions and preparing to attack. The British and German artillery had fired canister at the Americans, forcing them to fall back across Fish Kill again, but they took supplies and prisoners with them. Outposts of the two armies fired at each other all day. American artillery fired constantly from nearly all sides. Burgoyne's compact camp was an easy target, but in contrast any return fire into the dispersed and well-concealed American positions seemed to be a waste of shot and powder. Riedesel knew that this was the end game; the Americans would simply take one piece of the army after another, tightening the cordon as they did.[97]

9:00 AM, *John Burgoyne, British Headquarters*

Burgoyne and Hamilton grumbled for each other's benefit. They had nearly pulled off an inadvertent ambush of the overeager Americans. There had not been a spot on the ground north of Fish Kill where the British artillery would not have been able to decimate the exposed American troops, but they had slipped away at the last possible moment. "It is as bad as possible," said Hamilton. "The numbers of the army are few, their provisions short, their position not a good one owing to the nature of the country." Burgoyne agreed. "They must have formed under the fire of all our park artillery, within reach of grape shot, a cross fire from the artillery and musketry of the entrenched corps upon the hill. And the musketry of the 20th Regiment, which was at easy distance to be supported by the Germans in front. Added to this would have been the advantage of a charge upon an open plain." The bravado of proud but cornered soldiers continued, but it was just another lamentation of "if onlys."

The reality was that there was not a spot to be found in the whole village that was not now exposed to American cannon or rifle shot.[98] To protect their remaining oxen and horses the British had to bring them within their lines where there was no food at all for the poor animals. The forage was gone; the men were reduced to feeding them browse from the trees. The cattle were dying and there was no way to dispose of them. The stench in the confined camp was worse every day. As they gloomily assessed these realities a cannonball from an American gun barely missed Burgoyne and lodged in a tree. But it was clear that the Americans were not going to attack. It was a siege in the wilderness. The Americans knew that they only had to wait until all their enemy's food was gone, and with it Burgoyne's last hopes.

10:00 AM, John Fellows, East Bank of the Hudson

At ten o'clock the Americans on the east bank began pounding the bateaux again. They had cannons on a height that gave them clear shots at the bateaux and at many of the British and German positions in and around the village as well. The British returned fire and forced at least one American crew to pull back into the woods, but this was small comfort to the British.[99]

The American soldiers made a game of trying to cut out the boats closest to them. Some were taken, others retaken by the British guards. The harassment forced the British troops to finally finish unloading the remaining bateaux under fire and secure the provisions on the heights away from the river.[100]

11:00 AM, Horatio Gates, American Headquarters

Harriet Acland had long since come and gone. She was now safely at an Albany hospital with her wounded husband. Now, days later, Gates finally had the time to write a considered letter in response to Burgoyne's scribbled note that Harriet had brought with her when she crossed into the American lines. It was somehow at once magnanimous and peevish, qualities that seemed to join easily in this war. Gates was still annoyed by Riedesel's response on October 2 to his proposal for an exchange of Colonel Ethan Allen for a pair of German prisoners. This time he offered two British officers, Major Williams, who was still alive, and another major. He made no direct mention of Riedesel's ridiculous request that Gates send back two other German officers for a month so that they could settle the payroll accounts of their respective units. Gates sent the letter back to Burgoyne with Chaplain Brudenel and the two boats that had brought Harriet downriver two nights ago.[101]

Saratoga October 11th 1777

Sir

I have the honor to receive your excellency's letter by Lady Ackland. The respect due to her ladyship's rank, the tenderness due to her person and sex, were alone sufficient recommendations to entitle her to my Protection. Considering my preceding Conduct with respect to those of your Army, whom the fortune of war has placed in my hands. I am surprised that your Excellency should think that I could consider the greatest attention to Lady Ackland in the light of an Obligation.

The cruelties which mark the Retreat of your army, in burning the gentlemen's & farmers' Houses as they pass along, is almost among Civilized Nations, without a precedent. They should not endeavour to ruin those they could not Conquer. This conduct betrays more of the vindictive malice of a Monk, than the Generosity of a soldier. Your friend, Sir Francis Clark, by the information of Doctor Potts the director General of my Hospital, Languishes under a very Dangerous wound. Every sort of Tenderness & attention is paid to him, as well as to all the Wounded who have fallen into my hands, & the hospital, which you was [sic] necessitated to leave to my Mercy.

At the solicitation of Major Williams, I am prevailed on to offer him & Major Miborn in Exchange for Col^l. Ethan Allen. Your Excellency's Objections to my last proposals for the Exchange of Col^l. Ethan Allen, I must consider as trifling as I cannot but suppose that the Generals of the Royal Armies act in Equal Concert, with those of the Generals of the Armies of the United States.

The bearer delivers a number of Letters from the Officers of your Army taken Prisoners in the Action of the 7th instant.

 I am
 Sir
  Your Mo. Ob. Serv.
 H. Gates
  M. Genl.[102]

12:00 Noon, John Burgoyne, British Headquarters

Burgoyne had shifted his location to the main British camp on the Saratoga heights with the burning of Schuyler's house. He ordered the distribution of one day's fresh meat for Sunday morning, but said there would be no more for the week. The days were still warm, but the nights were cold. Water froze in canteens, yet the men had to lie outside in uniform and armed every night. Curiously, the cold air did not seem to produce more sickness. Even the men with dysentery were getting better. No one could explain this counterintuitive set of circumstances. After all, everyone knew that the bad air of cold nights was what caused many illnesses.[103]

Burgoyne also ordered that sailors who had been assigned to care for the bateaux should be released from those duties. Officers were still burning their baggage and the remaining supplies were being distributed to the men. The bateaux were being regularly holed by the Americans and there was no chance that any could be used to build a new bridge of boats. The bateaux were being abandoned, and the erstwhile sailors had nothing to do but walk around the soggy camp with long faces. Desertions continued, and the day's passwords were again changed midway through the day because of the hemorrhaging.[104]

The men continued to dig in as best they could. The Germans on the one flank still struggled with stony ground, still unable to get their trenches more than a foot or foot and a half deep. If the Americans cannonaded from this direction the ramparts would do more harm than good. Balls striking the stony berms would send secondary fragments flying, turning the defensive works into shrapnel. The men were digging in with the Hudson to their backs, expecting any American attack to come from the south, west, or north. But everyone knew that the Americans would continue to cannonade from across the river as well, perhaps even ford the river from that direction. At the very least, nearly all the troops could expect to be caught in cross fires.

Everywhere the Americans had dense woods to cover almost any approach. They were already too close to allow the men to move out from their lines and clear lines of fire. Riedesel sent out patrols of jägers to find out what was going on in the woods that lay just beyond their lines. Unfortunately for them, the Americans were as good at snatching up the patrols as they were at harassing the pickets and the wagons trying to secure supplies. It was all as clear as it could be to everyone who thought about it that the Americans could attack at will in a style with which they were already comfortable or could simply wait Burgoyne out and wear his army down by attrition.[105]

7:00 PM, Burgoyne, British Headquarters

In the evening Burgoyne summoned Riedesel and Phillips to consult with him. They discussed their options. Burgoyne said, "It is my opinion that it is as impossible to attack the enemy as to maintain our position either in the center or upon the right wing." At length, Riedesel said, "We could abandon the baggage and retreat on this side of the river during the night. Not to Fort Edward, but to ford the river four miles below and strike across to Fort George. The feat is still possible because the enemy has not yet occupied the road on this side of the river." Burgoyne and Phillips were skeptical. It had taken them two days just to retreat this far; a heroic escape, fighting on the run, seemed to them unrealistic at best.[106]

Each general thought privately about the desperation of his situation—for that matter, the desperation of any alternative course of action any of them could imagine. Phillips had already decided that Burgoyne had missed a chance to break through when he decided not to attack quickly in the days following September 19. Riedesel still thought that they should abandon the baggage and artillery, then push toward Fort George at the foot of Lake George. Phillips was also willing to consider an attempt to break out. He argued that they could conceivably reach Ticonderoga and dig in there for the winter. Burgoyne was not yet ready to consider this alternative. Ticonderoga had to be at least sixty miles away to the north. It might as well be ten times that far. Such a dash was hopelessly unrealistic. The meeting broke up with no agreement.[107]

By the end of the day another fifty British and German soldiers had been lost, most of them willing deserters. One entire picket of Germans, officers and men, went over to the Americans. As darkness descended many of the Canadian wagon drivers slipped away and were never seen again. Inside their lines the British and German soldiers dug ever deeper into the hard ground while beyond them the Americans became ever more numerous.[108]

SUNDAY, OCTOBER 12, 1777

8:00 AM, John Burgoyne, British Headquarters on the Heights

It was Sunday. There were no written orders. Burgoyne used Charles Stanhope as a sounding board for his ideas. It was not the first time that he had used the young lord this way, asking and answering his own questions. Should they force a fording of the Hudson? No, the Americans would pick them off like flightless geese. Should they try to cut through along the river road toward Albany? The American guns on Bemis Heights would surely cut them to pieces. Should they march by night to gain the fords above Fort Edward? Perhaps, but the Americans were positioned to cut them to pieces along this route as well. On top of those problems they both knew that the army was also perilously low on ammunition.[109]

9:00 AM, Horatio Gates, American Headquarters south of Fish Kill

The morning was clear and pleasant.[110] Gates spent the morning writing a three-page letter to John Hancock, detailing the great success of the Northern Army on October 7. He took pleasure in itemizing the cannons, ammunition, baggage, and supplies taken and in listing the British officers killed and captured. Deserters, especially Germans, were now coming over to the Northern Army in large numbers. This time he made special note of "Gallant Major General Arnold" before going on to cite the performances of other American officers.[111] There was no escaping it, Arnold had made a difference, and there was no point in pretending he had not. The fact that his wound would finally remove him from the Northern Army made it easy for Gates to be magnanimous.

A while later Burgoyne's terse response to Gates's long letter of the previous day came in.

> *L^t. Genl. Burgoyne presents his compliments to M. Genl. Gates, and will send an answer to his letter with the officers' baggage as soon as possible.*
> *Saratoga*
> *Oct. 12, 1777*[112]

Burgoyne could do little more than point out that he outranked Gates.

12:00 Noon, Daniel Taylor, at Kingston, New York

Daniel Taylor was hanged as a British spy from an apple tree near the church in Kingston on Sunday morning. The American General George Clinton evacuated the town and pulled his troops back northward toward Albany. Later that day the British Army under General Henry Clinton entered Kingston and found Taylor's body dangling from the tree. The British were outraged; the Americans would pay for this. In a few days they would burn the entire town, as some of its evicted inhabitants watched from the surrounding hills.[113]

Had he seen it, one man would have been more sobered by the sight of Taylor hanging from the apple tree than anyone else could be. It was Captain Campbell's duty to carry the same message to Burgoyne that the Americans had found in Taylor's little silver ball. His chances of being intercepted, found out, and hanged were as grim as Taylor's, yet it was his duty. Campbell worked his way upriver with his message to Burgoyne, north past Albany and on to Saratoga.

2:00 PM, Frederika Riedesel, the Lansing House

On this, her third day in the cellar, Frederika was able to put on relatively fresh clothes as the three wounded English officers protected her privacy. The men became friendly with the children, taking on the roles of protective uncles as good men do. When little Frederika cried during the night, one of them could quiet her with a perfect imitation of a cow or a bleating calf. The time passed slowly for everyone, but it was especially trying for the children.

Frederika's cook did well enough with meals, but clean water was in short supply. No one dared go to the water's edge. Instead, everyone, including the children, drank wine. General Riedesel insisted upon it even when water was available, which caused his faithful old servant to fear for him. "I fear that the general drinks so much wine because he dreads falling into captivity and is therefore weary of life." The wife of one of the soldiers eventually drew up the courage to venture to the river with a bucket. She returned safely and everyone decided that the Americans would not fire at a woman. That ended the water shortage and made the woman a heroine in camp. Another woman at the southern end of the village was not so fortunate. When she tried to take water from Fish Kill she was challenged by an American sentry on the other side. She refused to comply with his orders and he shot the poor woman dead.[114]

Frederika was constantly mindful that she was the only officer's wife still present whose husband had not been killed or wounded, and it weighed on her. While she continued to sleep inside with the children, Friedrich slept with his men in the cold damp around the watch fires.[115] Frederika kept herself from dwelling on the terrible danger all around them by staying busy with the wounded men with her in the crowded cellar. A Canadian officer came in nearly unable to stand and insensible from starvation. She took him in as well, and he revived. She made them tea and coffee, and shared her noonday meal with them, doing her best to ignore the growing stench from their infected wounds. One of the wounded was artillery Captain-Lieutenant Thomas Blomefield, General Phillips's adjutant. Blomefield had been shot through both cheeks on October 7, leaving him almost unable to eat or drink. Several of his teeth were shattered and the ball had grazed his tongue. Now, five days on, Frederika thought he would die of starvation before healing enough to eat again. She gave him broth and her Rhine wine. These seemed to soothe his wounds and numb his pain. He kept a dram of wine continuously in his mouth and seemed to be improving.[116]

Friedrich told Frederika that word had arrived that the Americans had cut the road to Fort Edward; indeed they occupied all posts along the road northward. It was clear that more and more Americans were joining the units already surrounding Saratoga. In the morning Burgoyne again ordered the distribution of provisions for six days. The village was now a prison. Whether they remained in place or not, it could soon be time for every man to depend upon his own resources.[117]

Friedrich had come by with Phillips to check up on Frederika and the girls. She could see that he still wanted to break out and was suddenly seized with the fear that he might attempt it with just the men in his command who were still fit for duty. She was terrified of falling into the hands of the Americans and begged him not to abandon her and the children. Friedrich promised again not to desert her. As Friedrich and Phillips walked away Phillips said, "No! Not for ten thousand guineas would I come here again. My heart is entirely, entirely broken."[118]

3:00 PM, *John Burgoyne, British Headquarters*

At three o'clock Burgoyne called a new council of war composed of nearly all his general officers. The previous meeting had been limited to Phillips and Riedesel. This time he had invited Hamilton and von Gall as well, but von Gall was not present. Burgoyne put the facts before them.

"The enemy in force, according to the best intelligence I can obtain, to the amount of upwards of fourteen-thousand of the enemy, and a considerable quantity of artillery, are on this side of Fish Kill and threaten an attack. On the other side the Hudson's River between this army and Fort Edward is another army of the enemy, the numbers unknown, but one corps which there has been an opportunity of observing is reported to be about fifteen hundred men. They have likewise cannon on the other side the Hudson's River, and they have a bridge below Saratoga Church by which the two armies can communicate.

"The bateaux of the army have been destroyed and no means appear of making a bridge over the Hudson's River, were it even practicable from the position of the enemy. The only means of retreat therefore are by the ford at Fort Edward, or taking to the mountains in order to pass the river higher up by rafts, or by another ford which is reported to be practicable with difficulty or by keeping the mountain to pass the head of Hudson's River and continue to the westward of Lake George all the way to Ticonderoga. It is true this last passage was never made but by Indians or very small bodies of men.

"In order to pass cannon or any wheel carriages from hence to Fort Edward some bridges must be repaired under fire of the enemy from the opposite side of the river, and the principal bridge will be a work of fourteen or fifteen hours. There is no good position for the army to take to sustain that work, and if there were, the time stated as necessary would give the enemy on the other side of the Hudson's River an opportunity to take post on the strong ground above Fort Edward or to dispute the ford while General Gates' army follows in the rear.

"The intelligence from the lower part of Hudson's River is founded upon the concurrent reports of prisoners and deserters who say it was the news in the enemy's camp that Fort Montgomery was taken, and one man, a friend to government, who arrived yesterday and mentions some particulars of the manner in which it was taken. The provisions of the army may hold out to the twentieth. There is neither rum nor spruce beer."

It was a long-winded statement of the obvious. The discussion moved on, slowly and carefully, as men do when they know what needs to be done but wish to avoid taking the lead. At last Burgoyne summarized the options open to them:

"Having committed this state of facts to the consideration of the council, I request your sentiments on the following propositions:

- First, to wait in the present position an attack from the enemy or the chance of favorable events.
- Second, to attack the enemy.
- Third, to retreat, repairing the bridges as the army moves for the artillery, in order to force the passage of the ford.
- Fourth, to retreat by night, leaving the artillery and the baggage, and should it be found impracticable to force the passage with musketry to attempt the upper fords or the passage round Lake George.
- Fifth, in case the enemy by extending to their left leave their rear open, to march rapidly for Albany."[119]

When he had finished Burgoyne said that he was ready in his own mind to attack the Americans and attempt a breakout. Riedesel repeated the proposal he had made the day before. Push north along the west bank, cross the Hudson four miles below Fort Edward, then push past Fort Edward to Fort George. The consensus of the other generals present was to retreat under cover of darkness. One pointed out that provisions could not hold out more than a week at best.[120]

Each option was discussed in turn. The consensus grew that the first option would only allow the situation to grow worse with each passing day. The Americans had declined to attack when the army was at its most vulnerable, and they were even less likely to attack now that defenses had been raised. The Americans could afford to wait and allow the army to starve.

The second option seemed desperate, even suicidal. The army was so badly outnumbered that an attack had no hope of success. All agreed that the third option was simply impracticable. There was no hope of extricating both the army and the artillery train, or what was left of it.

Phillips and Hamilton thought that the fifth option had some merit, but even they were easily convinced that any attempt to break out and make a sprint to Albany faced impossible odds. In the end the fourth option was the only one that seemed to have any chance of success. Burgoyne read out their resolution to somber nods. "Resolved, that the fourth proposition is the only resource, and that to effect it, the utmost secrecy and silence is to be observed, and the troops are to be put in motion from the right in the still part of the night, without any change in the disposition." That was it then. They would attempt to break out at night and make a run for Fort George.[121]

7:00 PM, *Canadians and Loyalists, the British Camp*

The annoying American harassment of the British camp continued without respite. Fish Kill was a natural boundary, but the American riflemen sniped at the British pickets on the north side so incessantly and so effectively that the pickets had to drop back to safer entrenchments. British scouts confirmed that the Americans now occupied the entire opposite side of the Hudson too, all the way to Fort Edward. Captains of the Loyalists and Canadians could see where it was all going and they were worried that their men would be badly treated by the Americans when the inevitable capitulation occurred. They asked Burgoyne for passes to withdraw to Ticonderoga, which they could do in small numbers with the help of the Mohawks. Burgoyne granted the request, and they began departing after dark.[122]

9:00 PM, *John Stark, East Bank of the Hudson*

This night John Stark reappeared with his Vermont militiamen, Bennington veterans, drawing up on the east bank of the Hudson opposite Saratoga. Congress had at last promoted him to the rank of brigadier general in the Continental Army on October 4, and the irascible Stark was at last willing to put himself under the commander of the Northern Army. Stark had left camp and gone home with his militiamen when their enlistments expired at midnight just hours before the battle of September 19. Now they were back, bearing the honors they had earned at Bennington, having helped retake Fort Edward farther up the Hudson, and ready to share in the American victory over Burgoyne. Stark's troops crossed the Hudson just north of the village and dug in. With that, they emphatically closed Burgoyne's last possible escape route northward, and then settled in to await the outcome.[123]

11:00 PM, *John Burgoyne, British Headquarters*

Earlier in the day the council had broken up and the generals had moved off to put their desperate plan in operation. It was the fourth option, to retreat by night, leaving the artillery and the baggage, and attempt the upper fords or the passage round Lake George. The sun had set at five-thirty, and it was dark a half hour later. There was a half moon; if the clouds were not too thick it would be light enough that night to move.

The colonels had queried the men of their regiments. The British soldiers seemed ready to fight regardless of the odds. The Germans saw things differently. They had fought enough. They said *nichts* to the money, *nichts* to the rum, and *nichts* to the idea of continuing the fight.[124]

If the mood of his rank and file came back to Riedesel he showed no evidence of it. Unlike most of the soldiers under his command Riedesel had been adamant. The other generals had not seen him like this before. They had been considering retreat for days. Riedesel had thought all along that it was their only realistic option, but here they were dithering yet again. "A retreat is now still practicable, but the slightest movement of the enemy will render it utterly impossible." His vehemence gradually brought the others along, and gradually a consensus formed around the idea of breaking out. But no sooner had they arrived at their decision than one of Burgoyne's aides leaned in to inform them that the six days' provisions Burgoyne had ordered distributed in the morning had still not been handed out. An exasperated Riedesel had pressed on. If the provisions could still be distributed tonight, the retreat should begin under cover of darkness. The generals had all agreed. Riedesel would lead the van; Phillips would bring up the rear guard. Riedesel's promise to Frederika and their daughters was pushed to the back of his military mind and forgotten.[125]

Riedesel rushed about prodding the quartermasters to get the provisions distributed, telling units to abandon everything not essential to life and prepare to march. At seven o'clock the men had again been receiving three days' supplies and orders had been passed to prepare to move out. Scouts had been sent out to probe every possible avenue of escape and the camp began to take on an air of muffled readiness. The moon would not set until after one in the morning. If they left soon they would have enough light even under the clouds to at least get started. At ten o'clock Riedesel had reported to Burgoyne that the dwindling provisions had been distributed and that everyone was ready.

Then scouts had arrived with new reports on the American positions. Stark's brigade had been detected on the north side of the village. The enemy now had so many units in play and Burgoyne's army was so completely surrounded that it would not be possible to move even a portion of the army without it being immediately discovered. Burgoyne countermanded his orders at eleven o'clock and called his generals back to tell them that even the desperate fourth option was now impossible. Burgoyne said, "It is too late."[126]

Burgoyne had been caught between the conflicting principles of his own personality. He could not bring himself to waste the lives of his officers and men, but neither could he tolerate the disgrace of capitulation. "The bulk of the enemy's army is hourly joined by new corps of militia and volunteers," he told his generals. "Their position, which extends three parts in four of a circle round us, is from the nature of the ground, unattackable in all parts. The enemy are entrenched opposite the fords and possess a camp in force on the high ground between Fort Edward and Fort George. With cannon! They have also parties down the whole shore to watch our motions, and posts so near to us upon our own side of the water as must prevent the army moving a single mile undiscovered." There was no remaining avenue of escape. They were completely surrounded. They had to remain in their present position. Riedesel said nothing.[127]

MONDAY, OCTOBER 13, 1777

6:30 AM, Friedrich Riedesel, British Headquarters

It was cold and cloudy at dawn on Monday. Riedesel and everyone else could now see that Burgoyne had been right. The Americans completely surrounded the army in overwhelming numbers. The only way to attack from their prison would be northwest across a marsh and up a steep hill, suicidal even if the armies were evenly matched, which they were not. Worse, any attempt to break out in that direction would leave the western shore of the Hudson open. The Americans could then easily come across to the undefended village in boats and attack them in their rear. No retreat was possible and provisions were down to enough for only five days.[128]

There were no written orders this day. Time dragged as they waited for the American attack that they knew would not come. The British and German troops were in the best positions that could be made, but they were inferior to those of the Americans, who were now all around them. All they could do was to wait, dressed and armed, day and night. The American riflemen shot at anyone who moved from what seemed like impossible distances. Grape and balls from American cannons raked the ground all day. The only consolation was that the army was so well dug in that the American artillery could do little real damage.[129] The British and German pickets did their best to return fire, as did the artillery, but without much effect. And so it went all day long.

Everyone knew that the last chance to escape had passed. Despite having left hundreds of sick and wounded behind to the mercies of the Americans five days earlier, the camp was now burdened again with newly sick or wounded soldiers. There was no way to establish a new hospital. The whole camp was open to American firepower. Destitute soldiers staggered from place to place, looking for food, medicine, or dressings for their wounds. Loyalists who had not already left for Ticonderoga bemoaned their fates and the fates of their families. All fodder was long since gone and the emaciated horses were lying down and dying from simple starvation. Most of those that remained upright were living skeletons. The exceptions were a few of the senior officers' mounts. Many soldiers were in rags, with no means to better clothe themselves or even wash what was left of their uniforms. Worst of all, there was no more brandy or tobacco to be had at any price.[130]

7:00 AM, *Horatio Gates, American Headquarters*

The clouds kept the warming rays of the sun away, and the wind cut through the men's light clothing. Gates fiddled with the deployment of his units, trying to get them placed in the most advantageous ways. Latimer's Connecticut militia regiment was moved to the left wing of the American Army, a march of about three miles around to the north side of Saratoga. Dearborn's light infantry was moved around to the north to finish sealing off the final British escape route along the west bank of the Hudson. Small detachments were set up at key points along the main road and smaller paths. The detachments soon took fifteen willing prisoners in the process. Other American detachments scoured the woods and skirmished with German jägers, who fled quickly, but not quickly enough for Dearborn's fleet young men. Ten were caught before they could make it back to the safety of their lines.[131]

Morgan's riflemen were also roaming the woods looking for stragglers and deserters. One scouting party saw a party of Germans and Canadians. One of the riflemen called out to them in German, "Kommen sie bitte hier." One of the German soldiers astonished the rifleman by throwing down his musket and running to surrender himself. He told the Americans that everyone in Burgoyne's army had drawn the last of the provisions, enough for seven days at the most. It seemed now to be every man for himself, and for this one the better choice was clear.

North of town American scouts intercepted nine men trying to make a break to Ticonderoga with their seven days of provisions. Each of them had been slightly wounded in the fighting on the seventh, not enough to be left behind in the hospital but enough to make them a hindrance to their army. The wounded men were turned around and made to take the shorter trip into American captivity.[132]

About thirty more deserters came across through the American lines over the course of the morning. To a man, the prisoners and deserters told the same story. Burgoyne's army had little in the way of either supplies or hope. Gates ruminated on this and said, "The accounts from every deserter and prisoner agree so well that I have reason to believe it. It is contradicted by none."[133]

But Gates also had Governor George Clinton's letter from New Windsor. Clinton had written it on the seventh, and that day had clearly not gone as well for him as it had gone for Gates. Forts Montgomery and Clinton had fallen, and Sir Henry Clinton's British forces were moving up the Hudson toward Albany. There had been hard fighting but the Americans had been outnumbered, and they had lost men, cannons, strong points, and ground.

Gates needed to help the governor and he did. He had already ordered Van Schaick's regiment back to Albany, and he had sent Brigadier General Gansevoort to Albany to take command of all forces there. He wrote to Clinton as charitably as he could.

> I am clearly with you in opinion that should the enemy's General push up the river, your force, in addition to the reinforcements I can give you, acting upon the west side, will so co-operate with General Putnam upon the east side, that Sir H. Clinton will not be able to effect any stroke of consequence; and, perhaps, may finally be as much embarrassed to retreat, as General Burgoyne most visibly appears to be. The two heavy brass twelve pounders taken from the enemy, with a very fine brass train, that I can spare for your succor, will be a good recruit for your artillery. I have already sent down the two Esopus regiments, the Tryon county militia, and most of the militia of Albany county, so that General Gansevoort may be able immediately to form a post the moment Van Schaick's regiment gets to Albany the cannon shall meet them there.[134]

Gates had not been able to persuade General Wolcott to also take his militia to Albany. The men in Wolcott's regiment had volunteered for the Saratoga action only, and would be leaving soon. Gates was thus losing men, either by design or circumstance. With luck, he would still have enough to force Burgoyne to surrender, but it would not be good if the British commander learned of the units that were leaving the Northern Army.[135]

12:00 Noon, American Artillerymen, the British Right Flank

The Americans set up a new artillery emplacement on a hill on the east side of the Hudson opposite the Hessen-Hanau Regiment on Burgoyne's northern flank. With this cover American troops occupied the island in the river just opposite the Hessen-Hanau men. At noon the cannonade began. The Americans fired ball after ball into the northern part of the village where the Hessen-Hanau men were dug in. Buildings full of sick and wounded men were repeatedly holed. But fortunately for the Germans, the two big 12-pounders that had nearly been lost in the early morning hours of Friday had been set up to support the Hessen-Hanau defense of this sector. The big guns began to fire and the smaller American guns were silenced. The British and German gunners enjoyed their technical superiority, and the small victory pushed aside the more general hopelessness of their situation for a few hours.[136]

7:00 PM, John Burgoyne, British Headquarters

Burgoyne would not make the decision alone. Even his council of generals was too small a group to share the burden. Field officers and captains holding their own commands were summoned and added to the reconvened council of war. Burgoyne reported on the previous night's meeting and its aborted outcome. He laid out the facts. "The enemy is entrenched at the fords of Fort Edward, and likewise occupies the strong position on the pine plains between Fort George and Fort Edward. I am ready to undertake at your head any enterprise of difficulty or hazard that should appear to you within the compass of your strength and spirit. I have reason to believe a capitulation has been in the contemplation of some, perhaps all, who know the real situation of things. Upon the circumstance of such consequence to national and personal honor, I think it a duty to my country, and to myself, to extend this council beyond the usual limits. The assembly present might justly be esteemed a full representation of the army. I should think myself unjustifiable in taking any step in so serious a matter without such a concurrence of sentiments as should make a treaty the act of the army as well as that of the general."[137]

Burgoyne paused and moved on. "I consider it an impossibility to attack the enemy. Even should we, against all probability, beat him, the lack of provisions will effectually prevent us from reaching Fort George. To retreat is equally impossible, unless each one for himself should make his way as well as he can through the pathless forests. We can, it is true, still maintain ourselves in our present position for five days. At the expiration of that time, however, our situation will be the same, our position in the center and on the right wing untenable, and the rout and dispersion of the army an event not only probable but certain."[138]

No one, not even Riedesel, could challenge the accuracy of this assessment. It was the end, and each knew now that it had been the end ever since the ball had struck Fraser six days earlier. Burgoyne went on, "No one but myself should answer for the situation in which the army now finds itself. I have never asked anyone for advice, but have only asked obedience to my orders."

Riedesel and the others were grateful for this absolution, but Riedesel wanted more. He said, "I beg all the English officers to bear testimony to that effect if at any time I should be called to account."

Burgoyne could do nothing but absorb the sting of Riedesel's remark. There was one last desperate option remaining, explained Burgoyne. Tell the army that it was every man for himself. The remaining supplies had been distributed and the men could be told to take to the woods and do their best to get back to Ticonderoga. Phillips knew it was too late for that now. Perhaps a few Mohawks or frontiersmen who knew the country could make it, but to simply scatter thousands of regular soldiers into the vast New York forests made no sense. None of them had enough supplies to last the several days it would take for them to reach Ticonderoga, assuming that they knew the correct trails. They would be picked off one by one, killed or captured by the more numerous and more skilled Americans. Streams were rising and the cold was deepening. The idea was nothing short of mass suicide. Even if they simply stayed where they were, they would be completely out of food in five days, seven at the most if they cut rations again. The Americans knew exactly what the situation was, and they were unlikely to attack when simply waiting would be effective. If they did attack, the army would surely be overrun and dispersed.[139]

Burgoyne presented the council with the first of three prepared questions. "Are there examples in military history of war that an army has capitulated in the situation in which ours now finds itself?" The members of the council agreed that there were. A few offered specific examples in which armies had capitulated in what were probably less serious circumstances. Three German surrenders were mentioned. A consensus formed that no one could have faulted the generals who had capitulated in circumstances that were in fact less severe than those currently faced here at Saratoga. Several said that the higher goal was to save the army.[140]

Burgoyne moved to the second question. "Is an army of three thousand five hundred fighting men and well provided with artillery justifiable upon the principles of national dignity and military honor in capitulating in any possible situation?" The men were of one mind. There would be no disgrace in capitulation given the present circumstances.

On Burgoyne's third question they were also of one mind. "Is the present situation of that nature?" Burgoyne stated the answer aloud and looked around for any sign of dissent. "The present situation justifies a capitulation upon honorable terms." He saw no hint of disagreement. They all agreed that they were ready and willing to fight to the end, but if nothing could be gained it would be better to seek an honorable surrender. No one thought it wise to simply wait to be attacked, scattered, and hunted down one by one. Several officers hastened to point out that if they saw any possibility of success they would gladly attempt it, even if they lost their lives in the attempt. But the situation was truly hopeless. It was better to save the king's troops than to sacrifice them in an effort everyone knew would be futile.[141]

Burgoyne turned to his writing desk. At length he finished a draft of a letter to General Gates. It was written in the third person, as if not by Burgoyne but by some impartial observer. The grim council approved its contents and Burgoyne turned it over to Major Robert Kingston, his secretary now that Francis Clerke was gone, so that Kingston could prepare a clean copy.

After having fought you twice, lieutenant general Burgoyne, has waited some days in his present position, determined to try a third conflict, against any force you could bring to attack him.

He is apprized of the superiority of your numbers, and the dispo-sition of your troops, to impede his supplies, and render his retreat a scene of carnage on both sides. In this situation he is compelled by humanity, and thinks himself justified by established principles, and precedents of state, and of war, to spare the lives of brave men upon honorable terms.

Should major general Gates, be inclined to treat upon that idea, general Burgoyne would propose a cessation of arms, during the time necessary to communicate the preliminary terms by which in any extremity, he, and his army, mean to abide.[142]

He wrote a second note, this one personal and directed to Gates alone.

L^t. General Burgoyne is desirous of sending a field officer with a message to M. Genl. Gates upon a matter of high moment to both armies. The L^t. Genl. Requests to be informed at what hour Genl. Gates will receive him tomorrow morning.[143]

The messages were handed to George Williams along with a white truce flag. Young George was the nephew of Major Griffith Williams, the cranky artilleryman who had been lost with his guns on the seventh. The boy was still a cadet, just twelve years old. He took the message and set off with a rattling drummer for Fish Kill and the American line.[144]

Burgoyne and his officers listened silently as the drumbeat faded in the distance, then stopped. Fifteen minutes passed, then a half hour, then an hour. At last the drum was heard again and the boy returned. The Americans had not cut his throat. They had acted like soldiers.

Gates had agreed. He would be pleased to receive a field officer from Lieutenant-General Burgoyne at the advanced post of the Army of the United States at ten o'clock the next morning. From there the field officer would be conducted to the American headquarters.[145]

11:00 PM, James Wilkinson, American Headquarters

Wilkinson got back to the hovel called headquarters after completing rounds, as he had on previous nights. Gates was already asleep, but he woke up when Wilkinson came in. He handed Wilkinson Burgoyne's notes. Then Gates showed Wilkinson his copy of the reply to Burgoyne he had written and sent back two hours earlier.

Wilkinson read the note and was worried by its implications. Both armies were mired in squalor, many men had died, and there was nothing to recommend any of their current circumstances, but proprieties had to be maintained even in difficult conditions, perhaps most of all in difficult circumstances. "Have you not condescended improperly in agreeing to receive the deputy of your adversary at your headquarters, within your guards, and between the lines of your army?" he asked.

Gates thought about this for a minute. "You are right, young man. I was hasty, but what's to be done?" Gates should have stipulated that tomorrow's messenger be met and dealt with by someone of equivalent rank, and between the lines, not with Gates himself in his headquarters. But now the invitation was on Burgoyne's table and it could not be withdrawn.

Wilkinson was ever ready to step forward, particularly when it would make him the center of attention. "I will meet the flag and endeavor to draw the message from the officer. But if he claims your engagement he must be admitted." "Agreed," said Gates. "Do so."[146]

12:00 Midnight, British Troops, Saratoga

The army had been lying dressed and on their arms for six days and nights. Their exhaustion was punctuated by an ever increasing number of cannonballs coming in from nearly all sides. They could see hordes of new militia joining the already swollen American Army all around them. New American cannons were now in place to ravage the grenadier lines. That night, soldiers who could set to work throwing up a traverse breastwork to protect them against this new threat, the men working with a desperation brewed from fear combined with resignation. Not far away the last of the Mohawks and most of the remaining Loyalists quietly left for Fort Ticonderoga. The stealthy irregulars slipped through the American cordon and faded into the vast northern forest.[147]

TUESDAY, OCTOBER 14, 1777

10:00 AM, Robert Kingston and James Wilkinson, at Fish Kill

It had been a very foggy morning. Dearborn's light infantrymen had continued the game of skirmishing and chasing down the slower German jägers in the mist. It was turning into a fine still day. Burgoyne had once again assembled his generals. Major Robert Kingston attended as

Burgoyne's new secretary. Kingston had started out the campaign as deputy adjutant-general. Now the loss of Francis Clerke had led to his promotion.[148]

Wilkinson went to the American advanced post on Fish Kill with Henry Livingston at the appointed hour and waited. The bridge had been destroyed, but one could still leap across the sleepers. Before long there was a chamade from a British drummer. Major Kingston appeared and hopped across on the fragmentary bridge. "Major Kingston with a message from Lieutenant General Burgoyne to Major General Gates," said Kingston. "Colonel Wilkinson on the part of General Gates to receive the message," said Wilkinson hopefully. Kingston thought about this for a few moments, then answered, "My orders direct me to Major General Gates." Wilkinson tried again. "It is to save time and trouble that I am authorized to receive the message you bear." Kingston hesitated. "General Gates has agreed to receive the message and I am not authorized to deliver it to any other person," said Kingston with as much finality as he could muster. Wilkinson was ready for this. "Well then, sir," said Wilkinson, "you must submit to be hoodwinked." Now Wilkinson pressed his advantage. "I understand there was nothing more common than to blindfold military messengers when they were admitted within the walls of a place, or the guards of a camp." Kingston knew that he had been bested in the exchange and groped for a face-saving condition. "Well, sir, I will submit to it, but under the express stipulation that no indignity is intended to the British arms." Wilkinson relished his partial triumph while he blindfolded Kingston with the man's own handkerchief.

The two of them then walked arm in arm for a mile to Gates's headquarters, past silent American soldiers. As they strolled Kingston talked at length about the beauty of the Hudson Valley and the charms of autumn in New York.[149] At last they gained Gates's marquee and Wilkinson ushered Kingston into the presence of General Gates. Kingston saluted and said, "General Gates, your servant." Gates smiled and said, "Ah! Kingston, how do you do?" Gates's omission of Kingston's rank was apparently unnoticed. They shook hands, took their seats, and exchanged pleasantries for a few minutes.

After a few minutes of small talk Kingston stood up and said, "I have certain communications to make to Major General Gates from Lieutenant General Burgoyne, and to guard against inaccuracy of memory I have committed them to paper, and with permission I will read them." Gates nodded and Kingston then read Burgoyne's communication. It was a long rambling rebuttal to Gates's letter of October 12. The charges of wholesale burning were unjust. Schuyler's house had been torched only after Americans approached and threatened to use it for cover. The barracks in Saratoga had burned by accident. That message safely behind him, Kingston turned to Burgoyne's second message and matters at hand.[150]

Kingston paraphrased Burgoyne's letter. "I am directed to you from General Burgoyne, that having fought you twice he has waited some days in his present situation determined to try a third conflict against any force you could bring to attack him. He is apprised of the superiority of your numbers and the disposition of your troops to impede his supplies and render his retreat a scene of carnage on both sides. In this situation he is impelled by humanity and thinks himself justified by established principles and precedent of state and of war to spare the lives of brave men upon honorable terms. Should Major General Gates be inclined to treat upon that idea General Burgoyne would propose a cessation of arms during the time necessary to communicate the preliminary terms by which in any extremity he and his army mean to abide."[151]

Wilkinson was apprehensive as Gates reached into his pocket without any further formalities, pulled out a paper, and handed it to Kingston. "There, sir, are the terms on which General Burgoyne must surrender." Wilkinson and Kingston were both taken aback by this breach of protocol. Where was the polite conversation expected of gentlemen? Where was the mannered give-and-take that must attend such a courtship?

The niceties were over and Kingston was stunned. The mortified Kingston read Gates's conditions. The flummoxed major objected. He could not in good conscience take such an insulting ultimatum back to Burgoyne. "I must beg leave to decline delivering this paper to Lieutenant General Burgoyne because, although I cannot presume to speak for him, I think the propositions it contains cannot be submitted to." Gates said smoothly that although he might be mistaken, there could be no impropriety in Kingston delivering the message. Kingston then tried to convince Gates to send the message by his own officer. Gates sighed and said, "As you have brought the message you ought to take back the answer." Kingston reluctantly agreed that this seemed like a good idea. Wilkinson, who still did not know the contents of Gates's letter, blindfolded Kingston again and led the stricken man back to the advanced guard. This time the conversation was less cheerful. Kingston was filled with reproach and chagrin, and he said so. The British Army was proud and spirited, its regiments had admirable reputations, and so forth. Wilkinson said nothing.

When he got back to headquarters, Wilkinson let Gates know about his uneasiness over the day's proceedings. "Did you not give Burgoyne an advantage by not waiting to receive his overtures before presenting your own terms?" Gates said that he could not think so. Wilkinson pressed the point. "Do you mean in any extremity to recede from the propositions you have made?" Gates shrugged again, and said that he was ready to back off several demands if it meant that he could get possession of the British Army's weapons. Wilkinson got to the nub of his concerns. By handing Kingston a statement of his conditions Gates had inadvertently let Burgoyne take control of the agenda. "In the capitulations of Cape Breton, Quebec, Montreal, and other places, which I have read, the propositions were made by the besieged, and were granted, modified, or refused by the besiegers, at their discretion. But having offered conditions by which you do not mean to abide, I am fearful Burgoyne will dictate the terms of surrender."

Gates thought about this for a while, then put his hand on Wilkinson's shoulder. "Wilky, you are right again. But it is done, and we must make the most of it. I shall be content to get the arms out of their hands."[152] So there it was. Gates had made a mistake in allowing Kingston to come to his headquarters in the first place, then he had made another by not requiring Burgoyne to make the first offer. Then word had spread that there would be a ceasefire at ten o'clock. By then both the fog and the distant gunfire were gone.

12:00 Noon, John Burgoyne, British Headquarters

Kingston handed Gates's message to Burgoyne. Gates's terms were brusque and lacking in the elegance, subtlety, and diplomacy of the polite discourse Burgoyne had expected.

1. *General Burgoyne's army being exceedingly reduced by repeated defeats, by Desertion, Sickness &c. their Provisions exhausted, their Military Stores, Tents and Baggage taken or destroyed, their retreat cut off and their Camp invested, they can only be allowed to surrender prisoners of war.*

2. *The Officers and Soldiers may keep the Baggage belonging to them; the Generals of the United States never permit Individuals to be pillaged*

3. *The Troops under his Excellency Gen. Burgoyne will be conducted by the most convenient Route to New England, marching by easy marches, and sufficiently provided for by the Way.*

4. *The officers will be admitted on Parole, may wear their side arms, and will be treated with the Liberality customary in Europe, so long as they by proper behaviour continue to deserve it; but those who are apprehended having broke their Parole (as some British Officers have done) must expect to be close confined.*

5. *All Public stores, Artillery, Arms, Ammunition, Carriages, horses &c. &ct. must be delivered to Commissaries appointed to receive them*

6. *These Terms being agreed to and signed, the Troops under his Excellency General Burgoyne's Command, may be drawn up in their Encampments, where they will be ordered to Ground their Arms, and may thereupon be marched to the River side to be passed over in their way toward Bennington*

7. *A Cessation of Arms to continue til sunset to receive General Burgoyne's answer.*

Signed
Horatio Gates

Burgoyne pondered the seven stark points in Gates's communication. Some of his officers were nearly convulsed with indignation. There was a chorus of outrage, the gist of which was that they would all rather die of hunger than agree to such disgraceful terms. Riedesel said, "Propose rather to General Gates that the troops should return to Canada without arms, and on the condition that they should not serve during this war against the Americans unless exchanged." Burgoyne said, "It is useless to think of it. Such a proposition would not be entertained by the enemy for a moment."[153]

At length Burgoyne drew Kingston aside and dictated responses to five of the seven points in Gates's message.

1. *Lieut. General Burgoyne's Army, however reduced, will never admit that their retreat is cut off, while they have Arms in their hands.*

3. *This Article is answered by Gen. Burgoyne's first proposal, which is here annexed.*

4. *There being no Officers in this Army under, or capable of being under the description of breaking Parole, this article needs no answer.*
5. *All Publick Stores may be delivered, Arms excepted.*
6. *This Article inadmissible in any Extremity; sooner than this Army will consent to ground their Arms in their Encampment, they will rush on the Enemy determined to take no Quarters.*

With these peevish codicils the council of war gathered around Burgoyne almost unanimously agreed. All of them held to the hope that providence, perhaps even Clinton, would intervene. There was still a little time for stalling and venting.

5:30 PM, Robert Kingston and James Wilkinson, at Fish Kill

Wilkinson met Kingston again at Fish Kill, and again they hiked to Gates's marquee. Kingston's second meeting with Gates began differently from the first. Kingston complained that Gates's propositions were inappropriate. The British Army was a proud institution. He asked Gates and Wilkinson to remember the feats performed by six British regiments at Minden, and so forth.

Kingston then read the response of Burgoyne and his council of officers. The council had made a mountain of article 6. Kingston declared, "If General Gates does not mean to recede from the 6th Article, the treaty ends at once. The Army will to a man proceed to any act of desperation rather than submit to that Article."[154] Burgoyne would allow his army to be disarmed, but not in their encampment. He insisted that they be allowed to march out of Saratoga and to ground their arms only then. Burgoyne had seized upon a distinction without a meaningful difference and had blown it up into a major issue. Gates saw the almost meaningless face-saving device for what it was. If revising this condition was all it would take to gain Burgoyne's capitulation, it was a tiny price to pay. Kingston went back to Burgoyne with the concession, and given that opening the British generals set to work crafting a set of alternative proposals.

Wilkinson thought that it might all end badly. Burgoyne proposed that the British Army should keep its accoutrements, its colors, and its payroll, and Gates seemed ready to let them have all that if only he could get their arms. It did not seem like a proper capitulation to Wilkinson, but it would probably do.[155]

Gates was clearly worried, but not about the negotiations. Some units of the Northern Army were already gone. Various militia units were starting to leave. The Hampshire County Massachusetts battalion went home today.[156] Albany County militia regiments were fretting, wanting to move south to defend Albany in case an attack from the south materialized. After all, so far as they could see Burgoyne was finished. But what if Burgoyne found out about these departures before negotiations were concluded? What might happen then?

WEDNESDAY, OCTOBER 15, 1777

7:00 AM, John Burgoyne, British Headquarters

It had been a quiet dawn. The weather was pleasant, and it appeared that it would probably stay that way all day. The ceasefire was still in effect and by mutual agreement would hold until two o'clock. Men began talking across the narrow no man's land. British and German soldiers began approaching American sentries and asking for water. Everyone around Burgoyne who was familiar with what had transpired was surprised at how easily Gates had yielded the day before. Was Clinton moving up the Hudson? Was Carleton coming south on Lake Champlain? Gates was agreeing to nearly everything Burgoyne had demanded. Then Gates had demanded that the British march out of their positions by two o'clock in the afternoon.

There had to be a reason why Gates was in such a hurry. Rumors were increasing that Clinton was advancing on Albany. Although he was still at a considerable distance, there were glimmers of hope that Gates would have to redeploy some of his army south to intercept Clinton. If Gates was so ready to agree to Burgoyne's terms, maybe there was some truth to the rumors.[157]

Now it was Burgoyne's turn to temporize. He convened yet another council of war. A new consensus emerged that they should accept the new proposal but with the condition that additional details be negotiated before any formal capitulation. Such a negotiation could not be accomplished that same day. Burgoyne sent the messengers back with the proposal that staff officers from both sides meet to settle the details and then arrange for ratification after they had done their work. Burgoyne appointed Lieutenant-Colonel Sutherland and Captain Craig to negotiate for the British. Some council members argued for withdrawing from the negotiations altogether, but in the end that idea was set aside.[158]

10:00 AM, Horatio Gates, American Headquarters

Wilkinson rode to Fish Kill to meet with Kingston at ten o'clock. They exchanged pleasantries and Wilkinson took the latest message from Burgoyne back to Gates. Here were ten counterproposals from Burgoyne.

Answers being given to Major General Gates's Proposals, it remains for Lt. General Burgoyne and the Army under his Command to state the following preliminary Articles on their part.

1. *The Troops to march out of their Camp with the Honours of War, and the Artillery of the Intrenchments, which will be left as hereafter may be regulated.*

2. *A free passage to be granted to this Army to Great Britain, upon condition of not serving in North America during the present Contest; and a proper port to be assigned for the entry of Transports to receive the Troops whenever Gen. Howe shall so order.*

3. *Should any Cartell take place, by which this Army or any part of it may be exchanged, the forgoing Article to be void so far as such Exchange shall be made.*

4. *All Officers to retain their Carriages, Bat Horses and other Cattle, and no Baggage to be molested or searched, the Lt. General giving his Honour that there are no Publick Stores secreted therein. Maj. General Gates will of course take the necessary measures for the security of this Article.*

5. *Upon the march the Officers are not to be separated from their men, and in Quarters the Officers shall be lodged according to Rank, and are not to be hindered from assembling their men for Roll-calling, and other necessary purposes of Regularity.*

6. *There are various Corps in the Army, composed of Sailors, Batteauxmen, Artificers, Drivers, Independent Companies, and Followers of the Army, and it is expected that these Persons, of whatever Country, shall be included in the fullest sense and utmost Extent of the above Articles, and comprehended in every respect as British Subjects.*

7. *All Canadians and Persons belonging to the Establishment in Canada to be permitted to return there.*

8. *Passports to be immediately granted to three Officers not exceeding the Rank of Captain, who shall be appointed by Gen. Burgoyne to carry despatches to Sir William Howe, Sir Guy Carleton, and to Great Britain by the way of New York, and the publick faith to be engaged that these despatches are not to be opened.*

9. *The foregoing Articles are to be considered only as preliminaries for framing a Treaty, in the Course of which others may arise to be considered by both parties, for which purpose it is proposed that two Officers of each Army shall meet, and report their deliberations to their respective Generals.*

10. *Lieut. General Burgoyne will send his Deputy Adjutant General to receive Major General Gates's Answer tomorrow morning at ten o'clock.*[159]

Burgoyne had to know that once his army was disarmed it would be at the mercy of the Americans no matter what pettifogging details the agreement included. Gates scanned Burgoyne's ten points and quickly wrote "agreed" in the margin next to most of them. The first was the most important, and this he amended.

1. *The troops to march out of their camp, with the honours of war, and the artillery of the intrenchments to the verge of the river, where the old fort stood, where their arms and the artillery must be left.*[160]

To the second he specified Boston. Article 9 was as important as article 1, so he rewrote it.

9. *This capitulation is to be finished by 2 o'clock this day, and the troops march from their encampments at five, and be in readiness to move towards Boston tomorrow morning.*

With that Gates signed the document, dated it "15th Oct. 1777," and sent it back with Wilkinson. Kingston was waiting to convey it to British headquarters.

12:00 Noon, John Burgoyne, British Headquarters

Still Burgoyne quibbled. He sent a new letter to Gates saying that while several points were agreed to, more time was needed to execute a final agreement. Burgoyne sent Kingston back with a letter specifying the points and saying that Kingston and another officer were authorized to settle the matter of where the two representatives from each side would sit down to work out the final details.[161]

1:00 PM, Horatio Gates, American Headquarters

The exasperated Gates relented, agreeing that final details could be worked out by delegates near the black ruins of Schuyler's house. Gates appointed Wilkinson to the task of completing final negotiations. After some discussion, they decided that Brigadier General Whipple of the militia would second him. Gates's aide would come along as secretary. Wilkinson and Kingston agreed that a tent would be pitched between the advanced guards of the two armies, just above Schuyler's sawmill. They would meet in the afternoon. The ceasefire would be extended. Nicholas Sutherland and James Craig would be there to negotiate for Burgoyne.

Sometime during the day the French commander of the detachment from the Second Continental Light Dragoons, Captain Jean Louis de Vernejoux, disappeared from the American camp. The troop was known mainly for its pretty uniforms. Its commander had never impressed Gates as being much more than a dandy, and there was probably not much to be done when a foreign volunteer decided to seek more comfortable quarters for the coming cold weather. Gates simply added this to the long list of annoyances that would need his attention in the coming days.[162]

2:00 PM, Nicholas Sutherland and James Wilkinson, at Fish Kill

The men came together and exchanged credentials. Then they sat down and talked for several hours. As men will, particularly when they speak the same language, they set aside animosity and allowed themselves to like each other. Tense formalities smoothed into easier conversation. At last, at eight o'clock at night, they exchanged articles of capitulation. With that both teams returned to their respective generals.

The men had agreed that they were all fully empowered to negotiate, and that the commanding generals of both armies would be bound by whatever agreements they were able to work out. The words of honor of each of them were on the table. In the end it was agreed that Burgoyne would sign for the British Army the next morning and that Gates would do the same. The men and their assistants returned to their respective camps feeling positive about their accomplishment and confident that tomorrow would be the day this all came to a satisfactory conclusion.[163]

11:00 PM, *James Wilkinson, American Headquarters*

Wilkinson made his usual rounds and did not reach headquarters again until eleven o'clock that night. Gates was already in bed and asleep. Wilkinson found a note from Captain Craig, written only a half hour earlier. It was florid, the handwriting perfect and the content as obsequious as it was wordy.[164]

Wilkinson woke Gates. There was just one more thing. In their zeal to complete their work the British negotiating team had inadvertently used the word "capitulation" where the word "convention" should have been used. If the Americans would generously agree to the correction of this oversight the British negotiators were prepared to meet at the stipulated time the next day with a signed copy in hand. Craig's note explained that an oversight had been made in their haste to complete the agreement. It might seem like a minor point to the Americans, but it was an important one to the British. The note went on:

> I hope, Sir, you will excuse my troubling you so late, but I thought it better than by any delay to prevent the speedy conclusion of a treaty, which seems to be the wish of both parties, and which may prevent the further effusion of blood between us.

This Craig had signed, dated, and noted the time as half past ten o'clock.

Wilkinson and Gates both agreed, knowing that whatever it was called the document was unlikely to have much practical value once Burgoyne's men laid down their arms. Wilkinson scratched a note to Craig saying that the alteration was agreed to.

> Colonel Wilkinson's Compliments to Captain Craig, Major-General Gates will admit the Alteration required. October 15th at night.[165]

The note from Gates was sent back across to the British camp. There, that had to be the last word. Gates slid back to sleep. Wilkinson stuffed Craig's letter into his pocket, dropped on to his own bed, and did the same.

12:00 *Midnight, John Burgoyne, British Headquarters*

Of course, it was not the last word. Late that night a ragged Loyalist from Albany slipped into the British camp with the news that General Clinton

had advanced as far north as Esopus almost a week ago. He was probably approaching Albany by this time. Still grasping at any faint hope,
Burgoyne let this tiny spark ignite optimism in him once again. He
seemed to put his full faith in the words of the man as he thought about
the possibility that he might be able to scrap the entire draft agreement
with Gates. Burgoyne and several others were made so giddy by this news
that for the moment, at least, they seemed ready to reject the ratification
and take their chances.[166]

Cooler heads drew the Albany man off for tougher interrogation. Had
he seen Clinton or any British troops? Where had he learned of Clinton's
success? Gradually he admitted that it was all hearsay. But Burgoyne had
enough new hope to put three new questions to the weary officers in his
war council.

"First, can a treaty finalized by authorized commissioners, which
I have promised to sign as soon as the commission has ironed out all rough
spots, be honorably broken?" The council debated the question, and after
lengthy discussion they voted fourteen to eight that because the treaty had
been negotiated in good faith, and all the specifics had been agreed upon,
it could not be broken without violating military honor.

Burgoyne pressed on with a second question. "Does the news just received advantageous to our situation suffice to break such an agreement?"
It was really the same question put another way, and Burgoyne received
the same advice from the same majority. Most of the council was incredu-
lous. The vote was split again, but many argued that the report was hearsay at best, and doubtful coming as it did from a deranged man who had
deserted to an army on the brink of annihilation. There was no courier
from General Clinton, no eyewitness account, no evidence that there was
time for Clinton to assist them. Even if Clinton had taken Esopus he was
still much too far away to provide any effective support. The situation at
Saratoga was unchanged.

Burgoyne persisted, framing his third question. "Does the army, particularly the private soldiers, still have enough spirit to defend their positions until the last man?" The British officers from the left wing said yes.
The German officers from the right wing were less optimistic. If the men
could attack the Americans they would do so, but if they had to defend
against an American attack, the same level of bravery could not be expected of them. Burgoyne thanked the men and the council dispersed.
The officers moved off to spend another fitful night in the cold.

THURSDAY, OCTOBER 16, 1777

1:00 AM, Friedrich and Frederika Riedesel, the Lansing House

The ceasefire had improved life for Frederika. She was able to move her children and maids upstairs and into a little parlor. She made up a bed in another room so that Friedrich would finally be able to get a good night's sleep. At one in the morning an adjutant came to speak with Riedesel, waking him from the first sound sleep he had enjoyed in days.

To the surprise of everyone, Captain Campbell had managed to return at last, somehow slipping through the relaxed American cordon around the British Army with a message from Henry Clinton. Friedrich thought that this would be better than hearsay from a crazy American deserter, but not much. Campbell could not possibly carry news that would change the current dire situation at Saratoga.

The adjutant's news did not please Riedesel in the least. Burgoyne was calling for another council first thing in the morning. He would be grasping at straws again, imagining once again that Clinton was close to attacking Gates from the south. Nonsense. Riedesel closed his eyes and went back to a grumpy sleep.[167]

At dawn Friedrich went back to his post and Frederika shepherded her flock back down into the cellar. Fresh meat was distributed and the women turned it into a wonderful stew for themselves and the men in their care. On most of the days previous to this they had eaten salted provisions, which the men thought aggravated their wounds. Frederika's appetite had disappeared and she had been subsisting on bread crusts dipped in wine. Now the wounded officers insisted that she take some of the soup and a good cut of meat. It would make them happy to have her join them in their first decent meal in many days. She declined and they put their plates down with mock rage and refused to eat any more until Frederika joined them. At length she relented. Then the men also relented and everyone ate with something approaching good humor.[168]

7:00 AM, John Burgoyne, British Headquarters

It had been another quiet dawn, dark and foggy at first, but becoming clear and pleasant after eight. The British war chest was opened in the morning and money was distributed to the soldiers. The ceasefire was still in effect and would hold until two o'clock. In the American camp Gates

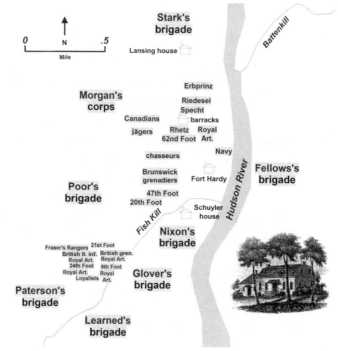

Figure 5.5 Disposition of the armies around October 16, 1777. Inset shows the Lansing House, after Lossing (1851: 89).

was content that he had an agreement, but in the British camp Burgoyne still vacillated. The British and German soldiers were unconcerned. They strolled about their encampment, venturing to the water's edge and to the limits of the pickets.[169] (See Figure 5.5.)

Word that Campbell was back in camp spread quickly. New rumors immediately began circulating that Clinton was advancing on Albany. Campbell had been gone since September 28, and Burgoyne had long since concluded that he had been caught and hanged. Now he was here and reporting that he and another courier named Daniel Taylor had left Clinton on the morning of Wednesday, October 8.[170] It had taken Campbell over a week to get here; nothing had been heard about Taylor's fate.

Burgoyne's delight at seeing his courier was quickly muted by what Campbell had to report.

Not having received any instructions from the commander in chief respecting the northern army, and unacquainted even with his intentions respecting that army, except his wishes that they should get to Albany, Sir Henry Clinton cannot presume to give any orders to General Burgoyne. General Burgoyne could not suppose Sir Henry Clinton had an idea of penetrating to Albany with the small force he mentioned in his last letter. What he offered in that letter he has now undertaken, cannot by any means promise himself success, but hopes it will be at any rate serviceable to General Burgoyne, as General Burgoyne says in his letter answer the offer (23rd Sept.) that even the menace of an attack would be of service.[171]

Campbell was dumbfounded by Burgoyne's reaction. Evidently, the false hopes raised late last night by the man from Albany still skewed the commander's thinking. After reading the message Burgoyne had brightened and said to his staff that though Clinton was still at a considerable distance there was still a glimmer of hope that Gates would have to redeploy some of his army south to intercept him. If Gates was so ready to agree to Burgoyne's terms, maybe there was some truth to the rumors of a British push up the Hudson. There was also some evidence that Gates was sending some units of the American Northern Army south. Several hundred New York militiamen appeared to have reached the ends of their contractual terms of service and were heading home, with or without Gates's permission.[172]

Burgoyne temporized, grasping at this one last straw. He sent a note to Gates accusing him of having detached a major part of his army while negotiations were going on in order to protect Albany from a British advance up the Hudson. Burgoyne demanded that Gates show two of his officers all the American encampments so that they could be assured that this was not the case. If the relative strength of the American Army was found to be still three or four times that of Burgoyne's army he would sign the treaty, but if such numerical superiority could not be demonstrated matters were at an end. The note, he thought, put the onus back on Gates. If Gates had sent men south, then it was Gates who was negotiating in bad faith, and it was Gates who would be responsible if the talks collapsed.[173]

8:00 AM, Horatio Gates, American Headquarters

Major Kingston delivered the letter to the American side. Gates was furious and rejected the demand out of hand. Gates sent Kingston back with Gates's assurance, on his word of honor, that the strength of the army was the same or greater than it had been at the time he had moved up to Saratoga, that he had in fact been reinforced by an additional brigade, and that to give a British officer a tour of his positions would be impolitic and dishonorable. He would not consider it. Then Gates scrawled a note to Burgoyne.

> General Burgoyne ought to think the matter well over before he breaks his word of honor and becomes answerable for the consequences. As soon, however, as the capitulation should be ratified I will be prepared to show General Burgoyne my whole army. I pledge you my honor that he will find it is four times stronger than his own, not reckoning the troops posted opposite upon the other side of the Hudson. However, I cannot grant him more than an hour's time for his answer. After the expiration of that time I will be forced to take the most stringent measures.[174]

Gates inventoried his army for Burgoyne. Could the man not see for himself that he was hopelessly outnumbered? Twelve brigadiers, forty-four colonels. The list went on. Well over three hundred first lieutenants and a like number of second lieutenants. There were five chaplains, eight surgeons and mates, almost fourteen hundred sergeants, and 636 drummers, an astonishing number. Altogether the roster boasted 13,216 rank and file present and fit for duty. Gates then accounted for the 1353 sick, the 3875 detached elsewhere, even the 180 on furlough. Perhaps Burgoyne would not believe them, but believable or not they were true numbers.[175]

Wilkinson quickly proposed that he go off to visit Burgoyne personally and carry the note directly. Gates agreed; now it was Wilkinson's turn to find a drummer to beat the chamade and pick his way across the ruined bridge over Fish Kill. As he was leaving, Gates called after him, "Tell Burgoyne if you are not back in an hour and a quarter I'll open every battery I have upon him."[176]

9:00 AM, Brothers in Arms, the Banks of Fish Kill

The 9th Regiment of Foot was posted with the core of Burgoyne's British forces on the heights overlooking Fish Kill. The soldiers of both armies had set aside their arms and begun to venture to the water's edge over the last day or two. It was a steep climb down on both sides, and it took the wary soldiers time to convince themselves that they would not be ambushed and picked off from across the narrow stream. But the kill was only thirty yards wide here, and once they made the descent without their arms the men began to relax; civilized conversation began to drift back and forth across the water. The men looked for connections, as strangers usually do, searching for commonalities, telling jokes, putting the horror of the battles behind them. More British soldiers joined the men of the 9th from their camp on the heights. Americans from Glover's and Learned's brigades began to line the southern bank of the kill, sometimes joined by men from Morgan's corps.

Private McGuire, an Irishman of the 9th Regiment, joshed with the rest, testing the waters of sociability, smoking, relaxing, laughing at the pleasure of it. This went on for hours. Eventually another happy Irish-accented voice drifted across from the American side, causing McGuire to jump to his feet, rigid, his eyes wide. So too did the American. Then without explanation the two men both jumped into the frigid water and waded toward each other with a fury that brought the rest of the men on both banks to their feet. After all they had been through, was this the beginning of a final battle, one set off by two ancient enemies? The two men grappled screaming in the middle of the river, the cold water splashing around them. They roared at each other in a brogue that the men on both shores found hard to understand. A few words were clear. "My brother! My dear brother!"

The McGuire brothers had not seen nor heard from each other since they had taken separate paths out of poverty. James had immigrated to America and was now part of Morgan's corps of riflemen.[177] His brother had joined the British Army and was here with the 9th Foot. Now here they both were, not knowing until this moment that each had twice done everything he could to take the other's life.[178] The brothers wept and laughed, hugged and shouted, cheered on by their friends on both sides of Fish Kill.

Elsewhere on the western side of the village, American scouts grabbed a Loyalist who was trying to get away before the capitulation. The man had deserted to the British when Fort Ticonderoga was taken in July, and he had been with them ever since. Now he had little choice but to run for it. Unfortunately for him, he did not run far enough before exhaustion overtook him. The scouts found him sleeping and brought him back to the American camp to face whatever indignities the men there cared to inflict on him. They put a noose around his neck and told him that they were going to hang him on the spot. He begged to be shot by a firing squad instead. Then the men removed the rope, tied him to a tree, and gave him a hundred lashes. When this was concluded he begged to be hanged. The consensus was that he should be lashed again a hundred times on each of the following two mornings. After that he could face trial by court-martial. This seemed to satisfy everyone but the unfortunate Loyalist, who gave up begging for anything at all.[179]

10:00 AM, James Wilkinson, at Fish Kill

After being met by a subaltern of the 21st, Wilkinson asked for Major Kingston and told him, "I am charged with a verbal message from Major General Gates to Lieutenant General Burgoyne." After some military ritual Wilkinson was allowed to pass between two log redoubts. Behind them stood Burgoyne, accompanied by Phillips, Riedesel, Hamilton, von Gall, and Specht.

Wilkinson was suitably impressed, and for a change intimidated, by the array of famous decorated generals standing before him. He was twenty years old and dressed in a plain blue frock with nothing more military about him than a cockade and sword. He recited his memorized message. "Major General Gates in justice to his own reputation, condescends to assure your excellency that no violation of the treaty has taken place on his part since the commencement of it. The requisition therefore contained in your message of this day is inadmissible, and as it now remains with your excellency to ratify or dissolve the treaty. Major General Gates expects your immediate and decisive reply."[180] He handed Burgoyne Gates's note.

Attached to Gates's note was the summary roster of the American Army. Burgoyne could hardly believe the numbers. Over thirteen thousand rank and file fit for duty? Just half that many would be an appalling number. He thought of his own current roster. No more than thirty-five hundred British and German rank and file were fit for duty.[181] Even if Gates was exaggerating and the numbers were twice the true strength of the American Army, Burgoyne's forces were still outnumbered two to one.

Burgoyne turned and talked in murmurs with his generals. Indecision drifted on and Wilkinson's brash courage started to come back to him. "Your excellency must entertain a humble opinion of Major General Gates's professional knowledge or you would not have demanded permission for two of your officers to critically examine his numbers, and of consequence his position, while the British Army has their arms in their hands. General Gates can not but conceive you are trifling with him."

Burgoyne replied, "Not only my own individual reputation, but the service of the King my master and the honor of the British arms enjoin on me the most cautious circumspection. General Gates has no idea of the principle and spirit which animates the army I command. There is not a man in it, I assure you Colonel Wilkinson, who does not pant for action."

But Wilkinson had the better of the argument. "But what can the courage of a handful of men avail against the numbers you see on the hills beyond the river, and those which surround you? I can assure your Excellency, they are with difficulty restrained from falling on you at all quarters in the hope of dividing the spoils of your camp. Be pleased, sir, to favor me with your determination."[182]

"I do not recede from my purpose. The truce must end."

"At what time, sir?"

"In one hour."

They all synchronized their watches. "After what has passed, General Burgoyne, there can be no treaty. Your fate must be decided by arms, and General Gates washes his hands of the blood which may be spilled."

"Be it so," said Burgoyne.

Wilkinson tried to be resolute as he walked back to the American lines. He had walked about two hundred yards when he heard Kingston calling after him. Wilkinson stopped and turned. Burgoyne wanted him to return. He had a few more words. Wilkinson and Kingston walked back.

Burgoyne was conciliatory now. "General Gates has in the business depending between us been very indulgent. I would hope for time to take the opinion of my general officers in a case of such magnitude to the two armies. As it is far from my disposition to trifle in an affair of such importance . . ." Phillips stepped in.

"Yes sir, yes sir, General Burgoyne don't mean to trifle on so serious an occasion, but he feels it his duty to consult his officers."

"What time will you require?" Wilkinson asked.

"Two hours."

They synchronized their watches again and Wilkinson started off.

Wilkinson found a messenger from an anxious Gates waiting at the American lines. What on earth had taken so long? Wilkinson briefed the man and sent him back to headquarters. He stayed at the charred ruins of Schuyler's house and waited. An hour, then two hours, went by. Gates sent another messenger.

Overall the whole of both armies seemed more relaxed. Men in both camps presumed that Gates and Burgoyne were edging toward an agreement and it seemed only a matter of time before something good came of it. The pickets from the two armies were having easy conversations, almost embarrassed by the loaded firearms they were still required to carry. But here and there serious rumors of a contrary kind began spreading. Burgoyne had distributed sixty rounds of cartridges to each of the British soldiers in preparation for a last stand. The British regiments were ready to do or die but the Germans had refused to accept the cartridges. Burgoyne was capitulating; Burgoyne was preparing to attack. Some American commanders were ordering their men to strike their tents in anticipation of renewed fighting. Some heard that if talks did not succeed a cannon would fire at one minute after noon to signal the end of the ceasefire. And so the contradictory rumors mated and multiplied.[183]

Another fifteen minutes. At last Sutherland appeared and Wilkinson motioned him to cross the kill. By this time the negotiators had almost become friends. At the moment they seemed to understand each other better than they understood their respective superiors. Sutherland had asked Wilkinson to save his fusee for him, a weapon he had owned for thirty-five years. He did not want to see it lost in the piles of arms that would accumulate when the British Army surrendered. Wilkinson had been happy to accommodate. It was the kind of favor friends did for one another. Now they were trying to broker the best solution available in the face of resistance from the man who had the most to lose. Sutherland shook his head with a wry smile.

"Well our business will be knocked on the head after all."

"Why?"

"The officers have got the devil in their heads and cannot agree."

"I am sorry for it, as you will now not only lose your fusee but your whole baggage," Wilkinson replied, trying to make light of it

But Sutherland was downcast. He said he could not help the situation.

Then Wilkinson suddenly remembered the note he had received from Captain Craig the night before. He pulled it out of his pocket and read it to Sutherland, who looked surprised. What Craig had written was clear to anyone reading it. The final impediment had been removed last night. Gates had agreed to substitute "convention" for "capitulation." The contents of the note confirmed that the deal was done. What possible excuse could Burgoyne use to claim otherwise?[184]

Sutherland immediately saw the opportunity the note provided. "Will you give me that letter?" Wilkinson was reluctant to part with it. "No. I should hold it as a testimony of the good faith of a British commander." Sutherland was desperate. "Spare me that letter, sir, and I pledge you my honor I will return it in fifteen minutes."

Wilkinson stared briefly at his new friend. He handed Sutherland the letter and watched the man run all the way back into the British camp. Wilkinson then turned and saw a messenger from Gates approaching. The note from Gates said, "Break off the treaty if the convention is not immediately ratified." Wilkinson told the messenger to tell Gates that he was doing the best he could; he instructed the messenger to come back in a half hour.[185]

Back at his headquarters the exasperated Gates issued fresh orders to Morgan. "March immediately and scale their works and spare no man you can find. The army is to follow and carry it through."[186] The messenger from Wilkinson arrived breathless, just in time for Gates to rescind the orders to Morgan.

At Burgoyne's headquarters there was a final vote. This time it was unanimous. Even the eight who had thought it might be possible to discard the treaty the previous night now saw that there was no alternative but to sign it.[187] Gates had accepted their last demand, that the agreement be called a "convention" rather than a "capitulation." Craig's note now committed them to the convention; every officer from Burgoyne on down was sure of it.

Sutherland came back, sweating but punctual, bringing Captain Craig with him. Craig handed the convention to Wilkinson, complete with Burgoyne's signature. There was an additional article, which Wilkinson assured them would be acceptable to Gates. This final problem was that Burgoyne had not been mentioned by name in any of the articles of the convention. Surely Gates would allow Burgoyne's name to be added. The men all shook hands and went their separate ways.

Wilkinson had been gone from headquarters for hours. Now he at last made his way back. He handed the convention to Gates with as much satisfaction as he had felt since the campaign had begun. Gates laughed at the codicil requested by Burgoyne and scrawled it at the bottom.

> To prevent any doubts that might arise from L^r. Genl. Burgoyne's name not being mentioned in the above Treaty, Major-general Gates hereby Declares that he is understood to be comprehended in it as fully as if his name had been Specifically Mentioned.
>
> H. Gates[188]

Wilkinson took everything back to Burgoyne. There were thirteen articles. Most of them were meaningless once the British troops grounded their arms, but the long dance had ended. The last article stipulated that the two generals would sign the convention at nine the next morning. The British troops would then march out and ground their arms at three o'clock in the afternoon. Burgoyne read Gates's note and asked Wilkinson for a few minutes to confer with his officers. When he emerged he told Wilkinson that the convention would be ratified the next morning. Burgoyne thought, it is calamitous, it is awful, but it is an honorable hour.[189]

6:00 PM, John Burgoyne, British Headquarters

Before night fell the men heard that the articles had been signed and sealed after all, and that Burgoyne's army would lay down its arms at nine the next morning. The American soldiers were not as certain as the British and German soldiers that it would happen, but they all hoped it would. They all laid on their arms all night and prepared to be up to parade at three in the morning.[190] Across the river to the east the moon rose full again for the second time since the two armies had approached each other. It was the hunter's moon. The time for fighting was past. It was time now for men to go home, to take up their autumn hunting and preparation for winter.

That night the British and German regimental colors and tassels were removed from their shafts and packed away. The shafts were stacked and burned. Frederika Riedesel helped sew the flags into pillows and other hiding places. With any luck the Americans would not capture their colors.[191]

FRIDAY, OCTOBER 17, 1777

8:00 AM, American Soldiers, Saratoga

The Northern Army was ready for any eventuality. The men had paraded early under a full moon at four o'clock, and again an hour and a half after sunrise at eight. It was dark and foggy at first, but it cleared as the American Army prepared to march out of camp to receive Burgoyne and his army. It was going to be a fine day.[192]

James Wilkinson sat astride a beautiful white horse. When the time came, all eyes watched him ride from Gates's marquee to Fish Kill, cross the stream, and disappear into the British camp.[193]

9:00 AM, John Burgoyne, British Headquarters

Burgoyne called a meeting of all the officers early in the morning. He wanted to explain the events that had led to this end. He spoke about his disappointment that the army had failed to receive support from Clinton in New York. Each officer, he said, could judge the decisions and the outcomes for himself. He then read the articles of the convention. "The terms are even easier than we could have expected from our situation." He concluded by saying, "I never would have accepted any terms, had we provisions enough, or the least hopes of our extricating ourselves in any other way."[194]

Lieutenant Colonel James Wilkinson rode his white horse into the British camp. His task was to witness Burgoyne's signing of the convention and then to accompany Burgoyne to the American headquarters on the other side of Fish Kill. The twenty-year-old colonel was the only American present.[195]

Burgoyne signed the capitulation at nine o'clock, under an American elm in the village. The elm would be known as "the surrender tree" for as long as it stood. An American Grand Union flag of thirteen red and white stripes, with thirteen stars in the canton on a field of blue, the first of its kind, hung from a crude pole nearby. The new American flag, making its first appearance in the field, had been patched together from scraps of military uniforms.[196]

The defeated army began leaving its entrenchments at ten o'clock. Some of the men broke the stocks off their muskets. Drummers stomped their drums to pieces. A few remaining Canadians and

Loyalists climbed into bateaux to head north up the river and back to Canada. The Canadians had promised the Americans that they would not participate further in the war. The shaken Loyalists were being sent into exile, their only comfort being Gates's assurance that their families eventually would be sent along after them. Some of them had letters that Simon Fraser had written for them weeks ago. These were designed to give the Loyalists some protection if they were captured, but the truth was that they could not expect to be treated as well as the British or German soldiers.[197]

After the signing, Wilkinson showed Burgoyne where the British troops would ground their arms. Then they rode down closer to the river, on ground visible from the other bank, where Burgoyne would not have dared venture a day earlier.

"Is it not fordable?"

"Certainly sir, but do you observe the people on the opposite shore?"

"Yes, I have seen them too long."

Wilkinson said nothing to Burgoyne's surly response. The man was facing the ultimate humiliation for a commanding general, and he could be forgiven. The two men guided their horses as they picked their way down the bank of Fish Kill. The horses waded across the stream and climbed the south bank with a few grunts and lunges. Burgoyne's horse struggled, the weeks without proper forage having taken its toll even on the commander's best mount. The reappearance of Wilkinson on his white horse triggered a murmured report that spread through the entire American Army in less than a minute. The surrender had been signed.[198]

Gates's marquee stood nearly a half mile south of Fish Kill. The sides of the marquee were rolled up. There was a long table set for dinner. As they drew closer Burgoyne looked over at Wilkinson and proposed that he be introduced to General Gates. Wilkinson fell back and Burgoyne rode forward with Kingston at his side and his aides-de-camp, Charles Stanhope and a lieutenant, following. Behind them on scrawny horses rode Phillips and Riedesel. Gates rode out to meet them at the edge of his encampment. His plain blue frock coat contrasted with Burgoyne's rich, glittering, royal uniform. At fifty, Gates looked like an old man. Burgoyne, taller and five years Gates's senior, looked young and trim even in defeat.[199]

Burgoyne reined in to a halt almost within sword's distance of Gates and raised his hat. Gates saluted. Burgoyne did not smile. "The fortune of war, General Gates, has made me your prisoner." The men dismounted. Burgoyne drew his sword and handed it to Gates, who took it with his left hand and at the same time extended his right hand. Gates glanced down at the weapon. The entire blade was inlaid with gold filigree, and near the hilt were the King's initials, G. R., and the royal coat of arms. It was a beautiful, impractical, glorious, and now impotent weapon.[200]

Gates shook Burgoyne's hand and said, "I shall always be ready to bear testimony that it has not been through any fault of your Excellency." Phillips rode forward, exchanged salutes with Gates, and shook hands. Riedesel did the same, then the remaining officers, each introduced by Burgoyne in turn.[201] (See Figure 5.6.)

After a few minutes of talking, Gates returned Burgoyne's sword. Then the other British officers delivered their own swords and had them handed back in the same manner. That concluded, they all made their way to the large table for dinner. Gates ordered up a detachment of the Connecticut Light Horse to serve as a bodyguard to Burgoyne. Burgoyne's officers noticed that this unit, at least, was nicely uniformed. Their blue

Figure 5.6 Surrender of Burgoyne by Frederick C. Yohn. Courtesy of the Chapman Historical Museum.

uniform coats were now topped off by bearskin caps having long white tails of horsehair.[202]

2:00 PM, an Anonymous Woman, the British Camp

The woman who had first fetched the water from the Hudson the previous Sunday and had continued doing it ever since was rewarded by the English and German troops as they gathered to march out. She had exposed herself to snipers over and over, but the Americans had allowed her to pass without incident every time. Everyone knew that she had been terrified but resolute all the while. Everyone who had any money threw some into her apron as they passed by. In the end she came away beaming, with over twenty guineas in her purse. It was not a bad way for her to enter American captivity.[203]

3:00 PM, John Becker, Fish Kill

At three o'clock the king's army began to march out, its drums beating the "British Grenadier March," its honor intact. The drumbeat that had so animated them in days past now seemed feeble, almost as if ashamed to be heard. Officers wept stoically; only their ingrained discipline kept them from breaking. The soldiers were silent except for the shuffling of their boots, and the men avoided all eye contact.[204]

British and German soldiers streamed by in long lines, laying their arms in piles along the route. Thousands of muskets were grounded in the ruins of old Fort Hardy at the edge of the village. It was a shrunken army. Over a thousand of its number were already prisoners. Over nine hundred had been wounded, and many of them still lay somewhere to the south in the care of the Americans. Over four hundred had been killed and were already in the ground. The flat ground where the army grounded its arms was strewn with the carcasses of dead horses, and the overwhelming stench only added to the humiliation felt by the defeated soldiers.[205]

The British light infantry came first, wading across Fish Kill next to the ruins of the bridge, their white breeches soiled by the muddy water. John Becker and his father stood close to the long, slow procession. A British officer stepped over to the elder Becker, drew his sword, and presented it. "You damned rebel, take this, I have no more use for it."[206] The officer was gone before the dumbfounded Becker could react. He stood there with a beautiful sword in his hands, not knowing what to do with it. Should he keep it? Should he turn it over to someone on Gates's staff? He could not decide. At length he took a friend's advice and put it someplace safe until he could decide what to do. But of course it was gone when he went back for it, and he never saw it again.

The Beckers ran ahead, crossing Fish Kill and running to Gates's marquee to see what would happen next. He had been in this army for nearly two years, but John was still only fifteen years old, and had the fearless enthusiasm of young men his age. He wanted a closer look, but John's uncle stopped him abruptly. "Remain here. There is mischief doing here. I have just heard one of the men say that if General Schuyler shows his face here he will put a brace of balls through him."[207] The older man wanted to go warn General Gates; John scoffed at the idea. No American would dare do such a thing; it was all bluster.

3:30 PM, Frederika Riedesel, the American Camp

Friedrich Riedesel had called for Frederika and the children to join him. She bundled the girls, her servants, and herself into the calash and joined the long, sad parade through the American camp. She had expected to be met with scorn and derision, but she was greeted by compassion, even admiration. When they approached the American tents, a distinguished General Philip Schuyler rode forward on his white horse, dismounted, stepped forward from behind the American officers, and helped them all down from the calash. He hugged the children like a grandfather as he did so. With tears in his eyes he said to Frederika, "You tremble. Fear nothing." She replied, "No, for you are so kind and have been so tender toward my children that it has inspired me with courage." They were led to Gates's tent where she found Burgoyne and Phillips having a friendly meeting with the Americans. Burgoyne said to her, "You may now dismiss all your apprehensions, for your sufferings are at an end." Her measured reply was, "I should certainly be acting very wrongly to have any more anxiety when our chief has none, and especially when I see him on such friendly footing with General Gates." With that the generals dined.[208]

Schuyler no longer had either a country mansion or a command, but there he was, serene and unharmed. The New Englander who had threatened to shoot him had long since stomped off. Schuyler turned again to Frederika and said, "It may be embarrassing to you to dine with all these gentlemen. Come now with your children into my tent where I will give you, it is true, a frugal meal, but one that will be accompanied by the best of wishes." Frederika was overwhelmed. These were not the American monsters she had feared, not at all. "You are certainly a husband and a father," she said, "since you show me so much kindness." The frugal meal included smoked tongue, beefsteak, potatoes, bread, and butter, which after weeks of deprivation seemed like the finest meal Frederika had ever eaten.

3:45 PM, Burgoyne and Gates, the American Camp

When the long column of defeated troops reached Gates's headquarters and began passing by, the generals got up from their dining table and came out to watch the parade. Burgoyne stood to the left of Gates; neither said much.[209]

No commissary kept a tally. No American officer checked for compliance. Some of the men kept their cartridge boxes and their belts; others did not. Gates stood next to Kingston for a while and noticed that many of the men were keeping their powder flasks. He asked, "Is it not the custom in time of war to surrender arms and powder flasks together?" Kingston replied, "No mention was made of it in the capitulation and you have a right only to what was stipulated." Gates said, "You are right." Gates then turned to some of his own officers and said, "If we wanted to have them we ought to have mentioned them in the treaty." That ended the matter. No one else took notice. The artillery, horses, wagons, and tents stood where they had been left. After a while the generals returned to the marquee. It would take three hours for all of Burgoyne's army to pass by.[210]

The Germans stole sidelong glances at the American soldiers. Apart from occasional colored epaulettes and cockades, they seemed dressed more for work or a night at the tavern than for soldiering. The officers were well dressed, but most were not wearing anything that looked like uniforms to the British and Germans trudging by. Burgoyne's officers noticed that the American officers wore whatever uniforms or pieces of uniform had come to hand. There were brown coats, blue coats, whatever they had been able to find. The facings of their lapels were red, straw, green, and a few other colors, and the colors clearly could not be used to identify what units they commanded. The militia officers looked like successful businessmen in need of a change of clothes. The generals had sashes to indicate their rank, but little else. Yet the American rank and file acted like soldiers, standing rigidly still, eyes forward, muskets shouldered with bayonets fixed, each man's right foot slightly advanced.

To the Germans, most of the Americans seemed unusually tall, slender, handsome, and sinewy, impressive despite their lack of flashy uniforms. These were not the cannibalistic barbarians they had been warned about. One German soldier made a mental note to write home that "quite seriously, English America excels most of Europe in respect to the stature and beauty of its men." There were wigs of all kinds or no wigs at all. Yet at the same time he had to admit that despite the comical array of wigs it had been no joke fighting these men. These were men with a talent for fighting.[211]

The defeated soldiers also noticed the American regimental colors. Many of the German soldiers could not read English, and many of the English soldiers could not read at all. Those who could noticed that the American regimental flags were imaginative and colorful, bearing coiled snakes and other totems of freedom, often along with English or Latin mottos in case anyone missed the point.[212] These struck them as being as much sarcastic as they were patriotic. Yet despite the acerbic messages on their flags, there was no sign of mockery, delight, or hatred from the Americans. Burgoyne had called them "rabble in arms" more than once, but here they were acting like a real army despite their lack of proper uniforms and equipment. Before them all was the new national flag of stripes and stars, one never seen before today by any of Burgoyne's soldiers.

Dearborn's light infantry were ordered to march in and take possession of the British camp as the defeated army marched out. This they did while the British and German soldiers finished grounding their arms.[213] At Gates's order the American fifes and drums stayed out of sight of the British in a little patch of woods, but played "Yankee Doodle" as the defeated men piled their muskets and rifles. It was a jaunty little tune that the fifers enjoyed, written almost two decades earlier by a British Army surgeon to make fun of American colonial soldiers. Today the joke was on the surgeon, some of whose younger descendants now stood at attention among the Americans.

Burgoyne and the senior officers were already at Gates's headquarters, but all other officers were at the heads of their respective commands. The brigade officers rode at the heads of their brigades, and the regimental officers led their regiments in turn. It was all very orderly. One by one the regiments moved down the bank, waded Fish Kill, and struggled up the south bank with as much dignity as they could manage. One of the German artillerymen led a young black bear on a leash. From time to time the animal reared up on his hind legs and roared. A tame deer trotted along behind a grenadier. A German jäger carried a pet raccoon. A pack of young foxes looked out over the crowd from atop a baggage wagon.[214]

Sergeant Lamb of the 9th Regiment of Foot was not a happy man. Disgust rose like bile in his throat as he marched past the Americans. The rebels had succeeded at nothing, he thought. They had never engaged Burgoyne in a fair fight, but had simply let time erode British provisions and turn the weather cold. From their commander on down, all ranks seemed to Lamb to betray an improper exultation. The rabble seemed convinced that they had overpowered and overwhelmed their brave British and German adversaries when in fact they deserved none of the laurels that are earned and worn by victors after hard-fought battles. Lamb did not like the taste of sour grapes.[215]

Watching them all were the American Continentals and militiamen. The American artillery was also there, lined up and orderly. Though they looked like rabble on the surface, they stood at rigid attention in straight lines, staring straight ahead like the disciplined soldiers that events had proven them to be. Their silence was absolute. There were no hoots or catcalls, not even a grin here or there. Every musket had its bayonet fixed in place, but there was no sign of hatred or mockery. Lamb, like nearly all of Burgoyne's soldiers, was amazed despite himself.[216]

Bringing up the rear were the ragged women who had followed and served husbands and boyfriends in Burgoyne's army all the way from Canada. Besides the wives and children of British and German officers, there were many such women with the army. There were at least 215 with the British troops and another eighty-two with the German troops. They came nearly last, trailed by a ragtag assortment of camp followers. The more refined ladies and gentlemen who watched them pass were horrified. The women of Burgoyne's army were dressed in rags, mostly barefoot, filthy, and loaded down with baggage. A few of Burgoyne's Indian men and their wives were there too, but under strong protective guard. The story of Jane McCrae still roused intense passions among the American militiamen, and the officers in charge wanted no vigilante justice to mar the occasion. Gates had to feed all of them, of course, at a full allowance for the women and half each for an uncertain number of children.[217]

6:00 PM, Horatio Gates, American Headquarters

Gates at last had a quiet moment. He started to draft a letter to his wife. He was as full of confidence and ambition as he had ever been. He would add more later; for now he wanted to get down some of his thoughts while they were still well formed in his mind. This former British officer was now thoroughly American, and as full of republican fervor as the men he led. His contempt for the privileged aristocrats he had beaten was balanced by his hope that he might actually convert some of them to his adopted political views.

> The voice of fame, ere this reaches you, will tell you how greatly fortunate we have been in this department. Burgoyne and his whole army have laid down their arms, and surrendered themselves to me and my Yankees. Thanks to the Giver of all victory for this triumphant success.
>
> Major General Phillips, who wrote me that saucy note last year from St. John's, is now my prisoner, with Lord Petersham, Major Ackland, son of Sir Thomas, and his lady, daughter of Lord Ilchester, sister to the famous Lady Susan, and about a dozen members of Parliament, Scotch lords, etc.
>
> If Old England is not by this lesson taught humility, then she is an obstinate old slut, bent upon her ruin.
>
> Tell my dear Bob not to be too elated at this great good fortune of his father. He and I have seen days adverse, as well as prosperous. Let us through life endeavor to fear both with an equal mind. General Burgoyne has promised me to deliver any letters I please to commit to his care in England. I think to send a few to some principal men there. Perhaps they may be a good effect for both countries. I would fain have the mother reconciled to her child, and consent, since she is big enough to be married, to let her rule and govern her own house.
>
> I hope that Lady Harriet Ackland will be here when you arrive. She is the most amiable, delicate little piece of quality you ever beheld. Her husband is one of the prettiest fellows I have seen, learned, sensible, and an Englishman to all intents and purposes; has been a most confounded Tory, but I hope to make him as good a Whig as myself before he and I separate.[218]

7:00 PM, John Burgoyne, Prisoner of War

Today there had been no password, no countersign, no field officer. There had not been any of that for days. In Burgoyne's orderly book there was a single sentence written this day: "Treaty of Convention signed." Final returns enumerated the losses of the British and German units on September 19 and October 7. It was done.[219]

Burgoyne had begun the expedition with over nine thousand men. Some had been left behind to garrison Fort Ticonderoga and Fort George. Many had been killed, wounded, taken sick, taken prisoner, or had deserted over the course of time. Now only 5856 marched behind him into captivity. He tried to tell himself how much worse it might have been. "The expediency of advancing being admitted, the consequences have been honorable misfortune."[220]

As Burgoyne had ridden forward toward Gates's tents, he had to admit to himself that the Americans had performed well. They had forced a convention that was a capitulation in every respect but its name. Call it what he might, it was still surrender. The bulk of Burgoyne's army would make it as far back as Freeman's farm today.

Some of the British troops camped again in the Great Redoubt. There they found the British hospital still standing and still occupied by the sick and wounded, who all praised the care and generosity the Americans had shown them over the past week. Burgoyne, Phillips, and Riedesel, surrounded by the sharply dressed dragoons of the Connecticut Light Horse, rode on to Stillwater.[221]

Those who found their way to where General Fraser had been buried were appalled to find that the grave had been violated. Officers found shovels and ordered men to refill the empty grave and tidy up the damage. This they did, but they could see that the general's body had been "taken up."[222]

9:00 PM, Horatio Gates, American Headquarters

That night Gates began drafting more letters that he would post on Saturday. It was time to send the American volunteers home for the winter. One of the letters went to Brigadier General Whipple.

> *Sir, I desire you will acquaint the volunteers of New Hampshire of the*
> *High sense I have of their merit & service in the Defence of the common*

cause & of the alacrity & spirit with which they have stept forth at this
critical and Important season to the Deliverance of their country. The
have now my Leave to return home with the Honorable Dismission
convinced they will be ready upon every Important Occasion to join the
Northern Army.

I am sir your affectionate Humble Servant
Horatio Gates[223]

One army marched off into captivity. Much of the other one went home. Sooner or later many of the German soldiers and some of the British ones would discard their uniforms and make new lives for themselves in America. The Continentals would go into winter quarters, but militiamen would be returning to their families and their occupations until the war started up in earnest again in 1778. Ahead of them waited Valley Forge and countless other hardships. But Saratoga had changed everything.

Epilogue

Defeat would be the ultimate fate of British arms in this unnatural conflict. The finest army in the world could not prevail in this vast wilderness. Amateurs the rebels may have been, but there were too many of them to be suppressed by British expeditions operating at the ends of long vulnerable supply lines. Even modestly equipped American leaders could lead hordes of ragtag volunteers successfully on this endless landscape. Burgoyne had to admit it to himself. "The militia are inferior in method and movement but not a jot less serviceable in the woods."[1] It was cold comfort, but dim apprehension was shifting to certainty that sooner or later the Americans would prevail.

It had been a good strategic plan, but it turned out to be badly flawed in its execution. At the end of the Saratoga Campaign it was clear to Burgoyne, as it should have been to his superiors, that American independence was all but inevitable. A British soldier who was there later said, "The misfortunes attending the campaign of General Burgoyne . . . gave a decisive superiority to the cause of the colonists, and prepared a highway for opening the gates of American independence."[2]

Saratoga was a turning point, but fighting would drag on for four more years. There were more victories, but many defeats as well, as the Americans fought to avoid losing long enough for the inevitable exhaustion of the British effort to play out. The American loss of Philadelphia, the awful 1777–1778 winter at Valley Forge, and many other hardships were still ahead. The 1781 Siege of Yorktown would finally convince the British that they would not prevail. When Prime Minister Lord North heard the news of the Yorktown surrender he said, "Oh God, it is all over." It was, and the 1784 Treaty of Paris finally made it official.

Both armies lost many men, and the list of casualties included more than a few of the officers mentioned in this book. The American losses were not trivial, but Burgoyne's army suffered many more. Of his more senior officers, Friedrich Baum, Heinrich von Breymann, Francis Clerke, and Simon Fraser all died during or soon after combat. Both sides lost several more junior officers. Of the notable people who survived the events of 1777 several had subsequent careers that are worthy of brief mention.

John Dyke Acland survived the wounds he received on October 7, nursed back to health for a third time by his devoted wife, Harriet. They returned to England after his recovery. Just over a year following Saratoga Acland challenged a young British officer to a duel because the latter had said disparaging things about Americans at a dinner party. Acland was killed in the duel, leaving Harriet a young widow with two small children. The title of John's father, the Seventh Baronet of Killerton, thus passed to John's infant son when the elder Acland died in 1785. The boy died a few weeks later and the title passed to his uncle. The Acland title and family line survive in Devon.[3]

Benedict Arnold recovered from the severe bullet wound to his left thigh but the wound and his reputation for volatility ended his combat career. In Philadelphia he met and in 1779 married Margaret "Peggy" Shippen, the daughter of a Loyalist sympathizer. Through her Arnold met British Major John André, and Arnold's eventual defection to the British side was set in motion. A court-martial and a rebuke from Washington further soured Arnold. He obtained command of West Point in August 1780, but he was already prepared to deliver the post to the British by way of André. The plot fell apart and André was hanged, but Arnold escaped and took up a brigadier-general's commission in the British Army. He fought on the British side until late in 1781, when he left with his family for London. While there he challenged Alexander Lindsay to a duel, in which neither was injured. After relocating to New Brunswick for a few years Arnold returned to London, where he died in 1801.[4]

John Brooks returned to medical practice after the war but remained active in military and political affairs. He served under Benjamin Lincoln in the Massachusetts militia and participated in putting down Shay's Rebellion in 1787. Brooks was a popular political moderate and was elected governor of Massachusetts in 1816. He was re-elected annually until 1823, when he retired. He died in 1825.[5]

Alexander Bryan moved from Waterford to Saratoga Springs in 1787, becoming its earliest permanent resident and establishing a new inn there. His son built a stone house on the same site in 1825, which was revived as the Olde Bryan Inn in 1979. It remains a popular restaurant.[6]

John Burgoyne and other British and German officers returned to England, while the enlisted men they had led became prisoners of war. Burgoyne was required to defend his conduct of the campaign before the House of Commons. He was eventually restored to his military rank. However, he spent much of his time practicing his avocation as a playwright. He wrote several popular plays and were it not for his defeat at Saratoga would probably now be best remembered for these accomplishments. Burgoyne and his wife, Charlotte, had a daughter, Charlotte Elizabeth, in 1754. He was a widower by 1777, but after his return to England he had four more children by his mistress Susan Caulfield. Burgoyne died suddenly in 1792 at the age of seventy.[7]

Joseph Cilley had fought previously with Rogers' Rangers in the French and Indian War. At the beginning of the War of Independence he was appointed major in the 2nd New Hampshire. When John Stark resigned command of the 1st New Hampshire Cilley took command and led the regiment during the Saratoga Campaign. He subsequently led the same regiment under Sullivan against Loyalists and their Indian allies in western New York. He held both military and political offices in New Hampshire following the war until his death in 1799.[8]

Henry Dearborn began his service at Bunker Hill and was captured in Canada during Arnold's abortive campaign there in the winter of 1775. He continued to serve after Saratoga and was present when Cornwallis surrendered at Yorktown. He served in the Massachusetts militia after the war and was elected to Congress. Dearborn served as secretary of war under President Jefferson and returned to active army duty during the War of 1812. Dearborn, Michigan, and several other places are named after him. His son, Henry Alexander Scammell Dearborn, later had his own distinguished legal, military, and political career. He rose to the rank of brigadier general in the War of 1812.[9]

Horatio Gates enjoyed credit for American success at Saratoga, but became a controversial figure during the course of efforts by others to discredit George Washington and replace the commander in chief with Gates. Gates's role in what is called the Conway Cabal remains uncertain. Gates commanded American forces in the 1780 Battle of Camden and was blamed for the embarrassing defeat his troops suffered there. Gates's wife Elizabeth died in 1783 and he retired to his estate, Traveller's Rest, the following year. Two years later he married a British immigrant, Mary Valens. In 1790, at the urging of his friend John Adams, Gates freed his slaves and moved with his wife to Manhattan. There he remained active in society and politics until his death in 1806.[10]

John Glover commanded a regiment from Marblehead, Massachusetts, during the 1775 siege of Boston. Because of his background in shipping he was the first privateer to be authorized by George Washington. Glover's regiment was made up mainly of fishermen, who were used in various amphibious actions, including ferrying Washington and his forces across the Delaware in 1776. After Saratoga he commanded in Rhode Island, then took up a position in the Hudson Valley north of New York City to prevent British expansion in that direction. Glover retired from the army in poor health in 1782 and died in 1797. His orderly book, a key document for the Saratoga Campaign, survives in the Library of Congress.[11]

William Hull fought at Saratoga and in several other battles. He was from Connecticut, a friend of Nathan Hale, and did much to publicize Hale's famous last words: "I only regret that I have but one life to give for my country." Hull was later appointed territorial governor of Michigan by President Jefferson. Still later he commanded the Army of the Northwest during the War of 1812. His surrender of Fort Detroit led to a court-martial over which Henry Dearborn presided. Hull was condemned to death by the court, but the sentence was later reprieved by President Madison. Both Hull and his daughter, Maria Hull Campbell, did their best to salvage his reputation in various subsequent publications. Hull died in 1825.[12]

Thaddeus Kościuszko volunteered his services as a military engineer to the American cause in 1776. He was a Polish-Lithuanian national who was born in what is now Belarus. His recommendations regarding Fort Ticonderoga were rejected, with disastrous results, early in the Saratoga Campaign. After designing the American fortifications on Bemis Heights he went on to improve the defenses of West Point in 1778. He served under Gates again in the Southern Department until Gates was replaced by Nathanael Greene following the defeat at the Battle of Camden. He served effectively under Greene in the South until the war ended. Kościuszko returned to Poland in 1784 and re-entered military service there four years later. He had liberal views and supported Poland's constitutional reforms of 1791. However, reactionaries asked for help from Russia's Catherine the Great, and this resulted in the Polish-Russian War of 1792. Kościuszko, now a major general, successfully led his division in various actions but resigned his commission when the king capitulated in the face of Russian superiority. Kościuszko left Poland for Leipzig and Paris in 1792, hoping to obtain support to resist the partition of Poland. The dismemberment of Poland continued. Kościuszko then went to Krakow to lead an uprising that came to bear his name. This had failed by 1794 and Poland ceased to exist as a sovereign nation for the next 123 years. Czar Paul I, Catherine's successor, pardoned Kościuszko in 1796. He fled to the United States, but felt compelled to assist family and allies in Europe, returning there in 1798 under a false passport provided by President Jefferson. His efforts on behalf of Poland were largely ineffectual. Kościuszko died in 1817 in Switzerland, age seventy-one.[13]

Ebenezer Learned formed a regiment in Massachusetts in 1775 and participated in the Siege of Boston under Washington's overall command. He took leave in 1776 for health reasons, but recovered to take command of a brigade at Saratoga in 1777. He later commanded Massachusetts troops at Valley Forge, but was again forced to step down for health reasons. Learned did not resume military service and died in Massachusetts in 1801.[14]

Benjamin Lincoln was born in Hingham, Massachusetts. He was at Saratoga long enough to displace Arnold and to be seriously wounded the day following the Battle of Bemis Heights. He returned to Massachusetts to recover from his wound and was considering resigning his commission when he learned that Benedict Arnold had been retroactively granted seniority over him. Lincoln returned to service and Washington put him in command of the Southern Department in 1778. He was forced to surrender to the British in Charleston, but was exchanged for British Major-General William Phillips in 1780. Lincoln later served as the nation's first secretary of war. In 1787 he was involved in both the ratification of the US Constitution and the suppression of Shay's Rebellion. He also served a term as lieutenant governor of Massachusetts. Lincoln died in 1810.[15]

Alexander Lindsay, Sixth Earl of Balcarres, was born in 1752 and began his military career at the age of fifteen. He commanded the light infantry battalion at Saratoga and was released from captivity as part of a prisoner exchange in 1779. He returned to England and married Elizabeth Keith. He was promoted to the rank of lieutenant-colonel in the 71st Foot. By 1793 he rose to the rank of major-general. He subsequently served as governor of Jersey and later as governor of Jamaica. By 1803 he had achieved the rank of general. On one occasion Lindsay snubbed Benedict Arnold in England because he regarded Arnold as a traitor. A duel resulted from this insult but neither man was injured. Lindsay died in 1825.[16]

Daniel Morgan, of Welsh descent, was born in New Jersey in 1736. He moved to Virginia after a family dispute when he was seventeen. He served with his cousin, Daniel Boone, during the French and Indian War, famously acquiring at that time 399 lashes as punishment for striking a British officer. The Virginia House of Burgesses chose Morgan to form one of ten rifle companies that were raised to support the Siege of Boston in 1775. He marched them there in only twenty-one days. Morgan was part of Arnold's grueling expedition to Quebec later that year and was captured in the fighting. He was exchanged early in 1777 and returned to duty. He had been promoted during his absence and was now ordered to raise a larger corps of riflemen. Washington assigned Morgan and his corps to Gates and the Northern Army, which led to his singular participation in the two main battles of the Saratoga Campaign. Failing to gain promotion, increasingly frustrated by Congress, and suffering the effects of long service in the field, Morgan resigned and went home to Virginia in 1779. After Gates's defeat at Camden, Morgan agreed to return to the army, and he was soon promoted to brigadier general under Nathanael Greene's overall command in the Southern Department. Despite Greene's instructions to avoid direct battle, Morgan decided to confront a major British force at the Battle of Cowpens. It was a brilliant victory for the Americans. After the war ended he served again in the effort to suppress the Whiskey Rebellion, at which time he was promoted to the rank of major general. Morgan later served in Congress. He died in 1802 at the age of sixty-six.[17]

William Phillips was a career British military officer who gained renown as an artilleryman. After serving as Burgoyne's second in command in the Saratoga Campaign he was detained with other British officers until arrangements were made to exchange him for Benjamin Lincoln in 1780. Phillips returned to service in the southern theater of the war, where he came into contact with Benedict Arnold. By that time Arnold was serving on the British side in Virginia. Like many others, Phillips fell very ill with typhus or malaria, such that Arnold had to take over for him. Phillips died in the spring of 1781 and was buried in Virginia.[18]

Friedrich and Frederika Riedesel survived the Saratoga Campaign, as did their three young daughters. After extensive service and a wound in the

Seven Years' War, Riedesel served the Duke of Brunswick (Braunschweig). Because of this he was promoted to the rank of major general and assigned the task of commanding the mostly Brunswicker troops sent to America to support Burgoyne's Saratoga Campaign. Following Burgoyne's surrender, Riedesel and his family were sent to Virginia with other German prisoners, and then to New York City. After a year of parole, he was exchanged under the same arrangement that involved William Phillips and Benjamin Lincoln. Riedesel continued his military career in Europe until his retirement in 1793. He died in 1800. Frederika's journal of the Saratoga Campaign was translated and published in the nineteenth century and has been an important source for historians ever since.[19]

Alexander Scammell served with distinction throughout the war. Some of his letters to Abigail Bishop, his beloved "Nabby," survive. Their marriage was postponed by his army service. Scammell led his New Hampshire men in several battles before and after Saratoga. In 1780 he was appointed executioner of John André, Benedict Arnold's British accomplice, an assignment that weighed heavily on him and led afterward to a request for reassignment. He was wounded and taken prisoner at Yorktown. He later died, still unmarried, in nearby Williamsburg, the most senior American officer to be lost in the final siege of the war.[20]

Philip Schuyler was a New York patrician of Dutch descent who had a long political and military career. His primary residence was a mansion in Albany that has been preserved as a New York State historic site. He also owned land and buildings, including a country mansion, in Schuylerville, then known as Saratoga. Schuyler was a natural choice to command the Northern Army in 1775, but ill health prevented him from conducting the invasion of Canada late in that year. Schuyler was relieved of his command after Fort Ticonderoga fell to the British in 1777, and he was replaced by Horatio Gates. Schuyler then threw himself into the task of ensuring a steady supply of food, ammunition, and equipment for the rapidly growing Northern Army. He later served in the New York State Senate and as a US senator, resigning for reasons of ill health in 1798. Schuyler died late in 1804.[21]

John Stark, "the Hero of Bennington," was born in New Hampshire in 1728. He served in the British Army during the French and Indian War, but quickly accepted the rank of colonel in the New Hampshire militia when the War of Independence broke out around Boston. He served ably at Bunker Hill. Land that later became Vermont was known as the New Hampshire Grants in 1775, and New England men who served as soldiers early in the war were often rewarded with small land grants for their service. This provided New Hampshire with a defense against counterclaims coming from New York. Stark and his men served in the failed invasion of Canada and then went south to serve in New Jersey as well. He became disgusted with the Continental Army after being passed over for promotion and went home to accept a post as brigadier general in the New Hampshire militia. He refused to put himself under the command of Lincoln, Schuyler, or any other Continental commander, but he did not hesitate to attack and defeat Burgoyne's side expedition to Bennington in August 1777. Stark was finally awarded promotion to brigadier general in the Continental Army on October 4, 1777, and his militiamen arrived in time to help seal Burgoyne's fate. He was later commander of the Northern Army three times before the war ended. Stark retired at the end of the war. He is still known for his motto "Live Free or Die," which later became the New Hampshire state motto.[22]

James Wilkinson was a young, ambitious, charming, cunning, and devious American officer. Of these traits he was able to retain all but his youth through a long military career. Gates sent him to brief Congress after the victory at Saratoga, but he kept Congress waiting while he dealt with personal business. When he finally appeared he embellished his own role and was brevetted as a brigadier general despite still being only twenty years old. He then lost credibility in the eyes of his superiors and was forced out of service. He subsequently became a brigadier general in the Pennsylvania militia. Still later he moved to Kentucky and worked to help it gain independence from Virginia. Wilkinson traveled to New Orleans in 1787, where he agreed to serve as an agent of Spain. He continued to receive secret payments for this service even after returning to a US military career. He became involved with the Aaron Burr conspiracy and continued to play a double game through the War of 1812. He secured a post as envoy to Mexico during its 1810–1821 war of independence from Spain, using his position to promote a land scheme. Wilkinson died and was buried in Mexico City in 1825. His voluminous 1816 memoirs were an attempt to salvage his reputation. Fortunately, they contain much information not otherwise available about Saratoga. Unfortunately, they must be used very carefully because lies and self-promotion were so easy for this flawed man.[23]

Notes

Frequently referenced manuscript repositories are abbreviated as follows:

DLAR   David Library of the American Revolution
LC   Library of Congress
MHS   Massachusetts Historical Society
NPS   National Park Service
NYHS   New-York Historical Society
NYPL   New York Public Library
WLCL   William L. Clements Library

INTRODUCTION
1. Scheer 1957.
2. Ranks designated by two words are often hyphenated in the case of British officers, but not so in the cases of German or American officers.
3. Cubbison 2012: 39–40.
4. Stanley, 1961: 115.
5. Mintz 1990: 18.
6. Horatio Gates to Matthew Vishter, October 4, 1777, WLCL.
7. Nelson 1976: 43.
8. Stephenson 2007: 55; Burgoyne 1780a: 135–136.
9. A *picket* was one or more men posted around a camp as a guard. The term is today used more often to identify activists in labor disputes.
10. Stanley 1961: 100–102.
11. "Copy of a Letter from Lieutenant-General Burgoyne to Lord George Germain, dated Head Quarters upon Hudson's River near Fort Edward, July 30, 1777." *London Gazette* (11808): 1.
12. Burgoyne 1860: 184.
13. Burgoyne 1780a: 106.
14. Burgoyne 1780a: 138.
15. Burgoyne 1780a: appendix xli.
16. Cubbison 2012: 93–99.
17. Burgoyne 1780a: 139.
18. Burgoyne 1780a: appendix xlii.

19. Cleve 1778: 103.
20. Pettengill 1924: 90–91.
21. Specht 1995: 135.
22. Burgoyne 1780a: appendix xliii; Luzader 2010: 111; Morrissey 2000: 53.
23. "Letter from Lieutenant-General Burgoyne to Lord George Germain, August 20, 1777." *London Gazette* (11818): 2–3; Burgoyne 1780a: appendix xxxix–xliv.
24. Burgoyne 1780a: 144–145.
25. Burgoyne 1780a: appendix lxxxiv; Luzader 2002: 40.
26. Burgoyne 1860a: 107–112.
27. Burgoyne 1780a: appendix xliv–xlix.
28. Burgoyne 1780a: 102.
29. Burgoyne 1780a: xlix.
30. Ideally, each brigade would be commanded by a brigadier-general and consist of three or more regiments, minimally around two thousand men. But brigade strengths varied considerably.
31. De Fonblanque 1972: 208–209.
32. Edwards 1953: 191–193.
33. The "von" that sometimes appears ahead of Riedesel's surname connotes German social rank. He was a baron, though he declined to use either the title or the honorific "von."
34. Burgoyne 1860: 103.
35. McGuire 2011: 103, 160.
36. Ketchum 1997: 322.
37. McGuire 2011: 107.
38. Päusch 1886; Cleve 1778.
39. "Copy of a Letter from Lieutenant-General Burgoyne to Lord George Germain, dated Head Quarters upon Hudson's River near Fort Edward, July 30, 1777." *London Gazette* (11808): 1.
40. Haiman 1932: 17.
41. Lossing 1851: 45.
42. Lossing 1851: 47.
43. Ketchum 1997: 350.
44. Luzader 2010: 163.
45. Nelson 1976: 66–67.
46. Morgan 1853. There is disagreement in the sources about the number of lashes; this source is the closest to Morgan's own telling of the story.
47. Hanger 1814: 122.
48. Higginbotham 1961: 55–61.

CHAPTER 1

1. The timing of sunrises, sunsets, moonrises, and moonsets have been adjusted to local time. I have assumed that in both armies those who had

watches did their best to check and reset them at high noon each day. Except for the two days on which major battles were fought, most of the times cited are approximations based on the known routines of armies in this era.

2. Stone 1895: 283.

3. Burgoyne 1860: 106–107.

4. Hadden 1884: 145; Kingston 1777; Stephenson 2007: 74.

5. Burgoyne 1860: 6.

6. Hadden 1884: xxxix.

7. Burgoyne 1780a: 97, 102, 153; "Extract of a Letter from Lieutenant-General Burgoyne to the Honourable Sir William Howe, dated Campt before Ticonderago." *London Gazette* (11798): 2.

8. Bateaux (sing. "bateau") are shallow-draft, flat-bottomed boats that were used extensively in colonial North America for moving freight.

9. Päusch 1886: 108.

10. "The cat" is the cat o' nine tails, a multitailed whip used to inflict corporal punishment in the British Army.

11. Darling 1971: 8–9.

12. Burgoyne 1780a: 96.

13. Burgoyne 1780a: appendix xxv; Horatio Gates to John Hancock, September 15, 1777, Peter Force Collection, LC; Wild 1890: 94.

14. Blake 1973; Luzader, 2010: 204.

15. Richard Varick to Philip Schuyler, September 12, 1777, Schuyler Papers, NYPL.

16. An *abatis* was a tangle of trees felled toward the enemy, the eighteenth-century equivalent of twentieth-century barbed wire coils, intended to slow infantry attacks and keep enemy soldiers under fire for as long as possible.

17. Lossing 1972: 58; Luzader 2010: 187.

18. Nelson 1976: 112.

19. Hitchcock 1900: 134; Henry Brockholst Livingston to Philip Schuyler, September 15, 1777, Schuyler Papers, NYPL.

20. Luzader 2010: 198; Horatio Gates to Benjamin Lincoln, September 15, 1777, WLCL.

21. Horatio Gates to John Hancock, September 15, 1777, Gates Papers, NYHS.

22. Lossing 1972: 84; Burgoyne 1860: 168; Linklater 2002.

23. Wilkinson 1816: 1:234–235.

24. Anonymous 1777a; Anonymous, 1777b; Anonymous, 1777c; Orderly Book, 15th Massachusetts, Glover's Brigade, Manuscript Division, LC.

25. Henry Brockholst Livingston to Philip Schuyler, September 15, 1777, Schuyler Papers, NYPL.

26. Boardman, 1879: 224.

27. Brandt 1994: 116–117.

28. Luzader 2010: 183.

29. Cushman 2010.

30. Matthew Clarkson to his cousin Susan Livingston, September 11, 1777, Livingston Family Papers, MHS; Richard Varick to Philip Schuyler, September 12, 1777, Schuyler Papers, NYPL.

31. Luzader 2010: 215; Arnold 1880: 167–168; Henry Brockholst Livingston to Philip Schuyler, September 15, 1777, Schuyler Papers, NYPL.

32. Hadden 1884: lvi, 149.

33. Hadden 1884: lxxv, 149–150.

34. Howitzers in this era were small mobile guns designed to lob exploding cast iron balls into fortifications or troop concentrations, similar to the larger and much less mobile mortars of the day.

35. Burgoyne 1780a: 92–94, 146.

36. Hadden 1884: 315; Spring 2008: 39.

37. Burgoyne 1860: 184; Hadden 1884: xci–xcii.

38. Riedesel 1867: 113–114.

39. Riedesel 1867: 131.

40. Riedesel 1867: 94–95.

41. Riedesel 1867: 96–98, 125.

42. Sparks 1853: 96–97.

43. Lamb 1811: 155–156.

44. Lamb 1809: 145–146.

45. Lamb 1811: 156–157, 178.

46. Specht 1995: 77; Cleve 1778: 112.

47. Anburey 1789: 206.

48. Hadden 1884: lxxii.

49. Spring 2008: 60.

50. Anburey 1789: 176–177.

51. Anburey 1789: 375; Lamb 1809: 185–186; Stone 1895: 126.

52. Acland 1993: 29; Anburey 1789: 406–407; Burgoyne 1780a: 172; Lamb 1809: 186.

53. Becker 1866: 86–89; Riedesel 1965: 120.

54. Dearborn 1971: 105; Hitchcock 1900: 134; Luzader 2010: 215; Stone 1895: 284; Wild 1890: 94.

55. Burgoyne 1860: 109–112; Stanley 1961: 144.

56. Wild 1890: 94.

57. Dearborn 1971: 105.

58. John Burgoyne to Horatio Gates, September 16, 1777, Gates Papers, NYHS.

59. Henry Brockholst Livingston to Philip Schuyler, September 17, 1777, Schuyler Papers, NYPL.

60. Horatio Gates to John Burgoyne, September 16, 1777, Gates Papers, NYHS.

61. Anonymous 1777a; Henry Brockholst Livingston to Philip Schuyler, September 17, 1777, Schuyler Papers, NYPL.

62. Digby 1887: 269.

63. Hadden 1884: xli–xlii.

64. Boardman 1879: 224.

65. Unlike the German "von," which connotes rank, the Dutch "van" connotes the geographic origin of the family.

66. Benton 2015.

67. Scammell 1889; Alexander Scammell to Abigail Bishop, March 22, 1777, Boston Public Library.

68. Dearborn 1929: 4.

69. Luzader 2002: 71; Luzader 2010: 210.

70. Henry Brockholst Livingston to Philip Schuyler, September 17, 1777, Schuyler Papers, NYPL.

71. Digby 1887: 269.

72. Hadden 1884: 152; Digby 1887: 269.

73. Specht 1995: 77–78.

74. Richard Varick to Philip Schuyler, September 17, 1777, Schuyler Papers, NYPL.

75. Digby 1887: 192; Moore 1858: 223–227.

76. Van Cortlandt 1878: 285

77. Van Cortlandt 1878: 285–286; Richard Varick to Philip Schuyler, September 17, 1777, Schuyler Papers, NYPL.

78. Stanley 1961: 144–145.

79. Stanley 1961: 144–145.

80. Hitchcock 1900: 147.

81. Gates 1777; Horatio Gates to Jonathan Trumbull, September 17, 1777, Gates Papers, NYHS.

82. Horatio Gates to the Chairman of the Committee at Bennington, September 17, 1777, and Horatio Gates to the Chairman of the Committee of the County of Berkshire and the Chairmen of the Several Committees West of the Connecticut River, September 17, 1777, Gates Papers, NYHS; Hadden 1884: lxxxiv; Nelson 1976: 112.

83. Horatio Gates to Benjamin Lincoln, September 17, 1777, Gates Papers, NYHS.

84. Baldwin 1906: 120.

85. Henry Brockholst Livingston to Philip Schuyler, September 17, 1777, Schuyler Papers, NYPL.

86. Hadden 1884: 152–153.

87. Hoppin 1976.

88. Lossing 1972: 44.

89. Hitchcock 1900: 148.

90. Boardman 1879: 225; Dearborn 1971: 105.

91. Wilkinson 1816: 1:236.

92. Wilkinson 1816: 1:241.

93. Brandt 1994: 132.

94. Glover 1863: 101.

95. Wild 1890: 94.

96. Alexander 1909: 211.

97. Alexander 1909: 21; Digby 1887: 269–270; Stanley 1961: 145, 692.

98. Specht 1995: 78.

99. Lossing 1972: 44.

100. Burgoyne 1780b: 23–24; Burgoyne 1860: 113–114; Hadden 1884: 16–161.

101. Stanley 1961: 145.

102. Burgoyne 1860: 17.

103. Specht 1995: 78.

104. Doblin 1985: 432; Hadden 1884: 152–159.

105. Neilson 1970: 133.

106. Simms 1845: 254–255.

107. Boardman 1879: 225; Wild 1890: 94; Dearborn 1971: 105; Wilkinson 1816: 1:235–236.

108. Wilkinson 1816: 1:248–249.

CHAPTER 2

1. I have used sixty-one specific time references in twenty-six sources to segment the flow of the battle through the course of the day. Not surprisingly, the sources frequently disagree, so like Ketchum (1997) I have trusted some more than others: those men who were relatively detached, likely had their own watches, were not following the leads of other sources, and who wrote before their memories dimmed are among the more credible observers.

2. Digby 1887: 270–271.

3. Luzader 2010: 230.

4. Päusch 1886.

5. Lossing 1851: 51.

6. Wild 1890: 94.

7. Wilkinson 1816: 1:249.

8. Lossing 1851: 44.

9. Wilkinson 1816: 1:237.

10. Neilson 1970: 146.

11. Neilson 1970: 146–147.

12. Luzader 2010: 228.

13. John Burgoyne to George Germaine (public), October 20, 1777, Auckland Papers, DLAR.

14. Luzader 2010: 230.

15. Hadden 1884: liv.
16. Spring 2008: 39.
17. Darling 1971: 9; Lamb 1811: 178–179; Lossing 1851: 47; Spring 2008: 40.
18. Specht 1995: 79.
19. Luzader 2010: 230.
20. Burgoyne 1780b: 22.
21. Spring 2008: 77, 88.
22. Anonymous 1995; May 1997: 18.
23. Hanger 1814.
24. Simms 1845: 389.
25. Mattoon 1895: 249; Silliman 1895: 122.
26. Neilson 1970: 136, 146–147.
27. Lossing 1851: 52.
28. Lossing 1851: 44.
29. Commager 1967: 581; Stone 1895: 152.
30. Specht 1995: 79; Richard Varick to Philip Schuyler, September 19, 1777, Schuyler Papers, NYPL.
31. Digby 1887: 272.
32. Hadden 1884: 164.
33. Dearborn 1929: 5–6.
34. Specht 1995: 79.
35. Päusch 1886: 133–134; Specht 1995: 79.
36. Specht 1995: 80.
37. Päusch 1886: 135; Specht 1995: 79.
38. Specht 1995: 79.
39. Specht 1995: 79.
40. Spring 2008: 161, 247.
41. Anburey 1789: 411; Burgoyne 1780a: 69, 82; Stanley 1961: 147.
42. A *batman* is a soldier assigned to an officer as a servant.
43. Lamb 1811: 191.
44. Neilson 1970: 140.
45. Houston 2006: 41.
46. Spring 2008: 142.
47. Lamb 1811: 190.
48. Hadden 1884: 164.
49. Lamb 1811: 199.
50. Caruana 1977: 21; Darling 1971: 7.
51. Caruana 1977.
52. Wilkinson 1816: 1:236–237.
53. Lossing 1851: 52; Wilkinson 1816: 1:237.
54. Richard Varick to Philip Schuyler, September 19, 1777, Schuyler Papers, NYPL; Wilkinson 1816: 1:237–238.

55. Wilkinson 1816: 1:238.

56. Kidder 1973: 35.

57. Snell 1950.

58. Spring 2008: 155.

59. The 21st Foot was an infantry regiment that was one of the first to adopt flintlock muskets, for which reason they were referred to as "fusiliers." The term was first used by the French in the seventeenth century. The 21st and some other fusilier regiments retained the name and their distinctive hat style even as all infantry regiments adopted flintlocks in the course of the eighteenth century.

60. Lamb 1811: facing 158.

61. Lamb 1809: 107.

62. Anonymous 1995.

63. Dalgleish 1886: 139.

64. Anonymous 1995.

65. Stephenson 2007: 158.

66. Spring 2008: 257.

67. Dearborn 1929: 5–6.

68. Alexander Scammell to Jonathan C. Chadbourn, September 26, 1777, James S. Schoff Collection, WCL.

69. Alexander Scammell to Jonathan C. Chadbourn, September 26, 1777, James S. Schoff Collection, WCL.

70. Moore 1858: 251.

71. Alexander Scammell to Jonathan C. Chadbourn, September 26, 1777, James S. Schoff Collection, WCL.

72. Kidder 1973: 34.

73. Kidder 1973: 34; Alexander Scammell to Jonathan C. Chadbourn, September 26, 1777, James S. Schoff Collection, WCL.

74. Campbell 1848: 93.

75. Neilson 1970: 148; Richard Varick to Philip Schuyler, September 22, 1777, Schuyler Papers, NYPL.

76. Van Cortlandt 1878: 285.

77. Wilkinson 1816: 1:239.

78. Campbell 1848: 93–94.

79. Campbell 1848: 94.

80. Campbell 1848: 95–96; Neilson 1970: 144.

81. Campbell 1848: 96.

82. Burgoyne 1780a: appendix lxxxvi–lxxxvii.

83. Burgoyne 1780a: appendix lxxxvii; Hadden 1884: 164.

84. Pettengill 1924: 100.

85. Neilson 1970: 140; Van Cortlandt 1878: 286.

86. Neilson 1970: 144.

87. Wilkinson 1816: 1:245–246; Neilson (1970: 144) was uncertain about the deployment of this single regiment from Gates's division, but it is confirmed, or at least repeated, by Lossing (1972: 54). Continental regiments were not officially numbered until later in the war, but their numbers are used here for clarity.

88. Päusch 1886: 135–136.

89. Burgoyne had to mean "on their (the American) right flank." Burgoyne 1780a: appendix lxxxv; Riedesel 1867: 99.

90. Päusch 1886: 136.

91. Riedesel 1867: 99; Specht 1995: 80.

92. Päusch 1886: 136–137.

93. Dalgleish 1886.

94. Digby 1887: 277–278; Glover 1863: 101; Lamb 1811: 199; Lossing 1851: 55; Wilkinson 1816: 1:244.

95. Lamb 1811: 191.

96. Wilkinson (1816) later said that no American general officers were in combat this day. The anecdote about Arnold and the rifleman, which might be imaginary (Moore 1858: 498), is almost alone as evidence to the contrary, but it must be remembered that Wilkinson sometimes embellished for his own benefit. Luzader (2010: appendix H) provides the best detailed analysis of how the American general officers behaved on September 19.

97. Anburey 1789: 423; Lamb 1809: 176.

98. Return of Lieutenant General Burgoyne's troops killed, wounded, prisoners, and missing in the actions of September 19 and October 7, 1777, MacKenzie Papers, WCL.

99. Pettengill 1924: 101–102.

100. Cleve 1778; Stone 1970: 114.

101. Riedesel 1867: 115.

102. Lamb 1809: 175.

103. Digby 1887: 340–341; Anburey 1789: 423–424; Lamb 1809: 176; Riedesel 1867: 114–115.

104. Boardman 1879: 225; Dearborn 1929: 5–6; Dearborn 1971: 106.

105. Squier 1878: 692.

106. Matthew Clarkson to his cousin Susan Livingston, September 21, 1777, Livingston Family Papers, MHS.

107. Wilkinson 1816: 1:239.

108. Campbell 1848: 97.

109. Stephenson 2007: 8.

110. Glover 1863: 101–102.

111. Hadden 1884: 166.

112. Wilkinson 1816: 1:239.

113. Lossing (1851: 54); Van Cortlandt (1878: 286–287); and Digby (1887: 273–274) detail these confusing disengagements.
114. Päusch 1886: 137–138.
115. Päusch 1886: 141–142.
116. Specht 1995: 81.
117. Pell 1927: 11.
118. Päusch 1886: 141–143.
119. A *tête de pont* is a military defensive work constructed on a bridge abutment. Riedesel 1867: 99–100.
120. Neilson 1970: 143.
121. Van Cortlandt 1878; Dwight 1895: 144; Alexander Scammell to Abigail Bishop, March 22, 1777, Boston Public Library; Wilkinson 1816: 1:242–246.
122. Coffin 1845: 86.
123. Alexander 1909: 212; Sanderson 1909: 164.
124. Horatio Gates to Benjamin Lincoln, September 19, 1777, Gates Papers, NYHS.
125. Richard Varick to Philip Schuyler, September 19, 1777, Schuyler Papers, NYPL.

CHAPTER 3

1. Wild 1890: 94.
2. Päusch 1886: 141.
3. Axtell 1980.
4. Dearborn 1929: 6–7.
5. Lamb 1811: 194.
6. Lamb 1811: 192.
7. Return of Lieutenant General Burgoyne's troops killed, wounded, prisoners, and missing in the actions of September 19 and October 7, 1777, MacKenzie Papers, WLC; Wilkinson 1816: 1:246.
8. Anburey 1789: 422.
9. Päusch 1886: 143.
10. John Burgoyne to George Germaine (public), October 20, 1777, Auckland Papers, DLAR.
11. Specht 1995: 81.
12. Pell 1927: 11.
13. Anburey 1789: 424–425.
14. Lamb 1811: 192.
15. Doblin 1985: 433.
16. Alexander 1909: 212.
17. Hitchcock 1900: 149; Squier 1878: 692.
18. Dearborn 1929: 6–7. Estimates vary, but while the number of American casualties in the battle was around three hundred, Burgoyne lost around twice that many.

19. Neilson 1970: 145–146.
20. Wilkinson 1816: 1:246.
21. Hitchcock 1900: 149; Wilkinson 1816: 1:243–244.
22. Wilkinson 1816: 1:249–250.
23. Wilkinson 1816: 1:250.
24. John Burgoyne to Henry W. Powell, September 20, 1777, Gates Papers, NYHS; Wilkinson 1816: 1:242.
25. Burgoyne 1780a: 163.
26. Doblin 1985: 433; Specht 1995: 81.
27. Päusch 1886: 145.
28. Päusch 1886: 145.
29. Wild 1890: 94.
30. Pettengill 1924: 102.
31. Päusch 1886: 145.
32. Wilkinson 1816: 1:251.
33. Specht 1995: 81.
34. Lamb 1811: 198.
35. Pettengill 1924: 102.
36. Smith 1816.
37. Päusch 1886: 151.
38. John Burgoyne to Henry W. Powell, September 20, 1777, Gates Papers, NYHS.
39. Bakeless 1959.
40. John Burgoyne to George Germaine (public), October 20, 1777, Auckland Papers, DLAR; Burgoyne 1780a: appendix lxxxviii.
41. Burgoyne 1780a: 24.
42. Burgoyne 1860: 116–117.
43. John Burgoyne to George Germaine (public), October 20, 1777, Auckland Papers, DLAR.
44. Burgoyne 1780a: 103–104; Specht 1995: 136–137.
45. Burgoyne 1780a: 162; Pettengill 1924: 102.
46. Burgoyne 1780a: 162.
47. Burgoyne 1780a: appendix lxxxviii; Digby 1887: 275; Stanley 1961: 149.
48. Neilson 1970: 148.
49. Wilkinson 1816: 1:246.
50. Horatio Gates to Betsy Gates, September 22, 1777, Gates Papers, NYHS.
51. Boardman 1879: 225.
52. Dearborn 1971: 107.
53. Digby 1887: 281; Wilkinson 1816: 1:243–244.
54. Moore 1858: 251–252.
55. Alexander Scammell to Abigail Bishop, March 22, 1777, Boston Public Library.
56. Matthew Clarkson to his cousin Susan Livingston, October 5, 1777, Livingston Family Papers, MHS.

57. Alexander 1909: 212–213.

58. Lamb 1809: 193.

59. Lamb 1811: 199.

60. Specht 1995: 82.

61. Hitchcock 1900: 149.

62. Pettengill 1924: 103; Stone 1970: 118; Cleve 1778.

63. Alexander 1909: 213; Boardman 1879: 225; Specht 1995: 82.

64. Wilkinson 1816: 1:246.

65. Smith 1882: 443.

66. Hitchcock 1900: 150; Wild 1890: 95.

67. Boardman 1879: 225–226.

68. Hadden 1884: xxvi; Päusch 1886: 149; Specht 1995: 82.

69. Digby 1887: 276–277; Päusch 1886: 148.

70. Boardman 1879: 226.

71. Horatio Gates to John Hancock, September 22, 1777, Gates Papers, NYHS; Wilkinson 1816: 1:244–245.

72. Horatio Gates to John Hancock, September 22, 1777, Gates Papers, NYHS.

73. Päusch 1886: 148; Specht 1995: 82.

74. Hitchcock 1900: 1500; Wild 1890: 95.

75. Alexander 1909: 214; Boardman 1879: 226; Hitchcock 1900: 150; Wild 1890: 95.

76. John Burgoyne to Henry W. Powell, September 20, 1777, Gates Papers, NYHS.

77. Wilkinson 1816: 1:241–241.

78. Digby 1887: 278; Specht 1995: 82.

79. Burgoyne 1780a: 105.

80. Päusch 1886: 149.

81. Digby 1887: 277–278.

82. Lossing 1851: 47.

83. Horatio Gates to John Hancock, September 22, 1777, Gates Papers, NYHS; Smith 1882: 88–89; Wilkinson 1816: 1:245.

84. Richard Varick to Philip Schuyler, September 22, 1777, Schuyler Papers, NYPL; Wilkinson 1816: 1:254–256.

85. Thatcher 1827: 401.

86. Richard Varick to Philip Schuyler, September 22, 1777, Schuyler Papers, NYPL.

87. Richard Varick to Philip Schuyler, September 22, 1777, Schuyler Papers, NYPL; Wild 1890: 95.

88. Alexander 1909: 213; Wilkinson 1816: 1:251.

89. Benedict Arnold to Horatio Gates, September 22, 1777, Gates Papers, NYHS; Wilkinson 1816: 1:254–256.

90. Neilson 1970: 152; Richard Varick to Philip Schuyler, September 22, 1777, Schuyler Papers, NYPL.

91. Riedesel 1867: 115.
92. Neilson 1970: 157–158; Stone 1895: 167, 291. The sources of this humorous story do not specify an exact date, but this was the day that Gates ordered a daily half gill of rum for every man, "this to continue a standing order until revoked." He revoked the order the following day, no doubt as a result of this risky escapade.
93. Digby 1887: 279.
94. Digby 1887: 279; Specht 1995: 83.
95. Wilkinson 1816: 1:251.
96. Horatio Gates to Benedict Arnold, September 23, 1777B, Gates Papers, NYHS; Wilkinson 1816: 1:257.
97. Horatio Gates, Pass for Benedict Arnold to John Hancock, September 23, 1777, Gates Papers, NYHS; Wilkinson 1816: 1:257.
98. Anonymous 1777a; Anonymous 1777b.
99. Digby 1887: 279.
100. Päusch 1886: 152; Wild 1890: 95.
101. Digby 1887: 279–280.
102. Specht 1995: 83.
103. Digby 1887: 280.
104. Stanley 1961: 150.
105. Benedict Arnold to Horatio Gates, September 23, 1777, Gates Papers, NYHS; Wilkinson 1816: 1:257–258.
106. Horatio Gates to Benedict Arnold, September 23, 1777A, Gates Papers, NYHS; Wilkinson 1816: 1:258.
107. Squier 1878: 692; Hitchcock 1900: 150.
108. Stevens 1777.
109. Nickerson 1928: 356.
110. Digby 1887: 281; Päusch 1886: 152.
111. Stanley 1961: 151.
112. Specht 1995: 83.
113. Hitchcock 1900: 151; Kidder 1973.
114. Anonymous 1777c; Charles Snell, "A Report on the Organization and Numbers of Gates' Army, September 19, October 7, and October 17, 1777, including an appendix with Regimental Data and Notes," NPS.
115. Schnitzer 2016.
116. Arnold 1880: 182; Boardman 1879: 226.
117. Hitchcock 1900: 151.
118. Boardman 1879: 226.
119. Stone 1895: 187; George Washington to Horatio Gates, September 24, 1777, Gates Papers, NYHS.
120. Specht 1995: 83; Stanley 1961: 151; Digby 1887: 281.
121. Päusch 1886: 156–157; Specht 1995: 83.
122. Boardman 1879: 226; Wild 1890: 95–96; Arnold 1880: 185.

123. Arnold 1880: 185.
124. Wilkinson 1816: 1:251.
125. Alexander 1909: 214; Hitchcock 1900: 151.
126. Horatio Gates to John Burgoyne, September 25, 1777, Gates Papers, NYHS.
127. Päusch 1886: 157.
128. Specht 1995: 83.
129. Päusch 1886: 157; Specht 1995: 83.
130. Specht 1995: 83.
131. Specht 1995: 83–84.
132. Kingsley 1998.
133. Arnold 1880: 184.
134. Digby 1887: 281; Päusch 1886: 158; Specht 1995: 84; Stanley 1961: 151.
135. Boardman 1879: 226.
136. Hitchcock 1900: 151.
137. Alexander 1909: 214; Wild 1890: 96; Hitchcock 1900: 151.
138. Henry Brockholst Livingston to Philip Schuyler, September 26, 1777, Schuyler Papers, NYPL.
139. Arnold 1880: 182–183; Henry Brockholst Livingston to Philip Schuyler, September 26, 1777, Schuyler Papers, NYPL.
140. Alexander Scammell to Jonathan C. Chadbourn, September 26, 1777, James S. Schoff Collection, WCL.
141. Hitchcock 1900: 151.
142. Glover 1863: 102.
143. Riedesel 1867: 125.
144. Stone 1895: 92.
145. Burgoyne 1777; John Burgoyne to Horatio Gates, September 27, 1777, Gates Papers, NYHS.
146. Wilkinson 1816: 1:258–259.
147. Transcript of Friedrich von Riedesel to Horatio Gates, October 2, 1777, Gates Papers, NYHS.
148. Alexander 1909: 214.
149. Päusch 1886: 158.
150. Boardman 1879: 227.
151. Digby 1887: 284; Specht 1995: 84.
152. Päusch 1886: 158.
153. Glover 1863: 102.
154. Glover 1863: 102.
155. Transcript of Friedrich von Riedesel to Horatio Gates, October 2, 1777, Gates Papers, NYHS.
156. Transcript of Friedrich von Riedesel to Horatio Gates, October 2, 1777, Gates Papers, NYHS.
157. Digby 1887: 284; Specht 1995: 84.

158. Hitchcock 1900: 151.
159. Boardman 1879: 227.
160. Wilkinson 1816: 1:251.
161. Wilkinson 1816: 1:251–252.
162. Specht 1995: 84–85.
163. Wild 1890: 96.
164. Specht 1995: 85.
165. Boardman 1879: 227; Glover 1863: 102; Hitchcock 1900: 152.
166. Glover 1863: 102.
167. Wild 1890: 96.
168. Digby 1887: 285.
169. Wild 1890: 96.
170. Hitchcock 1900: 152.
171. Dearborn 1971: 107; Squier 1878: 692.
172. Digby 1887: 285.
173. Digby 1887: 281–284.
174. Burgoyne 1860: 123.
175. Hitchcock 1900: 152; Wild 1890: 95–96.
176. Digby 1887: 285.
177. Digby 1887: 285; Specht 1995: 85.
178. Dearborn 1971: 107; Hitchcock 1900: 152.
179. Burgoyne 1860: 124–125; Hadden 1884: 321–325.
180. Benedict Arnold to Horatio Gates, October 1, 1777, Gates Papers, NYHS; Wilkinson 1816: 1:259–260.
181. Boardman 1879: 227.
182. Thatcher 1827: 99.
183. Wilkinson 1816: 1:264.
184. Boardman 1879: 227; Hitchcock 1900: 152.
185. Wild 1890: 96–97.
186. Specht 1995: 85.
187. Burgoyne 1860: 124.
188. Päusch 1886: 157.
189. Wilkinson 1816: 1:264.
190. Wild 1890: 97.
191. Stanley 1961: 156; Wild 1890: 97.
192. Specht 1995: 86.
193. Simms 1845: 257–258.
194. Specht 1995: 86.
195. Stanley 1961: 156.
196. Alexander 1909: 214; Boardman 1879: 227; Dearborn 1971: 108.
197. Riedesel 1777; Transcript of Friedrich von Riedesel to Horatio Gates, October 2, 1777, Gates Papers, NYHS.

198. Wild 1890: 97.
199. Stanley 1961: 157.
200. Burgoyne 1780a: 63; Hadden 1884: 325–326.
201. Lamb 1811: 163; Riedesel 1867: 101; Specht 1995: 86.
202. Specht 1995: 86.
203. Digby 1887: 285.
204. Burgoyne 1780a: appendix lxxxviii; Burgoyne 1860: 125–126.
205. General Orders for October 3, 1777, Gates Papers, NYHS.
206. Schnitzer 2016.
207. Wilkinson 1816: 1:263–265; Alexander 1909: 215.
208. Boardman 1879: 228; Digby 1887: 285–286.
209. Stanley 1961: 158.
210. Stanley 1961: 157.
211. Stanley 1961: 158.
212. Squier 1878: 692.
213. Digby 1887: 285.
214. Stanley 1961: 157.
215. Wilkinson 1816: 1:280.
216. Horatio Gates to George Clinton, October 4, 1777, Gates Papers, NYHS.
217. Horatio Gates to John Hancock, October 4, 1777, Gates Papers, NYHS.
218. Specht 1995: 87.
219. Specht 1995: 87.
220. Specht 1995: 89.
221. Thatcher 1827: 100.
222. Schnitzer 2016.
223. Burgoyne 1860: 127.
224. Specht 1995: 87.
225. Matthew Clarkson to his cousin Susan Livingston, October 5, 1777, Gates Papers, NYHS.
226. Horatio Gates to John Hancock, October 5, 1777, and Horatio Gates to George Washington, October 5, 1777, Gates Papers, NYHS; Wilkinson 1816: 1:266.
227. Squier 1878: 693; Hitchcock 1900: 152.
228. Riedesel 1867: 101.
229. Burgoyne 1780a: 5–6.
230. Riedesel 1867: 101–102.
231. Wilkinson 1816: 1:251–252.
232. Specht 1995: 87.
233. Riedesel 1867: 102.
234. Digby 1887: 286; Specht 1995: 87.
235. Hitchcock 1900: 152–153; Neilson 1970: 162–163.
236. Burgoyne 1780a: appendix lxxxix; Digby 1887: 291.

237. Nickerson 1928: 358–359.
238. Burgoyne 1860: 127–128; Nickerson 1928: 358.
239. Boardman 1879: 228; Hitchcock 1900: 152–153; Wild 1890: 97.
240. Digby 1887: 286; Specht 1995: 87.
241. Dearborn 1971: 108; Squier 1878: 693.
242. Digby 1887: 286; Specht 1995: 87.
243. De Peyster 1895: 263.

CHAPTER 4

1. Wild 1890: 97.
2. I have used twenty-five specific time references in thirteen sources to segment the flow of the battle through the course of the day. As for the September 19 battle, I have trusted some more than others. Those participants who were relatively detached, not following the leads of other sources, and not basing guesses on distant memories are among the more credible.
3. Burgoyne 1860: 128.
4. Moore 1858: 262.
5. John Burgoyne to George Germaine (public), October 20, 1777, Auckland Papers, DLAR.
6. McGuire 2011: 155; Fischer 1989.
7. Houston 2006.
8. Watt 2013.
9. Anburey 1789: 437.
10. Päusch 1886: 160.
11. William Wilkinson's map shows ten companies of light infantry deployed against the Americans by 1:30 p.m. leaving the Balcarres Redoubt almost undefended. I have chosen to accommodate this discrepancy by assuming that Burgoyne deployed men who were fit for duty from all light infantry companies and left the rest to hold the redoubt.
12. Burgoyne 1780a: 25–26.
13. Päusch 1886: 161; Specht 1995: 89; Wilkinson 1816: 1:269.
14. Burgoyne 1780a: 25–26, 105.
15. Boardman 1879: 225, 228.
16. John Burgoyne to George Germaine "public," October 20, 1777, Auckland Papers, DLAR; Pell 1927: 12.
17. Päusch 1886: 161.
18. Riedesel 1867: 102.
19. Cleve 1778; Digby 1887: 286–287; Pettengill 1924: 105; Stone 1970: 121.
20. Digby 1887: 286–287.
21. Lossing 1851: 60; Wilkinson 1777.
22. Päusch 1886: 165–166.
23. Brooks 1858: 273.

24. Brooks 1858: 275.

25. Wilkinson 1816: 1:267.

26. Wilkinson 1816: 1:267.

27. Wilkinson 1816: 1:267–268.

28. General Orders for October 3, 1777, Gates Papers, NYHS.

29. Wilkinson 1816: 1:267.

30. Wilkinson 1816: 1:267.

31. Mattoon 1895: 243.

32. Mattoon 1895: 243.

33. Alexander 1909: 215.

34. Arnold 1880: 198.

35. Arnold 1880: 205–206; Wilkinson 1816: 1:274.

36. Woodruff 1895: 227.

37. Walworth 1877.

38. Tilghman 1908: 169.

39. Neilson 1970: 165; Stephenson 2007: 139.

40. Arnold 1880: 197.

41. Stone 1895: 145; Neilson 1970: 168.

42. Dearborn 1929: 7.

43. John Burgoyne to George Germaine "public," October 20, 1777, Auckland Papers, DLAR.

44. Samuel Woodruff (1895: 225–226) wrote this in 1827. He makes no mention of Timothy Murphy nor would anyone else until Simms's book was published in 1845. Stone (1895: 212) says that Woodruff participated in the battles but his name does not yet appear on the online roster (Schnitzer 2016). Mattoon claims that Morgan's men were not ordered to pick off British officers on October 7 contrary to reports he attributes to James Wilkinson and Ezra Buel, the latter being a battlefield guide in 1835.

45. Dearborn 1929: 7–10.

46. Alexander 1909: 215.

47. Quaife 1930: 546.

48. Arnold 1880: 204.

49. Neilson 1970: 170.

50. Dearborn 1929: 7.

51. Burgoyne 1780a: 71.

52. Wild 1890: 97.

53. Alexander 1909: 215.

54. Alexander 1909: 215.

55. Lossing 1851: 76.

56. Neilson 1970: 181.

57. Spring 2008: 117.

58. Wilkinson 1816: 1:271.

59. Lamb 1809: 180.
60. Wilkinson 1816: 1:271.
61. Lossing 1851: 45.
62. Wilkinson 1816: 1:270–271.
63. Kidder 1973: 36.
64. Burgoyne 1780a: 42.
65. Specht 1995: 90.
66. Woodruff 1895: 226.
67. Creasy 1987: 316; Neilson 1970: 254–257. Timothy Murphy was first mentioned as the man who shot Fraser in 1845. Jeptha Simms (1845) had heard the claim from Murphy's descendants decades after Murphy's death in 1818. The claim was repeated by later writers but there is no earlier mention or independent confirmation. Fraser himself saw a rifleman in a tree before he was wounded and said later that he thought it was the man who had shot him (Lamb 1809: 178). Stone followed Simms at least partly because of Fraser's belief, but the detailed testimony of Ebenezer Mattoon who was there on October 7, 1777, has to be credited. I have to agree with Harrington (2013) that Fraser was not shot by Murphy.
68. Mattoon's testimony is crucial for refuting the Murphy claim. It might be argued that Mattoon was not present on October 7, 1777, because his name is missing from files recording the roster(s) of Ebenezer Stevens's Corps of Artillery, but so are a majority of the other captains and lieutenants who served in that unit. Mattoon later had a long and distinguished military and political career (US Congress 2005: 1518–1519). His crucial letter to Philip P. Schuyler was written in 1835 when Mattoon was elderly and blind, but his words reveal an acute long-term memory (Mattoon 1835).
69. Mattoon 1895: 244.
70. Mattoon 1895: 245. Mattoon specifies that a "hunting gun" was used. Hunters typically loaded such smooth-bore guns with small shot for fowl but used a single ball with a greased patch for bigger game. "This tightly fitted 'patched' ball could easily make a 10″ group within the normal range of 30 to 60 yds." (Neuman 2008). Thus the shot that mortally wounded Fraser was within the capabilities of both the militiaman and his gun. A failed search for Fraser's remains in 1973 was intended to recover the ball in order to settle the debate over whether he had been hit by a smaller rifle ball fired by one of Morgan's riflemen or a larger ball fired from a hunting gun or musket. The search for the ball was unsuccessful, but the effort confirmed a contemporary report that Fraser's remains had been removed from his grave within days of his death (Snow 2016).
71. De Peyster 1895: 259.
72. Burgoyne 1780a: 42.

73. Digby 1887: 289.
74. Burgoyne 1780a: 58.
75. Burgoyne 1780a: 71, 168; Lamb 1809: 164.
76. Burgoyne 1780a: 91–92; Lamb 1809: 180.
77. Burgoyne 1780a: appendix xc; Cleve 1778; Davies 1976: 232; Digby 1887: 286; Pettengill 1924: 105; Stone 1970.
78. Neilson 1970: 167; Wilkinson 1816: 1:270.
79. Mattoon 1895: 246.
80. Burgoyne 1780: 59.
81. Mattoon 1895: 246–247.
82. Burgoyne 1780a: 107.
83. Päusch 1886: 169–170.
84. Päusch 1886: 171–172.
85. Dearborn 1929: 8.
86. Campbell 1848: 102; Neilson 1970: 171.
87. Coffin 1878: 125; Thatcher 1827: 469; Wilkinson 1816: 1:273.
88. Riedesel 1867: 102.
89. Dearborn 1929: 8.
90. Lamb 1811: 199.
91. Dean R. Snow and Richard G. Wilkinson, "Archaeological and Osteological Analysis of Two Human Skeletons from Saratoga National Historical Park, 1986," NPS.
92. Burgoyne 1780a: appendix xci.
93. Van Cortlandt 1878: 287; Wilkinson 1816: 1:271.
94. Arnold 1880: 199; Mattoon 1895: 247; Van Cortlandt 1878: 287.
95. Putnam 1903: 68. Massachusetts Continentals from both Learned's and Nixon's brigades were present here but the action was so chaotic that it is not possible to know now the movements of individual regiments.
96. Neilson 1970: 176; Wilkinson 1816: 1:271–272.
97. Wilkinson 1816: 1:272.
98. Neilson 1970: 177; Thatcher 1827: 101.
99. Brooks 1858: 273–274; Putnam 1903: 67–68. The action was very confused and men tended to see and remember only what occurred in their immediate surroundings. Years later Putnam took umbrage at descriptions that credited Brooks's units while ignoring the contributions of his own regiments. Some of his writing was intended to correct the oversight but the accounts are in fact complementary, not contradictory.
100. Pettengill 1924: 107; Riedesel 1867.
101. Dangerfield 1960: 467; Dearborn 1929: 8–9; Wilkinson 1816: 1:273–274.
102. Dwight 1895: 106.
103. Boardman 1879: 228; Mattoon 1895: 247; Stephenson 2007: 227.
104. Doblin 1985: 433; Mattoon 1895: 247; Päusch 1886: 172.

105. Dearborn 1929: 9; Mintz 1990: 210. Some recent sources have erroneously claimed that the wound was to his right leg.
106. Arnold 1880: 212.
107. The location of the Taylor house site is controversial. If as some have argued "Great Redoubt" refers only to the fortification at Stop 9 on the modern tour road and Fraser's burial on October 8 occurred there, then the only archaeological candidate for the house site appears to lie too far north. However, based on documents and archaeology Fraser must have been buried in the next fortification north (Stop 10). William Wilkinson's 1777 base map shows only one house and an associated barn at the foot of the bluff where the northernmost of the three Great Redoubt fortifications is shown. The 1789 Lane lithograph shows a house in the same location and a funeral procession on the Stop 10 bluff. The house also appears in the expected place on the 1817 and 1819 canal maps, by which time it was known as the "Smith" house. There is only one candidate for cellar depression and artifacts from our test excavations there dated to prior to 1820, by which time (according to the 1819 canal map and other documents) the house had been moved closer to the river. The cellar hole is thus almost certainly the foundation of the Taylor/Smith house (Snow 2016).
108. Riedesel 1867: 119–120.
109. Lamb 1809: 178.
110. Anburey 1789: 439–440; Riedesel 1867: 119.
111. Anburey 1789: 441.
112. Brooks 1858: 274–275.
113. Burgoyne 1780a: 72; Specht 1995: 91.
114. Burgoyne 1780a: 72.
115. Mintz 1990: 211; Papet 1998: 78.
116. Dearborn 1929: 9.
117. Neilson 1970: 179.
118. Higginbotham 1961: 76.
119. Burgoyne 1860: 175.
120. Burgoyne 1860: 175; Wilkinson 1816: 1:269.
121. Dann 1980: 103.
122. Riedesel 1867: 120.
123. Anburey 1789: 439–440; Riedesel 1867: 120–121; Lamb 1809: 178.
124. Hitchcock 1900: 153; Neilson 1970: 180–181.
125. Stone 1895: 155.
126. Mattoon 1895: 248.

CHAPTER 5

1. Specht 1995: 91.
2. Specht 1995: 91–92.

3. Pell 1927: 13.

4. Burgoyne 1780a: 167, appendix xcvii.

5. Burgoyne 1780a: 133–134.

6. Burgoyne 1780a: 167–168.

7. Burgoyne 1780a: 168.

8. Riedesel 1867: 102–103.

9. Wild 1890.

10. Mattoon 1895: 248; Wilkinson 1816: 1:275.

11. Dearborn 1971: 109; Hitchcock 1900: 153–154; Wild 1890: 98; Wilkinson 1816: 1:279.

12. Digby 1887: 292–293; Wilkinson 1816: 1:279.

13. Biographical material on John Henry, Campbell Papers, College of William and Mary.

14. Acland 1993.

15. Thatcher 1827: 469.

16. Burgoyne 1780a: 168–169; Specht 1995: 92.

17. Lamb 1811: 163, 200.

18. Hitchcock 1900: 154; Lamb 1809: 163; Mattern 1995: 49; Thatcher 1827: 102, 401; Wild 1890: 98; Wilkinson 1816: 1:279.

19. Anburey 1789: 448–449; Snow 2016: 96–100.

20. The location of Fraser's grave is known. Lane's 1789 drawing shows it clearly (Lane 1789). Engineering maps dating to 1817 and 1819 locate it precisely, and several sources from the decades immediately following 1777 consistently refer to the same location. In 1973 an archaeological team from the University at Albany found the grave at the predicted location and discovered that it was empty. A thorough search found no other graves nearby. Dean R. Snow, "Report on the Archaeological Investigations of the American Line, the Great Redoubt, and the Taylor House, Saratoga National Historical Park, 1974," NPS. This finding is supported by Anburey's report that the burial was "taken up" by looters within days of burial. Anburey 1789: 31–32.

21. Mattoon 1895: 249.

22. Dearborn 1929: 10; Wild 1890: 98.

23. Burgoyne 1780a: 710.

24. Acland 1993: 32; Digby 1887: 393–394; Lamb 1809: 165; Specht 1995: 92.

25. I. M. Hayes Return of the British Hospital, October 9, 1777, Gates Papers, NYHS.

26. John Burgoyne to Horatio Gates, October 8, 1777, Gates Papers, NYHS.

27. Riedesel 1867: 121–122.

28. Wilkinson 1816: 1:280–282.

29. Wilkinson 1816: 1:280.

30. Alexander 1909: 215–216; Pell 1927: 13; Hitchcock 1900: 153.

31. Sparks 1853: 438–442.
32. Burgoyne 1780a: 710.
33. Burgoyne 1860: 129.
34. Wilkinson 1816: 1:281–282.
35. Digby 1887: 295–297, 302.
36. Riedesel 1867: 103.
37. Riedesel 1867: 123.
38. I. M. Hayes, Return of the British Hospital, October 9, 1777, Gates Papers, NYHS.
39. Alexander 1909: 216.
40. Wilkinson 1816: 1:326–327.
41. Wilkinson 1816: 1:326–328.
42. The Confession of Danial Taylor (a Spy) at New Windsor, Thursday, October 9th, 1777, Gates Papers, NYHS.
43. Wild 1890: 98; Wilkinson 1816: 1:282.
44. Alexander 1909: 216; Boardman 1879: 229; Hitchcock 1900: 154; Wilkinson 1816: 1:275, 284.
45. M. H. Campbell 1848: 107.
46. Hitchcock 1900: 154; Wild 1890: 98; Wilkinson 1816: 1:282.
47. Digby 1887: 297; Pettengill 1924: 107; Specht 1995: 93; Stanley 1961: 163.
48. Mattoon 1895: 249.
49. Riedesel 1867: 103.
50. Riedesel 1867: 125.
51. Becker 1866: 99.
52. Stanley 1961.
53. Digby 1887: 297–298.
54. Stanley 1961: 163–164.
55. Digby 1887: 298–300.
56. Specht 1995: 94.
57. Burgoyne 1780a: 44.
58. Lamb 1809: 188.
59. Becker 1866: 91–93; Burgoyne 1780a: 173; Lamb 1809: 188; Riedesel 1867: 123.
60. Alexander 1909: 216; Mintz 1990: 214; Wild 1890: 98.
61. Mintz 1990: 214; Pell 1927: 14.
62. Dearborn 1929: 10–11; Wilkinson 1816: 1:283.
63. Specht 1995: 94.
64. Doblin 1985: 433; Lamb 1809: 181; Lamb 1811: 201; Specht 1995: 94.
65. Mattoon 1895: 249–250.
66. Burgoyne 1780a: 174–175.
67. Riedesel 1867: 127.
68. Riedesel 1867: 103; Specht 1995: 95.

69. Dearborn 1929: 11.

70. Acland 1993: 32; Wilkinson 1816: 1:284.

71. Becker 1866: 99–103.

72. Mattoon 1895: 250.

73. Burgoyne 1780a: appendix xcii; Davies 1976: 233; Digby 1887: 300; Riedesel 1867: 103; Specht 1995: 94–95; Stanley 1961: 164.

74. Hitchcock 1900: 155; Sanderson 1909: 165; Wild 1890: 98; Wilkinson 1816: 1:284.

75. Becker 1866: 109.

76. Mattoon 1895: 249.

77. Riedesel 1867: 127–129.

78. Riedesel 1867: 130.

79. Mattoon 1895: 250.

80. Dearborn 1929: 11; Specht 1995: 94; Wilkinson 1816: 1:284–285.

81. Burgoyne 1780a: appendix xcii; Pell 1927: 13.

82. John Burgoyne to George Germaine (public), October 20, 1777, Auckland Papers, DLAR; Lossing 1851: 74.

83. Burgoyne 1860: 130; Digby 1887: 300–303; Hitchcock 1900: 155; Lamb 1809: 181; Specht 1995; Stanley 1961: 164.

84. Digby 1887: 303.

85. Digby 1887: 303.

86. Lossing 1851: 75.

87. Wilkinson 1816: 1:285–286.

88. Stanley 1961: 164; Wild 1890: 98.

89. Boardman 1879: 229.

90. Dearborn 1971: 110.

91. Campbell 1848: 107.

92. Dearborn 1929: 11; Wilkinson 1816: 1:286.

93. Campbell 1848: 108; Wilkinson 1816: 1:287–288.

94. Glover 1863: 103; Putnam 1903: 69.

95. Dearborn 1929: 12; Glover 1863: 104; Lossing 1851: 76; Putnam 1903: 69; Thatcher 1827: 103–104; Wild 1890: 98.

96. Riedesel 1867: 130–131.

97. Riedesel 1867: 103–104.

98. Burgoyne 1780a: 176.

99. Specht 1995: 95; Stanley 1961: 165.

100. Burgoyne 1780a: appendix xcii.

101. Transcript of Friedrich Riedesel to Horatio Gates, October 2, 1777, Gates Papers, NYHS. Original in NYPL.

102. Horatio Gates to John Burgoyne, October 11, 1777, Gates Papers, NYHS; Wilkinson 1816: 1:290.

103. Burgoyne 1860: 130; Specht 1995: 95.

104. Specht 1995: 95.
105. Specht 1995: 95–96.
106. Riedesel 1867: 104.
107. John Burgoyne to George Germaine (private), October 20, 1777, Auckland Papers, DLAR; Riedesel 1867: 104; Specht 1995: 96; Wilkinson 1816: 1:250–251.
108. Boardman 1879: 229; Digby 1887: 304; Stanley 1961: 165.
109. Burgoyne 1780a: 74; Stanley 1961: 166.
110. Wild 1890: 98.
111. Horatio Gates to John Hancock, October 12, 1777, Gates Papers, NYHS.
112. John Burgoyne to Horatio Gates, October 12, 1777, Gates Papers, NYHS; Wilkinson 1816: 1:291.
113. Baxter 1887: 33–34; Thatcher 1827: 105–106.
114. Hoyt 1895: 209; Riedesel 1867: 131–132.
115. Riedesel 1867: 131.
116. Riedesel 1867: 132.
117. Riedesel 1867: 104.
118. Riedesel 1867: 133.
119. Burgoyne 1780a: 160; Davies 1976: 212–213.
120. Lamb 1809: 167.
121. Burgoyne 1780a: appendix C; Davies 1976: 214; Lamb 1809: 167–168.
122. Digby 1887: 304.
123. Mintz 1990: 214; Stark 1860: 138–139.
124. Pell 1927.
125. Riedesel 1867: 104.
126. Specht 1995: 96.
127. Burgoyne 1780a: appendix xciii; Lamb 1809: 168; Riedesel 1867: 105.
128. Riedesel 1867: 105.
129. Burgoyne 1780a: appendix xciii.
130. Specht 1995: 96–97.
131. Dearborn 1929: 12; Dearborn 1971: 111; Squier 1878: 693; Wild 1890: 99.
132. Boardman 1879: 230.
133. Boardman 1879: 230; Dearborn 1929: 12; Hitchcock 1900: 156.
134. Wilkinson 1816: 1:278.
135. Wilkinson 1816: 1:279.
136. Specht 1995: 97.
137. Davies 1976: 214; Lamb 1809: 169.
138. Riedesel 1867: 105.
139. Specht 1995: 97.
140. Riedesel 1867: 106.
141. Davies 1976: 214; Lamb 1809: 169–170; Riedesel 1867: 106; Specht 1995: 98.
142. Lamb 1809: 170.

143. John Burgoyne to Horatio Gates, October 13, 1777, Gates Papers, NYHS; Burgoyne 1860: 132.

144. Riedesel 1867: 106–107; Stone 1970.

145. Burgoyne 1860: 132.

146. Wilkinson 1816: 1:299.

147. Digby 1887: 305; Specht 1995: 98.

148. Burgoyne 1780a: 94; Dearborn 1929: 12; Hitchcock 1900: 158; Wild 1890: 99.

149. Wilkinson 1816: 1:299–300.

150. Wilkinson 1816: 1:301.

151. Digby 1887: 306–307; Wilkinson 1816: 1:291.

152. Wilkinson 1816: 1:302–303.

153. Riedesel 1867: 107.

154. Burgoyne 1860: 135; Digby 1887: 308–310.

155. Wilkinson 1816: 1:303.

156. Schnitzer 2016.

157. Boardman 1879: 230; Riedesel 1867: 107; Specht 1995: 98; Wild 1890: 99.

158. Digby 1887: 311–312; Riedesel 1867: 108.

159. Burgoyne 1860: 136–138.

160. Wilkinson 1816: 1:306.

161. John Burgoyne to Horatio Gates, October 15, 1777, Gates Papers, NYHS.

162. Schnitzer 2016.

163. Specht 1995: 98; Wilkinson 1816: 1:309–310.

164. James Craig to James Wilkinson, October 15, 1777, Gates Papers, NYHS; Wilkinson 1816: 1:310.

165. James Wilkinson to James Craig, October 15, 1777, Gates Papers, NYHS; 1816: 1:310–311.

166. Riedesel 1867: 108–109.

167. Riedesel 1867: 133.

168. Riedesel 1867: 133–134.

169. Digby 1887: 312; Wild 1890: 99.

170. The Confession of Danial Taylor (a Spy) at New Windsor, Thursday, October 9th, 1777, Gates Papers, NYHS.

171. Wilkinson 1816: 1:252.

172. Thatcher 1827: 108.

173. Riedesel 1867: 109–110; Specht 1995: 99–100.

174. Riedesel 1867: 109–110.

175. Burgoyne 1780a: 110.

176. Becker 1866: 114.

177. Schnitzer 2016.

178. Lamb 1809: 193–194.

179. Boardman 1879: 231.

180. Horatio Gates to John Burgoyne, signed by Wilkinson, October 16, 1777, Gates Papers, NYHS.

181. Burgoyne 1780a: 111.
182. Wilkinson 1816: 1:313–314.
183. Boardman 1879: 231.
184. James Craig to James Wilkinson, October 15, 1777, Gates Papers, NYHS; Wilkinson 1816: 1:310.
185. Wilkinson 1816: 1:316–317.
186. Boardman 1879: 231.
187. Specht 1995: 100.
188. Note on the Saratoga Convention, October 16, 1777, Gates Papers, NYHS; Wilkinson 1816: 1:320.
189. Burgoyne 1860: 149–151; Miller 1948: 214; Wilkinson 1816: 1:320.
190. Squier 1878: 693.
191. Riedesel 1867: 111; Specht 1995: 100.
192. Hitchcock 1900: 159; Squier 1878: 693; Wild 1890: 99.
193. Quaife 1930: 546.
194. Digby 1887: 317–319.
195. Lossing 1851: 80.
196. Nelson 1976: 143; Stone 1895: 231–233.
197. Hitchcock 1900: 159; Specht 1995: 101; Stone 1877: 115, 128.
198. Quaife 1930: 547.
199. Mattoon 1895: 251; Squier 1878: 693.
200. Stone 1895: 118, 251–253.
201. Wilkinson 1816: 1:321.
202. Becker 1866: 117; Digby 1887: 321; Specht 1995: 102.
203. Riedesel 1867: 134.
204. Digby 1887: 230.
205. Letters from a British Army officer under General John Burgoyne, 1777 November 17 to 1778 December 10, (1)8, R. Stanton Avery Special Collections, New England Historic Genealogical Society; Burgoyne 1780a: appendix li; Heinrich Urban Cleve, journal, 1777–1778, Peter Force Papers, LC; Mattoon 1895: 250; Stone 1970: 128; Thatcher 1827: 109; Wilkinson 1816: 1:323.
206. Becker 1866: 115–116.
207. Becker 1866: 117.
208. Riedesel 1867: 135.
209. Becker 1866: 119.
210. Letters from a British Army officer under General John Burgoyne, 1777 November 17 to 1778 December 10, p.8: 1:38, R. Stanton Avery Special Collections, New England Historic Genealogical Society; Burgoyne 1780a: 119; Squier 1878: 694.
211. Heinrich Urban Cleve, journal, 1777–1778, Peter Force Papers, LC; Pettengill 1924: 111–112; Stone 1970: 128–129.
212. Specht 1995: 101.

213. Dearborn 1929: 12.
214. Becker 1866: 122; Stone 1895: 295.
215. Lamb 1811: 205–206.
216. Specht 1995: 101.
217. Hadden 1884: lxxxi; Neilson 1970: 222; Stephenson 2007: 181.
218. Moore 1858: 261–262.
219. "Return of Lieutenant General Burgoyne's troops killed, wounded, prisoners, and missing in the actions of September 19 and October 7, 1777," MacKenzie Papers, WCL; Burgoyne 1860: 130.
220. John Burgoyne to George Germaine (private), October 20, 1777, Auckland Papers, DLAR; Charles W. Snell, "A Report on the Strength of the British Army under Lieutenant General John Burgoyne, July 1 to October 17, 1777, and on the Organization of the British Army on September 19 and October 7, 1777," NPS: 87–88.
221. Specht 1995: 102.
222. Anburey 1789: 2:20; Dean R. Snow, "Report on the Archaeological Investigations of the American Line, the Great Redoubt, and the Taylor House, Saratoga National Historical Park, 1974," NPS; Snow 2016: 96–100.
223. Coffin 1878: 266–267.

EPILOGUE

1. John Burgoyne to George Germaine (private), October 20, 1777, Auckland Papers, DLAR.
2. Lamb 1811: 209.
3. *Harper's Encyclopedia of United States History*, s.v. "Acland, John Dyke."
4. Martin 1997.
5. Brooks, 1858 #4333: 273; Campbell, 1848 #4195: 93–94; Mattoon, 1895 #4064: 247.
6. Stone, 1895 #3989: 283–284.
7. Cubbison 2012; Mintz 1990.
8. Dearborn 1929: 5–6; Kidder 1973: 34; Spring 2008: 257.
9. Dearborn 1929, 1971.
10. Luzader 2010; Mintz 1990.
11. Billias 1960.
12. Campbell 1848.
13. Pula 1998.
14. Luzader 2010; Ketchum 1997.
15. Mattern, 1995.
16. *The Peerage* online, s.v. "General Alexander Lindsay, 6th Earl of Balcarres," http://www.thepeerage.com; Martin 1997.
17. Higgenbotham 1961.
18. Davis 1999.

19. Riedesel 1867, 1965.
20. Moore 1858; Alexander Scammell to Jonathan C. Chadbourn, September 26, 1777, James S. Schoff Collection, WLC.
21. Gerlach 1987.
22. Luzader 2010; Ketchum 1997.
23. Linklater 2010.

References

Unpublished or very obscurely published sources are fully cited in chapter end-notes but not listed individually here.

Acland, Harriet. 1993. *The Acland Journal: Lady Harriet Acland and the American War*. Edited by Jennifer D. Thorp. Winchester, UK: Hampshire County Council.

Alexander, David E. 1909. "Diary of Captain Benjamin Warren on Battlefield of Saratoga." *Journal of American History* 3 (2): 201–216.

Anburey, Thomas. 1789. *Travels through the Interior Parts of America*. London: William Lane.

Anonymous. 1777a. Lt. Col. Joseph Storer's York County, Massachusetts Regiment, New York and Pennsylvania. In *Early American Orderly Books, 1748–1817*. Woodbridge, CT: New-York Historical Society.

Anonymous. 1777b. Maj. Ebenezer Steven's Independent Battalion of Continental Artillery, New York. In *Early American Orderly Books, 1748–1817*. Woodbridge, CT: New-York Historical Society.

Anonymous. 1995. *The Militia-Man*. Schenectady, NY: United States Historical Research Society.

Arnold, Isaac. 1880. *The Life of Benedict Arnold: His Patriotism and His Treason*. Chicago: Jansen, McClurg and Co.

Axtell, James, and William C. Sturtevant. 1980. "The Unkindest Cut, or Who Invented Scalping?" *William and Mary Quarterly* 37: 451–472.

Bakeless, John. 1959. "General Clinton's Dumbbell Code." *American Heritage*, April.

Baldwin, Jeduthan. 1906. *The Revolutionary Journal of Col. Jeduthan Baldwin, 1775–1778*. Bangor, ME: DeBurians.

Baxter, James Phinney. 1887. "The Campaigns of Carleton and Burgoyne from Canada, 1776 and 1777." In *The British Invasion from the North*, edited by James Phinney Baxter, 1–79. Albany, NY: Joel Munsell's Sons.

Becker, John. 1866. *The Sexagenary: or, Reminiscences of the American Revolution*. Albany, NY: J. Munsell.

Benton, Geoff. 2015. "Henry Beekman Livingston, Black Sheep of the Livingston Clan." *Journal of the American Revolution*." February 2, https://allthingsliberty

.com/2015/02/henry-beekman-livingston-black-sheep-of-the-livingston-clan/ . Accessed Feburary 28, 2015.

Billias, George A. 1960. *General John Glover and His Marblehead Mariners.* New York: Holt, Rinehart and Winston.

Blake, Thomas. 1973. "Lieut. Thomas Blake's Journal." In *History of the First New Hampshire Regiment in the War of the Revolution*, edited by Frederic Kidder, 25–56. Hampton, NH: Peter E. Randall.

Boardman, Oliver. 1879. "Journal of Oliver Boardman of Middletown: 1777 Burgoyne's Surrender." *Collections of the Connecticut Historical Society* 7: 221–237.

Brandt, Clare. 1994. *The Man in the Mirror: A Life of Benedict Arnold.* New York: Random House.

Brooks, John. 1858. "Colonel Brooks and Captain Bancroft." *Proceedings of the Massachusetts Historical Society* 3: 271-277.

Burgoyne, John. 1780a. *A State of the Expedition from Canada.* 2nd ed. London: J. Almon.

Burgoyne, John. 1780b. *A Supplement to the State of the Expedition from Canada.* London: J. Robson, T. Becket, and R. Baldwin.

Burgoyne, John. 1860. *Orderly Book of Lieut. Gen. John Burgoyne from His Entry into the State of New York Until His Surrender at Saratoga, 16th Oct., 1777.* Edited by Edmund B. O'Callaghan. Albany, NY: J. Munsell.

Campbell, Maria Hull. 1848. *Revolutionary Services and Civil Life of General William Hull, Prepared from His Manuscript.* New York: E. R. Campbell.

Caruana, Adrian. 1977. *The Light 6-Pdr. Battalion Gun of 1776.* Historical Arms Series. Alexandria Bay, NY: Museum Restoration Service.

Coffin, Charles. 1845. *The Lives and Services of Major General John Thomas, Colonel Thomas Knowlton, Colonel Alexander Scammell, Major General Henry Dearborn.* New York: Egbert, Hovey and King.

Coffin, Charles Carleton, ed. 1878. *The History of Boscawen and Webster from 1733 to 1878.* Concord, MA: Republican Press Association.

Commager, Henry Steele, and Richard B. Morris. 1967. *The Spirit of 'Seventy-Six: The Story of the American Revolution as Told by Participants.* New York: Harper & Row.

Creasy, Edward Shepherd. 1987. *Fifteen Decisive Battles of the World: From Marathon to Waterloo.* New York: Military Heritage Press.

Cubbison, Douglas R. 2012. *Burgoyne and the Saratoga Campaign: His Papers.* Norman, OK: Arthur H. Clark.

Cushman, Paul. 2010. *Richard Varick: A Forgotten Founding Father.* Amherst, MA: Modern Memoirs Publishing.

Dalgleish, John. 1886. "Extract from Lieut. Dalgleish's Journal." In *Journal of Captain Pausch, Chief of the Hanau Artillery during the Burgoyne Campaign*, edited by William L. Stone, 139–140. Albany, NY: Joel Munsell's Sons.

Dangerfield, George. 1960. *Chancellor Robert R. Livingston of New York, 1746–1813*. New York: Harcourt Brace.

Dann, John C., ed. 1980. *The Revolution Remembered, Eyewitness Accounts of the War for Independence*. Chicago: University of Chicago Press.

Darling, Anthony D. 1971. *Red Coat and Brown Bess*. Alexandria Bay, NY: Museum Restoration Service.

Davies, K. G., ed. 1976. *Documents of the American Revolution, 1770–1783*. Vol. 14. Colonial Office Series. Dublin: Irish University Press.

Davis, Robert P., 1999. *Where a Man Can Go: Major General William Phillips, British Royal Artillery, 1731–1781*. Westport, CT: Greenwood Press.

Dearborn, Henry. 1929. "A Narrative of the Saratoga Campaign." *Bulletin of the Fort Ticonderoga Museum* 1 (5): 2–12.

Dearborn, Henry. 1971. *Revolutionary War Journals of Henry Dearborn: 1775–1783*. New York: Da Capo Press.

De Fonblanque, Edward Barrington. 1972. *Political and Military Episodes in the Latter Half of the Nineteenth Century: Derived from the Life and Correspondence of the Right Hon. John Burgoyne, General, Statesman, Dramatist*. Boston: Gregg Press.

De Peyster, J. Watts. 1895. "Gen. J. Watts de Peyster's Visit in 1880." In *Visits to the Saratoga Battle-Grounds, 1780–1880*, edited by William L. Stone, 257–273. Albany, NY: Joel Munsell's Sons.

Digby, William. 1887. "Some Account of the American War between Great Britain and Her Colonies." In *The British Invasion from the North*, edited by James Phinney Baxter, 79–361. Albany, NY: Joel Munsell's Sons.

Doblin, Helga B. 1985. "A Brunswick Grenadier with Burgoyne: The Journal of Johann Bense: 1776–1783." *New York History* 66 (4): 420–444.

Dwight, Theodore. 1895a. "Visit to the Battle Ground in 1820." In *Visits to the Saratoga Battle-Grounds, 1780–1880*, edited by William L. Stone, 141–148. Albany, NY: Joel Munsell's Sons.

Dwight, Timothy. 1895b. "Visit of Rev. Timothy Dwight, D. D., to the Battle and Surrender Grounds in September, 1779." In *Visits to the Saratoga Battle-Grounds, 1780–1880*, edited by William L. Stone, 105–109. Albany, NY: Joel Munsell's Sons.

Edwards, Thomas Joseph. 1953. *Standards, Guidons and Colours of the Commonwealth Forces*. Aldershot, UK: Gale and Polden.

Fischer, David Hackett. 1989. *Albion's Seed: Four British Folkways in America*. New York: Oxford University Press.

Gates, Horatio. 1777. "Horatio Gates to Governor Clinton, September 17, 1777." *Bulletin of the Fort Ticonderoga Museum* 6 (4): 155.

Glover, John. 1863. "A Memoir of Gen. John Glover of Marblehead." *Historical Collections of the Essex Institute* 5 (3): 97–130.

Hadden, James M. 1884. *A Journal Kept in Canada and upon Burgoyne's Campaign*. Albany, NY: Joel Munsell's Sons.

Haiman, Miecislaus. 1932. *Poland and the American Revolutionary War.* Chicago: Polish Roman Catholic Union of America.

Hanger, George. 1814. *Colonel George Hanger, to All Sportsmen, and Particularly to Farmers and Gamekeepers.* London: G. Hanger.

Harrington, Hugh T. 2013. "The Myth of Rifleman Timothy Murphy." *Journal of the American Revolution*, March 25, https://allthingsliberty.com/tag/timothy-murphy/. Accessed June 6, 2013.

Higginbotham, Don. 1961. *Daniel Morgan, Revolutionary Rifleman.* Chapel Hill: University of North Carolina Press.

Hitchcock, Enos. 1900. *Diary of Enos Hitchcock, D. D., a Chaplain in the Revolutionary Army.* Vol. 28 of *Publications of the Rhode Island Historical Society.* Providence: Rhode Island Historical Society.

Hoppin, Polly. 1976. "The Thomas Swords Family: A Perspective on the Loyalists of the American Revolution." Manuscript available in the Saratoga Public Library.

Houston, Wade L. 2006. *Fighting the American Revolution: Tactics, Battles and Battlefields.* Gettysburg, PA: Thomas Publications.

Hoyt, Epaphras. 1895. "General Hoyt's Visit to the Battle Ground in 1825." In *Visits to the Saratoga Battle-Grounds, 1780–1880*, edited by William L. Stone, 182–211. Albany, NY: Joel Munsell's Sons.

Ketchum, Richard M. 1997. *Saratoga, Turning Point of America's Revolutionary War.* New York: Henry Holt.

Kidder, Frederic, ed. 1973. *History of the First New Hampshire Regiment in the War of the Revolution.* Hampton, NH: Peter E. Randall.

Kingsley, Ronald F. 1998. "Letters to Lord Polwarth from Sir Francis-Carr Clerke, Aide-de-Camp to General John Burgoyne." *New York History* 79: 393–424.

Lamb, Roger. 1809. *An Original and Authentic Journal of Occurrences during the Late American War from Its Commencement to the Year 1783.* Dublin: Wilkinson & Courtney.

Lamb, Roger. 1811. *Memoir of His Own Life.* Dublin: J. Jones.

Linklater, Andro. 2002. *Measuring America: How an Untamed Wilderness Shaped the United States and Fulfilled the Promise of Democracy.* New York: Walker and Company.

Lossing, Benson J. 1851. *The Pictorial Field-Book of the Revolution.* New York: Harper Brothers.

Luzader, John R. 2002. *Decision on the Hudson.* Fort Washington, PA: Eastern National.

Luzader, John R. 2010. *Saratoga: A Military History of the Decisive Campaign of the American Revolution.* New York: Savas Beatie.

Mattern, David B. 1995. *Benjamin Lincoln and the American Revolution.* Columbia: University of South Carolina Press.

Mattoon, Ebenezer. 1835. "Letter to Philip Schuyler." *Saratoga Sentinel*, November 10, 3.

Mattoon, Ebenezer. 1895. "Visit of General Ebenezer Mattoon in 1835." In *Visits to the Saratoga Battle-Grounds, 1780–1880*, edited by William L. Stone, 239–255. Albany, NY: Joel Munsell's Sons.

May, Robin. 1997. *The British Army in North America 1775–83, Men-at-Arms*. Oxford: Osprey Publishing.

McGuire, Thomas J. 2011. *Stop the Revolution: America in the Summer of Independence and the Conference for Peace*. Mechanicsburg, PA: Stackpole.

Miller, John C. 1948. *Triumph of Freedom, 1775–1783*. Santa Barbara, CA: Greenwood Press.

Mintz, Max M. 1990. *The Generals of Saratoga*. New Haven, CT: Yale University Press.

Moore, Frank, ed. 1858. *Diary of the American Revolution*. 2 vols. New York.

Morgan, Daniel. 1853. "Letter from Daniel Morgan to a British Officer, November 28, 1781." *Virginia Historical Register and Literary Companion* 6 (4): 209–210.

Morrissey, Brendan. 2000. *Saratoga 1777: Turning Point of a Revolution*. Long Island City, NY: Osprey Publishing.

Neilson, Charles. 1970. *An Original, Compiled and Corrected Account of Burgoyne's Campaign*. Kennikat American Bicentennial Series. Port Washington, NY: Kennikat Press.

Nelson, Paul David. 1976. *General Horatio Gates: A Biography*. Baton Rouge: Louisiana State University Press.

Neuman, George C. 2008. "Hunting Guns in Colonial America." *American Rifleman: Official Journal of the American Rifle Association*. Online. Accessed May 3, 2015. http://www.jaegerkorps.org/NRA/Hunting%20Guns%20in%20 Colonial%20America.htm.

Nickerson, Hoffman. 1928. *The Turning Point of the Revolution: Or Burgoyne in America*. New York: Houghton Mifflin.

Papet, Friedrich Julius von. 1998. *Canada during the American Revolutionary War Lieutenant Friedrich Julius von Papet's Journal of the Sea Voyage to North America and the Campaign Conducted There, 15 May 1776 to 10 October 1783*. Translated by Bruce E. Burgoyne. Bowie, MD: Heritage Books.

Päusch, Georg. 1886. *Journal of Captain Pausch, Chief of the Hanau Artillery during the Burgoyne Campaign*. Translated by William L. Stone. Albany, NY: Joel Munsell's Sons.

Pell, Joshua, Jr. 1927. "Diary of Joshua Penn, Junior: An Officer of the British Army in America 1776–1777." *Bulletin of the Fort Ticonderoga Museum* 1 (6): 2–14.

Pettengill, Ray W., ed. 1924. *Letters from America, 1776–1779: Being Letters of Brunswick, Hessian, and Waldeck Officers with the British Armies during the Revolution*. Boston: Houghton Mifflin.

Pula, James S. 1998. *Thaddeus Kosciuszko: The Purest Son of Liberty.* New York: Hippocrene Books.

Putnam, Rufus. 1903. *The Memoirs of Rufus Putnam.* New York: Houghton, Mifflin and Company.

Quaife, M. M. 1930. "A Boy Soldier under Washington: The Memoir of Daniel Granger." *Mississippi Valley Historical Review* 16 (4): 538–560.

Riedesel, Frederika. 1867. *Letters and Journals Relating to the War of the American Revolution, and the Capture of the German Troops at Saratoga.* Translated by William L. Stone. Albany, NY: Joel Munsell.

Riedesel, Frederika. 1965. *Baroness von Riedesel and the American Revolution: Journal and Correspondence of a Tour of Duty, 1776–1783.* Translated by Marvin L. Brown, Jr. Chapel Hill: University of North Carolina Press.

Sanderson, Howard Kendall, ed. 1909. *Lynn in the Revolution.* Vol. 1. Boston: W. B. Clarke.

Scammell, Alexander. 1889. "Alexander Scammell to Abigail Bishop, June 8, 1777." *Collections of the New Hampshire Historical Society* 9: 197–199.

Scheer, George F., and Hugh F. Rankin. 1957. *Rebels and Redcoats.* New York: Mentor Books.

Schnitzer, Eric. 2016. "The Saratoga Campaign of the Revolutionary War: Tables of Organization." SaratogaNYGenWeb Project. www.saratoganygenweb.com/Sarato.htm.

Silliman, Benjamin. 1895. "Professor Silliman's Visit to the Battle Grounds in 1819." In *Visits to the Saratoga Battle-Grounds, 1780–1880*, edited by William L. Stone, 110–140. Albany, NY: Joel Munsell's Sons.

Simms, Jeptha. 1845. *History of Schoharie County and Border Wars of New York.* Albany, NY: Munsell & Tanner.

Smith, George. 1816. *An Universal Military Dictionary.* London: T. Egerton.

Smith, William Henry, ed. 1882. *Life and Public Services of Arthur St. Clair.* Cincinnati, OH: Robert Clarke & Co.

Snow, Dean R. 2016. "The British Fortifications." In *The Saratoga Campaign: Uncovering an Embattled Landscape*, edited by William Griswold and Donald W. Linebaugh, 81–104. Lebanon, NH: University Press of New England.

Sparks, Jared, ed. 1853. *Correspondence of the American Revolution.* 4 vols. Boston: Little, Brown and Company.

Specht, Johann Friedrich. 1995. *The Specht Journal: A Military Journal of the Burgoyne Campaign.* Translated by Helga Doblin. Edited by Mary C. Lynn. Contributions in Military Studies. Westport, CT: Greenwood Press.

Spring, Matthew H. 2008. *With Zeal and with Bayonets Only: The British Army on Campaign in North America, 1775–1783.* Norman: University of Oklahoma Press.

Squier, Ephraim G. 1878. "Diary of Ephraim Squier." *Magazine of American History* 2 (11): 685–694.

Stanley, George F. G. 1961. *For Want of a Horse*. Sackville, NB: Tribune Press.

Stark, Caleb 1860. *Memoir and Official Correspondence of Gen. John Stark*. Concord, MA: G. Parker Lyon.

Stephenson, Michael. 2007. *Patriot Battles: How the War of Independence Was Fought*. New York: Harper Collins.

Stone, William L. 1877. *The Campaign of Lieutenant General John Burgoyne*. Albany, NY: Joel Munsell.

Stone, William L. 1895. *Visits to the Saratoga Battle-Grounds 1780–1880*. Albany, NY: Joel Munsell's Sons.

Stone, William L. 1970. *Letters of Brunswick and Hessian Officers during the American Revolution*. Translated by William L. Stone. New York: Da Capo Press.

Thatcher, James. 1827. *A Military Journal during the American Revolutionary War*. Boston: Cottons and Barnard.

Tilghman, Tench. 1908. "Tench Tilghman to John Cadwalader, January 18, 1778." *Pennsylvania Magazine of History and Biography* 32: 167–170.

US Congress. 2005. *Biographical Directory of the United States Congress, 1774–2005: The Continental Congress, September 5, 1774, to October 21, 1788, and the Congress of the United States, from the First through the One Hundred Eighth Congresses, March 4, 1789, to January 3, 2005, inclusive*. Washington DC: Government Printing Office.

Van Cortlandt, Philip. 1878. "Autobiography of Philip van Cortlandt, Brigadier-General in the Continental Army." *Magazine of American History* 2: 278–298.

Walworth, Ellen Hardin. 1877. *Saratoga, The Battle-Ground-Visitors' Guide*. New York: American News Company.

Watt, Gavin K. 2013. "Continental Dragoons in the Schoharie Valley." *Journal of the American Revolution*. August 12, https://allthingsliberty.com/2013/08/continental-dragoons-in-the-schoharie-valley/. Accessed April 15, 2016.

Wild, Ebenezer. 1890. "Journal of Ebenezer Wild." *Proceedings of the Massachusetts Historical Society* 1: 78–160.

Wilkinson, James. 1816. *Memoirs of My Own Times*. 3 vols. Philadelphia: Abraham Small.

Wilkinson, William C. 1777. "Plan of the Position of the Army under the Command of Lieut. Gen. Burgoyne near Stillwater." LC., MS No. G3803. S3S3 1777.W5.

Woodruff, Samuel. 1895. "Samuel Woodruff's Visit to the Battle Ground in 1827." In *Visits to the Saratoga Battle-Grounds, 1780–1880*, edited by William L. Stone, 212–234. Albany, NY: Joel Munsell's Sons.

Index

Page numbers in *italics* refer to figures. Page numbers suffixed with "n" refer to notes. American, British, and German military unit entries show main subcategories in **bold**.